HAPPILY
SOMETIMES
AFTER

⚜

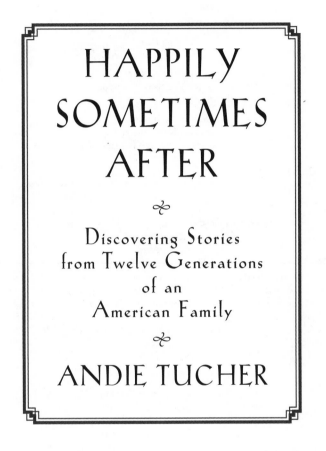

HAPPILY SOMETIMES AFTER

Discovering Stories from Twelve Generations of an American Family

ANDIE TUCHER

University of Massachusetts Press
Amherst and Boston

ISBN 978-1-62534-128-0 (paper); 127-3 (hardcover)

Designed by Sally Nichols
Set in Adobe Garamond Pro
Printed and bound by Sheridan Books, Inc.

Library of Congress Cataloging-in-Publication Data

Tucher, Andie.
Happily sometimes after : discovering stories from twelve generations of an
American family / Andie Tucher.
pages cm
Includes bibliographical references and index.
ISBN 978-1-62534-127-3 (hardcover : alk. paper) — ISBN 978-1-62534-128-0 (pbk. : alk. paper)
1. Woodson family. 2. Tucher, Andie—Family. 3. Oral tradition—United States.
4. Intergenerational relations—United States. 5. Pioneers—United States—Biography.
6. Pioneers—Kentucky—Biography. 7. Kentucky—Biography. 8. United States—Biography.
9. United States—Genealogy. 10. United States—History—Philosophy. I. Title.
CT274.W643T83 2014
305.20973—dc23
2014021801

British Library Cataloguing-in-Publication Data
A catalogue record for this book is available from the British Library.

To my niblings
Trina, Clark, Will, and Dan

❦

and to the memory of my parents
Albert and Doris

CONTENTS

❧

ACKNOWLEDGMENTS

⤜

THE FRIENDS, ACQUAINTANCES, COWORKERS, SCHOLARS, RESEARCHERS, students, and bystanders who have talked with me over the years about their families' stories and how they worked all rightfully own a little piece of this book. But for enlightening conversations along the way and thoughtful comments on all or parts of the manuscript, I am particularly grateful to Dan Bischoff, the late James Carey, Ann Fabian, Kathy Roberts Forde, Michael Schudson, Robert W. Snyder, and Albert Tucher. Rob Tucher lent a welcome hand with photographic work. I am both happy and relieved that I can finally proclaim my thanks to Leslie Clark, Ruth Ford, Todd Gitlin, Nick Lemann, and my students and colleagues at the Columbia Journalism School for their encouragement, moral support, and patience. I am also grateful to the Journalism School for helping to fund my research travel.

After years of work on this project I can confidently confirm that *not* everything can be found online, and I owe a great debt to the informed and responsive guidance of librarians, curators, and archivists at dozens of libraries and historical societies from Albany to Richmond and from Brooklyn to Louisville. And the deft crew at the Columbia University Interlibrary Loan department can, I am convinced, find *anything*.

At the University of Massachusetts Press, Clark Dougan, Carol Betsch, Mary Bellino, Amanda Heller, Jack Harrison, and Sally Nichols handled my manuscript—and me—with great intelligence, care, good cheer, and good sense. My warmest thanks also go to my agent, Joe Spieler.

This book had its genesis in the work my mother and I began long ago on our family history, and I am grateful to the legions of generous and dedicated genealogists with whom we have traded information over the years. I'm sure they will share a tired and knowing smile when I point out that some of what follows represents interpretation and informed guesswork, not certainty. But I'm also sure some will note with dismay that at times I don't seem to know this or that well-known "fact." Actually, after all these years I'm pretty sure I do, but most of the time, if I couldn't confirm a claim (that, say, the first Mrs. Josias Payne was born a Fleming) or found that it was inaccurate (it was actually a *different* Sampson Trammell who married Kerhappuch Garrett), I've simply dropped or corrected the misinformation rather than engaging in debate, which is not my purpose here. I hope my fellow family historians will forgive me for challenging cherished stories and will take pleasure in discovering new ones.

I am grateful beyond words to my family for their never-failing love and support. My mother was my first research partner, my father our bemused and dauntless chauffeur, and I sorely miss indulging in the pleasure of handing them this book and basking once more in their button-bursting pride. And to all those generations of greats and great-greats and beyond: thank you for prevailing.

An earlier version of part of chapter 4 was published as "Soldiers' Tales: 'What Did You Do in the War, Great-Great-Great-Great-Great-Grandpa?'" in *Common-Place* 4, no. 3 (2004), www.common-place.org.

Figure 1 was originally published in Calder Loth, ed., *The Virginia Landmarks Register,* 4th ed. (Charlottesville: University Press of Virginia, 1999), 196, and is reproduced by permission of the Virginia Department of Historic Resources.

HAPPILY
SOMETIMES
AFTER

☙

INTRODUCTION

⚯

FOR TWELVE GENERATIONS, MEMBERS OF AN AMERICAN FAMILY HAVE BEEN telling stories. They have told of impassioned elopements and heartbreaking kidnaps, of hairbreadth escapes and bloody murders, of an eerie propensity for grievous wounds to the head. They have told of enormous riches and miserable poverty. Of changeling children, defrauded heirs, lost treasures, battlefield heroes, bigamists, bastards, Indians, avengers, bandits, moguls, floods, fires, drunkards, Rebels, Patriots, and how the great-grandmother of Chief Justice John Marshall married the pirate Blackbeard by mistake.

The stories as they survive today are full of incomplete sentences and unfinished paragraphs, enigmatic characters, unreliable narrators, and endings without conclusions. Some are verifiably accurate, some that seem fantastic weren't, some have been revised or embroidered, and some are, in the most scholarly sense of the word, "bullshit"—that is, not in the least concerned with truth.[1] Some lived on in a luxuriant range of variations, while others left little more than a fossilized imprint behind, a barely visible tracing to show where a living, breathing story once was. But since these twelve generations were, it turns out, my ancestors, all of these stories were what *they* wanted to tell *me.*

They almost failed. I didn't grow up on the stories. I never heard them while eavesdropping on the veranda as the katydids cried or snuggling on some ample and aproned lap as the cookies baked. My grandmother Grace, a taciturn and joyless Kentucky native who had left her past behind in 1919 to marry the New Yorker she'd met while doing war work, never said—or possibly even knew—much more about her ancestors than that they were supposed to have been related to Daniel Boone. (They weren't.) But years ago, when I started helping my mother put together a family tree as a diversion for Grace in her great old age, we were astonished to find ourselves pushing back, and back, and back into America's past, through the Civil War soldiers and the western pioneers and the Revolutionary Patriots and the Chesapeake tobacco moguls, all the way back to a set of my tenth-great-grandparents, John and Sarah Woodson, who arrived at the Virginia Company's ragged little Jamestown settlement in the spring of 1619, a good year and a half before the Pilgrims ever showed up on their ballyhooed rock. Grace's people, we discovered—my people—have been living in the place now known as the United States just about as long as any non-indigenous family possibly could.

While simply having ancestors is hardly a feat worth celebrating, the ability to put names to more than a handful of them tends to be confined to either griots or royal heirs. Records are muddled, records are lost, records are never kept in the first place. People don't care, or forget, or prefer to forget. People leave no trace, or erase others' traces. African Americans whose roots in the New World could be every bit as deep as mine may never know for sure, and my casual mention of a four-centuries-dead forefather drew a long sigh from a friend of mine whose parents had lost their histories along with their families in the Holocaust. Only chance (and the southern American penchant for pre-serving family lore) made me an offspring of ancestors rather than of shadows. Most of them—like most people—were nobody special.

But for me as a journalist and historian—as someone professionally and profoundly interested in the ways people create, share, and use stories—the real stroke of luck lay in acquiring a family that had not just witnessed almost the entire sweep of the English American experience but also left behind stories about it. As I turned up bits and shards of my ancestors' tales on online gene-alogy bulletin boards and databases, or scoured local libraries and historical societies for privately printed family chronicles (with magnificent titles like *From the Caesars to the Cresaps*), amateur family newsletters stapled together on the kitchen table, and carbon-copied typescripts of some ancient worthy's reminiscences, I found myself reveling in the same sort of gratitude and lust that must have gripped Howard Carter when he thrust his candle through the hole in the sealed door and peered for the first time at the "wonderful things" in the dim depths of Tutankhamen's tomb. Much more appealing to me than the possibility of filling in another blank on the *Ahnentafel* was the wide-open opportunity to eavesdrop on what generations' worth of people who happened to be my ancestors *said* and *thought* about the American lives they'd led—and those they wished they'd led.

People use stories to explain things—sometimes the way things are and sometimes the way they aren't. We all use stories to organize reality: to think and reason about what's going on, to review situations and compare them with what's happened before, to make the unknown familiar, to impose order on the buzz of events going on around us. At its most basic level the story—the narrative form—is an acknowledgment of time: it accepts that we all live moving forward from "now" to "later" and experience events in a chronological sequence, and that where we stand at this moment has something to do with where we stood before, whether twenty minutes ago or twenty years. A storyteller chooses and orders the events, characters, and scenes that illuminate what that relationship might be, and in stories for everyday use those choices are often streamlined and familiar. As Charles Tilly put it in his elegantly titled *Why?:* "When humans began creating stories, they fashioned one of their great social inventions. In our complex world, causes and effects always join in complicated ways. . . . [S]tories enormously simplify the processes involved." Stories offer reasons for what happened before, models for what is happening now, and predictions for what might happen again.[2] They defy the mindlessness of fortune's caprices.

People tell stories to explain *themselves,* too: to envision and test themselves as a particular kind of person rather than another kind, to present themselves to the world in a way that feels true, to make sense of their pasts and plot their futures. Everyone lives life as a story, say philosophers and psychologists alike, and choosing the stories that describe or explain our lives is an essential part of choosing the lives we want to live. In fact a case could be made that America's founding ideals had a special resonance for the storyteller—that an offspring of the natural rights to life, liberty, and the pursuit of happiness is something like a right to tell our own stories. During and after the Revolution the new ideas about individual as well as political rights inspired a riot of personal storytelling, much of it revolutionary in its own right. For the first time, countless ordinary Americans—from working people to veterans to convicts, the sort of people unused to thinking of themselves as interesting, important, or independent— opened their mouths or took up their pens and publicly claimed the right to tell about (and direct) their own lives, some in works that were published and widely read. Many of my ancestors did indeed glory in that opportunity. Others, however, like the feckless soul who might have begun his life in the United States as a transported convict and ended it as a penniless veteran, would probably never have opened his mouth to anyone at all if the new post-Revolutionary government hadn't *made* him talk.[3]

And people tell stories to explain things—or themselves—*to others*. The point of a story is to be shared; it is a negotiation between the teller, who offers a vision of some piece of the world, and the reader or listener, who decides whether or not to accept that vision. I turned up two different kinds of stories told about and by my family. Some were small, personal, and circumstantial, embedded in earthbound sources like court records and applications for veterans' pensions. Intended for a specific purpose and a known audience, they were utilitarian and finite, offering intriguing but limited flashbulb glimpses into daily life. The drunken partygoer hauled into court on charges of having bitten another in the buttocks, for instance, was explaining himself to the judge who would decide his punishment, without a thought for the bemused descendant who would find the record of his peccadillo nearly three centuries later.

But another kind of story aspires to something more. The stories that families create for themselves not only acknowledge time but also defy it, and seek to shape not just their own present but also the presents of their future kin. A story can tell how things were for this particular group of intimately connected people, this one group out of all the groups in the world. It can preserve the knowledge of where they came from and where they had hoped to go. It can spread their triumphs, and justify or excuse or revise their failures. It can bridge the chasm between past and future. It can be the most personal protest possible against the heartless limits of the lifespan.

Historians, who spend a lot of their time with the dead, are painfully familiar with those limits too. All good scholars are conscious of what historical evidence doesn't say, humbled by what they can no longer recover, and resigned to dealing with sources and evidence that can be ambiguous, incomplete, contradictory, even deceitful. It's not just History's Greatest Mysteries that tantalize, those classic jigsaw puzzles that lack a couple of critical pieces right at the center of the picture (what was Stonehenge for? what happened to Ambrose Bierce?) and that—truth to tell—can be so pleasurable to ponder that any final resolution could well prove a disappointment. It's also the questions of interpretation and perspective (was Hiroshima necessary?) that will be argued and reargued indefinitely. Or the enigmas of the individual soul (why didn't Nixon destroy the tapes?) that invite as much psychiatric speculation as historical. Or the actions so firmly rooted in past assumptions and attitudes (why did Salem execute witches?) that they come close to defying the imagination of those who come after. It's the challenge of understanding clearly and representing fairly the splendidly varied and maddeningly unpredictable experiences of humans who are past speaking for themselves.

As "found" history consisting only of whatever raw materials happen to have been preserved through the generations, family stories like mine are both especially fragile and peculiarly valuable. Considered purely as sources for biographical or historical facts, they are frustrating in the extreme. Almost always pocked with gaping holes and slashed through by abrupt silences, they also tend to be studded with strange little factoids and nuggets so far removed from their contexts (where did my fifth-great-grandmother get the forename Derecter?) that they will never make sense to anyone again, and the historian simply has to decide to let the indecipherable bits go before they become obsessions. Out of self-preservation I have learned to file these bits away as what I call Musgraves, after the Sherlock Holmes story "The Musgrave Ritual," which tells of the tradition that every Musgrave heir on his twenty-first birthday must be ceremonially taught a nonsensical-sounding jingle whose meaning has been long forgotten. The shrewd butler who figured out that the jingle pointed to the hiding place of the ancient Stuart crown ended up, of course, dead.

But stories told by people about their own experiences can offer something remarkable to the adventurous historian: an entry point for understanding not so much the historical facts of human lives as the much less accessible landscape of human hearts and minds. The mere survival of these stories, in fact, in however imperfect a form, is what makes them important, commanding attention precisely for whatever it was that preserved them. Those may well have been the stories that offered the most useful or congenial explanations for life's predicaments. As such they can tell us something about *what happened* but also about what the people involved thought or wished or hoped or feared happened, what they saw as the deepest *truth* of the matter—which is not always the same as the simple facts of the matter. They can show us how people talked about what they valued, what they had lost, how they judged their own lives and found meaning in them.

They can even, perhaps, offer a glimpse into what may be the most basic yet elusive question about any human beings: Were my ancestors happy?

It's hard to say; they never told us directly. But it's a valid question, given my family's long, strong roots in a nation whose founders deliberately embedded the idea of happiness in the revolutionary document that became its "sacred text."[4] Indeed America has long been seen as the place where you can throw off the trammels of tradition and free yourself from everything but your own hopes, aspirations, talents, demons, and flaws. Even in the earliest years of its settlement, when prevailing religious and philosophical teaching tended strongly toward the conclusion—empirically justifiable to be sure—that earthly happiness was more a snare, a delusion, or a phantom than something a human being might expect to achieve, many of the people who chose to make their lives in the brave New World were also willing to entertain the idea of a more worldly happiness, something they could grasp, *should* grasp, should seize upon and admit to enjoying here and now. And even those Americans whose religion was strictest often found themselves struggling to reconcile God's strictures against secular pleasure with their achievement of worldly success. Famously, the Puritans, true to their Calvinist roots, were always wary of the temptations and delusions of prosperity but ended up accommodating both gains and God, figuring that since working hard and honoring one's calling gave glory to the creator, earning temperate rewards in that work was a sign of his approval.

The Declaration of Independence itself embodied a worldly point of view. Thomas Jefferson didn't specify exactly what he meant by a natural right to pursue happiness, but he would later insist he hadn't been proposing anything extraordinary. The Declaration, he wrote in a letter near the end of his life, was "an expression of the American mind" that derived its authority from "the harmonizing sentiments of the day"—simply the things people were talking about, writing about, and reading about in works by thinkers from Aristotle to Locke. Among those harmonizing sentiments was the enlightened idea that human beings were born with certain inherent rights that no government could meddle with. On everyone's list of rights were life and liberty, but closely following was a cluster of other rights to what was variously called happiness or property or security or ease—life's foundations, liberty's fruits, and the essential elements of a well-ordered society—and government had no business interfering with the efforts of its citizens to pursue whatever they thought a good life should include.[5]

Over the years the expanding economy, the evolution of ideas about civil and human rights, and the activism of government have helped increase the opportunities for happiness of millions who would never have had a shot at it in Jefferson's America (or in many other Americas either). Happiness has come to seem so accessible, so normal, that scrutinizing the state of one's own is now something of a national preoccupation. Books parsing its every aspect from the historical to the how-to enjoy brisk sales and serious reviews, websites offer happiness questionnaires, NBC's flagship *Nightly News* once broke the urgent story that the "secret of happiness" is "finding the things that make you happy and keep you that way," and the study of positive psychology is staking out its turf as a serious academic endeavor, Claremont Graduate University having started the world's first program to offer what wags inevitably call a "Ph.D. in Happiness." And of course these days there's an iPhone app for that, though users were reporting that the frequent crashes of the "Live Happy—A Happiness Boosting Positive Psychology Program" were not making them particularly happy.[6]

Yet this hopeful and happy America has also long embodied a quieter, darker side, an unofficial yet also deeply American undercurrent of melancholy that Andrew Delbanco has called the "dark twin of hope . . . [that] shadows the hopeful promise of our exuberant democracy."[7] A land that promises so much, that so extravagantly encourages expectation of *any* kind, also has the potential to be the most disappointing place in the cosmos. Disappointment is the tax Americans pay on hope.

It began at the beginning, with the first permanent English American settlement in the New World. The Virginia Company's expectations for its Jamestown colony were almost as enormous as the wreckage it left in the end. After the colony yielded no gold or jewels, few heathen converts, and an epic death rate, Captain John Smith acknowledged that "all the world doe see a defailement" of the effort.[8] And my Woodson tenth-great-grandparents were among the tiny percentage who survived the wreckage.

Ancestors of mine went on to live through other of the most iconic of American experiences. Flemings, Tarltons, Paynes, and Trammells numbered among the thousands who wagered that they could outlive their indentureships in the brutal tobacco fields of the seventeenth-century Chesapeake, while a few Ballards and Randolphs lorded over them. Whartons, Maupins, Flemings, and Mullinses risked their lives, their fortunes, and their sacred honor to side with the Patriots against Great Britain, and some of them lost heavily in the first two categories. Ballards, Conways, Daughertys, and Duckers pressed over the mountains to the Kentucky frontier that was America's first great West, and found that the promised land was a dark and bloody ground. Robertses and Daughertys fought on both sides of the Civil War and then fought almost as hard to survive the peace. McManuses and McDonalds had a moment of Gilded Age splendor before a series of their own personal "defailements" brought everything crashing down.

The hopes of most of them must have been heavily taxed indeed. But like so many others, they used their stories to recalibrate their hopes, redeem their disappointments, and explain to themselves and others the way things *really* were. In this story of American stories I analyze some of the surviving tales told by and about ancestors of mine ranging from the Jamestown settlement to the Gilded Age metropolis and beyond, and trace how ideas evolved about what made people happy and what made selves whole; how people built relationships with their past and used them to explain the present on behalf of their future; and how they confronted the persistent tensions between hope and disappointment in a nation that by making happiness thinkable also made unhappiness regrettable.

Most of the stories I examine have wandered far from whatever form they first took decades or centuries ago. Like most tales that have been passed word-of-mouth from person to person, they often became palimpsests of misunderstandings, revisions, re-rememberings, and dismemberings that ended up bearing only cryptic relationships to the events that inspired them. A story about a toddler who was the sole survivor of an Indian attack, for instance, acquired a set of rococo details from a teller three generations down the road who also seems to have confused Virginia with Poughkeepsie. And the tale of how Chief Justice John Marshall's great-grandmother went to the altar with Blackbeard was only one of the sensational legends I found about marital misadventures ranging from bigamy to insanity in the family of my famous six-times-removed third cousin—legends that would have sounded familiar to readers of certain nineteenth-century best-sellers, too.

But it's the wayward-seeming evolution of the stories that is precisely what makes them so interesting. In the layers of an old family story, suggestive hints often linger as to how and when the tale changed in response to new social and personal needs and how its tellers put it to work explaining the happiness or unhappiness of their own lives and those of their forebears. My aim was never to catch out my forebears in a lie, but rather to use other versions of the events based on other kinds of evidence as the foil against which to consider why the stories my family constructed and passed on made better sense to their tellers, their hearers, or both.

The oldest tale in my family's arsenal, for instance, or at least the one that *seems* the oldest, is set during the American Indians' mass assault on the Virginia settlements in 1644 and involves one of the most traditional and consoling of themes, the redemption of tragedy and loss through heroism. But closer investigation also turns up what appear to be clear traces of its service in comforting the father of a Revolutionary officer taken prisoner by the British, with embellishments by an aging and still unreconciled Confederate veteran. And an elderly cousin's letter that turned up among my grandmother's papers rehabilitated an embarrassing uncle by appropriating someone else's story for him, though our cousin's choice put him in good company: a president of the United States found his happiness in appropriating exactly the same story for *his* uncle.

All stories yearn toward conclusions, whether "the rest is silence" or "they all lived happily ever after." Present-day readers of this collection of narratives have a great advantage over the people who experienced or told them: we can see more of how they came out. We can take a spiky pleasure in knowing that a powerful and conniving eighth-great-grandfather of mine, who in the lethal political turmoil of late seventeenth-century Virginia was uncannily skillful at maintaining lucrative friendships with two warring factions at once, would probably have been nonplussed to know of the fecklessness of his heirs: a grandson was illiterate, a great-great-granddaughter illegitimate, and a great-great-great-great-grandson so hapless he blew himself up while blasting a well, leaving, as his anonymous obituarist noted, "his brains scattered promiscuously over the ground."[9] We can smile at the irony that the prosperous fifth-great-grandparents of mine who lived with their four children in publicly and defiantly unwedded bliss would number among their descendants a university president who banned from his campus the grave sin of dancing. And we can pause to marvel that my grandmother, a woman with a three-century-old American past who herself claimed no past, had the gumption to create a different future for herself. That rather than *telling* a story that made sense of her life, she *lived* one, making a definitive break from her history that would redirect her descendants' lives more radically, and shape their chances at happiness more definitively, than any single step any other ancestor had taken since John and Sarah Woodson boarded their ship to Virginia nearly four hundred years ago.

Pull your chair closer and let me tell you a story . . .

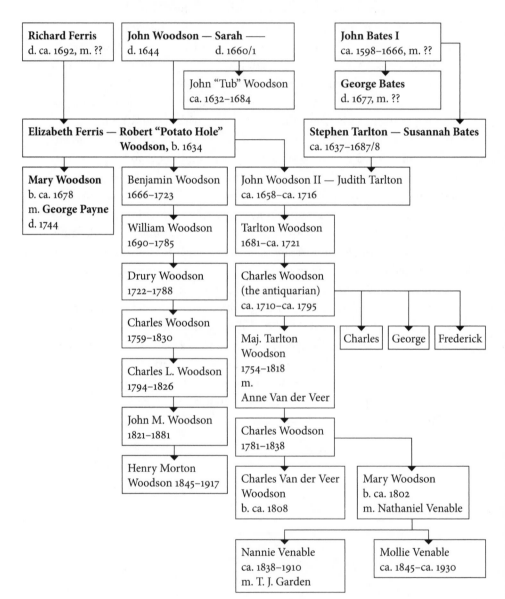

Names in **bold** represent direct ancestors. Other names are included on if relevant.

CHAPTER 1

Seeking Paradise in the New World

⚭

Snookered

On the 18th day of April 1644, the Indians made a sudden attack upon the [Virginia] settlements and killed about three hundred of the colonists before they were repulsed.

At this time Dr. John Woodson's two sons, John and Robert, were respectively twelve and ten years of age.

There is a cherished family tradition that, on the day of this second massacre, Dr. John Woodson, while returning from visiting a patient, was killed by the Indians in sight of his home. The Indians then attacked the house which was barred against them and defended by his wife, Sara, and a man named Ligon (a shoemaker) who happened to be there at the moment. The only weapon they had was an old time gun which Ligon handled with deadly effect. At the first fire he killed three Indians, and two at the second shot. In the meantime two Indians essayed to come down through the chimney; but the brave Sara scalded one of them to death with a pot of boiling water which stood on the fire: then seizing the iron roasting spit with both hands, she brained the other Indian, killing him instantly.

The howling mob outside took fright and fled; but Ligon fired the third time and killed two more, making nine in all.

At the first alarm, Mrs. Woodson had hidden her two boys, one under a large washtub and the other in a hole where they were accustomed to keep potatoes during the winter, hoping in this way to save them in the event the Indians succeeded in entering the rude log cabin in which they lived.

From this circumstance, for several generations, the descendants of one of these boys were called "Tub Woodsons" and those of the other were designated as "Potato Hole Woodsons."[1]

SOMETIMES I WISH I HAD GROWN UP KNOWING THAT STORY. BEING A Potato Hole Woodson child might have changed my life; it might have made me a different person entirely. If on slow afternoons long ago my grandmother Grace had fed me cookies, lemonade, and the epic of my forebears, how could I not have grown up bolder, brazener, cheekier? If I'd been able to eavesdrop on some old grizzled colonel in a string tie declaiming on the porch in the summer twilight as he caressed with gnarled fingers a silver cup redolent of bourbon and mint, how could I have borne to shut myself up with books all the time? If all along I'd known my tribe, my people, my history, been on first-name terms with hundreds of people living and dead, every one of whom clearly wanted me born, how could I ever have felt alone? If I'd understood that once, centuries ago, only a dank earth pit smelling of spuds had stood between oblivion and the possibility of *me,* how could I not have known I was special?

Yet Grace, my maternal grandmother, the remotest ancestor I knew, never told me or my four siblings the Woodsons' story. As far as I can remember, Grace rarely told us any stories at all, not even "Cinderella" or "Rumpelstiltskin." Not one of those jolly, snuggly grandmothers of legend, never at ease with herself or lavish with her affections, Grace neither invited nor divulged confidences. She was sharp and skinny and tall, at least when she was standing on her gnarled and arthritic size 10AAA feet, which at some point in my childhood she decided she'd done long enough, and thereafter from her wheelchair she predicted her imminent death for a quarter of a century before finally getting it right a month before her ninety-sixth birthday. When all those years ago my mother, Doris, and I started poking into our family history, we didn't expect any surprises. We weren't the sort of family that *had* surprises; we lived in New Jersey.

So we were shocked to discover that in this nation of newcomers, where so many people we know are either immigrants or nearly descended from them (among them my own father, whose parents came from Nuremberg and Vienna during the Ellis Island era), and where getting in touch with one's roots usually involves learning to cook with some fragrant herb or spice that smells like

Granny's kitchen, so much of our family had been American for so long. Even my mother's father's people, the late arrivals at the party, have been here for a century and a half, having shown up fifteen or twenty years before the Civil War. But no one had expected to find that every one of my mother's mother's immigrant forebears had arrived here before the Revolution, let alone that some of them had beaten the *Mayflower* here. No wonder that when I started adding garlic to *my* cooking, Grace had no idea what it was.

We were even more shocked to discover, after all those years in school learning to thank heaven we New Jerseyans were on the side of Ulysses S. Grant, Abraham Lincoln, and the good guys in blue who freed the slaves of the bad guys in gray, we weren't victors after all. While my grandfather Joe's Irish and Scottish forebears had embraced—and wrung good Yankee profit from—those good Yankee values like grit, ambition, and drive in the gritty and ambitious New York cities of Albany and Troy, virtually every one of Grace's ten generations' worth of American forebears had been a southerner.

That was a legacy she did know a little something about, and she was perfectly happy to have put it all behind her. In the 1930s, when her two daughters were small, the family made an annual journey by car all the way from their home in New York City to Kentucky to visit the many relatives still living in and near Covington, Lexington, and the tiny Pendleton County town of Falmouth that lay between them. The journeys didn't leave much of an impression on either my mother or my aunt. Doris was generally bored by the endless jaunts over bleak back roads to be presented to yet another Cousin Virgie, while her sister, Virginia (aka Ginny or Gina—she refused to be a Virgie too), cherished the memory of Aunt Gertrude's Kentucky beans with bacon. But in general Grace apparently believed that old times there were best forgotten. By the time I knew her, the only trace she still betrayed of her southern roots was the way she would offer a steaming cup of "coh-feh." Everything else she had meticulously shaken off when World War I offered her the chance to get out of her provincial town and take a government job in Washington.

There, while waiting in line for a flu shot, she met a young mechanical engineer, a Yankee from the remote and exotic city of New York, who in good storybook fashion could take her away from *all that*. Joe Clark had been barred from combat because of his terrible eyesight, and he, too, had come to Washington looking for adventure and hungry to seize on some piece of the war at home. After the Armistice, Grace took Joe back to Kentucky just long enough for a wedding by the Baptist preacher in her aunt Clara's parlor, then moved with her husband to New York, where she soon renounced the Baptists for Joe's Episcopalians (for whom Joe's mother had earlier renounced the Catholics) and never cooked grits again.

And never told stories again—or, perhaps, ever. So rarely and reluctantly did Grace talk about her past that we could never tell how much she even knew about it, and by the time I had become interested in learning more about her Kentucky roots, the few remaining ancient relatives who were neither vanished nor dead had no more interest than she in digging up so un-modern a past.

So it was in a privately published volume of Woodson family lore pulled off a library shelf, not at my grandmother's knee, that I first came across the story of the death of John Woodson. It was while sitting in the gloomy splendor of the New York Public Library genealogy room, not rocking gently on the porch in the summer twilight, that I read about how my tenth-great-grandfather had been killed in the second "Great Massacre," the mass attack on the Virginia settlements in 1644 led by Powhatan's successor Opechancanough, who was nearly one hundred years old, so weak his aides had to hold his eyes open as he lay on his litter, and determined that this time he would manage to drive the white interlopers away forever. Perhaps, though, it's just as well that the story came to me not entangled in the intimate and complicated bonds of my own flesh and blood but embedded in the liberating impassiveness of a fat and musty old book. If I actually *had* grown up knowing that story, it would have been much more difficult to step back and look beyond the drama and tragedy to the story of the story—to explore how Woodsons had created it, shared it, preserved it, and passed it down through the generations. It would have been harder to acknowledge that this story, like *all* stories people tell, is not a sacred text, but rather has evolved over the generations in ways that responded to the individual interpretations and needs of its tellers. The saga of John and Sarah Woodson offers above all a wide-open opportunity to explore the many and varied ways that successive members of one spectacularly long-lived yet otherwise ordinary family used the memory of one antique misfortune to ponder, define, and continually redefine their own American pursuit of happiness.

No account of John's murder and Sarah's heroics turns up in any of the standard histories of the Virginia settlement or the Powhatan Confederacy. Nor does the story either claim or possess any authority other than family tradition. Given the loss or destruction of most of Henrico County's records from the era of the assault, just about the only fact confirmable in other sources is that people named John and Sarah (or Sara) Woodson did once live in the

Jamestown settlement. In an official census of the colony's inhabitants and their possessions taken in early 1625, the couple, at that point childless, was listed as having arrived in 1619 aboard the *George* and as living at Peirseys Hundred, the "particular plantation" originally established under the name Flowerdew Hundred by their fellow passenger Governor Sir George Yeardley. Persuasive but purely circumstantial evidence ties John and Sarah to the increasingly bet-ter-documented generations of Woodsons that began with their putative sons, Robert, generally understood to have been "Potato Hole," and John, the "Tub." And while a vivid on-the-scene account published by the Virginia Company preserves to this day the horror of Opechancanough's *first* "Great Massacre," which in March 1622 had wiped out more than a quarter of the European pop-ulation of Virginia, no contemporary description survives of the 1644 assault, leaving it even less discernible than the Woodsons in the historical record.[2]

By the early eighteenth century, the family was clearly visible in the orbit of Virginia's planter elite, owning slaves and substantial tracts of land, generally marrying well though rarely brilliantly, and holding a variety of minor colonial offices. Other Woodson descendants would include Dolley Madison, a proslav-ery acting governor of "Bleeding Kansas," Lincoln's attorney general, Stonewall Jackson's stepfather, and the outlaw whose full name was Jesse Woodson James.[3]

We can only guess at how much the first five or six generations of American Woodsons knew or thought about their deep roots in the New World. Probably not much; Americans before the nineteenth century tended to be indifferent to their history and to dismiss genealogical pursuits as elitist and irrelevant. In fact one of John and Sarah's great-great-grandsons, a Charles Woodson who died at an advanced age around 1795, was memorialized as a man of "eccen-tric disposition" because he *did* carry out extensive historical research into the Woodson history, compiling a list of the Jamestown couple's descendants that survives to this day.[4]

The earliest published version of the attack story that I know of came out only in 1887, nearly two and a half centuries and seven generations after it happened—by which time it had the air more of a mythic founding epic than a historical event. An article in the *Richmond State* newspaper titled "Two Old Relics" quoted reverently from what it said was an account of the catastrophe jotted down in the family Bible by an unnamed Woodson relative, apparently Charles's great-grandson Charles Van der Veer Woodson, who was born in the first decade of the nineteenth century. The bachelor Charles Van der Veer seemed either uninterested in or unfamiliar with the exploits of the women and the children; he called the heroic wife by the name of one of her descendants and never even mentioned the little boys or their hiding places. But he reveled in the details of the cook pot and the roasting spit and was fascinated by the old gun, which he claimed to have in his possession along with a second "relic," a walnut-framed mirror once owned by another ancestor. According to "tradition," the article said, the musket, so big "that it strikes everyone who sees it with utter astonishment [and] looks like it was made for one of the sons of Anak," had been brought from England by Dr. John Woodson himself.[5]

A maverick variation popped up in 1903 in Mrs. H. D. Pittman's genealogical encyclopedia *Americans of Gentle Birth and Their Ancestors.* Hannah Daviess Pittman, who claimed descent from Alfred the Great and William the Conqueror as well as the Woodsons, insisted that her work was not a "fashionable fad of the moment" but rather "an encyclopedia of authenticated pedigrees of people of to-day, whose ancestors, by their gentle birth and noble deeds, entitle them to a place in its pages."[6] Actually it *was* quite fashionable, given that era's fascination with genealogical matters, but "encyclopedia" it really wasn't; that seems entirely too respectable a term for so phantasmagoric a work.

Although Mrs. Pittman asserted in her preface, which she grandly called her "Proem," that she had spent four years of "painstaking care and investigation" gathering her information, many of her family trees are hopelessly tangled, based more on wish and whim than evidence.[7] She skips generations, manhandles dates, and shanghais innocent bystanders as ancestors, and the reader soon learns to understand that the recurrent phrase "There is no doubt that" actually means "The author really, really hopes."

Her version of the Woodsons' story in fact belongs to someone else entirely; in classic oral tradition style she had folded Sarah's name into a similar but much more famous adventure, reported in a best-selling nineteenth-century compendium of pioneer tales, that had featured a Mrs. John Merril and had taken place in frontier Kentucky in 1787. That story, too, had the Indians incapacitating the heroine's husband and gaining her rooftop, but this time the brave little woman's weapons were not kitchen utensils but bedclothes: she threw the feather bed onto the fire to send thick black smoke billowing up the chimney. Overcome by the fumes, the intruders tumbled senseless onto the hearth, where she quickly dispatched them with an axe. (Nor was Mrs. Pittman the only family historian with a soft spot for that story: a cousin of Harry Truman's whom the president once called "a nut" about genealogy told a very similar tale involving an *hors de combat* husband, a heroic wife, and a burning feather bed on the hearth, but this one was attributed to their great-great-grandmother Margaret Tyler, one of the first residents of what is now Shelby County, Kentucky.) Mrs. Pittman's boudoir-based telling, however, seems to have gained no traction among Woodson family historians, of whom there was an increasing horde. In 1912 the Order of First Families of Virginia was founded by a Woodson descendant and populated almost entirely by her kin, nineteen of the twenty-one original members claiming Woodson blood.[8]

But it was Henry Morton Woodson's version, the one I'd read in the library in his huge tome published in 1915, that quickly became the definitive one, *the* telling, his details now accepted as canonical. He said nothing about the provenance of the "cherished family tradition" with which he proudly prefaced his generation-by-generation account, but he did take care to describe the scrupulousness of his research. He cited both of the surviving censuses of the early Virginia settlement, for instance—the 1625 muster as well as the rudimentary headcount from the previous year—in support of his conclusion that John Woodson, surgeon and Oxford graduate, had bought six of the twenty-odd Africans traded by the Dutch merchant ship that had wandered up the James River in 1619, which made our ancestor a party to what is usually called the first slave transaction in English America.

And Henry proudly described his correspondence with hundreds of family members seeking their recollections about dead relatives, taxing their memories about a trove of family papers that some feckless cousin had tragically lost, laboriously copying out the old wills and letters they did manage to preserve, and working with patience and discretion to reconcile "contradictory statements" from "widely separated" informants. It was a labor of love that occupied ten years (he finished the book just in time, dying at the age of seventy-two barely two years after its publication), and he performed it not for a mass and faceless audience but rather on behalf of his own community of "dear kinspeople," the sort who would recognize exactly what one correspondent meant when, in an attempt to characterize an aunt, he settled on "she was—well, she was a Woodson."[9]

Plenty of present-day Woodson descendants, now at least ten or eleven generations removed from John and Sarah, know of the attack story, and take as much pleasure as any of Henry Woodson's contemporaries in aligning themselves with either the Tub tribe or the Potato Hole clan. But the tale has long since passed from the realm of oral tradition to be disseminated mainly in print—almost exclusively Henry Woodson's print—and most of my many-times-removed cousins came upon the story as serendipitously as I did. The Internet, however, has radically heightened the consequences of that sort of serendipity. When my mother and I started our labors, the prime sources for trading family information were privately published genealogical newsletters, whose telltale purple ditto machine ink betrayed the slimness of their circulation. Now online genealogy bulletin boards and personal websites send out a flood of discoveries, citations, and documents as well as misapprehensions and misinterpretations, all of them circulating much more quickly to much wider audiences. Surfing through Woodson forums, I found frequent messages from posters sharing with their newfound cousins the thrill of having discovered "We are Potato Hole Woodsons!"—which in turn elicited responses from both grizzled veterans smiling at their fresh enthusiasm and dazzled newbies demanding to be let in on the family legend.[10]

But in virtually all of the references to the story made in the past generation or so that specifically name a source—in newsletters going back thirty years, in online postings, in my conversations and correspondence with active family historians—the citation is not to Great-Grandpa but rather to old Henry's big book or to some other publication directly derived from it. Although occasional Woodsons of my generation or younger did tell me that they had first heard the story from an older relative, those older relatives had themselves found it only through a random encounter with Henry's book.[11]

The book has never been hard to find: it is held by libraries popular among genealogists, it has been microfilmed and issued on CD-ROM, it has been reprinted by a specialty publishing house, and in 2008 it debuted on Google Books. And it's not just family members who have found it, either. Henry's book has been cited uncritically by academic historians and has even shown up, verbatim, in a respectable medical journal, in a tribute to Sarah, "the first wife of a doctor to come to our new land." Even a rare writer who dared apply her own imaginative touches to the story still sheltered herself under the authority of the canonical version. The author of a popular 1967 history of the women behind famous doctors wove a romantic thirteen-page fantasia on Sarah's travails as she surmounted the loneliness and dislocations of moving to the New World with her selfless doctor husband and gradually attained serenity, lace cuffs, and a houseful of slaves who sang at their work. In her endnotes, however, the author cited as the only source for her preposterous fantasy the medical journal article that had in turn essentially been copied from Henry Woodson's pages.[12]

The basic plot of this wide-traveling and durable story, that John Woodson was killed by American Indians, is very likely true; that happened all the time to English people in Virginia in the early years. Plausible, though less certain, is that his death came during the mass assault of 1644 that left four or five hundred of the roughly eight thousand colonists dead. On the one hand, since oral historians find that people seeking bearable explanations for tragedy often conflate their personal calamities with larger events, it's not impossible that John was simply struck down in some workaday encounter too mundane for his grieving descendants to accept.[13] On the other hand, the extravagance of the carnage—the suggestion that it had taken more than nine "savages" to overcome the lone white man, and the immediate, humiliating, and effortless vengeance that a lone woman and a humble artisan achieved against them with the "civilized" weapons of superior technology and quicker wits—does hint at a determined attempt to grapple with the otherwise inexplicable horror that so many Europeans could have fallen prey to such primitive havoc.

But almost every other word Henry Woodson wrote about the attack is either unconfirmable, inaccurate, or unlikely.

John Woodson was neither an Oxford graduate nor a doctor nor a slave owner nor, apparently, a success at anything, and his widow, Sarah, died poor too. In the detailed census of 1625 John has no title while "Doctor John Pott" does, no accident in a hierarchical society where even "Mister" had to be earned, and Virginia Company records strongly suggest that Pott was the only physician in the colony in the 1620s. The inventories of each household's arms and provisions that were included in the census, moreover, show that although Dr. Pott was rich in possessions—including two houses, ten "peeces" of small arms, twenty barrels of corn, and seven hundred preserved fish—the Woodsons' cache of four bushels of corn and a few odd armaments made theirs one of the skimpiest recorded in all Virginia. The census also clearly lists all seven of the Africans in Peirseys Hundred (including a child) not in the Woodson household but in that of the cape merchant Abraham Peirsey, the richest man in Virginia. John Woodson is totally invisible in other contemporary records, leaving no trace of ever having held any office or witnessed any documents or formally claimed any land, one hundred acres of which would have been due to whoever had paid for his and Sarah's passage. In fact, since John and Sarah voyaged out with Governor Yeardley and settled, with their meager possessions, on the governor's land, they most likely numbered among Yeardley's tenant farmers, just a small social and economic step above the indentured servants.[14]

At some point, according to a wayward legal document recently discovered, the widowed Sarah Woodson seems to have married and outlived a second husband, a man named Johnson. In January 1660/1, the estate of "Sarah Johnson widdow deceased" was inventoried and distributed according to her directions; the four legatees, whose relationships weren't specified, included John Woodson, Robert Woodson, and an otherwise unknown Deborah Woodson, who may have been their sister, with John as executor. But if this Sarah was indeed the Jamestown immigrant, her second marriage hadn't raised her much in the world. The deathbed inventory shows only a sorry puddle of possessions: some tailor's implements, a feather bed, a chest, a few dishes, some "ould Clathes," and four cows, one so "ould" it could "be killed at [John's] pleasure." The inventory also includes a pot and a spit—the most common of household utensils, they were also the ones Sarah supposedly turned against the attackers—though it doesn't, I note, list a huge gun.[15]

Almost every detail of the Indians' assault itself falls apart under a moment's thought. Ligon the shoemaker, for instance, was supposedly able to take down seven fleet and furious attackers with three blasts from his musket. But that would have been a miraculous feat for even the nimblest marksman using the matchlock or snaphaunce of the day, which required long minutes to load and fire and which was notoriously balky and inaccurate, effective only in close-range volleys, prone to misfiring (generally about one shot in every four), and impossible to aim with anything approaching precision. According to some estimates, fewer than half a percent of the shots fired from a musket actually hit their targets, and a seventeenth-century shooter would have considered "he couldn't hit the side of a barn" not a taunt but a tranquil acknowledgment of the limitations of technological and human capabilities alike. The only recorded Ligon in the colony in 1644, moreover, was no lowly artisan achieving his one moment of greatness but rather a wealthy cousin of Governor Berkeley's who carried the title "Colonel" and who would later serve as a burgess for Henrico County.[16]

The behavior of the attackers was peculiar, too: no one would have been so brainless as to slide down a chimney while a fire was burning down below. The little boys' hiding places under the tub and in the potato hole were implausible for a raw riverfront settlement where no one would have owned an unessential luxury like a washtub and no one could have eaten a potato, a vegetable unknown in Virginia in 1644. Nor is it credible that a very humble household of four happened to own something as preposterously extravagant as an Indian-size cook pot, then kept it boiling on the hearth on a warm April day just in case a brainless Indian-size guest should come calling on the roof.

Some of the parts of the story in fact sound more archetypal than historical, literally fairy-tale material. Sarah's cook pot–and–chimney maneuver vividly recalls the trick the Third Little Pig pulled on the Big Bad Wolf, while the musketeer's coolly efficient slaughter of the massed forces of darkness bears echoes of such tales of magical prowess as "Seven at One Blow" (a feat accomplished, we remember, by a lowly artisan, a tailor) or "Jack the Giant-Killer" (who was a poor widow's son). And once the potato gained acceptance in the eighteenth century as a staple crop and a versatile food, the potato hole began to figure as a classic hiding place in all manner of local and family lore, a rustic haven that never failed to shelter innocence from evil, whether it be Indians, Redcoats, Yankees, slave catchers, tornadoes, or flames.[17]

The mirror that was one of the "Two Old Relics" described in the 1887 newspaper article has apparently been lost, but the miraculous musket survives to this day, carefully preserved at the Virginia Historical Society in Richmond. Records at the society show that in 1929, nearly three hundred years after it allegedly worked its "deadly effect," the "Woodson gun" was placed on deposit there by Francis L. Venable, whose surname links him to a Prince Edward County clan that frequently intermarried with Charles Van der Veer Woodson's branch of the family. More than seven feet long, the fowling piece was recently restored with the help of contributions from Woodson descendants and now stands on display in a tall glass case. Carefully acknowledging both legend and scholarship, the label notes forthrightly that the wooden stock of the gun dates from the 1740s and the flintlock bears the mark of a lock maker active in 1758, but "it is just possible that the barrel only may coincide with the earlier Woodson legacy." The re-stocking of the gun, the label adds, would also explain the absence of Ligon's name, which, according to Henry Woodson, had been "rudely carved" on the original stock.[18]

It isn't just the details of the Woodsons' life that are off the mark, however; the general notions of most Woodson descendants about life in seventeenth-century Jamestown, which showed most explicitly in the rosy history of the famous doctor's resourceful wife but thrums as an obbligato throughout the other versions as well, pictured my ancestors and their fellow English Americans as having gathered their happiness as gently as if they were cupping a butterfly in their hands. That wasn't the story at all. Virginia did indeed make extravagant promises of happiness, but to most people Virginia delivered little more than tragedy, trouble, and despair.

Like nearly all of the first waves of settlers who set out for what would end up as the first permanent English settlement in the New World, my tenth-great-grandparents John and Sarah Woodson doubtless signed up for the voyage for one reason only: to get rich, or at least less poor than they'd been. (The unsourced story I found on several online genealogy sites that John Woodson renounced his baronial title and came to the New World so that his Quaker wife could freely practice her religion is, of course, another fantasy: although later generations of Woodsons did become Quakers, the Religious Society of Friends wasn't formed until 1647.) Improving their situation didn't seem an implausible hope. For more than a century, Europeans had been hearing vague but dazzling reports of the treasures and marvels and perfect happiness to be found in the prelapsarian paradise across the sea. The English were growing ever more determined to claim their part of both happiness and loot even as their first efforts met disappointment after fiasco after defeat: beaten to the best spots by the papist tyrants of Portugal and Spain, balked by the strange elusiveness of the Northwest Passage, baffled by the mysterious fate of the Roanoke colony, whose entire population, more than one hundred men, women, and children, had been lost or killed or spirited away and not a single soul found to tell what had happened.

Jamestown was going to be different. Underwritten by the Virginia Company, a private joint-stock corporation under royal charter, it was open to anyone who wanted to risk some spare cash (or, if he preferred, his own body and labor) in return for a proportionate share of whatever profits the Company earned. And both legend and the Company promised enormous ones. There would be spiritual dividends, to be sure, in helping to bring Protestant Christianity to the New World; there would be social benefits in having a rigorous and remote preserve where England's idle poor could be put to worthwhile work. But it was the prospective financial rewards that really dazzled—the gold, silver, copper, and pearls, of course, but also silk, spices, dyestuffs, medicinal plants, furs, wine grapes, timber, tar. The Americas, everyone said, would be a convenient backyard larder, hothouse, and treasure chest combined, a one-stop bazaar brimming with all the riches of Africa, Asia, and Europe.

Even a gentleman's son with an Oxford education and training in medicine—even the man John Woodson was *not*—might have felt tempted by visions of paradise to abandon a life of applying plasters and leeches to the ills of Dorsetshire. And for the man John Woodson most likely *was,* a farmer's son facing a life of little more than producing more farmer's sons, how could paradise have looked any more appealing? So John and Sarah signed on. In the deep winter of January 1619 my forebears left behind everything and everyone they knew and with a hundred other intrepid souls including the new governor, Sir George Yeardley, crammed themselves aboard the *George* for a wretchedly uncomfortable three-month sea voyage that killed off fourteen passengers and three members of the crew. That wasn't so bad. You always lost some people to illness or mishap aboard ship. At least the *George* wasn't boarded by pirates or blown hopelessly off course or scuttled by a storm; at least it didn't meet the fate that soon afterwards overtook the *Abigail,* an epidemic so virulent that "after a while," one of the harrowed survivors wrote her sister back home, "we saw little but throwing folkes ouer boord." The *George* arrived safely in Virginia in the last days of April, and the Woodsons and their surviving fellow travelers set foot at last on land.[19]

Or, more likely, *in* land. Jamestown was built mainly on a bog, and the unwary tended to sink.

Their hearts undoubtedly did too when Sarah and John took their first good look around the twelve-year-old settlement. The Virginia Company had snookered them. Paradise turned out to be a bleak and mangy place, populated by about a thousand souls, including a handful of children and nowhere near enough women to go around. And in Virginia, it soon became clear, prospering didn't mean being wealthy; it meant being alive.

At least the "starving time" was over by the time the Woodsons arrived, that terrible winter of 1609–10 when the supply ships failed to come, the meager food stocks dwindled completely away, the vigilant Indians shot at any settler who ventured outside the stockade to forage or hunt, and the desperate inhabitants were reduced to digging up corpses to eat. The shocking rumors that soon began circulating about one enterprising fellow who was said to have killed, dismembered, salted, and slowly eaten his pregnant wife marked a turning point in the image of the New World as a place of peace and plenty. But while the famine was caused in part by the colonists' improvidence and the Indians' hostility, it was made even worse by the freaks of nature. Clues found in centuries-old tree rings, lake beds, and glacial moraines have been adding weight to the on-the-spot accounts suggesting that the Virginia Company could not have chosen a less auspicious moment to plant its paradise: just as the southern seaboard was being ravaged by some of its coldest weather ever and its worst drought in centuries.[20]

Only at the very last minute was the entire English experiment saved from going belly-up. An unexpected fleet bearing reinforcements, fresh supplies, and a new governor arrived like a perfect nick-of-time prototype of the U.S.

Cavalry, rounding Point Comfort at the mouth of the James at exactly the right moment to intercept the few dozen gaunt survivors of the dreadful winter who had finally decided to pack up, go home, and forget the whole preposterous idea of America. Few of the weary colonists, however, seemed particularly happy about their narrow escape from escaping.

That timely deliverance did not relieve Jamestown of its other perils, either, one of which probably came as a particularly cruel shock to anyone expecting another Eden. Not so long before, a Spanish physician called Nicolás Monardes had thrilled readers throughout Europe with a widely translated account of how the natural wonders of the Indies could cure any ill. Oil from something called the fig tree of hell could "heale a windy Dropsie." Tobacco was a surefire remedy for everything from pains in the head, breast, or stomach to labor pains, kidney stones, snakebite, and bad breath. And sassafras cured anything at all; so reliable was its potency that the Spanish explorers had no fear of "the evilles which are present, nor have any care of them that be to come, and so they have it for a universall remedy, for all manner of deseases." In the New World, if you believed Dr. Monardes, no one would ever be sick.[21]

But the colonists seemed to be sick all the time—sick in ways that, like the good doctor's pharmacopoeia, were special to the New World; sick in ways that no root or bark or bone could cure. Hundreds of hopeful new settlers were inveigled every year by the promoters and pamphleteers, but they died by the score, soon after their arrival and much to their surprise, if not from malnutrition then from malaria, typhoid, dysentery, scurvy, or salt poisoning from drinking the slimy, brackish river water that was all they could get on their ill-chosen marshy peninsula. Experience suggested that anyone who managed to live through an entire summer in Virginia would be "seasoned," as they put it, to the muggy heat and the alien and inadequate diet, and somewhat less vulnerable to disease. No one, though, ever felt entirely free from fear of the "evilles" of the place.

Nor was disease the only danger. No amount of seasoning could prevent the deaths of scores more settlers by Indian attack, drowning, or accident, like the nearly fatal gunpowder explosion in 1609 that sent Captain John Smith back home to England for good. Some years later Smith would establish himself as a prototype of the distastefully bumptious American. His published accounts of the settling of the New World heavily featured his own wisdom, derring-do, and singular importance, including his deathless tale of how the love-struck Indian princess Pocahontas had shielded his body with her own just as her father, the chief Powhatan, was raising his war club to dash out the gallant captain's brains. The princess was actually ten or twelve at the time, a curious and playful child who wandered around the English fort stark naked and used to demonstrate the art of turning cartwheels to a rapt crowd of boys in the market square, and if the war club episode happened at all, it may, some historians say, have actually been not a real threat at all but rather a symbolic gesture intended as part of a ceremonial adoption. Scholars now generally agree that Smith's role in keeping the precarious little colony from going under was every bit as vital as his own swaggering prose insisted, but they have been arguing for nearly four hundred years about how much to believe of his other swashbuckling adventures around the globe, including various other timely rescues by various other besotted highborn ladies. But as one of the first writers ever to embark on the task of fashioning a public story and a public *self* out of an American experience, the chesty Smith ended up with the last laugh at his critics: although he spent only about two and a half years in the colony, his most unprepossessing of names is probably the only one belonging to a Jamestown settler that four centuries later the average American can dredge up.

For their part, the settlers who stayed in Virginia had so little power to fashion anything and so little to be happy about that some actually died of despair; some simply turned their faces to the wall and faded away. Company officials safe at home in England denounced them as lazy and weak-minded, but the colonists themselves, wiser in the ways of Virginia, spoke of their companions' "Melancholye," their "distracted and forlorne" condition. In fact historians have speculated that those forlorn souls, weakened by a lethal combination of physical malnourishment and the emotional burdens of hopelessness, boredom, isolation, and fear, succumbed to the ailment that centuries later American prisoners of war in Japan and Korea would dub "give-up-itis": a loss of the will to live.[22]

The Virginians who didn't die quickly lived meanly. They found no gold. They found no silver. The pearls disappointed; the wine grapes fizzled; the silkworms died. The cargo ships that were expected to return to England in triumph bulging with New World treasure instead toiled modestly up the Thames loaded with clapboards, potash, pitch, and so much sassafras that prices in England plummeted. There's no evidence that illness did too. Then, shortly before he consummated English America's first-ever mixed marriage by wedding the now teenaged, Christianized, and well-clad Pocahontas in 1614, the resourceful John Rolfe introduced the colonists to the cultivation of tobacco and demonstrated that the leaf might have magical healing powers after all. The colonists were soon cultivating the stuff with such single-minded ferocity, sowing it everywhere from the fields to the market square and the streets, that they had to be forced to take time out for less beguiling chores like fishing or hunting or tending corn.

As a married couple who arrived together, John and Sarah were still something of a rarity in a place so top-heavy with men, and the Company tried hard to impose a semblance of normal domestic life on its colony of unruly gallants far from home. Investors gathered up several shiploads of widows, orphaned girls, and other females at loose ends, all of whom, they said, had furnished testimonials of good character, and invited any lonesome colonist who could plunk down 150 pounds of tobacco for her passage to take his choice. Most of the brides, however, proved to be bad bargains; within five years of their arrival, the seasoning and the Indians had killed off something like three-quarters of them. In 1619 a wayward ship described as a Dutch man-of-war wandered into anchor at Jamestown and, desperate for food and supplies, offered to barter its only spare merchandise: some twenty African Negroes. That human cargo would turn out to be a much more productive buy for the Jamestown planters.

Reading history can be just as messy and complicated as telling it. If you believe the historian Robert Beverley, writing in 1705 about the founding of Virginia a century earlier, it was right about this time in this goldless, silkless, comfortless, and outlandish New World that the inhabitants were beginning to think themselves "the happiest People in the World."[23]

In some ways, daily life did seem to be looking up by the time John and Sarah Woodson came ashore. The ferocious regime of martial law was ended, and in the summer after their arrival the House of Burgesses, the first representative legislature in English America, began meeting and deliberating on everything from tobacco prices to gambling and drunkenness. A truce with Powhatan along with Rolfe's marriage to Pocahontas, a highly visible if rare success story in the Company's project to convert the Indians to Christianity, seemed to put an end to the constant skirmishing with the natives. Even though King James himself had publicly called the custom of smoking "lothsome to the eye, hatefull to the Nose, harmefull to the braine, daungerous to the Lunges," shipments of the noxious weed were rising every year, while Company officials were vigorously recruiting vignerons, ironworkers, and glassmakers.[24] And some settlers had left the fetid and boggy Jamestown peninsula behind to move upriver or across the bay, where the sweeter air and water made the seasoning a little easier.

The Company had also recently come up with a brilliant gambit for attracting more stable and productive settlers for its straggling colony: land. Under the new "headright" system, well-to-do newcomers could become instant proprietors, receiving fifty acres of land for each person they transported to the colony at their own expense, whether family members, tenant farmers, or servants. And even people of modest means who could never have afforded either their own land in England or their own fare to Virginia—people, probably, like John and Sarah Woodson—now had the opportunity to become property owners too. If they pledged to work as tenant farmers for seven years, the Company would pay for their passage, give them a half share in the profits of their labor, and at the end of their service allow them to claim their own fifty acres of Virginia soil. The Woodsons were joining a surge of new arrivals that reached more than 3,500 between 1618 and 1621—a distinctly mixed blessing, given the slender resources available to support them.

The boom in land, settlers, and tobacco also turned out to be a cheap way for a lucky and ambitious few to build substantial fortunes, and a small clutch of Jamestown's citizens was growing very fortunate indeed, often at the expense of the Company, fellow colonists, or both. Upon their arrival the Woodsons settled at Flowerdew Hundred, the plantation owned in turn by two of the most successful. George Yeardley, who arrived in 1610 owning nothing more valuable than his soldier's sword, ended up a three-time governor with a knighthood and a reputation for cheating the help, and the merchant Abraham Peirsey used his position in charge of the Company's magazine to amass the handsomest estate seen in the colony.[25]

Virginia soon paid for its first pink dawnings of success. The native inhabitants, who for years had endured streams of white newcomers pouring in, pushing ever farther afield, taking up more and more land, consuming or wrecking more and more of the country's resources, cheating and harassing and killing their women and children as well as their men, had begun to understand that the English were not about to give up and go away on their own. In the spring of 1622 Opechancanough, who had become chief after the death of his brother Powhatan, plotted a drastic remedy. Although a friendly Indian's warning had placed the city of Jamestown on alert and a few other communities got the news in time, most of the settlements that spread for miles along the river saw no cause for alarm on the morning of March 22, when bands of unarmed Indians arrived, as they often did, to barter their venison, turkeys, and fruits. Some of the natives even sat down calmly and shared breakfast with the settlers.

Then suddenly, as the English went about their daily business in their homes and fields, doing their planting, gardening, brickmaking, and sawing, the Indians turned on them and "basely and barbarously murthered" them by the score, as the Company's account of the event put it, "not sparing eyther age or sexe, man, woman or childe; so sodaine in their cruell execution, that few or none discerned the weapon or blow that brought them to destruction." Most of the whites were struck down with their own tools. "Not being content with taking away life alone," the account went on in righteous fury, "they fell after againe vpon the dead, making as well as they could, a fresh murder, defacing, dragging, and mangling the dead carkasses into many pieces, and carrying some parts away in derision, with base and bruitish triumph." By the time the sun set, roughly 350 of the 1,240 or so colonists lay dead. "God forgiue me I thinke the last massacre killed all our Countrie," William Capps wrote home. "Besides them they killed, they burst the heart of all the rest."[26]

That was John and Sarah Woodson's *first* massacre.

As Jamestown teetered on the edge of disaster, Company officials saw clearly how hazardous the wrong story could be to their enterprise, and America's first English fathers became America's pioneer spin doctors. Not only did they churn out cheery promotional tracts, ballads, and broadsheets to keep inveigling new settlers; not only did they rigidly censor what those new settlers could write home once they had arrived in Virginia, and mete out drastic punishments to anyone who dared murmur against the authorities; but also Company men were deliberately peddling outright lies about what was going on in the settlement. The colony's leaders, it was said, would routinely write "double and contradictorie" reports to the folks back home, cheerily discoursing on abundance and prosperity in the letters they intended for the public while frankly describing the settlement's misery in private correspondence within the Company itself.[27] And even after the Indians' strike, with the Company practically bankrupt, the colony nearly annihilated, and the settlers' retaliatory campaign against Opechancanough's people waxing even more savage than their attackers had been, Company officials continued to insist that the only way to repair Jamestown's fortunes was to get more and more settlers to come— by whatever means necessary.

Come they did. In 1623, the dismal year after the great assault—when the few survivors of the disease-ridden ship *Abigail* were spreading the contagion among their new neighbors with such diligence that the epidemic killed even more settlers than the American Indians had, when the hungry and demoralized

Virginians were vainly awaiting succor from the supply ship *Seaflower,* which had been blown up by a careless smoker roistering in the gunroom during a stopover in Bermuda—another of my ancestors, a Canterbury youth named John Bates, heard the Company's siren song. He signed his body and soul over to Abraham Peirsey, promising the merchant the next five or so years of his life in return for a suit and a couple of pairs of stockings, some meager rations, £5 or £6 for his passage on the *Southampton,* and the chance to plant his feet on the soil of the New World.[28] Or the bog. All told, in the seventeen years that it managed the colony, the Company sent perhaps seven thousand settlers to seek their fortunes in paradise. In February 1624, just months before the exasperated Crown shut down the Virginia Company and took over the colony itself, officials counted fewer than 1,300 inhabitants. That made for a mortality rate of upwards of 80 percent.[29] Seldom has a hope of happiness been so lethal.

Traditions

None of the vast chronic unhappiness that was the Virginia settlement made it into the Woodson family's antique tale of the second "Great Massacre." The story that later generations of Woodsons cherished and passed along to their children wasn't about the misery, the fear, the squalor, and the brutality of everyday life. It did allude to a moment of historic and personal tragedy, but the killing of John Woodson during the mass assault seemed little more than a plot point to invite his wife's heroic act.

In fact the story was barely about John and Sarah at all. Like so many other "cherished family traditions," the Woodsons' says more about the lives, hopes, and histories of its tellers than about its long-dead heroes. And it's the story *behind* the story that has more to say to the historian—and the descendant as well—than does either the tale itself or the event at its heart.

The Woodsons' epic, it turns out, probably took its current shape not in the wake of the mass attack but instead more than one hundred years later, toward the end of the eighteenth century, and is more revealing about the tumult of the Revolution than about the woes of Governor Berkeley's Virginia. Its survival into the twentieth century had more to do with what an unreconstructed Confederate preferred to believe about African Americans and Yankees than with anything it stated about American Indians. And the persistent appeal it enjoys in the twenty-first century arises from the peculiar phenomenon that present-day Woodsons are *merely* telling it.

The key player in the saga of the story was John and Sarah's great-great-grandson Charles Woodson, the "eccentric" family historian, who died at an advanced age around 1795. He was the first documented owner of the famous musket that, though said by later family members to have been used in 1644, was actually manufactured in whole or in part a century later, during his own life-time. He would have known his grandfather, who was Potato Hole Woodson's oldest son. And his marriage to a third cousin would make their seven children Potato Holes twice over.

Other clues implicating Charles Woodson as the story's shaper are essentially archaeological: neither potato holes nor washtubs would have been anachro-nisms in his Virginia, and the new weapon that would come to be known as the Kentucky rifle, which made bull's-eyes at one hundred feet not just possible but routine, could have turned even the most human shooter into a magical marksman. The demotion of the gun-toting Ligon from colonel to shoemaker could have been something of a pointed joke among neighbors whose closeness bred both affection and rivalry; for decades Ligons and Woodsons lived near enough each other at Curles on the James River to share in several lawsuits over property as well as in at least one wedding, around 1772. And the elevation of John Woodson into selfless pioneer physician might have been intended as a gesture of support for another Woodson whose medical skills had been publicly impeached. In 1766 Constant Watkins Woodson, a Prince Edward County neighbor married to a cousin of Charles's, had been granted a £100 reward by the House of Burgesses for having developed some undescribed cure for can-cer. She took to the newspapers to cheekily advertise her superiority over the local doctors, but was soon denounced in the same papers by the husband of a relapsed patient, who warned readers that his poor wife "hath been much worse with that disease since [Constant] dealt with her than she ever was before."[30]

After Charles's death, his progeny stepped in as custodians of the tale. All the names associated with its very first published version—the author of the 1887 newspaper article, the owner of the old gun who had jotted the notes in the family Bible, the first owner of the old mirror, and the granddaughter-in-law of Sarah's who was misnamed as the heroine—belonged by blood or marriage to Charles's immediate family. In fact as late as 1936, a descendant of Charles's five generations removed was telling a brief version of the story, chronologically askew but still clearly recognizable, to Mrs. Bessie Thompson, a researcher for the federal government's Works Progress Administration. Mrs. Thompson had come to Prince Edward County asking the local old-timers about the history of "Brooklyn," the dilapidated old two-story weatherboarded house built by Charles Woodson's son and inhabited for at least a century afterwards by his descendants. As she relayed the Woodsons' story in her official report, the bloody work of wielding the roasting spit against the attackers had decorously devolved from Granny to a faceless "old slave," and the whole affray, her informant seemed to believe, had taken place in that very house. Impossible, as Mrs. Thompson dutifully remarked, since the property had been bought in 1776 and the house built in 1812, but a further confirmation of the story's chain of custody.[31]

Another set of clues into the social uses of the story is more inferential than verifiable, suggested by the general Enlightenment-era shift in the ways people thought about themselves as independent, their will as free, their lives as worth telling, and their happiness as their right. Any woman in any epoch could have acted decisively to protect her children or avenge her husband. But *making a story* out of the deed—in effect choosing to remember and celebrate not an archetypal larger-than-life hero but rather an ordinary person, this particular ordinary person named Sarah, who *acted,* who exerted her will to seize control of her destiny—is an enterprise particularly resonant with, perhaps even unlikely before, the revolution in consciousness and the rise of new ideas about autonomy, identity, selfhood, and natural rights that rippled through the later seventeenth and eighteenth centuries. From that revolution also sprang a mighty new way of telling stories, the modern novel, and a new kind of protagonist, the ordinary individual person whose actions had causes and effects: a Clarissa Harlowe or a Tom Jones, not an Everyman, and a plot, not the workings of Providence.[32] In all these evolving ways of making connections among history, humans, selfhood, and story, the Woodsons' epic participated as well.

And finally, the larger message of that particular story, rooted in massacre, vengeance, dark-skinned marauders, and female prowess, is peculiarly Revolutionary in spirit. The hoary genre of the Indian captivity narrative surged back into prominence during the American War for Independence. Accounts first published by Puritans a century earlier, like the story of Mary Rowlandson's capture in 1676 during the apocalyptic King Philip's War, were frequently reprinted during this period. But the stories held very different meanings for American Patriots than they had for readers in Rowlandson's day.

The Puritans' tales had been meant to teach a religious lesson: that captivity among the devilish savages was God's way of testing the steadfastness, faith, and submissiveness of his people, while their return to civilization symbolized their redemption. During the Revolution, however, those old stories of Indian war and captivity were understood in a light not religious but political, as American Patriots struggled to liberate themselves from the warlike outsiders who were invading, tyrannizing, capturing, even "massacring" (see Boston, Paoli, Waxhaw) the innocent. The new editions of Rowlandson's narrative used exactly the same text as the originals, but some included illustrations showing the supposedly submissive Rowlandson in a pose that made nonsense of the Puritan message, boldly defending her liberty by firing her musket at attackers dressed more like Redcoats than "red devils."[33]

That the brave and warlike Woodson of the tale happened to be a woman was not unusual for this era either. Some captivity tales had begun to feature a different type of heroine, the "deputy husband," who, in the absence of her man through death, war, or travel, was called upon to take over the traditionally male duties of protecting her hearth and children. Faced with Indian attack or captivity, these women did not simply *endure* until the men came home; they did not simply wait out threats to their freedom. Instead they took action to preserve or reclaim it. In 1697 Hannah Duston of Haverhill, Massachusetts, the most famous example of the Amazonian heroine, was carried off by Indians just days after giving birth to her eighth child, but she soon found an opportunity to kill ten of her twelve captors, take their scalps for the bounty, and make her escape by canoe. With their deeds of manly prowess, these women embraced, at least symbolically, the Patriot cause, and underscored America's steadfastness, virtue, and willingness to fight.[34]

Sarah Woodson's story must have had a personal appeal for the antiquarian Charles as well. As a third-generation Quaker whose family was steadily falling away—a daughter married a non-Quaker, a son enlisted in the Continental Army, and Woodsons everywhere were wrestling with their consciences over the Friends' recent move toward abolitionism—he probably felt deeply ambivalent about warfare. Telling Sarah's story could have given Charles the vicarious pleasure of expressing his patriotism and joining the fight without having to acknowledge a martial spirit of his own. It's tempting, though perhaps too pat, to argue that the story itself was also deeply ambivalent about warfare: Sarah herself hadn't actually *shot* anybody, having deployed only household utensils, and only against those attackers who had bodily invaded her house and threatened her children. She left the bloodier defense duties to Ligon, the male laborer, and the carving of *his* name on the musket might have made it a more acceptable heirloom for a Quaker family. In any case, Sarah's deeds in *preventing* captivity for herself and her sons also had a special resonance for her great-great-grandson Charles in his role as the father of young Major Tarlton Woodson, who was taken prisoner by the British during a raid on Staten Island. During the three years Tarlton spent fretting in captivity in Brooklyn, he carried out a vigorous epistolary debate with a brother over whether America had enough virtue to prevail in the fight for independence.[35]

We'll never know exactly what Sarah was doing on that spring day in 1644 when the Virginia settlements came under assault. We can, however, easily understand why, during the military, moral, and political crisis of the 1770s and 1780s, as Charles and his sons debated the strength of American virtue and made their sacrifices on its behalf, he might have found his own happiness in restoring, revising, or even creating a story of how the grandmother of his grandfather had confronted the hopes and perils of a new world, turned her feminine plowshares into arms, and redeemed the sufferings of her family with an unlikely victory over a bestial foe. In a revolutionary era that was particularly hospitable to new notions of individual personhood, that in fact was dedicated to securing the right of individual persons to define their own happiness and the liberty to fashion their own lives accordingly, this story about the personhood of an ancestor whose life had so many parallels with his own, whether or not all its facts were strictly and confirmably accurate, could also have been a way for Charles to help himself negotiate his own place in the terra incognita of the United States of America. Telling his foremother's story of devotion, virtue, and triumph, in other words, was a way to narrate what he saw his own life to be.

The wide dissemination of the story in the twentieth century came almost entirely from its inclusion in the huge and detailed family history published in 1915 by Henry Morton Woodson of Memphis. And it takes little imagination to conjecture why this Woodson found a story allegedly from 1644 to be so appealing two and a half centuries later.

Unlike the "eccentric" Charles Woodson's, Henry's interest in his ancestors was highly typical of his (and the encyclopedist Mrs. Pittman's) time. By the end of the nineteenth century and the beginning of the twentieth, genealogy was becoming something of an obsession among the many nostalgic Americans anxious to claim and control a golden national past in the face of a present they saw as increasingly ungovernable, impersonal, and tinny. No one could deny that the nation was hurtling along a path more urban, more industrial, more commercial, more Yankee-fied, where everything seemed bigger, faster, louder, dirtier. Many old-stock white Americans, especially those in the middle class, felt increasingly beleaguered by the growing population of freed slaves, immigrants,

city dwellers, and other people who seemed either unreliably American or, perhaps, reliably un-American—people, they felt, who neither appreciated the old
traditions and values nor understood why they needed protection against the
new order. Springing up around this time were dozens of heritage organizations—the Colonial Dames, the Daughters of the American Revolution, the
Mayflower Society, and the Woodsons' own First Families of Virginia— that
restricted their membership to people who could confirm their descent from the
earlier immigrants and fostered a sense of communion, exclusivity, and safety in
the service of filiopiety. And family historians were laboring long into the night
to establish the *right* descent: in 1869 the Library of Congress had just 414 genealogical publications in its collection, but by 1909 the shelves were groaning
under nearly 3,500 new acquisitions.[36]

Henry was also a southerner through and through, another traditional pre-
dictor of deep interest in family and history. Born in 1845 in Mississippi and
educated at a military school in Tennessee, he was still a month shy of seventeen
when he enlisted in his uncle's company of the Thirty-fourth Mississippi, which
was badly mauled at Chattanooga. His family history appeared in an era still rife
with romantic Lost Cause revisionism and in the very year the release of the D.
W. Griffith film *Birth of a Nation* helped focus the festering postwar grievances
of the white southerner and spark the revival of the Ku Klux Klan.[37]

Bitterness runs riot throughout Henry's book. To "prove" that his ancestors
numbered among the first people ever to have bought and owned slaves in
America required a misreading of the two Virginia censuses that, given his otherwise careful research in primary sources, was very possibly willful. But Henry's
reinterpretation offered him two golden opportunities: to claim a preeminence
in *two* of the most highly valued areas of achievement for many southerners—
ancestry and slave owning—as well as to reinforce the general and still seething
southern resentment over the Yankees' harmful and ignorant meddling in their
way of life. Henry also included a paean to his great-grandfather's "kindly sympathy and generous treatment" of the toilers on his plantation, which inspired
them with "absolute devotion," and he took care to point out that all Woodsons
had been "humane masters" to their slaves, many of whom, "not having any
patronymics of their own, adopted that of their former masters and cling to it
to this day with an affection and pride that is pathetic." Among the "pathetic"
descendants of one Woodson family's slaves, by the way, likely numbered Carter
G. Woodson, Ph.D. Harvard 1912, who would become known as the founder
of African American studies.[38]

So for the aging rebel Henry Woodson, the Indians seem to have been fulfilling a dual fantasy, representing both another dark-skinned "Other" bowing to white superiority and another invader whose triumphs white southerners still could not quite admit and whose wrongs they still burned to avenge. But while Charles Woodson could have seen in his family's story both a prefiguration and a celebration of his own Revolutionary experience of sacrifice and victory, Henry Woodson's "cherished family tradition" was, whether or not he was able to acknowledge it, a fairy tale at heart, singing of a great conquest he himself had notably failed to achieve and erecting and claiming a mythic happiness that could never actually be his. Telling his foremother's story of vengeance and vindication was a way to narrate what he wished his own life had been.

What, then, is the appeal of the story now, to the current generations of John and Sarah's descendants who have come across it on a website or in a family history library? If Charles Woodson used it two hundred years ago for self-fulfillment and Henry a century ago for wish fulfillment, what is it doing for present-day Woodsons? Or perhaps, as a Potato Hole Woodson myself, I should rephrase the question. What is it doing for *us*?

Woodson descendants have heartily embraced the story, generally treating it as uncritically as if they were hearing it at Grandfather's own knee and passing on the tale to other Woodsons like a fraternity handshake. While a few have delicately questioned aspects of the tale, pointing out, for instance, the anachronism of Potato Hole's nickname, others have resisted and even resented the slightest challenge to its truth. After a skeptic scoffed that an upside-down washtub was a silly place to hide since any Indian could have turned it over, an indignant descendant refuted him by drawing on her experience as a mother. "I would take any measure to protect my brood," wrote the editor of the *Woodson Watcher* newsletter in 1983, "including hiding my son under a tub, hoping that it would be overlooked in the excitement and flury [*sic*] of battle. THREE CHEERS FOR SARAH!!!!"[39]

Subscribers to the active RootsWeb e-mail list for the Woodson family have frequently revisited the tale over the years, but they rarely challenge its basic premise, confining their questions to such imponderables as which son was put into which hiding place. Not even the doubts publicly expressed by so august a genealogical authority as the Colonial Dames of America, which decided in 1999 to designate Robert and John as the first qualifying Woodson ancestors because the link to their putative father, Dr. John, had never been documented, could persuade some diehard Woodsons to loosen their grip on their "beloved" ancestor and his story. The old Woodson family tradition, it seems, which carries traces of possible service to litigious neighbors, sidelined Revolutionaries, questioning Quakers, embarrassed mountebanks, and embittered states' righters, has achieved something unexpected for a story so deeply rooted in oral history. It has become inviolable.

There's nothing inherently pure or sacred about Henry Woodson's particular version; it's one exemplar of an old story, one version out of many, one that emerged by accident and that might well have ended up wrapping fish heads if it had appeared only in the ephemeral pages of a newspaper instead of in a hardy 760-page volume. Yet while Henry Woodson himself reported that he had often had to reconcile his relatives' "contradictory statements" about their family history, once he had pickled his version in the brine of print, it became a sacred talisman that family members passed from hand to hand with its canonical details, even language, carefully intact, vigilantly defending it from challenge not just by other Woodson kin but also by outsiders. While so many efforts to embody historical memories—in holiday commemorations, schoolbooks, monuments, in the Smithsonian's exhibition of the *Enola Gay* and Oliver Stone's movie about JFK, in the four-hundredth anniversary of Jamestown and the first anniversary of September 11—give rise to public conversations about identity and values, conversations that range from the formative to the contentious to the obstreperous, the Woodsons' tale is protected by a community that has chosen simply to *tell* it rather than to converse, ponder, or debate about it.

It's a commonplace that communities are defined by—are in fact created by—the sharing of stories and collective memories. As the historian David Carr nicely put it: "A community exists wherever a narrative account exists of a *we* which has had a continuous existence through its experience and activities. . . . [W]here such a community exists it is constantly in the process . . . of composing and re-composing its own autobiography."[40] A community made up entirely of distant cousins brought together by their genealogical research, however, produces an autobiography of a particular kind. Most of them—most of us—have had no continuous existence as conscious Woodsons, no common activities, and no experience in the communitarian composition, let alone recomposition, of our autobiography.

We don't recall the dramatic events at the heart of our story, we don't know anyone who recalls the events, and few of us know anyone who personally recalls anyone else's recollection of the events. We share no visible identifying marker, not even the surname in question; my own family married out of the

Woodson name back in 1704. Our "memory" was not passed down still trailing the faint aura of Great-Grandmother's clove sachet; it was disinterred. While we seem to love identifying ourselves on family websites or bulletin boards as either Tubs or Potato Holes, we know our clan only because we looked it up. And our *we* doesn't have the slightest idea what "she was—well, she was a Woodson" actually means. Initiation into the community of Woodsons, in other words, has one prerequisite only: an interest in family strong enough to lead the seeker to Henry's tale. And continued membership requires one task only: the acceptance of the founding story as told by our bard.

The rub, of course, is that the story that is doing all this work to make us a *we* is, at bottom, distasteful, rooted in fear, suspicion, and condescension toward darker-skinned "Others," both the brainless American Indians so easily trounced by a lone woman and the African Americans for whose pioneering enslavement one Woodson actively stole the credit. I certainly don't want to suggest that present-day Woodsons embrace their story *because* of its racially loaded messages; I don't for a moment mean to assert that family historians are reactionaries at heart. Although genealogy has always exerted a notorious appeal for would-be elitists and exclusionists, living Woodsons who describe their feelings about the story mention most often their pride in their foremother's courage and their surprise and pleasure in discovering so deep a connection to the nation's history. I suspect, in fact, that many Woodsons see the story more as an heirloom to cherish—very much like, say, a seven-foot-long antique musket visible but untouchable in a glass case—than as a narrative to interpret, and don't think much about its deeper meanings at all.

Nor would I argue that the Woodsons' diligence in protecting their story from challenge is somehow either deceptive or bizarre. Families, nations, religious sects, and ethnic groups of all kinds are equally defensive of their founding stories, which almost always serve purposes more ceremonial than informative. With stories like these, the ritual of sharing knowledge is more important than the knowledge itself, and *what it's about* matters much less than *that it is*. The essential (and important) product of this kind of storytelling is a community, not an answer.

Answers, however, are exactly what historians do want, and if my distant Potato Hole cousins are "underreading" the story, as the literary scholar might put it—if they are not absorbing all the information the narrative contains— then I am happy to "overread" it in the hope of teasing out motives, ideas, or judgments that aren't directly expressed.[41] If it's true that the tale survived for generations because it filled important needs, there's a corollary: that other versions, other parts, other aspects that did *not* fulfill needs have faded away.

And that includes almost anything at all about Sarah Woodson. The ostensible heroine of the tale, she is all but invisible in its current version, a *dramatis persona* whose entire life has been reduced to a single moment and then pressed into the service of progeny centuries removed. It's the rest of her story, the part that's been lost, that most intrigues me—the part about how she might have seen her future once she arrived in Virginia, how she dealt with the disappointments of her new life, whether she regretted her move, how she talked to her sons about living in a world so raddled by loss, and whether she really, genuinely, deep in her heart of hearts, had expected to improve her happiness by voyaging over the seas in the first place.

We know nothing definite about her origins or birth family, but that's scarcely a surprise; we know nothing definite about the private lives of most women of that era, whose vital statistics were always a little less vital than their husbands' and fathers' and brothers' and sons'. It was the men who wielded the economic, political, and legal power in any community, the men who controlled the marital property and the children's future, the men who bestowed their names on their offspring, the men who left the biggest and most conspicuous footprints in the pages of history. The women . . . the women married the men. At least Sarah Woodson bears the tiny human dignity of a first name. Many of her female contemporaries, whose entire lives are summed up in the old genealogies with some tidbit like "he is thought to have married a Miss Williams before 1680," lost theirs centuries ago.

What I'd like to know even more than her birthdate, though, is how she felt about her life after she kissed her family and friends good-bye forever, boarded the *George,* and sailed off toward the sea monsters to pursue happiness in the company of a man she may not have known very well or even liked very much. Was it adventurousness that drove her? Or desperation? A hope that life could be happier, or the conviction that it couldn't be worse? She had probably never traveled much past the borders of whatever quiet little country village was hers before the day she embarked on the hazardous journey to the remote and savage place where anything she wanted she either raised or built herself or waited a year for a ship to bring it from England. And once she'd settled in Virginia, she may never have heard from England again; tenant farmers like herself and John and their families were probably not literate enough to make letter writing and letter reading anything but a chore.

Having arrived toward the beginning of the big surge in immigrants lured by the offers of cheap land, she watched shipload after shipload of hopeful newcomers stagger onto dry land, and die: of every five new people she met, the odds said that four would be dead before long. She survived disease, deprivation, *two* shattering massacres, and two or three childbirths (or more; since her first known child was born more than a decade into her marriage, she may well have lost a row of babies before one finally lived). Every day she fought with loneliness, overwork, grief, fear, and the killer "melancholye." She mourned at least a pair of husbands. And for all that, not only did she and John never make their fortune, but also there's no record they ever got the hundred acres of land that should have been theirs for finishing their term of service with Governor Yeardley, who was known for exploiting his tenants. The tailor's implements listed in the deathbed inventory of her possessions suggest she was scraping a living by sewing.

Then again, though her circumstances were modest in the extreme, they weren't in the least unusual, and especially after the Virginia Company years, with more and more emigrants arriving as indentured servants contracted to labor for a number of years at a master's command, she was probably no worse off than most other Virginians and better off than many. And if the outline of her biography we can glimpse is true, she was married to the same person for at least a quarter of a century at a time when it wasn't unusual to run through two or three spouses a decade. She saw two sons grow to manhood and become sturdy landowning citizens. She met their brides. She held in her arms the first three or four of her dozen grandchildren, a progeny so fecund and hardy that in the diligent but inevitably incomplete catalogue of her descendants he published in 1915, Henry Morton Woodson would count up 4,324 of them. And she died with her boots *off,* if not in her bed then doubtless somewhere near it, at something not far from the biblical threescore and ten. Hardly a one of the richest and most powerful citizens of the colony had achieved anywhere near as much.

So was she happier in Virginia than she would have been in England?

That's a story waiting to be told.

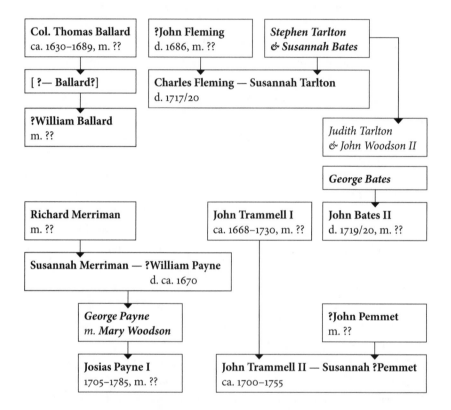

Names in **bold** represent direct ancestors; names in *italics* have been introduced in a previous tree. Other names are included only if relevant. For Ferris, see chapter 1; for Mullins and Via, see chapter 3.

Sources from this era offer conflicting and incomplete biographical data, and I take issue here with some of the conventional genealogical wisdom. Not charted at all is the intricately intermarried and impossibly complicated network of Eastern Shore families, including George Smith (d. 1648/52), his sons George II (d. 1703) and John (d. 1677), and John's daughter Derecter, who have a web of connections to William Hickman (d. 1673), an ancestor of Derecter Hickman Smallwood (see chapter 5); Robert Huitt (d. 1677), his wife, Mackall, and their daughter Mary, wife of George Smith II; Huitt's sister Mary, wife of Rowland Savage (d. 1717); and John Roberts and Robert Watson (d. 1703), who also connect at several points with the Smiths and Hickmans.

CHAPTER 2

Camelot in the Tobacco Fields

⚘

Blue Bloods

FOR MOST PEOPLE WHO WERE ALIVE IN THE SEVENTEENTH-CENTURY Chesapeake, their stories will wait forever to be told; hardly anything authentic either by or about them has survived. Yet the historian's loss seems to have become the descendant's boon. This notoriously brutal era turned out to be, wildly against the odds and much to my surprise, in some ways the best of times for my ancestors, and as a historian I can only lament the disappearance of any shred of evidence for how so many of them managed to claw their way to an astonishing level of the kind of material happiness that would come to define the American dream at its pinnacle. But if the whole story of my long-lived and long-suffering ancestors' only real moment in the sun had been coolly and truly retold to their descendants generations down the road, it would have been both impossible to ignore and uncomfortable to accept. These forebears were their happiest, it seems, when they were their most heartless, and waiting forever for *those* stories may not be such a bad fate for their progeny after all.

Then again, their progeny have been left perfectly free to invent their own stories out of whole cloth—and they have.

The first century of the Virginia and Maryland colonies makes up the most complicated of studies for anyone interested in the possibility of happiness, and plays host to the most enormous, most egregious gap between story and reality in my family's long history. On the one hand, that particular past does seem to be another country and the experience of its individual citizens almost impenetrable; hardly anyone who actually lived during that era left any personal words to enlighten the historian. Most of what anyone knows about those people, my own ancestors and everyone else, too, comes in bits and fragments and at second or third hand. Few residents of the Chesapeake either told or figured in anything that could be called a contemporary narrative, and they don't show up much anywhere else, either. For many citizens, the only evidence that they ever lived and died was an erratically spelled name captured in some court record, will, or headright claim, while others—perhaps most others—left no trace at all of their passage on earth. The circumstances of most lives ranged from wretched to loathsome and raise complicated, unsettling questions about the larger social costs of individual achievement and the relationships between the people who are happy and the people who are not.

On the other hand, people who know nothing about the seventeenth-century Chesapeake tend to find it irresistible. It has been a favorite storyworld for nostalgic Americans many generations removed, especially the disgruntled Hannah Daviess Pittmans, Henry M. Woodsons, and other romancers from around the turn of the last century, who created an alternative society there that they vastly preferred to their own and that they populated with romantic heroes and heroines they liked much better than their neighbors. In these stories the Chesapeake was the place where you lived if you'd lost your keys to Camelot. Just about every man in Virginia and Maryland, the legend went, held his head high despite having been driven out of his home (or, even better, castle) by some tragedy, some injustice, some gloriously mad fidelity to a gloriously hopeless cause. It was a land both buoyed and beset by causes lost long before the emergence of the Lost Cause, a land where all the tears shone unshed and all the blood ran blue.

The inhabitants of this other Camelot were special in another way: besides being the heirs of nobility, all of them also seemed to be the ancestors of genealogists. I can trace about a score of forebears to this era, and for just about every one of them I've found a claim by some descendant somewhere along the line that our mutual ancestor left behind titles and noble demesnes to come to North America. These remote cousins of mine rarely told any genuine stories about their American blueblood kin, no narratives of the lives their ancestors led in the New World. Their point was simply the emphatic and repeated assertion of their noble connections, as if the connection itself provided all the drama anyone could require.

Our Paynes, for instance, according to the genealogical encyclopedia that Mrs. Pittman, with no sign of a blush, called *Americans of Gentle Birth,* descended from the family of Hugh de Payen, a twelfth-century Norman who was one of the founders of the Order of Knights Templar, dedicated to protecting pilgrims on the Crusades. Our Mullinses, who according to one family historian used to be Normans named de Moulins-la-Marche or Desmoulins, also included among their numbers a Crusader, this one the Grand Master of the Order of St. John the Baptist Knights Hospitallers, who was martyred by "Saladin the Seljuk Turk" on the very slope where Christ had delivered the Sermon on the Mount.[1]

Our Trammells, according to a legend vaguely attributed to someone in the DAR, were the rightful earls of Bute, descended from the five-year-old heir who was kidnapped from Scotland in the 1670s and smuggled aboard a ship bound for America to keep him from succeeding to the title. (Fellow passengers christened the nameless little stranger "Trammell" because of the "trials and hardships of his early lot.") Our Ferrises, assert their descendants, spring from the loins of the noble Norman family of de Ferrieres, who came to England with William the Conqueror and were later rewarded with the earldom of Derby. Present-day Ferrises seem serenely untroubled by the wide-open secret that, as correspondents on a family Web forum have noted, an undocumented gap of three hundred years separates the de Ferrieres crew from the English gentleman named Farrar they claim as the progenitor of the American Ferrises.[2]

Our Ballards, other descendants point out proudly, trace back to a servant of Richard II, who shortly before the cataclysmic collapse of his reign rewarded this underling's fidelity with the sumptuous gift of four manors. Our Savages haven't managed to hook themselves up with the celebrated Ensign Thomas Savage, the Jamestown immigrant generally credited as the ancestor of the oldest English family in the United States (and, with a splendid tidiness, occasionally credited as a descendant of Charlemagne, too), but some claim a lineage even more romantic: a twelfth-century Norman conqueror of Ulster, a knight who built dreamy Killyleagh Castle in County Down, and finally one Rowland Savage, who with his brother was driven out of their crenelated home during the civil wars by envious and conniving Catholics. And many of our Flemings claim descent from "Sir Thomas Fleming, second son of the Earl of Wigton," who was said to have arrived in Jamestown in 1616, and from him back through Robert the Bruce, Henri I of France, and William the Conqueror to the tenth-century French monarch Hugh Capet. It was a foregone conclusion: we were really lords a dozen times over, and even though we'd been deprived of our castles and our coronets, we were simply by nature finer, truer, happier than the ordinary run of mortal. We were happier than, for instance, *you*.[3]

Genealogists are drawn to their pastime by all sorts of reasons, and as a hobby it seems ubiquitous nowadays. In 1976 the celebration of the nation's bicentennial and the publication of Alex Haley's gripping (and much embellished) best-seller *Roots* helped kindle the latest in a long line of genealogy booms, this one more recently gaining renewed vigor from the proliferation of amateur-friendly websites bursting with digitized and easily searchable databases of all kinds, from census returns and military records to passenger lists and land deeds. Previously that kind of information could have been collected only by genealogists whose supplies of time, patience, dust masks, and dollars were all endless. The potential profits for those who cater to the armies of hobbyists now seem endless, too. The largest of these websites, Ancestry.com, was acquired in 2012 for $1.6 billion by a private equity firm.

Some of the most diligent genealogical burrowers are moved not by profit but by religious purpose. Mormons are assiduous trackers of others' ancestors as well as their own in order to baptize them posthumously and fill all of heaven with Latter-Day Saints; but in the process they seem to have found and taken copies of every bit of moldering paper that ever bore a human's name in every parish hall, courthouse basement, registration office, and ministry in the world. Others simply enjoy their hobby as a brain-teasing pastime as endlessly absorbing as Sudoku or crossword puzzles, and seem happy with anything that fills in another blank line on the *Ahnentafel.* I was enchanted a while back to come across a work by a distant cousin in a branch of the family that included a few modest luminaries such as the second governor of Missouri. "Every individual person wants to be 'somebody'!" my remote cousin wrote with bracing good cheer. "What is better than to be a member of the Bates family?"[4]

Many genealogists, however, are seeking, or at least feeling a tickle of hope for, something more: the happiness of proving that Gramps's old tales of past glories or special tribulations were true, or of finally claiming a place in a national history that may not have been very welcoming before, or of borrowing a sense of personal importance from a link to a "somebody" rather grander than a Bates. And sometimes they actually find it. DNA evidence, for instance, has come as close as scientifically possible to confirming the Hemings family's stories, long dismissed as both impossible and offensive, that Thomas Jefferson fathered at least one of the children born to his slave Sally Hemings—a spectacular personal vindication for her descendants as well as a radical revision in the traditional story of the third president of the United States.

Yet even the science that so resoundingly validated the Hemingses won't necessarily win a debate against Gramps.[5] On the four-part PBS program *African American Lives* that aired in February 2006, the Harvard literary scholar Henry Louis Gates confronted a cousin with the results of a DNA test that disproved their old family story about a white forefather named Brady. "I don't know about the tests, the science, but I know what my grandfather said, what your father said, and what my uncle said, that was always the history," the cousin told Gates. "I still tell the Brady story. . . . I mean the DNA story's one story, and the Brady story's the other."[6] And still other genealogists are seeking not a confirmation of a particular family story but a connection to something much more sublime. I once found a website, now vanished, on which a California accountant traced his lineage all the way back, without losing a single generation, through Henry III, Ethelred the Unready, Alfred the Great, Odin of Asgard, Priam, Abraham, and Methuselah, to Adam himself, who "died about 3070 B.C."

Claims of exalted lineage were flourishing long before the hobbyists ever came along; they were serious business as far back as the beginning of recorded history and probably deeper into antiquity than we will ever know. The Egyptian pharaohs, the Sumerian kings, the Chinese feudal lords, the Hebrew patriarchs, the Elizabethan aristocrats all created impressive pedigrees as tools for invoking what the historian J. H. Plumb has called "the overwhelming authority of the past" to secure and burnish their standing in the present, to keep peasants and workers in their place, and to stave off challenges from upstarts and *nouveaux.* Inflation was a routine part of the process. "Where the service of the past has been urgently needed," Plumb noted wryly, "truth has ever been at a discount."[7]

Even though the authority of heredity was one of the things Americans had fought a revolution to free themselves *from,* within a couple of generations of their rebellion many of them, too, were finding an urgent need for the service of the past. By the 1830s, aristocratic lineage had been planted as the foundation for one of the South's most cherished and enduring stories, the contention that, in the face of an ever-widening gulf in culture, outlook, and values between North and South, their heritage put the southern planters on the sunnier side. The myth of the Cavalier was an explanation both congenial to the South's own obsolescent agrarian society and also oddly appealing even to the southerners' nemesis, the crass and bourgeois Yankees, who seemed to accept the South's preeminence in life's graces as a fair exchange for their own dominance over the nation's industries, markets, and banks.[8]

The myth encouraged every southern planter to believe that he was descended from Old World gentlemen, preferably King Charles I's gentlemen, those noble Cavaliers with the lace collars and the flowing locks, while the Yankee was relegated to a much baser kinship with the pinched and graceless Roundheads. Blood told, clearly: Cavaliers were courtly and refined, Yankees crude and common; Cavaliers were men of honor, Yankees creatures of commerce; Cavaliers were carefree and generous, Yankees dour and envious.[9] Created out of antebellum nostalgia for the seventeenth century, propelled by Gilded Age nostalgia for the antebellum era, the Cavalier legend, like other tales of important connections, still finds occasional uses in today's present among those who see the past as the last best place to pursue their happiness.

Mrs. Pittman and the others were lucky in one thing: they were spinning their fantasies about principals who had kept their own mouths shut and offered no challenge to the preferred version. The generally unbureaucratic, modestly educated, and largely printing press–free seventeenth century in America produced little surviving paper of any kind, little official documentation, and even less of the sort of personal account that illumines individual experience or provides hints about personal happiness. Some New England Puritans recorded in introspective poems or journals the soul scrutiny that was a spiritual obligation of their religion. The former captives who described their ordeals among the Indians also cast the experience mainly in religious terms as God's test of their faith. Travelers and explorers spun stories about their adventures, usually in places safely remote from anywhere their readers would see and judge for themselves.

But because people of the time were not accustomed to thinking of their *selves* as either unique or particularly interesting, little else in seventeenth-century America (or Europe, either) even remotely qualified as self-revealing writing or allowed any insights into how people felt and thought about their daily lives. On the cusp of modernity, as the likes of Descartes and Locke were exploring new ideas about reason, selfhood, free will, and natural rights, most people still saw themselves in the traditional way as parts of an interdependent social whole carrying out roles assigned by a higher power without regard to personal character or happiness. Rare, too, among ordinary people was any real sense of connection with their own family history or forebears. The high death rate that constantly remade household units, the long distances that often separated kinspeople from one another, and the practical importance of daily networks of friends, neighbors, co-religionists, and other non-relatives made the very idea of "family" both expansive and ambiguous. Most people knew little and cared less about any ancestor more than two generations back and couldn't have come up with the name of a single great-grandparent, let alone a story about one. Few people, and certainly few Americans preoccupied with survival in a raw and remote colonial settlement, would ever have gotten around to pondering, recording, preserving, or simply even *having* life stories or family stories of their own.[10]

So my later kin were happy to do most of the talking for their Cavaliers, and I was sure that once I began looking into other kinds of sources, I would find that none of the tales of blue blood would turn out to be true. It seemed inevitable that I'd have no moldering overseas castles in my past, just a long string of undistinguished and unhappy forebears who'd spent their lives grubbing in the soil and producing scads of children, of whom perhaps three or four from each generation managed to grow up and one or two to improve their lot a bit. It seemed inevitable that the romancers would prove to be deluded.

And deluded they largely were, at least about the blue-blooded heart of their story. The tale of the peopling of the Chesapeake with lords errant has always been topped with large dollops of fantasy. During the Puritans' dominance in England, Governor Berkeley did do his best to set up an alternative throne room in the Virginia wilderness by luring a clique of broken-hearted Royalists and envious younger sons. Some of them went on to found powerful dynasties: the Randolphs, the Carters, the Masons, the Marshalls, the Lees all had roots in the English gentry or aristocracy.[11] But most emigrants to the Chesapeake during the seventeenth century, as many as three-quarters of them, began their American lives not as gentle exiles but rather as indentured servants, contracted to work, usually for four or five years if they were adults or even longer if they were under twenty-one, in return for their transatlantic passage and their (very modest) keep.

That's what nearly all of my ancestors were, too, not gallants but servants who arrived under obligation to someone else. Many of them in fact probably did descend from Charlemagne, though that feat is scarcely worth mentioning; just about *anyone* with any European ancestry can legitimately claim Charlemagne as an ur-grandfather. Anyone can persuasively claim Mohammed, too, for that matter, as well as any number of kings, queens, artists, rascals, charlatans, courtesans, villains, and thugs. Researchers have come up with mathematical models and computer simulations showing that everyone with European roots probably had a common ancestor who died as recently as 1000 or even, perhaps,

1400. In a bounded society people inevitably marry people to whom they are already somehow related, whether or not they know it, because there aren't enough unrelated people to go around.[12]

But while all those royalty-besotted genealogists would thus have had no rational reason to consider their blood any bluer than anyone else's, not one of the particular noble forebears claimed by my later kinfolks checked out. The progenitor of our American Paynes was so obscure it's not even clear whether he was a Richard, a John, or, my hesitant bet, a William—which might matter more if it weren't also true that the Knights Templar was a holy order, all of whose members, including our alleged forebear Hugh de Payen, took monastic vows of not just poverty but also chastity, which *should* have rendered impossible both Mrs. Pittman and me. That three-hundred-year gap dividing the English gentleman Farrar from the de Ferrieres line of noble Normans was trivial compared to the impossible chasm between that selfsame Farrar and his alleged but completely undocumented grandson, the Richard Ferris who came to Virginia as an indentured servant and eventually married his daughter to "Potato Hole" Woodson.

Even the self-proclaimed descendants of Saladin's victim acknowledge that no evidence ties the martyred Grand Master of the Order of St. John the Baptist Knights Hospitallers to John Mullins, indentured servant. The story of a kidnapped underage seventeenth-century earl of Bute is chronologically impossible, since the earldom wasn't created until 1703, at least a generation after the Trammells arrived. The tale of little Trammell's surprise sea voyage, furthermore, bears a striking resemblance to a notorious real-life case. James Annesley, who in 1743 made a dramatic appearance in Dublin to accuse his uncle of having kidnapped him twelve years earlier, shipped him to the colonies as a servant, and stolen his earldom, is widely thought to have inspired Robert Louis Stevenson's novel *Kidnapped*. He was probably not the only fantasist to be galvanized by young Annesley's sensational adventure.[13]

I did find Savages, including many generations of Sir Rowlands, among the powerful Anglo-Norman baronial families that lorded over Ulster for centuries. But there's no evidence any of them ever left their little fortified tower houses in County Down for the wilds of Virginia, and dreamy Killyleagh, built by John de Courcy in the twelfth century, has belonged not to the Savages but to the Hamiltons since the first decade of the seventeenth century. And no record whatsoever survives of either an American-bound second son for the earl of Wigton or the arrival of any Fleming, "Sir" or otherwise, at Jamestown anytime near 1616. Although some Fleming descendants have publicly acknowledged the American earl to be a figment, the deathless claim periodically reemerges on Fleming family websites and ignites the debate all over again.[14]

Virginia as a paradise of lords was only the beginning of the romance. Not even the Chesapeake's elite, the men who did wield the power in the new land, lived in ways that Mrs. Pittman would have been willing to share if she'd been magically relieved of the indignities of life in the twentieth century. She and her ilk seem to have been laboring under illusions even more fantastic than the one about all those unbroken lines of descent: that gentle birth means gentle manners; that blue blood guarantees strong hearts, wise brains, and fat purses; that everyday life was gracious and leisurely, adorned with elegant ladies fluttering their deft white hands among the silver tea things; that happiness came with the territory.

But not even the European nobility she so admired would have fulfilled her fantasies. It was the vast quantities spilled, not the color, that most distinguished *their* blood, and very few of them met fates that any sane person would have considered bearable, let alone happy. The Savages of Ulster, for instance, inhabited a brutal land that perfectly complemented their name; they and their fellow Norman overlords had helped turn their part of the island into a place of "troubles" long before the Irish Republican Army ever came on the scene. The old annals are full of episodes of treachery and violence: a Savage hostage murdered even after his kin paid the ransom, Savages murdering the hostage taker as he hid in a church, an O'Neill blinding and castrating his Savage captive, a Savage murdering a Savage. And the Flemings were a turbulent, melodramatic lot always in the thick of plots, feuds, hostage takings, treacheries, and those periodic awful battles with the English that left the flower of Scotland dead on the reeking field nearly every time. They did, however, have great stories. John, for instance, the second Lord Fleming, was suspected of poisoning a breakfast dish served to his own wife and her two sisters, one of them the mistress of James IV, and was himself later assassinated while out hawking by someone named Tweedie of Drummelzier.

Even the seventeenth-century Chesapeake was better than that, but it still was not much of a place for a silver tea service. Anyone who managed to prosper in the raw and punishing environment of Virginia and Maryland would very likely have been what anyone nowadays could call heartless. In fact, in that day and age a man would probably have had to be heartless in order to end up wealthy, powerful, and, presumably, happy.

To my shock, many of my ancestors did.

They could even have been called uniquely happy and heartless, or happy and heartless in a unique way that was never again duplicated. Many of society's leaders in the mid-seventeenth-century Chesapeake—and a stunning number of my particular forebears—were members of a singular generation: those who had achieved the most symmetrical possible version of what would become known as the rags-to-riches American dream by rising from a position of absolute powerlessness to one of absolute power. They had begun their American lives during the peak years of the system of indentured servitude, a bondage that was both total and temporary. As young adults they had endured a term of labor under conditions closely approximating slavery and often marked by ferocious exploitation and abuse, then found themselves among the lucky (or rugged) bare majority who were freed from their terms by survival rather than by death. And they had done so early enough in Virginia's development that toughness, ambition, diligence, and luck could still suffice a freedman as the seed capital for material happiness. So when my ancestors acquired absolute power over their own absolutely powerless servants, they would have known—precisely, intimately, and possibly gleefully—the cost their success was exacting from others very much like themselves.

By dubbing them heartless I am, perhaps, being disrespectful of the reality that in that time and place, where you could never be sure that any of the friends, patrons, or kinfolk who greeted you fresh and blooming one day wouldn't be dead and stiff the next, where the economy depended on one fragile and finicky plant that ripped through land and servants like some insatiable Minotaur demanding his tribute, you couldn't have gotten far in your search for happiness without being shrewd, gutsy, thick-skinned, hard-hearted, and cold-blooded. And if you weren't one of the rich and happy few, you were probably miserable most of the time. In that time and place even more than most, money and power essentially *defined* happiness.

It's true, too, that the institution of white indentured servitude did not particularly rattle the conscience of an age whose sages included Thomas Hobbes. The practice incorporated echoes of the home country tradition of apprenticeship, which bound young, dependent unpaid laborers for lengthy terms to masters who in return provided their basic necessities and instructed them in the art and mystery of some craft (one that was usually, however, rather more mysterious than working a hoe). The master-servant relationship did not disturb long-held assumptions about the deference due from the lower ranks to the higher or the rights and obligations of the higher ranks to control the lower. The relegation of great numbers of fellow citizens to a life largely devoid of opportunity or autonomy did not challenge the reigning premise that one's place in the social order was appropriately determined by birth (and therefore by God) rather than by one's personal qualities, talents, or desires.

Stern discipline of the labor force did not seem particularly harsh to a society that routinely punished debtors with prison and vagrants with expulsion, expected orphans barely out of leading strings to help earn their own keep, and sent out press gangs to "recruit" common seamen by forcible kidnap. In those years of chronic overpopulation and unemployment, transportation to the colonies was often seen, by prospective servants as well as officials, as a reasonable if not welcome escape from alternatives even worse. And it seems fair to conclude, as the historian Thomas Haskell does, that the ability of seventeenth-century society to get along perfectly well without the word "responsibility" (its first recorded usage came in 1788 during the debate over the Constitution) is just one sign that people in that era held a different set of assumptions about causation, free will, moral behavior, and the human consequences of choice.[15]

But these heartless people are *my* people, and perhaps it's my obligation as a historian-descendant to rescue them from their too adoring chroniclers, to balance accounts by posing a corrective to the happy fantasies long exercised on their behalf, and to allow them the complicated, difficult lives they actually lived, nasty and brutish though they probably were, unhappy though they sometimes may have been. And if, as the analyst Hans Loewald has said, the goal of psychoanalysis is to transform ghosts into ancestors, perhaps one goal of history can be to look those ancestors in the face, judge them, and restore what it is about them that *ought* to make us scared.

Accepting such people as kin to me *is* scary, though it may be even more incomprehensible than frightening. Among my immediate family have been people who refused to return to the store a gift they didn't like because the prospect of disappointing not only the giver but also the store clerk was too awful to contemplate. I am kin to people who were known to order an entrée they didn't want from the waiter's endless recital of today's specials just so the poor guy wouldn't feel that his arduous performance had gone to waste. And while my own decision to become a journalist might seem a liberating career choice for someone trained never to *bother* other people, I cunningly stuck to television documentary units that focused mainly on ideas, culture, and history and that featured people who were either thrilled to be noticed or dead. In the seventeenth-century Chesapeake, we would have lain down and died of softheartedness.

How could we be kin to the likes of Mackall Huitt, accused of stealing gowns by a niece who loathed her, and her husband, Robert, convicted of stealing hogs from neighbors who despised him? Stephen Tarlton, who knocked up one servant, was sued by another for reneging on his promised wages, and joined a crowd of drunken rioters chopping down their neighbors' tobacco plants? George Smith, who hosted a party so bibulous that before the end, two of his guests had bitten another in the buttocks so badly as to draw blood? Thomas Ballard, the "Fellow of a Turbulent mutinous Spirit" who betrayed both sides in turn during Bacon's Rebellion?[16]

Well, how could we have ended up born at all when anyone who survived had to be like that?

Fortune's Wheel

Actually, would-be Americans didn't *have* to be like that; there were other choices. If they were devout enough to risk all for their faith (and solvent enough to afford the journey, which was usually part of the deal), they could set out instead for Plymouth or Massachusetts Bay, and leave their descendants a welcome legacy of nicer ancestors and pleasanter stories: the *Mayflower,* the friendly Squanto, cranberries and turkey, plentiful harvests. True, the Pilgrims and Puritans who dominated the New England settlements weren't paragons. Their celebrated ardor for religious freedom rarely extended to anyone who disagreed with their own religion, while their ferocious theology offered two stark alternatives for eternal life—ineffable bliss in the sun of God's presence or interminable agony in a pit of fire—and then assured you that nothing you did for good or ill would have any effect on where you ended up. But even so, the pioneering generations of New Englanders have always gotten better press than their southern neighbors, offering as they do a more comfortable vision of American aspirations and successes than did the heartless Virginians who preceded them to the New World.

New Englanders have generally been seen as more communitarian, more orderly, more benevolent, more selfless than the Virginians. New Englanders were driven (frequently) by love of God, Virginians (often) by love of money. New Englanders were smarter, or at least more intellectual; within sixteen years of their first landfall they had built a university that survives to this day, while Virginians took more than eight decades to do the same thing. New Englanders arrived mainly in families, not in shiploads of dangerously young, poor, solitary, and celibate males. They inhabited snug and sociable towns, not sprawling plantations; they built a stable and relatively homogenous society of laborers, farmers, and tradesmen, not a kleptocracy that rewarded the ruthless accumulation and exploitation of servants and land. Later in the century they did not forgo the ownership of slaves, and some profited handsomely from the trade in them, but their brand of oppression seemed somehow less sociopathic than in the brutal universe of the tobacco farm. They had a deep respect for authority, but they didn't go overboard. While the earliest Virginians laid down martial law, the first New Englanders laid down covenants.

Yet even though the sober and pious New Englanders in their steeple hats may have ended up with the most respectable stories, and Mrs. Pittman and her friends certainly had the most romantic ones, real-life Virginia—with its heat, torpor, disease, and tobacco plants, with its heartless planters and its miserable servants and its sloppier God—had stories of its own worth the telling, too, stories that drove to the heart of what American happiness meant. If the first generations of Chesapeake settlers had had the time, inclination, and self-awareness to talk truthfully about their lives, this is what they might have said.

The most basic human challenge remained unchanged from the Jamestown years: to grow old. Disease was still a constant marauder, the average lifespan still piteously fleeting. Children born in the colonies, like little Robert "Potato Hole" Woodson, in effect went through their seasoning at birth, so if they survived that ordeal, they tended to be healthier and to live longer than their immigrant parents. But since men still vastly outnumbered women, and most women were deep into their twenties before the completion of their indentures freed them for marriage and (legitimate) childbearing, relatively few of those sturdier natives were getting themselves born. Not until the next century did the ratio of men to women reach something like a balance.

Those who survived hoped to build some sort of stability and accumulate a little property. In fact those survivors could reap something of a bonanza from the grisly mortality rate, for the high turnover in spouses meant that the hardier partner might accumulate several marriages' worth of property in one lifetime. In childbirth women faced dangers men did not, but they often seemed better able to bear the climate and the seasoning than men, and if motherhood didn't kill them, they might well outlive their spouses. And a fresh widow rarely spent long in mourning before she—along with whatever property her late husband had managed to scrape together—was snapped up by a new man who doubtless appreciated her dowry as much as her charms.

Tabitha Scarburgh, the well-dowered daughter of one of the nabobs of Virginia's Eastern Shore, was widowed for the first time before she was twenty-one and for the fourth time when she was sixty-one, at which point she called a halt to husbands and lived unattached for two decades more. Her third spouse, the wealthy merchant and planter Major General John Custis, brought to their marriage his inheritances from his two previous wives, the second of whom had brought to *their* marriage her share of the lands and possessions of her three previous husbands, one of whom had himself been enriched by his own first marriage to a prosperous two-time widow. Most of the evanescent couples in this chain hadn't even left children of their own to splinter the legacies, while the few surviving offspring tended to keep things in the family, too: Tabitha's only heir, her granddaughter by her first marriage, married a nephew of her third husband.[17] By the time General Custis's great-grandson Daniel died in 1757, the family estate had grown to gargantuan size, making Daniel's widow, Martha, a prize catch for the struggling young planter George Washington.

This is where the philosophically inclined tend to pipe up that money does not necessarily buy happiness, and there's plenty of evidence that sometimes money actually bought woe. That, however, was probably no warmer a comfort to the threadbare neighbors of the rich than it ever is to the envious poor. Daniel Parke Custis's parents were famously, operatically miserable in their nine-year union, in part because of their constant wrangling over money, property, and the promises and debts—both of them enormous—sent their way by the bride's irascible father. Years after the wedding, Frances and John Custis signed articles of agreement that included among other provisions her promise to stop calling him "vile names." When Frances died of smallpox before her thirtieth birthday, rumors circulated for years that she'd caught the disease from an infected dress presented to her by her exasperated spouse. Her widower in turn ordered an inscription on his tombstone telling the world that only during his bachelor years had he ever been happy.[18]

Besides a good marriage or two or three, the other key to prosperity was, still, sotweed. Tobacco became the currency of daily life, though a fragile and often heartbreaking one. And even though differences in wealth, power, and status quickly became evident between the large planters and everyone else, Chesapeake society for a brief time was open enough, and good land was available enough, that white newcomers could cherish a not unreasonable hope of working their way toward material happiness.

Although that way was, for many, long indeed, my people did have two great advantages over thousands of the other folks in like circumstances bent on the New World: their sturdy constitutions and their timing. It's unclear exactly how common it was for servants who reached the first great goal of surviving their terms to go on and achieve other milestones of happiness such as acquiring land and servants of their own, holding office, or dying rich. For a time in Maryland, a freedman's odds of achieving modest success were a bit better than long shot: one historian has calculated that of 275 servants who had arrived by 1642, more than one-third died, fled, returned to England, or otherwise vanished from the records without ever earning their freedom, but around half of the 158 who *did* live through their terms were known to have ended up landowners in Maryland, while at least some of the others moved on and bought land elsewhere. The experience in Virginia is not as well documented, but there, where the boom was over quicker, the land tended to be pricier, the masters often seem to have been harsher, and the freedom dues for former servants were stingier, opportunities were generally bleaker. Despite some inspiring anecdotal evidence here and there—seven men who were listed as servants on the 1624 muster, for instance, were sitting in the House of Burgesses five years later—in some Virginia counties at some times, fewer than 10 percent of all freed servants were known to have eventually acquired land of their own.[19]

But scholars generally concur that the odds in both colonies were best of all for those who arrived when most of my own people did, between around 1630, after the Crown had taken over from the chaotic Virginia Company, and around 1660, by which time a small group of wealthy elites had wrested near-total control over most of the colony's powerful offices and the supply of good, available, and accessible land had begun to plummet along with the returns from tobacco farming. Maybe that makes my kinsmen Rowland Savage and Amer Via, who came later than the others but ended up successful anyway, the most heartless of the bunch. Certainly that makes *all* of them—what? Is it sufficient just to say lucky, hardy, tough enough to have beaten both the long odds against surviving and the even longer odds against prospering? No one is more surprised than I at my ancestors' apparent and astonishing triumph over the bleak statistics in favor of success.

Rooting, poring, poking, querying, reckoning, presuming, I've managed to pry out of headright claims, wills, deeds, court records, and other documents the names of more than a dozen men who came to the Chesapeake around the middle third of the century and for whom I can advance reasonable evidence that they were direct or collateral ancestors of mine. Some of the links are impossible to prove positively, the consequence of an underdocumented age, but just listing so many *likely* names at all feels like a splendid victory over the oblivious weight of three and a half centuries: Savage and Via, Thomas Ballard, Richard Ferris, William Payne, John Roberts, John Fleming, William Hickman, Richard Merriman, John Mullins, George Smith, Robert Watson, Robert Huitt, Thomas or John Trammell, either Stephen Tarlton or his parents, and John Pemmet, said to have been a Frenchman and thus the only non-Briton I know of from this era. And if these are indeed my ancestors, Ballard is the only one I feel sure did *not* arrive indebted to someone else.[20]

I can imagine without stretching far the sort of people these men and the other, nameless ur-great-grandfathers must have been. I can posit something about all those nameless great-grandmothers, too, though with most of them we'll never know anything more specific than that they had husbands and children. Most of the prospective servants who embarked for the Chesapeake in the seventeenth century were single, in their late teens or early twenties, and from southwestern England or London. Emigrant men still outnumbered emigrant women, now by two or three to one, a statistic that amuses me every time I contemplate the sort of extravagantly Darwinian aggressiveness our male ancestors must have displayed to make possible the existence three and a half centuries later of the three young men to whom our grandmother earnestly confided that the secret to being "the life of the party" was to play the piano with dash.

The conventional idea that only riffraff sold themselves into servitude—only the scourings of the gutter, the hopelessly unhappy with nothing left to lose—has turned out to be something of an exaggeration. Historians have debated over what the skimpy available data mean, but it seems clear that prospective servants came from a broad swath of English society. Many were indeed poor, unskilled, and footloose, but others were farmers or yeomen, a good number were tradesmen or artisans, and more than a few could read and write.[21]

We'll never know what drove John Roberts or John Fleming to rewrite his life so radically in return for such an ambiguous shot at happiness. Some immigrants had no choice. Vagrants, incorrigibles, orphans, and prisoners of war were routinely dumped overseas by exasperated parishes, overstretched uncles, or the vengeful Lord Protector Cromwell himself. Children, drunkards, and bumpkins were preyed upon by a flourishing new breed of entrepreneurs known as "spirits," who tricked or kidnapped countless unwitting souls into servitude far from home, leaving friends and family as baffled as they were bereft.[22]

For others, however, the choice seemed clear. England in the middle decades of the seventeenth century was for many a place of insecurity and distress, with jobs disappearing, prices rising, and danger or even death threatening for those who practiced the wrong religion or embraced the wrong politics. The disruptions and upheavals of civil war, rebellions in Scotland and Ireland, and wars abroad with the French, the Dutch, and the Spanish had accompanied rising food prices and an alarming long-term spike in population growth that had set loose frightening swarms of ungovernable vagabonds to clog the roads and infest the villages. Poverty was more evident and less tractable. The establishment of infant industries like cloth making, the efforts of large agriculturists to reshape the landscape for their own profit, the irresistible drainage of money, markets, and business toward London and other big cities, all were challenging the traditions of village life that had endured for centuries.

Yet if reports from the colonies across the sea were to be believed, life could be happy even for the indentured servant. "What's a four years Servitude," George Alsop, a self-proclaimed graduate of an indenture in Maryland, asked his readers jauntily, "to advantage a man all the remainder of his dayes?" Yes, conceded the promotional tract *Leah and Rachel* in 1656, the southern colonies did have a scary reputation, but the Chesapeake was no longer the "nest of Rogues, whores, desolute and rooking persons" it had once undeniably been. The work there, the author assured his readers, was easier than that of a farmer or craftsman in England; in the summer everyone could take a five-hour nap at midday, and in the winter no one worked at all. In fact the region was now "a place of pleasure and plenty" so rewarding that the writer could only "pitty the dull stupidity" of any English person unwilling to make the move.[23]

So if Richard Merriman was a farmer's younger son not so stupid that he didn't know he would never inherit his father's land, he could well have seen a persuasive prospect of happiness in the chance to wrest some of his own; if William Payne was a fresh graduate from an apprenticeship in some overcrowded trade, he may well have seen opportunity in the underpopulated colonies. A lovelorn Jane or Elizabeth may have seen in the male-heavy New World an open bazaar of possible mates even for those who, as Alsop put it (with a visible smirk, "for I ought to know"), would otherwise have kept their virginity "until it had been mouldy."[24] Some Mary or John who had found an *un*suitable spouse may even have looked to the New World to grant practically what was nearly impossible legally: a divorce.

When they got off the ship as someone's indentured laborer, however, Fleming, Merriman, Payne, and others would quickly have been disabused of the boosters' happy visions. They could have been, and probably were, treated very much like chattel slaves during their terms of service. They did whatever work their master demanded of them, they ate what their master fed them and wore what he gave them; they could be handed over to a new master without their consent or bequeathed as property in a dying one's will; and if they were caught committing any infraction at all, from killing a pig to running away, their terms of service could be dragged out for months or even years. There were tasks to be done all the year round, and the only place you could get away with a leisurely midday nap was on your deathbed. The work the servant did was so hard and the conditions so harsh that more than one-third and perhaps more than one-half of the indentured laborers in the Chesapeake died before finishing their terms.[25]

Except on the smallest farms or during the busy planting and harvesting seasons, white female servants weren't used primarily as field laborers, but their household chores were scarcely lighter or less relenting: washing and mending, gardening and cooking, hauling the wood and the water, caring for the young and the ill, tending the poultry and the dairy, making the cider and the soap.[26] Since indentured servants were generally forbidden to marry until they had completed their terms, servant women did, in theory, have one advantage over the wives of small planters or freedmen, who had to handle the same chores for their own families even when they were heavy with child. But prohibition of wedlock is no contraceptive, and illegitimate pregnancies among servant women were commonplace. Years could be added to the term of any woman who inconvenienced her master by lying in—even if he himself was the father.

The servant's experience varied according to the character and situation of the master. On a small holding with only a servant or two, they probably lived very much as the master's family itself did, sharing the house and eating at a common table. On larger plantations, however, servants saw much more of one another than they ever did of their masters, and there the institution of indentured servitude had its own peculiarities that made it not worse or better than, certainly—that judgment would be grotesque—but consequentially different from the chattel slavery that by the end of the century was displacing it.

Slaves, who saw their lives stretching ahead endless and changeless, had every incentive to live in the *now* because the future was no less unbearable. And though some fought back with intransigence, defiance, or passivity—after all, what was left to forfeit?—many lightened the burdens by sharing them, forging bonds of mutual assistance if not affection, risking the bittersweet comfort of loving a spouse or children they daily feared to lose. Indentured servants, however, unlike slaves, knew that if they could just hang on long enough, their bondage would someday end. Living contingently, focusing all their desires and energies on the very dicey proposition of surviving their terms, counting down the days until their real lives could start, ineligible even to *have* a spouse and children to fear for, they might well have resisted squandering any precious resources, whether corn or compassion, on any person, emotion, or thing that didn't contribute to getting them where they wanted so desperately to be. For the indentured servant, hope could have made humanity too expensive.

The historian can be left wondering about the humanity of the free citizen, too. Many of my forebears hailed from the Eastern Shore of Virginia and Maryland, which happens to possess an unusually long and full run of early court records that were preserved mainly by chance. The documents offer rare glimpses into everyday life—glimpses that are intimate if not quite firsthand, storylike in structure if rarely complete with beginning, middle, and end. By their very nature, most of these tiny stories of legal actions involve conflict. Every offer of protection to a dear friend's orphan, every cow given to a godson "out of love," is overwhelmed by a dozen episodes of violence, cupidity, or ill will. Faithless guardians, reluctant relatives, abusive spouses, false accusations, misappropriated legacies, free-for-all brawls, perfidious bargains, and a riotous variety of unsanctioned sexual activities all invite or require official interventions that leave paper trails; quiet friendships, contented marriages, and spontaneous acts of kindness usually do not.

Still, the picture they weave of life on the Eastern Shore seems remarkably short on ordinary happiness. The sense of constant abrasion, irritation, and acrimony that arises from the documents is almost tangible even now, raising provocative questions about the simple contentment, even basic bearability, of everyday life. A six-year-old orphan was grotesquely beaten, burned, and half drowned by her female guardian because she had dirtied the bed. In the middle of the night someone delivered a rude doggerel verse to the house of Sarah Hinman, around whom swirled exotic rumors about her sex life with Indians and multiple husbands. Roger Mikell, a "knowne pirate and robber" with a history of abusive quarrels with his wife, returned from a long trip to

Barbados with a new eighteen-year-old bride, having wagered that the first wife had died in the meantime. (She hadn't.) The newly freed servant Richard Jones had a boisterous sexual encounter with the wife of Robert West as several neighbors peered giggling through the peephole and West's furious little son berated Jones to get off his mother. When an Irish servant named Thomas who worked for the grand Custis family was found dead in a well with a gash in his neck, an inquest determined that the enterprising fellow had "willfully made himself away": he had jumped into the well to drown himself after botching an attempt to cut his own throat.[27]

One is left wondering: Could any Shore residents pass a month without encountering someone they had once maligned or been maligned by? Someone they had cheated or been cheated by? Someone they had sexually betrayed or been sexually betrayed by? Someone who had once lorded over their life and labor or someone they had once lorded over themselves? While we all have modern examples, even personal experiences, to help us understand how those Virginians might have coped (or not) with all that suing, cheating, and betraying, it's the consequences of the lording—the institution of indentured servitude, which underlay so many of the Shore's relationships and which allowed the lucky to graduate from near-slave to near-despot over a new batch of near-slaves—that three and a half centuries later seem almost impossible to imagine. No former servant could have forgotten the harshness and impotence of that life, and we can only guess at what sort of psychic turmoil the achievement of absolute power might have brought to new masters who could remember their own powerlessness. And it's the total and unique perfection of that role reversal—the precision of the turn of fortune's wheel that crowned with material happiness those who best learned to do unto others the same brutality that had been done unto them—that may help to explain why so many of the transactions of daily life were churned by undercurrents of vengefulness, rage, and, indeed, heartlessness.

The only one of my direct relations who seems to have begun his American life already at the top of fortune's wheel was my eighth-great-grandfather Colonel Thomas Ballard, and although the records about his life and background are the usual spare and enigmatic specimens, they also carry suggestions that his happiness was much more abundant than his personal charms. His first documented appearance in Virginia, as clerk of York County, dates to 1652, and he may have been the Thomas Ballard who was born in 1630 in the tiny Worcestershire village of Inkberrow.[28] It was less than a year after Cromwell's forces battled

Charles II to a halt at Worcester and then viciously sacked the strongly Royalist town that Thomas Ballard first showed up in Virginia's records.

He did very well for himself. He was apparently able to afford his own passage, and snagged the clerkship of York County while presumably only in his early twenties. He traded vigorously in land, transported dozens of servants, and owned substantial tracts in several of the richest counties. He advanced steadily, appointed to positions of power and visibility: high sheriff, commander of the James City County militia, vestryman of the influential Bruton Parish church in Williamsburg, justice of the peace, burgess, councilor, and Speaker of the House. None of that he could have achieved without the right friends, specifically the very best friend any ambitious Virginian could have. Governor Sir William Berkeley was a gentleman, a scholar, an author (of one play, a "tragy comedy" called *The Lost Lady*). He was also a devoted Royalist who had been knighted on the field at Berwick and who, upon his appointment as royal governor to Virginia in 1641, actively recruited other like-minded gentlemen to join him in perhaps the last British outpost loyal to the House of Stuart. In 1670 Berkeley gave Thomas Ballard a seat on his council of advisers, the pinnacle of power in Virginia and, full as it was of the various perks and opportunities of office, a smooth road to great wealth.

In a romantic mood one could imagine that Thomas himself had been one of the Worcester Royalists, that maybe he had even fought under the king's flag in the battle of Worcester, had shared the anguish of that decisive defeat, and was rewarded for his fealty by the king's disappointed supporters across the sea. But it would be absolutely safe to assume that since Ballard came on his own dime, took on an important official position while still young enough to live nearly forty more years, rose steadily through the political ranks, owned huge tracts of land, was extravagantly favored by the governor, and died rich, *something* he was, or knew, or said, or did, or bought, won him the notice and approbation of the all-powerful Royalists of Virginia.

Whatever that something was even won him forgiveness for what appears to have been an act of either opportunism or treachery against the governor during the crisis known as Bacon's Rebellion, the murky uprising of 1676 driven by a volatile stew of populist resentment, economic insecurity, and European fears of American Indian aggression.[29]

The rebellion, or anyway rebelliousness, had been building for years, as aspiring lords of the land continually encountered more and bigger potholes in their road. One of the gravest problems was the very commodity that had saved the colony from extinction in its first decades. Everybody was producing tobacco, everybody wanted to finish his indenture so he could produce tobacco for himself, and as more and more millions of tons were sent overseas, prices wallowed downward, measurable in shillings no longer but rather in pence per pound, even as taxes, duties, fees, and levies continued to rise and often disappear swiftly into the pockets of the powerful.

By then, too, the great planters had snapped up most of the best land as well as the political power, driving many of the later comers and smaller farmers to the fringes of both subsistence and civilization—where conflicts with the Indian tribes were growing ever hotter—so anyone who wasn't *already* rich was less likely to drudge his way there. And the rich were finding it harder and harder to get good drudges. With a king back on the throne in England and economic stability returning to the home country, fewer English yeomen looked upon selling themselves into temporary slavery as a step up in life.

So the planters were turning more and more eagerly to another kind of labor they had not yet fully exploited: permanent slavery. The advantages of using Africans had become obvious. Though initially more expensive to purchase than English servants, once bought they would stay bought. They would not need replacing every four or five years, they could be worked harder than white servants, they reproduced themselves, they were easily visible if they ran away, and they were, after all, heathens, marked by God with dark skin as a sign of their inferiority. It was about this time that enslaved Africans became entrenched as a currency of daily life crucial to the happiness of the southern planter, including many of my forebears.[30]

In the eyes of their masters, black slaves held another advantage over white servants: they weren't expected to expect any happiness. By the 1660s and 1670s, more and more of the yeomen who *had* sold themselves into indentureships, worked their time, paid their dues, and finally gone free were finding their opportunities more shrunken and their happiness less complete than they'd planned on. After four or five years of brutal toil under mean and squalid living conditions, subject to constant and grievous abuse at the heavy hands of masters with the powers of potentates, the newly free laborers were discovering that the sustaining vision of a vine and fig tree of their own (as a favorite image from the Book of Micah had it), along with a family of their own, was scarcely nearer than it had been the day they put their marks to the indenture papers. Undomesticated, unsatisfied, and virtually uncontrollable, weathered veterans of the arts of exploitation and abuse, and quite possibly panting for the chance to play exploiter and abuser themselves for a change, they have been called by the historian Edmund S. Morgan the "terrible young men."[31]

Meanwhile Governor Berkeley, by then seventy and tired, was vainly begging the king to replace him with a younger man, and the locals were sniggering that his feisty and much younger wife was wearing him out with insatiable demands, only some of which were for money. The touchstone to the rebellion came over Berkeley's reluctance to authorize an expedition against aggressive American Indians in the frontier county of Stafford. In the governor's dithering Nathaniel Bacon glimpsed opportunity. Two years earlier, in 1674, that troublesome young gentleman, a cousin of Lady Berkeley's, had been packed off to the colonies by his family to escape a string of scandals at home. The arrogant and ambitious Bacon had already mounted one unauthorized Indian hunt on his own, and seeing the agitation of the settlers, he defied the governor, gathered a band of volunteers, and set out to hunt some more. As more and more restless and resentful freedmen, small farmers, new gentry, and terrible young men came flocking to Bacon's banner, their mission snowballed from punishing the Indians to plundering the homes and estates of the powerful and demanding fiscal and governmental reform. After attempts at both confrontation and accommodation, Berkeley fled to the Eastern Shore, while other powerful Virginians saw safety or profit or both in joining the rebel.

After five months of chaos, however, during which Jamestown was burned to the ground, Bacon, and his uprising with him, were undone by Virginia's curse: the great rebel died, suddenly, of some disease variously described as "bloody flux" or "lousey fever." As the rebellion sputtered out, Berkeley took an extravagant revenge. Although in the interests of order and tobacco planting the king was willing to pardon most of the insurgents, the governor was not; he hanged some two dozen of Bacon's followers, sold "free" pardons to many more, doubled the term of servitude for rebels who had been indentured, and confiscated the property of those who'd had any.

Our happy Colonel Ballard, however, adroitly managed to come out of the rebellion ahead after ricocheting back and forth between publicly supporting his patron the governor and openly working on behalf of his patron's mutinous opponent. But after Bacon's death, Governor Berkeley seems to have readily forgiven Ballard's apparent perfidy, even giving him a seat on the courts-martial of Bacon's biggest supporters, where my ancestor cast votes that helped condemn to death some of the very men he had enticed into joining the rebellion.

I wish I knew how he'd done it. I'd like to believe it was his raffish charm, though I suppose something like intimidation, ingratiation, favor trading, or bribery is more likely. In any case, he continued to arouse suspicion and support in equal measure. After Berkeley returned to England, where he soon died, Ballard was dismissed from the council by the new lieutenant governor, who called my ancestor "a Fellow of a Turbulent mutinous Spirit, yet one that Knowes how to bee (at every turne) as humble low and penitent as Insolent and Rebellious, and is for these Virtues called by Sir William Berkeley his Mary Magdalene. But he was before Bacons chiefe Trumpett, Parasite Subscriber . . . and an Emminent abettor of the late Rebellion."[32] Unfazed, the House of Burgesses promptly elected the parasite to the speakership.

The best we could say of our colonel through all this, I suppose, is that he was an unswerving and eagle-eyed pragmatist, the worst that he was either an agent provocateur purposefully setting up the betrayal of his friends (or perhaps his political rivals), or a two-time traitor whose zeal carefully tracked his prospects. Either choice carried a clear logic in precarious times; either one could have seemed to him nothing more or less than the necessary means of preserving his happiness—which his lavish landholdings clearly show him to have done. But to Ballard's terminally softhearted descendant, either choice offers ample confirmation of his heartlessness.

The skimpy documentary evidence about my less illustrious forebears, all those former servants, makes it impossible to say how so many managed to beat the terrible odds against surviving at all, let alone succeeding—except to feel certain that whatever it was, my siblings and I didn't inherit it. They were, we can assume, happy, at least in the material sense. Yet given the conditions of life in the Chesapeake, my ancestors could not have achieved that happiness without smothering it in others. They must have managed to induce steady streams of other people to put themselves entirely in their power and do interminable, filthy, backbreaking, and often lethal labor for them. And even though the system was generally considered the natural order of things, my ancestors, who had started exactly that way themselves, had an intimate knowledge of what life under that order was like. They had borne their own masters' whims and wrath (and perhaps their beatings), endured the gnawing of hunger and cold and sexual desire, faced the awful choices about whether defiance would be worth the punishment it would invoke; they could well have known fellow laborers who had been worked to death, starved to death, punished to death, wearied to death. They had stored up years' worth of anger, resentment, and frustration that until then had found no outlet. Once free, they would have had little incentive, little reason, and little precedent to act in any other way than their own employers had acted. And they *would* have been well acquainted with the rewards that were reaped by the devious, the brutal, the stony, the heartless.

And yet: they prevailed. Having begun their American lives with nothing, not even the power to choose the task they'd do that day or the confidence they'd live to the end of the week, they had managed to build both fortune and family, and could probably provide, for themselves and their kin, just about any of the comforts or possessions they had ever lusted after during the long lean years of privation and toil. Smart, lucky, and tough, they had risen in the world much further than they ever could have hoped to do in the hidebound and hierarchical society back home in England or even in the orderly little towns of New England. Not only do I owe them personal thanks for not having lain down and died of softheartedness, but also I suppose I should congratulate them for having numbered among the first people in the world to achieve their wildest American dream.

As the seventeenth century drew to a close, my ancestors seemed poised to flourish forever. My tenth-great-grandparents John and Sarah Woodson, those first immigrants whose obscure lives left traces only because they were so dramatically avant-garde, left two boys, too, Robert and John, "Potato Hole" and "Tub," who were apparently the sort of citizen best described by the adjective "sturdy"; neither held any significant public office, neither could write his name, and several of their sons and sons-in-law made their living as carpenters, a calling that could have left them quite comfortable but probably neither powerful nor influential. Both Robert and John did, however, manage to acquire their own modest plots of land, which their murdered father and threadbare mother had never been able to do. And true to the dream, the next generations rose even higher. Robert Woodson's daughter Mary married George Payne, who filled the useful positions of justice and high sheriff of Goochland County, and two of their sons, my seventh-great-grandfather Josias and his brother John, served together for eight sessions in the 1760s as Goochland's two burgesses. Josias was able to bequeath nearly 3,500 acres of land and at least twenty-eight slaves to his eight children.[33]

Within a generation or two of the founding immigrants' arrival, many of my families—the Merrimans, the Smiths, the Hickmans, the Ferrises, the Trammells—ended up in the generally comfortable circumstances of Tub and Potato Hole Woodson, practicing a useful craft or vocation and owning enough land and personal property to require a will. Others, however, wrote success

Tarlton Fleming's house at Rock Castle, Goochland County, Va., built ca. 1732. Virginia Dept. of Historic Resources.

stories so splendid as to sound more like romance than biography. Another tenth-great-grandparent, John Bates, also arrived in the Virginia Company's colony as a young bonded servant, and unlike the Woodson couple, he had embarked on his new life completely on his own, with no family members to sustain him. Forty-odd years later he died a prosperous merchant in prosperous Williamsburg. Among *his* grandsons was one who, on his death around 1720, lavished on his heirs a glorious bequest of more than 2,500 acres of land in three counties, two mills, livestock, furniture, silver, and thirty-seven slaves, named one by one in his will and parceled out in small groups, ones, and twos. My seventh-great-grandmother Hannah got the slave girl who shared her name, and the promise of £470 sterling when she turned twenty-one.[34]

John Fleming, a ninth-great-grandfather, came from nowhere (certainly not the earldom of Wigton), lived obscurely, took a nameless wife, and left few and muddled records. Nonetheless, he too served as a burgess of Goochland County, and acquired several thousand acres in New Kent, which also meant a generous stock of slaves. His son Charles accumulated splendid holdings of more than ten thousand acres and an equally splendid collection of in-laws, as his children married into such fabled families as the Randolphs and the Bollings, descended directly from John Rolfe and Pocahontas herself. And Charles's son Tarlton Fleming, who married Hannah Bates (along with her £470), was master of a house at Rock Castle in Goochland County, built around 1732 and still standing as a National Historic Landmark. Except for its alleged ghost, a Yankee named Pierson who died in a car wreck in 1922 soon after buying the place, I don't suppose Fleming's Rock Castle property—which took its romantic name from the large outcropping of rock on the nearby riverbank—would have satisfied the cravings of those distant descendants searching for links to Camelot. But for ordinary eighteenth-century Virginians, accustomed as they were to cramped squalor, the compact but sturdy white frame house, with plenty of good-sized glass windows, extensive wood paneling, damask wall coverings, and a fine Georgian staircase that climbed to the second half story lighted with dormer windows of its own, doubtless merited the name.[35]

Even the hapless Stephen Tarlton, another ninth-great-grandfather, who had once been fined more than a year's income for impregnating a servant girl and who had humbled himself to beg for a pardon after being "seduced," he said, into joining the terrible young men of Bacon's Rebellion, had reason to be happy in his children's success.[36] One Tarlton offspring took as her husband a sturdy son of "Potato Hole" Woodson, and two more, including my eighth-great-grandmother Susannah, made grand marriages to members of the prosperous Fleming clan. And the obscure scapegrace Stephen Tarlton left a much sturdier legacy even than land, which can be sold, or houses, which can fall. His heroically prolific offspring were so fond of their family name that the researcher can't dip a finger into the records of central Virginia without stirring up yet another Tarlton Woodson, or Tarlton Payne, or Tarlton Bates, while the Tarlton Flemings are both legion and immortal. A live-and-well Tarlton Fleming can be glimpsed on some of the genealogical websites.

Those were the folk, these heartless and flourishing weed barons, who have inspired their descendants' most creative efforts to find for them blue blood, royal lineage, gentle birth, and the keys to Camelot.

Hannah Daviess Pittman, the author of *Americans of Gentle Birth,* was not the only lady at the turn of the last century to have found such happiness in romance and exclusiveness. And surely in its more benign manifestations the cult of ancestor worship may have contributed to building a sense of community, tradition, and rootedness that, while admittedly artificial, is scarcely less so than the United States itself, the first modern nation to agree itself, however contentiously, into being.

But no one can deny that ancestor worship has often included immense helpings of xenophobia, elitism, egotism, and self-delusion or that it has caused pain, if not real harm, to those dismissible as less than gently birthed. Many of the heritage romancers of Mrs. Pittman's era were consciously erecting their bulwarks against people they firmly dubbed inferior: the recently freed slaves and the swarms of odd, dark, and unintelligible new immigrants from Europe's less familiar corners who were bringing their outlandish habits, religions, cuisines, and clothes to the streets of America's cities. Henry Morton Woodson with his big book of *white* family lore, and heritage societies like the DAR with their doors strongly barred against outlanders, were reactions as characteristic as Mrs. Pittman's genealogical encyclopedia, no eccentric aunt's hobbyhorse but an embodiment of its times.

That embodiment was shot through with fantasy. Mrs. Pittman earnestly assured her readers, for instance, that having blacksmiths or weavers among their ancestors was no indication of "plebeian blood." Since "an education in these crafts was an absolute requirement of eligibility to office," argued the ingenious author, and since after all King James I had been a member of the Clothworkers Guild, ancestral membership in an artisans' guild was "rather a proof of gentle birth than otherwise." Furthermore, she insisted, all the *real* gentlemen had left Europe behind to come to America, so anyone who still held an actual title back in Europe was obviously second-rate.[37]

Even the bloodline-besotted Mrs. Pittman, it turned out, did not manage to impress her views on her own blood. Her two sons were dismissive of her genealogical labors, once joking that they'd buy her "old book" only to burn it up. The disrespect, Mrs. Pittman confided in a letter to a literary friend, "has broken me down." But even if that grave disappointment never made her think critically about her claim to superiority by heritage, anyone interested in the pursuit of happiness in America can easily glimpse some wrinkles in the insistence of the Mrs. Pittmans and their friends on ancestor worship. If admirable achievement was simply a reflection of the virtue of one's forebears, what did it matter how virtuous one was oneself? (That old radical Tom Paine, in *Common Sense,* put it pithily: "When we are planning for posterity, we ought to remember, that virtue is not hereditary.") And what would have been the point in the seventeenth century of coming to America at all, which was perhaps the only place in the world where your virtues alone—or your heartlessness—could actually achieve for yourself the sort of transformation from pauper to plutocrat that everywhere else would be, literally, a fairy tale?[38]

Featuring my ancestors in a romantic story of blue blood, in other words, would hardly make them any less heartless than they already were. But the real story of the lives of my seventeenth-century forebears is that only in America—in fact only in the Chesapeake—would so many who had not been born to it been able to achieve either their heartlessness or their happiness.

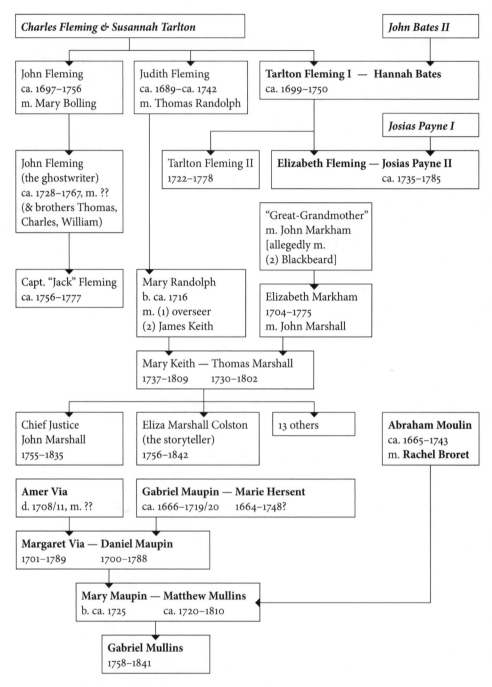

Names in **bold** represent direct ancestors; names in *italics* have been introduced in a previous tree. Other names are included only if relevant. For the Woodsons, see chapter 1; for Ballard, Wharton, Collins, Conway, Ducker, and Daugherty, see chapter 4; for Nichols and Roberts, see chapter 5.

CHAPTER 3
Declaring Independence

⚬

Cassandra's Heirs

Around the middle of the eighteenth century, an outbreak of Cassandras gripped the Chesapeake. In Virginia and especially in Maryland in the decades leading up to the Revolutionary War, dozens of parents named their brand-new baby girls after the princess of ancient Troy, Priam's loveliest daughter and one of the most inauspicious female namesakes in Western literature.

Cassandra had prevailed on her divine suitor Apollo to grant her the gift of prophecy. But the sun god's courtship gift did not come without strings, and when Cassandra refused to yield the expected quid pro quo, the spurned lover retaliated by poisoning his gift: she would still see the future with perfect clarity, but no one would ever believe her. So she knew exactly what was coming when the Greeks who had been besieging the city for ten years left a great wooden horse at the gates of Troy and apparently sailed away. She knew about the Greek soldiers who would pour out of its belly, about the ravage and slaughter that would ensue. She also knew that the victorious Agamemnon would claim her as war booty and carry her home to Mycenae, where both she and the king would be murdered by his vengeful queen, Clytemnestra. And there was nothing she could do about it.

Millennia later it would be senescence, not betrayal, that would carry off my mother's mother's mother's mother's mother's mother, Cassandra

Roberts Nichols, at the age of "100 years and 3 days," according to her obituary in the Paris *True Kentuckian* of April 6, 1866. That nice round number may have been cooked; just six years earlier she'd been only eighty-eight, or so noted the census taker for Harrison County. But even if she was merely an octogenarian, she'd surely be in the running for Maryland's oldest pre-Revolutionary Cassandra, and probably the sturdiest as well, since the obituary added that she had always "enjoyed unusual good health, having never paid a doctor's bill, or taken any medicine." As a girl, however, she would have been just one Cassandra among many. In the 1776 census of Maryland alone (as imperfect as it is, lacking, among many others, my Cassandra herself and her family), her name was shared by some fifty girls and women, one born as early as 1711 but more than half of them after 1759. Even more Cassandras can be spotted wandering through newspapers, wills, land records, and other documents of the period.[1]

Names don't always tell stories, and sometimes fads are just fads. On the one hand, "Cassandra" may simply have been considered euphonious, chosen by Chesapeake parents with no more concern for the legend attached to it than modern parents feel over the association of their darling Madisons with our puniest president or their little Taylors with the one who died in office after overindulging in pickles, cherries, and ice-cold milk. On the other hand, all those eighteenth-century princesses of the Chesapeake bore a name that was uncannily appropriate to their time. It *was* an era of anxiety and distress, shadowed by alarms, invaders, betrayals, and threats, and the dozens of Cassandras would have had ample reason to echo their doomed and demented namesake's warning to watch out, watch out, everything's coming apart, and no one is going to live happily ever after.

By the time my own Cassandra was born in the late 1760s or early 1770s, the Chesapeake's Golden Age had lost much of its luster, having given way to an unsettling period of political and economic turmoil. The French had formed a diabolical alliance with Indian tribes on the North American front of their war against the British, but as soon as that conflict ended, officials in London began treating their fellow Britons across the water in ways that made the colonists feel like enemies themselves. With protests, boycotts, mob actions, and passionate political meetings, pressure was visibly building toward the taking of some sort of decisive and radical action—action that, when it came in 1776, would be explained to a candid world in the unprecedented but somewhat imprecise terms of a society's relationship to the happiness of its members. At the same time, expectations about the everyday satisfactions and pleasures of private life—in love, marriage, family, lifespan—were also changing in ways that could be as bewildering as they were liberating. In fact the very idea that an individual, a person, had an "inner self" that could make its own choices, exercise control over its own emotions and state of mind, and shape the contours of its own journey into the future was growing and flourishing throughout this period.[2] A happy life, in short, was becoming not necessarily more attainable but certainly more *discussable*.

For my own family, this complex and dramatic period would be a vital turning point in more ways than one. Many of my kin did in fact discuss, even experiment with, new ideas about the meaning of both political and personal happiness. I am inordinately proud that most of them would support that decisive and radical action of 1776, and equally pleased that some of them were drawing remarkably bold contours for their own individual journeys. But though they clearly foresaw the new nation's special promise, they were never able to pursue their happiness as successfully as they had *before* Americans launched a revolution on behalf of their right to try.

This era marked a small turning point for me, too, in my search for my family's stories: for the first time, some of my kin begin to speak for themselves. In part because more records managed to survive from this era, but also because the evolving understanding of the meaning of selfhood made more aspects of life *worth* recording, I was able to find many more traces of my forebears' presence, sometimes even their own stories from their own hands. Here was a small clutch of letters written during the war, there a journal kept by a famous neighbor, here an application for a military pension, there an accused housebreaker's feeble explanation to the court, there again a newspaper account of a battle or a death. And a couple of my relatives featured yet again in adventures so exotic that their kin continued for generations to tell and retell and embellish and re-embellish their stories.

Yet many of these records, papers, and legends could be deeply frustrating, too, filled with those indecipherable little nuggets I call "Musgraves" and revealing just enough of the story to leave me starving for the denouement that would never come. *Why* did this particular young dead soldier inspire such public mourning? *Why* did the Quaker turn his back on his faith to enlist? What *did* happen to the uppity overseer? And what on earth was going on with Great-Grandmother, the pistols, the pirates, and the orgies? More and more women of this period, too, appear in their own names with modest but evident histories of their own—the lovesick eloper, the romantic recluse, the Brooklyn girl who went south—not just as some man's Mrs. Those few whispers make possible, or at least irresistible, some speculation about the path that led to the most decisive event of a woman's life—her marriage to this man, not that one—in an era when ideas about the proper basis for a marriage were teetering along with so many other beliefs and habits on the cusp of change.

Virginia, America, and the prospects for happiness were looking very different than they had to the earliest immigrants. In the seventeenth century, at least one of my ancestors had arrived with property and powerful friends already at his command, but a surprisingly large number of them had followed essentially the same script: poor boy or girl gambles all, crosses the sea, sells self into servitude, manages not to die, probably acts heartlessly, gets land, gets servants, gets slaves, marries (often advantageously), gets more land and more slaves, and upon the deathbed has good reason to consider life happy, or at least happier than many others'.

During the late seventeenth and eighteenth centuries, however, the cluster of people who didn't know they were all my ancestors began compiling a whole anthology of scripts, dividing themselves into the categories that were coming to feel like the stratifications of class. Many of those who had become rich after arriving in Virginia or Maryland continued to flourish, or at least they looked as if they did. One or two of the more recent immigrants still managed to claw their way into prosperity. Others, including the Protestants who fled persecution in France, arrived in modestly comfortable circumstances and remained there. But those who were poor when they came were much more likely to stay poor; gone were the days when ambition and sweat and good health alone could plausibly carry any hardy Smith or Roberts from the depths of poverty to the heights of happiness.

For the big merchants and planters, including my Flemings, Ballards, Bateses, and Paynes, life generally seems to have been happy for the *first* half of the century. Though the elite accounted for at most about 10 percent of Virginia's white male population and perhaps 5 percent of Maryland's, their control over the political and economic institutions of power was nearly total. They were living handsomely, consciously modeling themselves and their estates after the English gentry, and in the 1720s and 1730s many had begun building the beautiful riverfront mansions that to this day whisper "aristocrat" to the tourist.

They hired tutors for their sons or schooled them in England, collected books and enjoyed polite literature and the classics, imported elegant furniture and plate, dressed their wives (and themselves) lavishly, laid out gardens, kept coaches and wine cellars. They enjoyed active social lives, with entertainments ranging from genteel exchanges of visits to vigorous, even brutal sporting events like horseracing and cockfighting. Anglicanism was Virginia's official faith, but formal religious strictures generally lay lightly upon the conduct of daily life. And it was around this time that Williamsburg, Virginia's elegant new capital and one of North America's first planned towns, became a cultural and social center as well as the political one, home to dozens of well-stocked shops and well-populated taverns (one of them owned by my seventh-great-grandfather Gabriel Maupin), a public hospital, a theater company, and the South's first surviving college.

After a long period in which life had often felt harsh, alienating, and terrify-ingly provisional, in short, swaths of Tidewater society were putting down rich networks of roots and fully expecting they would take. Achieving happiness, at least for members of the gentry class like my kinsmen (though less so for my kins*women,* the daughters and wives whose everyday happiness the men largely controlled), had come to mean something more complicated than not dying tomorrow, something more social than piling up acreage, servants, and hogs-heads. A cluster of ideas about *how* one ought to live, shaped in part by European Enlightenment thought but given a Tidewater seasoning, began to take on the form and force of a widely accepted cultural ideal, though like many ideals, this one was sometimes more honored than obeyed. A man ought to conduct himself with moderation, reason, and self-discipline; he ought to be conscious of his proper place in the community and render whatever services it required; he ought to maintain his family in safety, order, and comfort, enjoying its affection and support in his private life but finding his central role as a public man.

And building a society based on these values could also preserve as well as serve a greater goal, one that had always beckoned at the heart of the American experiment: the achievement of personal independence, the sense of being at peace under one's own vine and fig tree with none to make one afraid. Nothing should stand in the way of, and society should in fact operate to encourage, the right of every man (the limitation by gender was no accident, and no one even had to mention the tacit qualifier "white") to choose, seek, attain, and enjoy his own vision of comfort and security. Or, as Thomas Jefferson would soon put it so much more elegantly, to pursue his happiness.[3]

As usual, however, the pursuit had a snag or two to it. One was tobacco, the root of the region's very identity, the emblem as well as the guarantor of the social order. Though the lives of the planter and his family had acquired outward graces and flourishes that would have astounded their heartless seventeenth-century forebears, by the middle of the eighteenth century the fortunes of many were noticeably rickety at their core. No specially gifted Cassandras were necessary to see the pervasiveness of the economic unhappiness.

The reasons were complex. Most planters were spending heavily with British merchants to support the everyday work of their enormous estates, as well as to supply the generous and hospitable lifestyle that being a "planter" required. At the same time, a string of bad crops, produced by thinning soil and seasons too dry or too cold, meant that even an abstemious producer might be unable to recoup enough to cover what he owed. England's wars with the French were also upsetting both markets and currencies, sometimes causing strapped merchants to call in their debts or demand payment in sterling. The distress rippled through the ranks of the planters, from the great ones to the small.

So by around the middle of the century, more and more tobacco producers were finding themselves floundering under mountains of IOUs. While Virginians accounted for only about one-fifth of the entire population of the thirteen colonies at the outbreak of the Revolution, they were eventually responsible for nearly half of the £3 million in American debts claimed by British creditors after the war. In 1776 ten Virginians owed at least £5,000 apiece, an enormous sum considering that the fabled Colonel Landon Carter—who had a well-deserved reputation for moderation and thrift but also a large family, as many as four hundred slaves, vast landholdings, and an elegant manor house to keep up—noted with wonderment in March 1771 that for several years his annual expenditures to maintain his household "in everything, tools etc." had not been less than £400.[4]

The growing sense of uneasiness in the Tidewater by mid-century could not have been helped by the presence of the elephant in the room. As they had been in the seventeenth century, the comfort and prosperity of the elites were rooted in heartlessness: the exploitation of a dependent labor force kept under control with tactics of repression and brutality. By now, however, the vast majority of unskilled laborers were not white Britons under temporary indentures but enslaved Africans under life sentences. White indentureship was not yet dead, especially for skilled laborers, and some small and middling planters took the gamble of using British convicts who had been transported for labor in the colonies. Though unsavory, they were cheaper than Africans, and their terms were normally longer than those of other indentured whites.

But the white faces in the quarters grew increasingly rare throughout the century, and planters began to fashion a new relationship with this new kind of workforce no longer made up of Johns and Margarets from whom they would wring the last stroke of work before setting them free to become anything from threadbare malcontents to in-laws. Most masters came to characterize their relationship to their black "people" as something benevolent and familial. In their eyes it was a mutually beneficial lifelong association: duty required them to give to a simpleminded and childlike workforce the fatherly care and discipline it desperately needed in return for its loyal labor. That "paternal" care could be in some ways more sensitive to slaves' basic physical needs—a slave for life was a bigger investment than a servant whose term of indenture wouldn't outlast four or five pairs of shoes—but also more emotionally remote from the lives of beings it was already too easy to consider alien, a different order of human. Paralyzing ambivalence or carefully compartmentalized thinking about slavery was not at all unusual, and many Virginians, among them George Washington (whose will directed that his slaves be freed after his wife's death) and Thomas Jefferson (who liberated only a token number, including his putative sons Madison and Eston Hemings), expressed uneasiness with an institution that felt both entrenched and wrong.

Many of my ancestors owned slaves during the first half of the century, some of them dozens. Even the Quakers did; it wasn't until around the 1750s that the Friends began to embrace abolitionism, and that's about the time when most of the Quakers among my Bates and Woodson kin gradually began to discard not their enslaved people but rather the increasingly inconvenient faith of their fathers. My own large planters were never *great* planters; they never reached the happy heights of the Carters, Byrds, and Randolphs, though they were closely tied to that social circle by both friendship and marriage. It would have been hard not to be. Everyone, it seemed, was connected to the powerful and prosperous Randolphs, the Virginian equivalent of Queen Victoria's vast brood, whose dynastically provident marriages would make Victoria the grandmother of most of the crowned heads of Europe. Six sons and two daughters of William and Mary Isham Randolph married and spawned with such gusto and, usually, good taste that within a couple of generations, everyone who was *anyone* in Virginia could boast links to the Randolphs, often twice and thrice over as cousins kept marrying cousins, because everybody worth knowing was already kin. Among those kin were Thomas Jefferson, whose mother, Jane, was born a Randolph (she married "down"), and Judith Fleming, the sister of my seventh-great-grandfather Tarlton Fleming, who in 1712 took Thomas Randolph as her husband. Judith definitely married "up."

I suspect that Tarlton Fleming and his family always felt overshadowed by the well-wed Judith, who with her Randolph husband dwelt ("lived" seems too pale a word here) at Tuckahoe, a large plantation just a few miles west of present-day Richmond. The house, which grew from a single wing into a spacious and elegant H-shaped mansion beautifully finished inside with elaborately turned and carved woodwork, was, it was said, built for entertaining: the family lived in one wing and kept the other for guests. Thomas Jefferson, who lived at Tuckahoe for several years as a child when his father became the guardian of a brood of orphaned Randolphs, had a complicated attitude toward his own mother's "superior" connections; just about the only reference to her in all his surviving writings is a jibe in his autobiography at her claim to a long pedigree.[5]

Although Tarlton's property at Rock Castle, a good day's ride on horseback farther up the James, was much more modest than his Randolph brother-in-law's, even so it soon turned into a liability for his only son as well as a prime example of the kind of financial unhappiness that was perplexing many elite Virginians of the time. In his 1750 will, the elder Tarlton directed his namesake heir to give £500 to each of his four sisters, one of whom was my sixth-great-grandmother Elizabeth Fleming, soon to be the wife of Josias Payne II. Nine years later, the younger Tarlton petitioned Virginia's House of Burgesses for permission to raise the money by selling some of his entailed land. Selling the lands he held in fee simple wouldn't fetch enough to meet his obligation, he told the burgesses, so if he couldn't dock the entail on Rock Castle, he would have no other choice but to put "the greater part" of his slaves on the market.[6]

Even that didn't solve the problem. In 1773 Tarlton put up fifty-one slaves as security against a loan of more than £2,000 from the Glasgow merchant George Kippen & Co. Though his estate would be valued at £13,646 in paper currency after his death in 1778, his heirs would number among the many Virginians pursued by British creditors, and depreciation would reduce the worth of their inheritance to little more than the principal and interest on the debt to Kippen. After Tarlton's son was reduced to selling the Rock Castle property, a family of "beggared orphans" among Tarlton's grandchildren was left in such bad shape that their cousin Martha Jefferson would beg the president to find one of them a place as a midshipman.[7]

Yet for all Tarlton's struggles with his cash flow throughout his life, he by no means lived impoverished, and we have a clear idea of the sorts of purchases that had helped to bring his troubles down upon him. The inventory of his estate showed that besides his 1,900 taxable acres, more than eighty Negroes listed by name, dozens of head of livestock, and a huge assortment of farm tools and implements, his possessions included a chariot and four bay horses, a collection of books worth £25, a spyglass, china, walnut furniture, a set of ivory-handled knives and forks, a German flute, and a violin. Tarlton could literally have been fiddling while Rock Castle sank.[8]

Constant worries over money were distracting enough for anyone striving to live up to the ideals of gentlemanly conduct. But the Fleming family was also implicated in another challenge to those touchstone values of reason, self-discipline, and moderation in daily life.

The first teller of this story was the famous gossip William Byrd II of Westover, keeper of the notorious "secret diary" chronicling his daily life in an obscure shorthand that doesn't quite disguise the brisk banality of most of the entries: he breakfasted on milk and strawberries, he exercised, he read some Hebrew and some Greek, he doctored and disciplined his "people," he quarreled with his wife and then rogered her. Luckily, however, the story about Mary Randolph comes out of the more expansive part of his writings, a small group of essays on his travels that he had evidently intended (though never felt quite ready) to publish.[9] Though it does elide a number of critical details, the passage about Mary is chatty enough to provide a glimpse into some of the new ways of thinking about love, marriage, and personal freedom and prepares us to follow the long, loud, astonishing echoes down through the generations of one young woman's defiant pursuit of a different happiness—and at the same time to watch how a story that started out titillating grew into one that was positively lurid.

Byrd described how, on a journey to Fredericksburg in 1732 to inspect a new iron mine, he was trapped at Tuckahoe for two days by a nor'easter. Grumbling that there was no liquor in the house, he "killed the time" by reading *The Beggar's Opera* aloud and discussing herbal remedies for dysentery with his hostess, the widowed Judith Fleming Randolph, who, he reported, "smiled graciously upon me," and her guest, her sister-in-law (and my seventh-great-grandmother) Hannah Bates Fleming, the wife of the elder Tarlton. Hannah Fleming was chafing and complaining that the rain was delaying her reunion with her husband, whom she was supposed to join at Rock Castle now that they had finally, after seven years of indecision, resolved to move to "that retired part of the country." Byrd tried gallantly to comfort her, pointing out that married couples could find a brief separation good for romance. But privately he was dismissive. That "fond female," humphed Byrd, "fancies people should love with as little reason after marriage as before."[10]

Another "fond female" in the family, however, had recently been seized by some even more eccentric ideas about marriage, which Byrd described in his essay. As they waited for the weather to clear, he wrote, Judith Randolph told him "the tragical story of her daughter's humble marriage with her uncle's overseer." Though Byrd referred to the episode as if it was common knowledge, this condensed version is the only surviving contemporary written record of the scandal that for years lived in rumor and whisper, growing ever more sensational, before relatives and biographers of the impulsive bride's grandson, Chief Justice John Marshall, finally addressed it openly.

All Byrd tells us is that the family was "justly enraged" at the "senseless . . . prank" pulled by Judith Randolph's daughter Mary, my first cousin eight times removed, who was then no older than fifteen or sixteen. "Besides the meanness of this mortal's aspect," Byrd wrote heatedly, "the man has not one visible qualification except impudence to recommend him to a female's inclinations. But there is sometimes such a charm in that Hibernian endowment that frail woman can't withstand it. . . . Had she run away with a gentleman or a pretty fellow there might have been some excuse for her, though he were of inferior fortune; but to stoop to a dirty plebeian without any kind of merit is the lowest prostitution."[11] Randolph females were supposed to be captivated by Bollings and Lees and Wormeleys and Beverleys. Randolph females weren't supposed to be captivated by *Irishmen.*

Byrd's comments suggest that Mary's elopement with the overseer had taken place not long before his visit in September 1732. But around 1734 Mary gave birth to the first of her eight children with her apparent second husband, a parson named James Keith, who had something of a stormy history of his own. In October 1733 Keith had resigned under pressure as minister of Henrico Parish and taken temporary refuge in Maryland after he was accused of fornication with an unnamed "young Gentlewoman" whose family was apparently both powerful and irritable.[12] We don't know for sure that his partner in that particular sin was Mary, but more mysterious is the question of what happened to her first husband that allowed her second marriage. Only a century and a half later do written accounts begin to address the question publicly—often with a remarkable gusto, given the shadow cast by the episode on the tellers' own eminent family.

W. M. Paxton, a great-nephew of the chief justice through both his mother and his stepmother, spent months traveling to visit his kin and solicit information for his 1885 genealogy of the Marshall family, a "labor of love" and "tribute of affection," as he described it, that bestowed the "kindest words . . . on those I knew and loved." Mary Randolph did not fall into that category. After primly cautioning that "stories are told of this lady that need confirmation," Paxton enthusiastically threw himself into telling them again, in several variants. "She is said to have first secretly married a subaltern in the British army," Paxton began, "and when her marriage and hiding place were discovered, her husband and child were murdered by her brothers. It is charged that her marriage to Parson Keith was concealed from her brothers, and that she stole away to accompany her husband, when he returned to Scotland for orders."[13]

But his preferred version, the purple tale he labeled "LEGEND OF THE RANDOLPHS," was apparently drawn from relatives' recollections of an old story told many decades earlier by the chief justice's sister Eliza Marshall Colston. Eliza, who died forty-three years before Paxton's book appeared, had been the notorious Mary Randolph's oldest granddaughter and daily companion, as well as the firstborn girl in the vast brood of fifteen little Marshalls. Eliza "became the teacher of her younger brothers and sisters," wrote Paxton, "and they ever regarded her with deep veneration."[14]

Mary Randolph, Paxton's tale went, was barely into her teens when she was "induced" to elope with Tuckahoe's bailiff. For some time, the searches mounted by her frantic family and furious neighbors were fruitless, but the couple was finally discovered hiding on Elk Island, a large island far up the James. "The angry brothers came upon them in the night," Paxton wrote, "murdered the bailiff and the child, and brought their sister home. The deed of blood and cruelty so affected the wife and mother that she became deranged." With care, however, and utter silence about the episode of the bailiff, Mary's family managed to restore her health. She married Parson Keith, raised their children (among them the daughter who would marry Colonel Thomas Marshall and give birth in 1755 to the future chief justice), and seemed to have forgotten her early escapade.

Then, years later, a letter arrived, purportedly from none other than the murdered bailiff. "It stated that he still lived," Paxton went on, "that he that was left as dead, had revived, had changed his name, and had fled to foreign countries; after years of wandering had returned to look upon his lawful wife; had found her married and happy; that he would not afflict her by claiming her as his own, but advised her to be happy and forget him, who had more than died for her love, for she should hear no more from him." The shock "unhinged" poor Mary's mind all over again, Paxton concluded. "Her wierd [*sic*] form and the wild expression of her eyes, gave color to the ghostly stories told of her. But in her old age she was doubtless deranged."[15]

Whew. The story reeks not just of melodrama but also of nonsense. This harrowing tale of blood and vengeance doesn't sound as if it had anything to do with the "senseless prank" described during Byrd's stormbound visit by the girl's own mother and aunt, who were also perfectly able to talk composedly to their guest about comic operas and bowel disease. Nor is it likely that such a memorable event as an honor killing by one of the first families of the colony would not have been recorded *somewhere* or left some visible consequences *somehow*. Or that Mary's sole brother (not "angry brothers"), who was just nineteen and whom Byrd dismissed as spoiled and "pretty," was the Javert who had single-mindedly hunted the couple down. Or that a pregnant young gentlewoman and her husband would have hidden for months on an island in the wilderness rather than simply slipping easily over some county or colony line, where no Amber Alert or milk carton photograph could have betrayed them.

As in the Woodsons' tale of the Indian attack, the germ of this story is probably true, too. It's inconceivable that William Byrd, fond as he was of gossip, would have invented the scandalous story of the "humble marriage" out of whole cloth just to confide it to a journal he never got around to publishing. Nevertheless, rather than murdering Mary's dirty, "plebeian" first husband, the proud Randolphs probably employed a much tidier and equally time-tested method for ensuring his quick disappearance: cash. That, however, left the obvious problem that the bride would still have been legally married, reason enough for her kin to have strenuously discouraged the clerical suitor who next came calling for her, perhaps even to the extent of using their influence as vestrymen to have him banished from the parish. If the flighty young woman then revealed a pregnancy, the suddenly necessary marriage to Parson Keith would have been bigamous and all their children illegitimate.

Who it was who added the embellishments can never be proved, but we can guess. Eliza was demonstrably of a romantic turn of mind: she had indulged in years' worth of retirement from society, "sorely distressed" over the death of a lover during the Revolutionary War, before finally marrying at the advanced age of twenty-seven. As she grew older, Paxton noted, she loved to retell the old stories, and one of the younger relatives who used to sit spellbound "at her feet" passed on to Paxton yet another of her weirdly lurid family legends, this one relating how Eliza's great-grandmother Markham had married the pirate Blackbeard by mistake.[16]

That lady, according to Eliza, had been left a rich widow with many children after the death of her first husband, John Markham (who had himself been a seducer, a bigamist, and a murderer, but that's another story). In her loneliness she became "infatuated" with a handsome young man wearing the uniform of a British naval officer. Only after the wedding did she discover that he was actually the infamous pirate, but by then poor Great-Grandmother Markham was so utterly besotted that she began to join in the pirate's "orgies," and "on one occasion, when two villains intended to assassinate Blackbeard, and were seated at table, one on his right and the other on his left, she held two pistols beneath the table, and drawing a trigger with each hand at the same moment, the miscreants fell dead at the feet of her unworthy lord." During another drunken revel not long afterwards, the ungrateful brute kicked her so hard that she died. By then, however, the former Mrs. Markham's beautiful, accomplished, and gently educated daughter Elizabeth had been sent for her own safety to her uncles, where she was soon befriended by a local widow named Marshall and the widow's highly eligible son. This paragon of young womanhood would become Eliza Colston's other grandmother, Elizabeth Markham Marshall, whose son Thomas Marshall would marry the parson's daughter.[17]

As with the overseer elopement story, more than one version survives. "Tradition has gone wild," noted Paxton, with evident delight, over the career of Great-Grandmother's husband; in another variant he's simply piratical, not Blackbeard, but he's also the father, not the stepfather, of Mrs. Markham's seventeen daughters and only son. In any case, said Paxton, "all authority agree in pronouncing him a handsome, dashing and fascinating gentleman, and a daring, cruel and adroit villain." He clearly fascinated Paxton's younger stepbrother Thomas M. Green, the editor of the *Maysville Eagle* of Kentucky. "A shrewd, money-getting, out-breaking, lawless, self-witted, large-brained, devil-defying man was this John Markham, if all accounts be true," Green wrote, "respecting neither God nor man, and fearing neither; and every now and then there breaks out in his race the genuine Markham streak."[18]

Little is known about the family of Elizabeth Markham. One prominent Markham of the time, a cousin of William Penn's who served two terms as deputy governor of Pennsylvania in the 1690s, had some pirate connections; he protected the local buccaneers for a fee and even allowed his daughter to marry one, a union that was perhaps a distant inspiration for the Randolphs' tale. No evidence other than the shared name, however, ties the governor's family to the justice's vanishingly obscure Markham ancestors in Virginia's Northern Neck.[19] And the Blackbeard part of the story is clearly humbug.

Blackbeard, whose real name is usually given as Edward Teach or Thatch, spent most of his land-bound time not in northern Virginia but in North Carolina and the Bahamas. His career was meteoric but brief. He is said to have been born in Bristol and to have served on a privateering vessel based in Jamaica during Queen Anne's War, which ended in 1713. By 1717 he was capturing and commanding ships of his own and preying on seamen and landlubbers alike, at one point blockading Charleston and taking a group of prominent citizens hostage. In November 1718 a naval expedition sent by Virginia's governor caught up with the pirate off North Carolina. Blackbeard boarded one of the pursuing sloops and engaged in a wild sword and pistol fight with Lieutenant Robert Maynard and his men, one of whom, a Highlander, swung his broadsword and whacked the pirate's head from his shoulders. The severed noggin, its long and luxuriant beard doubtless twisted into its trademark pigtails, was stuck on the bowsprit and the body thrown overboard, whereupon, later legend insists, it swam several times around the ship before sinking from sight.[20] Little is known about the family of Blackbeard, either, except that he was said to have had fourteen wives—almost as many brides as John Markham had daughters.

Exactly what possessed Eliza Colston to create for the chief justice of the United States a family tree that embraced a notoriously savage pirate and a murderous female orgiast is an open question. In fact the parade of tales about the chief justice's ancestors on *both* sides is astonishingly ripe, full of the sorts of melodramatic murders, elopements, bigamies, sordid revels, and nighttime adventures that would be right at home in the best Victorian blood-and-thunder novel. It's possible that the truth about her villainous great-grandfather John Markham was both common knowledge at the time and so lurid that Eliza Colston hoped to improve his reputation by contrasting him with a legendary pirate who no one could deny was even worse. But she didn't seem to mind that her story made her quick-drawing great-grandmother look almost as bad, or that her family tales cheerfully acknowledged the presence of foolish and "infatuated" foremothers on *both* sides of her family.

For Eliza's younger male relatives, at least, having a black sheep in the family seems to have been even better than having an earl. By the time Paxton and Green came along in the late nineteenth century, the romantic stock of the bold and independent master of the seas was rising even as the real threat of pirates was fading, and Robert Louis Stevenson's swashbuckling tale *Treasure Island,* a wild best-seller in the United States, hit its peak of popularity exactly when Paxton was working on his own book. Commandeering a shrewd, fearless, devil-defying (and lusty) great-grandfather for Chief Justice John Marshall, one of the most respectable Americans who ever lived, could have been happiness itself for editor Green, who lived quietly with his mother in Kentucky, far from pirate waters, and who, according to Paxton, had never been able to take his rightful role as a leader of society because he was hard of hearing.[21] Thomas Green clearly did not himself embody the latest outbreak of that "genuine Markham streak."

Eliza Colston's story endowing the Marshall side of the family with a genuine crazy-bigamist streak actually makes a sort of utilitarian sense. When Eliza's big brother John was named the most important judge in America, she could well have been moved to press the tale of the unmurdered bailiff as a cannily half-accurate but disarmingly romantic explanation of what seem to have been persistent rumors about their grandmother Keith's first marriage. Here's where the poverty of the written record and the fragility of "common knowledge" become painfully clear. We can't now eavesdrop on the after-dinner gossip or the servant-quarters murmurings; we don't know how tenacious or damaging those rumors may have been. But we can surmise, on the basis of Paxton's apparently plentiful encounters with versions of the story among even distant relatives, that enough people thought the mother of the chief justice was a bastard to prod the family into addressing the issue.

And as damage control, Eliza's version is, in its own loony way, inspired: it endows the sinner Mary with a sympathetic exculpation of her youthful lapse— why shouldn't she have felt free to take a second husband after witnessing and extravagantly mourning what she thought was the brutal murder of her first?— while not sparing her the classic divine retribution of madness. It lifts all stain from Eliza's grandfather, the man of God, Parson Keith. And while not shrinking from violence in the name of honor, it quietly elides what Byrd, at least, had decades earlier considered the most unforgivable part of the whole affair: the overseer's nationality. Randolphs could murder, but Randolphs couldn't marry *Irishmen*.

From the moment Paxton broke the news, relatives and chroniclers of the chief justice have been fretting about how, or even whether, to acknowledge it. In 1916 Marshall's admiring biographer Albert Beveridge dismissed in a foot-note the "highly colored" tale of "an elopement, the deadly revenge of out-raged brothers, a broken heart and resulting insanity . . . [and] a fraudulent Enoch Arden letter," and said no more about it. The more recent efforts of Jean Edward Smith to analyze the story in his biography of Marshall, however, inad-vertently illustrate the enduring consequences of a silly error. Smith mistook Enoch Arden as the overseer's name, not having understood that Beveridge's footnote referred to Tennyson's narrative poem of that name about a husband, presumed lost at sea, who returns home after years as a castaway and finds his wife remarried. Unlike Mary Randolph's boorish husband, however, Enoch Arden, upon seeing for himself that his wife is happy, considerately decides not to reveal himself to her, arranging that she should be told only after his death.[22]

Tennyson's poem was an old warhorse almost from the moment of its birth in 1864 and for decades inspired countless imitations, takeoffs, and pastiches, including an Agatha Christie mystery and a Cary Grant screwball farce.[23] The high fame of Tennyson's verses may even have contributed to the gusto with which the Marshall descendants embraced and perhaps embellished Mary's story; like the present-day observer who tells the TV reporter that the outlandish event he happened to witness was "just like a movie," family members could have found narrative satisfaction and dramatic familiarity in seeing Granny's escapade as "just like a poem!" But as time passes and familiarity fades, so can sense. After Smith's book appeared, the "true identity" of the overseer quickly made the rounds of the Keith and Randolph online genealogy forums, and Arden now regularly pops up in the family trees on Ancestry.com as the name of Mary's first spouse.

None of these stories, however—not Byrd's contemporary sketch, not the versions handed down in the family, not the ones unearthed by scholars—tell us *why* young Mary did what she did, or where she got first the idea and then the courage to pull her senseless prank in an era when conventional wisdom, especially among families with property and standing at stake, still held that love and happiness could, should, and would follow a decently deliberate marriage, but need not precede one. (We can only guess at *how* the underage Mary managed to get herself married without either her guardian's permission or the required publication of the banns, though other ardent couples of the period found relief in a quick trip to Maryland.)

Any imaginative reader could propose a host of scenarios: adolescent rebelliousness, sexual curiosity, retaliation against a faithless suitor, the allure of the forbidden, a desire for adventure, the vulnerability of a recently fatherless young woman to an attentive older man. Yet while any of those would make sense applied to an elopement, the underlying theme common to all those possibilities is one Mary might not even have had the words to articulate for herself. A member of a powerful family expected to marry advantageously, a daughter taught to be passive and obedient to her father or guardian, an Anglican schooled to distrust passion of any sort, a Virginian raised in a culture that valued order, duty, and due deference, an Englishwoman conditioned to disdain the Irish, a gentlewoman who should have had nothing to do with the field help, Mary, by running off with the overseer, defied almost everything she was supposed to know and be. Though she probably did not even put it in those terms, in essence she was deciding to tear down the life that was expected of her in order to claim and pursue her own vision of what happiness might mean. I stand in awe of the gumption of my many-times-removed cousin—even as I acknowledge, with a pang, that her pursuit of this particular happiness was probably doomed from the start.

That's something Cassandra would have known.

Virtue

By the time of the outbreak of the rebellion that would formally acknowledge the pursuit of happiness as a worthy life goal, many of my forebears seem to have needed all the encouragement they could get to seize some for themselves. In the end, maybe they just weren't virtuous enough to keep their grip.

Ancestors of mine kept arriving in the southern colonies until the very brink of the Revolution. As usual, none of them had been born aristocrats, but nobody was becoming a plutocrat anymore, either. The century or so before 1776 was the era of my middling immigrants—Duckers, Segars, Nicholses— most of whom chose the calmer if humbler possibilities of rural Maryland over the disorderly extremes of Virginia. Modest, hardworking farmers, tailors, and millers, they often managed to acquire a bit of property, but they rarely held any significant office or exercised any visible social power and were more likely to be considered salt of the earth than lords of the land. Meanwhile the Robertses, the Hickmans, the Trammells, the Mullinses, and other early arrivals who had never been more than lordlings were beginning what would become the long sidle westward, away from the dwindling opportunities of the Tidewater and Eastern Shore settlements and into Maryland and the Virginia mountains.

My forebears were also becoming a little more multinational. Among those arriving in Virginia at this time was at least one family of Huguenots, the Protestants who fled France in droves beginning in 1685, when Louis XIV resumed the persecution of non-Catholics. But around this new kind of immi- grant would soon cluster some old and familiar-sounding stories. Descendants insisted that my seventh-great-grandfather Gabriel Maupin was not just a general in the army of Navarre but also a prince twice over, one of his great-grandfathers having been the king of Navarre and another a Capet of the French royal house.

Gabriel himself, they said, had married a daughter of Earl Spencer of England. Untrue again: Gabriel, born near Orléans, was a tailor and his bride a rope maker's daughter from a small town outside Dieppe. In the New World their fortunes were equally modest: Gabriel ran a tavern in his home in Williamsburg, one son was a saddler, and a grandson was in charge of military stores in the capital city during the Revolution.[24] Most Maupins, however, settled into farming, eventually wandering west from Williamsburg into the newly settled county of Albemarle, up against the Blue Ridge Mountains, where they began assiduously marrying the Mullinses, Vias, and Ballards they found there and producing huge families. My fifth-great-grandmother Frances Ballard, at least three generations and many social and economic rungs downstream from the royal governor's lofty and lordly friend Colonel Thomas Ballard, was an exception: she produced a daughter, Rachel, even though she married no one at all.

But even today, three centuries after the arrival of the immigrants Gabriel and Marie, some Maupins are still telling another kind of tale that among my kin was surprisingly rare: the divine miracle. The story goes that as the family was crossing the sea in the spring of 1701, a mighty storm tore a great hole in their ship. The despairing crew abandoned the pumps, but when a minister offered up a prayer, the waters subsided from the hold and the ship straggled safely to port—where a huge fish was found wedged like a stopper into the gash in the timbers.[25] The Maupins were, to be sure, the only forebears I know of who had suffered serious persecution because of their faith and for whom that iconic American promise of religious freedom would have been a true beacon of happiness. But this solitary mark of divine favor seems a paltry record for a tribe that spent four centuries pursuing happiness in a place as generally close to God as the United States has always been, and raises the niggling question of whether other forebears may have felt distinguished more by God's distance from their lives than by his presence.

As my wealthy kin faced tumult and loss, and my middling kin struggled to keep their prospects middling, yet another category of ancestor was arriving during the eighteenth century. All the folks I'd been able to trace so far came from the respectable side of my grandmother's family—Grace's mother's side, Alice's ancestors, who, as she used to tell my mother vaguely, "were *somebody.*" Now for the first time I was picking up the scent of the other side, Grace's father's people, and even if I hadn't already heard that Arthur Dougherty was something between a scapegrace and a scoundrel, I couldn't have escaped the conclusion that many if not most of Grace's paternal ancestors fell into those unhappy categories too.

These people came poor and stayed poor. Some were simply obscure, their passages traceable mainly through the imagination; others doubtless would have preferred obscurity to the immortality they achieved in such sources as delinquent tax lists, court actions for debt, and desperate pension applications. That's mostly where I found Ralph Collins, for instance, who reportedly came from Durham, in northern England, and who settled in Virginia probably as a teenager and likely just in the nick of time before the outbreak of the Revolution put a crimp in immigration. He spent the next decade or so in footloose and hapless wandering through Virginia's settled places, at one point perching in Loudoun County just long enough to default on his taxes. Loudoun officials marked him down as having "gone away."[26]

But many of those who arrived during the eighteenth century had a different kind of plan for life in the New World. Like most new Americans, they were looking for wider opportunities and a fresh start, but for them, pursuing happiness didn't seem to mean choosing the increasingly difficult and unlikely path of working their way up in the settled parts of civilization like Loudoun. It meant lighting out and making new communities for themselves in the remoter parts of the colonies, escaping not just the restrictions, exclusions, and oppressions of the old country but also those they saw in the new.

These immigrants, some 200,000 or more of them, came in waves between 1717 and 1775, fleeing the multiplying miseries of Ulster, Scotland, and the north of England: the wreck of the linen and wool trades, a string of dry years and bad crops, drastic food shortages, steep rises in rents, a revival of official pressure against Presbyterians in northern Ireland, the collapse of the Jacobite rebellion in highland Scotland. The immigrants tended to be tenant farmers, laborers, small tradesmen, semiskilled craftsmen, and their families—people whose always modest means had shrunk to the positively bashful. And they brought with them a long tradition of stiff-necked bellicosity, of suspicion toward authority, of resistance to the English and, often, savage defeat at their hands, of pride in their difference and intolerance toward others', of fierce loyalty to their clans and families that transcended fidelity to any state or monarch. In his book *Born Fighting*—an epithet clearly meant to be complimentary—the former navy secretary and future senator James Webb wrote unapologetically about the innate and pervasive pugnacity of his ethnic group that essentially disallows forgiveness of any kind. The Presbyterians among the Scots-Irish added to that mix a deep Calvinist belief in personal responsibility and firmness of principle that sometimes seemed to make ordinary civility morally impossible.

Most of them made straight for the remotest backcountry, first the Pennsylvania frontier and then south and west into the Shenandoah Valley and the Carolinas, where they hoped to be left alone. They usually were.[27]

The single most unhappy immigrant ancestor of this period, whose life would unroll as one long string of failures, disappointments, and debts, may also have had the least hopeful arrival in the New World. Rooting through the incomplete but plentiful contemporary records of immigrant newcomers, I found two William Whartons arriving south of New England at this time. Both of them were convicted criminals who had been transported to Maryland to be sold as servants or laborers, one sent in 1771 for fourteen years and the other in July 1770 for life.[28]

Shipment to the colonies was a common sentence for British offenders throughout much of the century. It was a good way, or so British officials thought, of ridding the kingdom of its least productive and desirable citizens. The colonists tended to hold a different opinion about serving as Britain's back-yard privy pit, the dumping ground for its least mendable trash, and anxieties ran high that transported convicts would bring with them disease and moral corruption, would murder and pillage their unwilling hosts, and would even incite slaves to rebellion.

Most of the convicts had actually been found guilty of modest crimes not considered worth the hangman's time, the commonest being grand larceny: stealing shop merchandise worth a couple of shillings could send a man over the water for seven years. The stiffer sentences of both of the William Whartons, however, suggest they were guilty of something worse, and indeed the proceedings of London's Old Bailey show that on a single day at the end of June 1770—just before the Wharton convicted for life was hustled aboard the *Scarsdale* bound for Maryland—a man by that name and several confederates were tried for three separate episodes of housebreaking. Working at night, the gang would target a house, wrench the shutters off with crowbars, and hand or lift Wharton, who was perhaps the youngest or most agile of the gang, through the window. He would then let the others in, and all would quickly scoop up their booty and flee. From the innkeeper Thomas Ayre, for instance, they expropriated a stash of ha'penny coins and a miscellaneous array of fenceable items—ruffles, stockings, teaspoons, tongs—along with a quart of gin. Wharton was acquitted in the first two cases, with no details given, but during the third burglary his intended victim had caught him red-handed standing under a broken fanlight in the entrance hall. Wharton had a story ready in his defense: he'd been forced to break into the dwelling, he said, by a pair of strangers who came upon him in the street at one o'clock in the morning and held a pistol to his head. "I own I was in the house," he told the court, "but it was against my inclination." The court, doubtless having heard that story before, found him guilty and sentenced him to hang, but like many capital criminals, he was "reprieved" for transportation.[29]

If this was indeed my William Wharton, he must have managed to escape from his master sometime after his arrival—not an uncommon feat, as attested by the constant newspaper notices asking for the return of runaways—and make his way to his nearest compatriots, the Scots-Irish of backcountry Pennsylvania, where a wartime army soon offered its traditional and uninquisitive welcome to the down-and-out and footloose. The Wharton who I know was my fifth-great-grandfather enlisted in Pittsburgh in 1776, and nothing else I've discovered about the rest of his ragged life challenges the premise that he began his American experience about as close to the bottom as anyone could get.

My north English and Scots-Irish fourth- and fifth-great-grandparents— William Wharton, Ralph Collins, James Callahan, John Conway, the Daughertys—were the last of my grandmother Grace's forebears to arrive from overseas. By the time the thirteen colonies declared themselves independent of Great Britain in 1776, her people were all here. They ranged from frontier Pennsylvania to the Carolinas but clustered most heavily in Virginia and Maryland. Most were English, many Scots-Irish, a few of French extraction. Some of them lived with their pampered families and their wretched slaves on extensive plantations and struggled against mountains of debts; others squatted in backcountry clearings, were likely to greet strangers with hostility, if not the barrel of a gun, and probably had as few debts as they did possessions. The most recent immigrants among them were no doubt living so precariously that almost any change could have looked promising. The others, despite their debts and frustrations, had much more at stake, and at risk, in that hot summer when every sheriff in Virginia was directed to proclaim the Declaration of Independence at the courthouse door on the next court day.

Like all national founding myths, the stories Americans tell of their revolution are often most revealing about who they *wish* they were. Even as the United States grew into the most powerful nation in the world, the stories of heroic little-guy defiance against the forces of tyranny continued to form as intimate a part of the memory bank of anyone who was a child in America as the steamy tomato sauce smell of the school cafeteria: the Boston Massacre, the shot heard 'round the world, the Christmastime surprise sprung by Washington's scrawny and shoeless troops against the slumbering Hessians, the giddy wonder of Saratoga and the epic misery of Valley Forge. Nor do adults escape the imagery, even those who fail to make a visit to a shopping mall in mid-February or early July. The political discourse has been permeated by the language of the Revolution, but it is often used with all the precision that Alice's Humpty Dumpty displayed—as when Ronald Reagan strove to reflect the glow of the Founding Fathers onto their "moral equivalents," the Nicaraguan contras and the Afghan mujahideen.

And the war that looms so large in our national imagination takes just as hefty a place in the family stories told generations later by my kin. At least five forefathers or cousins were said to have been present at the war's great punctuation mark, the surrender of Cornwallis; three supposedly had brushes with the war's great villain, the fearsome Colonel Banastre Tarleton; and one reportedly served as scout for the war's great hero, General Washington, in his time of greatest need at Valley Forge, Pennsylvania, during the winter of 1777–78. "Many the time," says a present-day researcher about "Tough Daniel" Maupin, "he left bloody tracks on the frozen ground and flinty snow when the rags which bound his feet wore away. And often he spent foodless days and freezing nights that our country might survive."[30]

In fact most of my kin had left the army by the time Cornwallis surrendered in 1781; the encounters with Tarleton are impossible to deny or confirm; and Tough Daniel's service records show that he enlisted as a sergeant in a local regiment in 1780, more than two years after Valley Forge, and never left Virginia. Which was perhaps a more shining record than that of another Daniel Maupin, Tough Daniel's cousin, who paid a convict named Edward Miller to serve in his place. Miller, the records show, "served the three years made a good soldier and returned home."[31]

Still, Tough Daniel, or more likely his descendants, can hardly be faulted for seizing on that powerful image of the bloody footprints in the snow; after all, everyone else did. First mentioned by Washington himself in a letter to Congress describing the army's dire need for shoes and other basic supplies, over the next century the tracks of blood made their way into speeches and writings by antiquarians, by travel writers, by local politicians, by the great orator Daniel Webster. The image neatly and poignantly summed up everything that an increasingly nostalgic America was finding so appealing about the great founding struggle—the triumph against all odds of humility, sacrifice, courage, and faith. Adding to its magnetism, the image even included a glimpse of the great Washington, *"not a man but a God,"* whose virtue soared ever higher the further the war receded into the past. For Tough Daniel's descendants and for so many others, the step was both small and easy from worshiping the "founding fathers" to inserting their own fathers among them.[32]

But like the lust for blue-blooded forebears, the drive to forge a personal connection to the defining event of United States history, benign and even praiseworthy as it often can be, has earned a bit of a bad odor from its intimate association with exclusivity, self-importance, downright meanness, and on top of that, witlessness. The Marian Anderson flap of 1939 is just one of the many examples of the DAR's tacit willingness to extend its members a sanctuary free from foreigners, servants, vagabonds, convicts, and drunks, or in other words, exactly the sort of people most likely to have served as common soldiers during the Revolution they claim as their sire. It's often so difficult to disentangle the exploitation from the reality that historians who pride themselves on being clear-eyed may hesitate to allow themselves the simple pleasure of admiring what was indeed an amazing political, social, and human feat.

So it took me a while to confess to myself that I was thrilled to be a small-d daughter of the Revolution half a dozen times over, thrilled that my dutiful searches found no evidence of any Tories in the family tree. Most of my male kin apparently supported the Revolution, either by serving on Committees of Safety or by actively joining the fighting, though there's no record of how any of the women felt about it. Some of my soldiers moreover paid for it in very hard currency: several spent years as prisoners of war, some died, and one of the dead inspired the composition of at least two extravagant elegies in verse that were widely published in the newspapers.

I was thrilled, but I was also, again, surprised. For two centuries Americans' embrace of their Revolutionary story seems to have been rooted in a casual conviction that any of us transported back to 1776 and faced with the same choice between treason and stasis would have cheerfully and without hesitation come down on the side of the traitors. But in fact if the colonists had been able to put the prospect to a democratic vote, they might well have chickened out. John Adams later estimated that perhaps a third of all Americans supported independence from Britain, a third actively opposed it, and another third didn't care, or notice, one way or the other. So once more, a classically American story that my ancestors had claimed and that my historian's eye greeted with skepticism turned out, against the odds, to be true after all.

Americans were, moreover, right to contemplate the prospect of war with wariness. Of concern were more than such predictable issues as lingering loyalty to the mother country, uncertainty over the validity or even decency of engaging in rebellion, fear of death or injury, or anxiety over economic disruption. Many, including some of my own kin, were also concerned about questions that went to the heart of America's special relationship to happiness.

One of those doubting kinfolks was George Woodson, a great-great-grandson of Potato Hole, a son of the family antiquarian Charles Woodson, a second or third cousin several times over to my direct Payne and Fleming forebears, and one of the ancestors who two centuries after his death spoke out directly to me, in small collections of wartime letters preserved in several Virginia libraries.

George himself apparently never fought, remaining on his Chesterfield County plantation throughout the war, but he had been disowned by the local Quaker Monthly Meeting along with his two younger brothers, Tarlton and Frederick, after all three were reported to have defied the Friends' pacifist teachings to enlist as soldiers. Although the brothers were fourth-generation Quakers, great-grandsons of a man who had become a Friend at great cost when religious dissent was liable to punishment in Virginia, their family faith was clearly on the wane. The soldiers' disgrace came shortly after their sister had been disowned by the Meeting for marrying a non-Quaker, and shortly before the oldest brother, Charles Jr., a noncombatant, was thrown out for nonattendance.[33]

The surviving letters suggest that Tarlton, at least, was an idealist as well as a fighter. To the middle brother, Frederick, who served only briefly as a lieutenant, George wrote mainly about stockings, turnip seeds, taxes, and "the fair Annabella," and chivvied him drily for not writing more often: "I have not heard from you so long I hope you are neither dead nor sick but your long silence gives me reason to fear that you are both."[34]

But with Tarlton, George opened his heart. You've probably heard, George wrote in May 1776 to his youngest brother, then encamped with the First Virginia at Kemp's Landing, that the Virginia Convention had voted for independence, which is what you were hoping for. But George confessed himself ambivalent. "If we indisputably had the Virtue to deserve freedom," he wrote,

> I should not hesitate to pronounce it a measure productive of the greatest good consequences. . . . If we have not Virtue to deserve freedom Independency will be a measure replete with misery to this Country, for if we should gain our point against Great Britain and should not after that have sufficient Virtue and publick spirit to maintain our acquisition, wherein shall we be benefited? Our Treasure will be wasted—our substance

consumed, our young Men the flower of our country slain or cut off by disease.... My doubts and fears arise from the importance of what we have at stake, our lives, our liberties, our properties, our all now depend upon our exerting all the Virtues necessary for a free people to have.[35]

This anxiety over virtue was pervasive, shared by many of those in the forefront of the Revolutionary movement. More than bullets, more than soldiers, more than generals, Americans needed virtue if they had any hope of prevailing in their great quest to form the first successful republic since antiquity. Quite simply, as John Adams put it, "public Virtue is the only Foundation of Republics." A government that derived its legitimacy not from intimidation or force but from the consent of the governed, colonists believed, would flounder and fail unless its citizens were willing to practice the cardinal public virtue of subordinating their private interests and desires to the greater good. Tending to the greater good, moreover, would enrich the life of each individual citizen, since public and private happiness were mutually reinforcing and mutually dependent.[36]

Particularly in comparison with doddering, decadent, and tyrannical Great Britain, Americans liked to believe they *were* specially virtuous, that they had a unique ability to put aside selfishness and greed on behalf of the commonweal, and that the fight against Britain was nothing short of the necessary combat of Virtue against Vice. But some, notably Adams, would sooner or later find themselves constituting a chorus of Cassandras as they came to the dismaying conclusion that America was no more virtuous and no less endangered than any other nation. And during the chaotic postwar period of the Confederation, many of the Americans surveying what they had wrought would listen closely to James Madison's argument that if men were angels, no government would be necessary—and would support the government he would help construct.

George's letter suggests a split between the brothers, with Tarlton cheerfully enrolled in the Party of Hope while he himself was already an Adamsian skeptic. Conceding that Tarlton might feel different about independence because he spent most of his time among soldiers who declared the "strongest attachment" to their country, George concluded gloomily that he feared "we have not as much Virtue as we should have." Like Cassandra, George and his pessimistic compatriots were both disregarded and right; many of their worries about insufficient virtue have come true. But if Tarlton and his more hopeful comrades had listened to them, then Tom Paine would never have been right either when he told Americans that they had the power to begin the world anew.[37]

The Woodsons may have had mixed feelings about the war, but on another branch of the family tree I was intrigued to turn up an entire family of wild-eyed radicals and downy-cheeked heroes devoted to the cause of life, liberty, and the pursuit of happiness. The younger Tarlton Fleming, the master of Rock Castle who was then in his fifties and who would die just three years into the war, served Goochland County on its Committee of Safety and then, in 1776, in the House of Delegates. His sister Elizabeth, my sixth-great-grandmother, married Josias Payne II, who served as a lieutenant in Goochland's militia through-out the war, and the couple's son Tarlton Payne became a captain in the First Virginia. Elizabeth's first cousin William Fleming, a college mate and lifelong friend of Thomas Jefferson's, was a delegate to the Virginia Conventions in 1775 and 1776, served in the Continental Congress in 1779, and ended up an influential judge on the Court of Appeals. William's brothers Charles and Thomas received battlefield commissions as colonels, and the brothers' young nephew Jack was a captain.[38]

Yet another of Elizabeth's first cousins, John Fleming, a lawyer, burgess, and militia colonel from Cumberland County, was a quiet but genuine revolutionary. This Colonel John was a brother of William, Charles, and Thomas, the father of young Captain Jack—and, as ardently told by Mrs. Pittman, a proud Patriot heir who refused to accept as his rightful inheritance the foreign earldom of Wigton and died fighting for his native land.[39] (In fact he died at home before the war, not on the field during it, and of course he had nothing at all to do with Wigton.) He was also, according to one account, the secret true author of one of the most inflammatory documents to emerge from that inflamed decade leading up to Bunker Hill. In 1765, after the passage of the Stamp Act, Patrick Henry made a fiery speech in the House of Burgesses that, according to legend, was interrupted at one point by other members appalled that he was evidently winding up to lump George III into the same category with such toppled tyrants as Caesar and Charles I. Stopped by their cries of "Treason!" he made a neat rhetorical save in mid-sentence: King George, he said, "may profit by their example. If this be treason, make the most of it."[40]

Henry was a very young and to some eyes unpolished lawyer who was emerging as a leader of the more radical backcountry faction, often to the dismay of conservative Tidewater interests. The resolutions he introduced in the speech, protesting the Stamp Act and opposing taxation without representation, were widely reprinted and helped fuel Revolutionary sentiment throughout the colonies. The great speech, however, is preserved only in several paraphrased versions, one of which, by an anonymous French traveler who happened to be passing through (and who wrote in English), challenges the legend of the firebrand orator by noting that after the interruption he apologized contritely to the House for having gone too far.

The story of the drafting of the resolutions survives in clashing versions, too. Henry left notes for his executor describing how he, "alone, unadvised, and unassisted," had determined to step forward and protest the act when it became clear no one else was willing.[41] Other observers, however, had other stories. A contemporary later recalled that Henry had shown the resolutions to two members, one of them John Fleming, before presenting them to the House; another said the resolutions had been drafted at Lewis's tavern by a small conclave of backcountry members including Henry and Fleming, "but who held the pen I never knew or heard." And Edmund Randolph—who was still a child in 1765 but who would spend decades at the center of state and local politics—stated in the history of Virginia he drafted around 1809–10 that the resolutions were "understood to have been written by Mr. John Fleming, a member for Cumberland County distinguished for his patriotism and the strength of his mind."[42] But John Fleming never had a chance to put his patriotism and strong mind to the service of an independent America; he died just two years after the conclave at the tavern. He was not yet forty.

I confess: I want to believe Edmund Randolph's version is the true one. I want my first cousin eight times removed to have been the true brains behind the resolutions, Patrick Henry's ghostwriter, the gadfly to the firebrand. If I can brand other ancestors as heartless, I can also allow myself to be proud of a true radical stouthearted enough to talk about the implications of liberty long before anyone could be at all sure that "our side" would win.

The story of John Fleming's only son, Captain John "Jack" Fleming, also seems to merit stern efforts to surmount postmodern cynicism. Jack Fleming, who had been about eleven at the time of his father's death, would become something of a hero too, except his great moment came in bloody combat, not heated debate, and the credit *he* got was extravagant. Captain Fleming's First Virginia Regiment had joined Washington's army on Harlem Heights in September 1776 and had taken part in the long retreat through New Jersey into Pennsylvania. On Christmas night the First Virginia numbered among the frozen and threadbare troops who silently pushed their way across the icy Delaware River and marched through snow and sleet the nine miles to Trenton. The sun next morning was obscured by thick clouds as the Americans loomed out of the squalling snow, fell upon the startled Hessians, and routed them, bringing the Continental troops the smashing victory their morale (and the public's) so desperately needed. Just a week later, after Washington had managed to cajole half his troops into reenlisting for the new year, British forces under Lord Cornwallis massed before Trenton for a counterattack. But Washington with most of his soldiers tiptoed around the main enemy force at night and marched twelve miles to Princeton in the dark to prepare for an attack on the British rear.

At Princeton on the third day of the new year, the twenty-one-year-old Captain Jack Fleming was thrust into the command of the tattered remains of the First Virginia, all of his superior officers having been either wounded or killed. The first clash came when General Hugh Mercer's vanguard, which included the tiny First Virginia contingent, emerged from a sunken road and was surprised by Colonel Charles Mawhood's column of British troops. As an unnamed officer would describe the encounter in a letter to Dixon and Hunter's *Virginia Gazette* of January 31, 1777, just ten yards in front of the enemy Captain Fleming ordered his men to "dress," or form a line. Defiantly, the British "black guarded our people, and damned them, 'they would dress them,' and gave the first fire. Our men placed *their* fire so well, that the enemy screamed as if many devils had got hold of them," and soon "were forced out of the field by the braver Americans."

But in the exchange the "gallant officer" Fleming "nobly fell . . . at the head of his company, in defence of American freedom," as Dixon and Hunter's *Gazette* had reported in its first notes on the battle on the twenty-fourth. In a letter from Baltimore published in Purdie's *Virginia Gazette* of January 24, an anonymous correspondent wrote that among the dead "is JACK FLEMING, who behaved and died as bravely as a Caesar could have done, ordering his men to dress before they fired, though the enemy were within 40 yards of him, advancing fast with abusive threats what they would do. However, they were mistaken, and most of them cut to pieces."

Voicing even more extravagant laments were two newspaper elegists. An eighteen-line verse in rhymed couplets published on March 1, 1777, in the *Pennsylvania Evening Post* celebrated the memory of Fleming and another young officer of the First Virginia, Lieutenant Benjamin Yeates, commemorating "How *well* they fought, how *well* they fell" in the battle against "base tyrannic hands." And Lewis Littlepage, a fourteen-year-old schoolboy from the Flemings' neighboring Louisa County, must have been thrilled when Purdie's *Gazette* printed his twenty-eight-line ode to "the brave, lamented, much-lov'd FLEMING":

With gayest hopes of happiness possess'd,
With every smile of flattering fortune blest.
Just as the spring of life began to bloom,
And manly virtues sadder makes the tomb,
In all that health, and energy of youth,
Which promis'd honours of maturer growth,
When his full heart expanded to the goal,
And promis'd victory had flush'd his soul
He fell, —his country lost her earliest boast,
His lovely sisters a fond brother lost.[43]

It's not immediately obvious why Fleming in particular seems to have inspired such extravagant mourning. He was young, certainly, but so were most dead captains. He came from an important family, but his uncle Colonel Thomas Fleming died in the field around the same time with much less notice. The public was doubtless moved by the familiar yet dramatic tale of a youth facing a fateful challenge who with his death helped buy a victory as surprising as it was sweet, and as a concrete expression of that gratitude, his heirs, two sisters, were granted the land bounty normally awarded a major.

But most newspaper accounts of the day, which, not surprisingly, focused on the glorious and badly needed triumph, did not reveal the poignant reality of his position. It was a particularly nasty engagement, the Americans had come close to abandoning the field in sheer terror, and Captain Fleming, as an inexperienced officer in charge of an understaffed regiment undersupplied with everything from bayonets to biscuits to boots, could hardly have been expected to do anything other than die. Official records, contemporary eye-witness accounts, and later historical analyses of the battle, including one in George Bancroft's magisterial United States history alluding to the death of the "gallant" captain, describe a situation of chaos and panic on the American side for some time before the enemy began that devilish screaming.[44]

After an exchange of several volleys, the British charged with bayonets, sending the Americans running. Fleming was probably killed not "at the head of his company" but at what had become its rear during his no doubt valiant but vain attempt to stop its flight. General Mercer, too, was fatally wounded, and Washington himself, pelting up with additional troops and shouting over the din, found himself for a few moments in the crossfire; his aide covered his eyes with his hat so as not to see his commander fall. Even hardened veterans were unnerved by the sight of so much bright red blood slithering across the hard-packed white snow.[45]

And the British attackers were particularly savage. After Mercer was knocked from his horse, he was surrounded by enemy troops who stabbed him with bayonets and clubbed him with muskets, finally leaving him for dead; he lingered for nine days. Lieutenant Yeates declared in a deathbed affidavit to Dr. Benjamin Rush that a Redcoat came up to him as he lay wounded on the field and sneered, "Oh damn you are you there." As Yeates begged for quarter, the enemy soldier "loaded his Muskett deliberately, & Shot him thro' the breast, & afterwards Stab'd him in 13 places with his Bayonett." He took a week to die.[46]

Only after the main American columns appeared did the British finally break and retreat. The last enemy holdouts holed up in Nassau Hall, home of the unprepossessing little college that would become Princeton University. They were routed by an American cannon shot fired by Captain Alexander Hamilton's artillery that, as Princeton upperclassmen were assuring us wide-eyed freshmen nearly two hundred years later, smashed right through the wall of the stone building and decapitated the portrait of King George II hanging inside. (Not *exactly* a tall tale: though the twenty-six-inch-thick exterior walls show no trace of an actual hole, one still bears a visible cannonball scar, and contemporary evidence suggests that a ball flying in through the window may indeed have achieved some patriotic damage.) I did not know then, in my days as a zealous classicist who secretly considered anything that happened after 476 A.D. to be merely derivative, that I was conjugating my Latin near the spot where my poor young second cousin seven times removed had been transformed from cannon fodder into a symbol of young America's triumph over tyranny. But I hope now that as the boy soldier, deserted by his men, faced the enemy bayonets alone, he was able to find some comfort in the lines any well-educated young man of the day would have known by heart: *Dulce et decorum est pro patria mori.*

Yet another poem now graces what might be Jack Fleming's tomb. In May 1917, just after the United States joined Great Britain on the battlefields of the Great War, a stone patio was installed over the place where 140 years earlier twenty-one British soldiers and fifteen Americans, all casualties of the battle of Princeton, had been buried together in one grave. Carved into the patio are four lines from a poem composed for the occasion by, I was nonplussed to see on a recent visit, Britain's poet laureate, Alfred Noyes. The lines were typically mawkish

Princeton Battle Monument, Princeton, N.J., near where Captain Jack Fleming was killed. Photograph by the author.

monumental fare, all "ere" and "paled" and "wrath" and Freedom peering with eyes aglow into the future while laying friend and foe side by side. I wasn't sure in the first place that I liked the idea of my poor Jack spending eternity snuggled shoulder to shoulder with the enemy invaders who had killed him. I was even less happy that his lofty demobilization had come from an alien poet best known for a breathless clippety-cloppety ode to Bess, the landlord's black-eyed daughter, who had died for love of her highwayman with the bunch of lace at his chin.

But it was a glorious morning in early spring, billows of daffodils were blooming around the patio and the nearby Ionic colonnade, and no stranger would have believed that just a mile or so beyond those trees thrummed a garish Walmarted and Holiday Inned stretch of Route 1. I was surprised at how many weekday tourists were wandering the battlefield still squishy from the previous day's hard rain, pausing earnestly at the historical markers, stepping a stately dance as they worked out exactly where "You Are Here" was. In the calm their voices carried. They were British.

The poem, suddenly, didn't seem in the least corny.

Some of my other kin made sacrifices too. A brother of my fourth-great-grandfather Gabriel Mullins was said to have died in battle. Ensign Joseph Payne, a first cousin of Josias Payne II, was captured at Germantown and imprisoned for more than three years. After surrendering at Charleston in 1780, Sergeant Charles Woodson and thirty comrades managed to escape "by means of their own invention" and walk all the way home to Virginia, hiding by day and moving only at night.[47]

But for others, the war seems to have held more drudgery than drama and had little visible connection to virtue. Collins, Wharton, Nathaniel Ducker, the Maupins, the Mullinses, the Conway sons, and probably a Daugherty were common soldiers, privates, which meant that some of them may have been drafted into the Continental service while others may well have seen in the army, and especially the bounties of land most recruiters offered as a sweetener, a better-paying job than they'd find anywhere else. That magnetic vision of soldiers' pay, however, often turned out to be precisely that: a vision. Land bounties were in fact the deal of the century for some lucky soldiers, an otherwise unimaginable boost up the economic ladder on the order of the college educations the GI Bill would make possible for another generation. And big states like Virginia, which claimed its north and south boundary lines ran straight across the continent to wherever the western ocean might be, were delighted to discharge their burdensome debts in the only commodity they possessed in plenty. Soon after the war, Private Gabriel Mullins gathered up his wife, the illegitimate Rachel Ballard, and his children to join the rush west and take up his modest chunk of Virginia's distant Kentucky territory. But land claims were of no use to a soldier who didn't survive the war, and many others, strapped for cash, found themselves forced to sell their warrants to speculators. William Wharton unloaded his without using it for himself.[48]

Whatever salary anybody did receive was well earned. Being a soldier was miserable. Like all men at war, the soldiers of the Revolution were often scared and often injured or ill. And like men at war throughout most of America's history, many of them—especially Virginia's recruits, of whom more than three-quarters were natives of the state, and half of the county where they'd enlisted—had rarely traveled anywhere distant or unfamiliar and weren't used to being away from home.[49] Virginia boys who wintered with General Washington at Valley Forge would eventually earn (as opposed to usurping) the right to dine out on the story for the rest of their lives. But along with the physical wretchedness of that dreadful winter, many must have wrestled with the imponderable question: What on earth am I doing in *Pennsylvania?*

And this war, like all wars, had its moments, days, weeks of idiocy. In the pension application he submitted fifty years after Yorktown, Gabriel Mullins, who couldn't remember whether he'd enlisted in 1776 or 1777, recalled little else either about his service as a private in the Virginia militia: he had guarded prisoners, he said, and he had been "generally engaged in marching from one place to another."[50] Gabriel's closest encounter with real fighting came during the famous summer 1781 lightning raid of Lieutenant Colonel Banastre Tarleton, notorious for the "Waxhaw massacre" the previous year, in which his mounted troops had pursued, caught, and butchered a Virginia infantry regiment that was retreating north after the American disaster at Charleston.

Tarleton was also notorious in my own family; online genealogy bulletin boards still tell the old tale of how, when the remorseless colonel invaded the Rock Castle house built by my seventh-great-grandfather Tarlton Fleming, he became so enraged at seeing the Tarletons' coat of arms carved over the mantel in a Patriot home that he hacked it out with his sword. Problems: "Bloody Ban" and Tarlton Fleming's family don't seem to be related at all; no Tarletons in Britain even *had* a coat of arms until the aging Banastre, whose people had been Liverpool merchants, won his long-desired baronetcy in 1816; and if anyone had hacked such a tyrannical emblem as a coat of arms out of the wall, it would, you'd think, have been a staunchly patriotic American Fleming.[51]

Even with all the bustle, anxiety, and excitement of Tarleton's 1781 raid, however, Private Gabriel Mullins managed to miss out on the entire affair. His regiment, as he noted later in his pension application, was redirected out of Tarleton's
path to secure and guard a cache of arms near Richmond. They hid the arms in a
mill and went home. I wish I could have been listening in years later, as Gabriel
regaled his Kentucky neighbors or his ten children with the exploits of his youth,
to hear how the tale of *his* brush with the malevolent Tarleton came out.

Cousin Tarlton Woodson had the most exotic wartime story, though he
doubtless didn't think so. Having enlisted in defiance of his family's religious
tradition, the young Quaker made a large sacrifice for his country, but in the
end it rewarded him with unexpected and romantic happiness. In May 1777
he was commissioned a major in General Moses Hazen's regiment. Less than
four months later, on August 22, Major Woodson was a prisoner of war, captured with seven other officers and 127 enlisted men during a bungled raid on
British-held Staten Island when an enemy unit they hadn't expected caught
them without enough boats to make their escape.[52]

Many of the American soldiers captured by the British endured grotesque
suffering. Considered rebels, the Continentals were generally treated by their
captors as traitors, not prisoners of war, and imprisonment on the notoriously
squalid and disease-ridden prison hulks in what would become the Brooklyn
Navy Yard was more lethal than combat. But captured officers, including
Tarlton, often had an easier time. A captain taken prisoner with Tarlton on
Staten Island reported that some of them did spend twelve days aboard a prison
ship themselves, when fears of an American incursion drove their anxious jail-
ers to secure them more closely for a while. Even then, however, despite the
cramped quarters, the meager provisions, and the shortage of cooking facil-
ities, the officers were able to keep their spirits up with whist, singing, and
"sometimes with dancing on the quarter deck, as some of the gentlemen were
performers on the violin." When the time came to move the prisoners back to
Brooklyn, no fewer than three of them managed to "elude the vigilance of the
guard" and make their escape in a small boat.[53]

The rest of Tarlton's confinement passed equally calmly. His prison house
seems to have been the whole of Brooklyn, and his word of honor the only bars.
As he wrote to his sister Sally Clark, the disowned Quaker who had moved to
Scotland with her non-Friend husband, "confinement but indifferently suits
well the human mind which frequently finds the whole world too small for the
immensity of its projects to promote future happiness . . . [but] I have little

cause to complain as I now injoy as great an island as any Prisoner can reasonably desire for carousal it being about six miles in length."[54]

Any captivity, however, even one under moderate circumstances, is stressful, demeaning, and fraught with uncertainty. Though rumors and assurances that Tarlton would soon be exchanged run through the surviving letters, the haggling and finagling by both sides over acceptable terms for prisoner exchanges helped stretch his term to more than three years. And George Woodson never stopped worrying about his captive brother. Don't be concerned about Mother, he wrote Tarlton; she can take some relief now in knowing that you're unlikely to be injured in battle. Don't think that our delay in sending you money is due to "the want of Brotherly affection in me"; it's hard these days to get specie. And please, please, don't be unhappy in your imprisonment. In May 1778, after yet more disappointing news about the possibility of an exchange, George wrote Tarlton a long letter pondering the possibility of happiness in adversity. "The subject of this letter," he wrote, "shall be to convince you that you should conform and acquiesce cheerfully to your situation, you should think yourself happy compared with others." Freedom, he pointed out, did not necessarily bring happiness; "the active mind is ever reaching after something which it cannot obtain," which can make it miserable, "but might it not have been miserable had it obtained all it desired?" In short, he wrote, "it is my opinion that happiness consists as much in the pursuit as in the fruition of any good, therefore it is the duty of every person when they find it out of their power to follow any favourite scheme to adopt another, and I would recommend it to you that you would apply yourself to something that may hereafter be usefull to you."[55]

George's argument was then, and still is, a classic response to adversity, familiar in both religious and philosophical traditions and a comfort to sufferers, prisoners, and exiles from Cicero to Viktor Frankl and beyond. Happiness, George told his captive brother, was not contingent, not dependent on luck or the gods or whatever his circumstances happened to be, but rather achievable by an act of personal will: by considering himself happy, he could *make* himself happy. But then, after all his careful work to cheer Tarlton up, George suddenly thudded back to earth. "I do not pretend to say," he concluded, "that you can be as happy in your situation as in some other. The nature of the case will not permit it, all that I desire is that you should not think yourself miserable, which I am doubly interested to do both on your account and on my own for if you were miserable I am sure I should be very unhappy."[56] Philosophy had its limits—and so, decided the perennial skeptic, did happiness.

Typically, however, Tarlton showed himself more hopeful than his brother, and much more adventurous in pursuit of his own happiness. Local records show that in December 1779, nearly a year before he would finally be released, the major lightened the burden of his imprisonment by taking a wife, a local girl named Anne Van der Veer. Here, it seems, was one of those newer-fangled marriages, a union based more on affinity and romance than on the strategic pursuit of alliances or land or power. Or at least a young Virginia gentleman like Tarlton could not have expected much along those lines from marriage to a girl from Brooklyn.[57]

And Anne, we can imagine, must have been swept off her feet. Except for two or three transient Pennsylvanians, she is the only born Yankee I know of among my grandmother's closest kin: she lived in the Flatbush section of Brooklyn, a rural community heavily populated by descendants of early Dutch settlers. Anne had probably never even seen a southerner before, let alone heard the distinctive vowels of one, though since many farmers in the area owned slaves (including her own father, Jeromus, who reported a female named Jude in the 1755 slave census), the South's most distinctive characteristic would not have been entirely unfamiliar to her.[58] Her vision of the South would have been shaped mainly by rumor, travelers' letters and tales, snippets from newspapers, whatever she heard about George Washington, and, in an age when outlooks and loyalties were almost entirely local, the innate wariness any New Yorker (or Georgian or Rhode Islander) would have felt toward anyone who wasn't one. Her decision to marry a man who would someday carry her back to the foreign country that was Virginia would have been a leap of faith almost as daring as that of Sarah and John Woodson when they crossed the sea to Jamestown in 1619. Her inevitable disorientation and home-sickness upon her arrival might have been eased but probably wasn't erased by his touching gesture of naming their Virginia plantation "Brooklyn."

By the time Tarlton was finally exchanged and sent home, in November 1780, the newlywed had had enough of soldiering. He was carried on the muster rolls for some time longer, and later claimed (or was claimed by others) to have been present at the surrender of Cornwallis, but his official records consistently listed him as being on furlough. But as frustrating as it had been for Tarlton, the war ever afterwards loomed large in his memory and his life. According to a grandson who "remember[ed] him well," he was known throughout his life by the affectionate (and inflated) title of "General," though with becoming and perhaps Quaker-inflected restraint he often remarked that "he never received a wound, and was never sure that he had slain an enemy with his own hand."[59]

And Tarlton knew the kinds of stories his audience wanted to hear. The grandson recalled listening to the General reminisce about the "many engagements" in which he'd participated and relate "thrilling anecdotes of military adventure, and hairbreadth escapes." We need not dwell on how many such adventures and escapes could actually have fallen to the lot of a man who had spent most of the war as what his own captors called a model prisoner, let alone one who had emerged from his ordeal not maimed or pockmarked or starved but married. But we can gather what kind of stories the old soldier did *not* tell about his days in the army. No one, reported Henry Morton Woodson in his big volume of family history published nearly a century after the major died, knew whether Tarlton had married Anne during the war or after it.[60]

For generations after his death in 1818, Tarlton had continued to star in, and sometimes usurp, the Woodsons' stories, in part because of his family's rather un-American propensity for staying put. When Tarlton brought his bride home after the war, he built her the home he called Brooklyn on the land his father had bought outside Prospect, Virginia, but in 1812 a sturdy new Brooklyn replaced the original. Consisting of two stories and an attic with gabled windows, it had eight rooms, three Flemish-bond chimneys, high mantels simply carved, and wide heart-of-pine plank floors. And it would be home to Tarlton's heirs for the next one hundred years. (It stands to this day, restored and recently having seen service as a B&B.)

For a while the house was bursting with family: on census day in 1850, for instance, those eight modest rooms were home to Tarlton's son's seventy-year-old widow, her sister, one of her sons, three daughters, three small grandchildren, and a step-grandchild, while the census taker seems to have overlooked her son-in-law, who was alive and well.[61] But over the years, as this branch of Woodsons manifested a remarkably dogged resistance to wedlock and childbearing—only one of Tarlton's six grandchildren ever married, and she herself was survived only by step-grandchildren—Brooklyn acquired the air of an old age home, full of spinster sisters, bachelor brothers, unattached nieces, and maiden aunts.

Directly descended from the "eccentric" antiquarian Charles, who was the first traceable teller of the Jamestown Indian attack story, this houseful of childless old folks did its best to preserve their ancestral glory; they were the ones who cherished the immense old gun, inscribed the yarn in the family Bible, told it to inquiring newspapermen and, doubtless, to visiting children, too. In 1936, after the last ancient niece had died and the house had been sold out of the family, an elderly step-great-great-grandson of Tarlton's still living in the neighborhood was eager to share the old Woodson legends with the researcher from the WPA who came knocking on doors seeking information about the history of the shabby old building. But in addition to apparently believing that Brooklyn was the very house that had been defended against the Indians with musket and roasting spit, the researcher's informant also asserted confidently that the victim struck down by warriors in sight of his home had been Major Tarlton Woodson himself.[62]

Tellers of historical tales often compress time, misplace generations, and populate their stories with old relatives they'd heard of instead of the even older ones they hadn't. And there in the house that Tarlton built, brimming with people who could call him Grandpa, no one could wonder that the war hero loomed larger than life. But part of what made him so memorable, or possibly part of what made the legend that accidentally attached itself to him so memorable, was another kind of story entirely, not about tragedy and heroism, not about wartime adventure, but about another classic component of American stories of happiness: money. Or rather, about money lost, that eternal and usually fanciful tale of the fortune that *almost* was—a tale that my kin, like many others' kin, would tell again and again about different *almosts* ranging from destroyed deeds to lost bags of money to torched houses to burned boats to property abused by the army quartermaster.

At the end of the war Major Woodson had submitted a claim for an officer's military pension, which Congress had briefly set at half pay for life before commuting that alarmingly generous offer to five years' full pay. And Tarlton submitted his claim for a pension again and again, sometimes varying it with a request for back pay, in formal petitions to army officials and to Congress over the years. After Tarlton's death his son took up the battle, around 1840 the torch passed to his granddaughter's husband, and eventually the Jarndycean quest spread into the Court of Claims as well. The last documents on the case I found were a Senate committee report dated 1901 and a bill tracking report dated 1904. That last hurrah came 123 years after Cornwallis's surrender, eighty-six years after the old major's death, and twenty-odd years before his last blood descendant, an unmarried great-granddaughter well into her eighties, finally faded away in the old house he'd built so long ago.[63]

No wonder the Woodsons were obsessed: in all that time, said the senators, the pension claim "was never allowed, but was never expressly rejected," by officials who claimed they didn't have the authority to act. Reject it they finally did, however, and they even explained why: Tarlton's Canadian-based regiment had not been an official part of the Continental line that qualified for pensions, and in any case he hadn't fulfilled the requirement of having served all the way through to the end of the war. The Senate committee did acknowledge that through a bureaucratic error the major had never been paid for his final year of service, when he'd been on furlough, and recommended that Congress pass a special bill allowing his heirs to receive $600 plus interest. Not as lavish a return as the accumulated heap of pension funds they'd hoped for, but it was a rare moral victory nonetheless, a fortune-hunting tale that wasn't entirely a fairy tale. The victory, however, remained moral only. Congress never passed the necessary bill, the heirs never got their $600, and the Woodsons, it seemed, never gave up their grudge, even as they gradually lost track of exactly what it was they were angry about. As late as 1936, Tarlton's four-generations-removed step-descendant, a rural mail carrier, was telling the researcher from the WPA that the major "was never paid for his service in the war."[64]

Tarlton Woodson came of age around the same time as two of the greatest ideas of the modern world: the United States of America and the conviction that the ordinary person had a right not just to pursue his happiness but also to name it, to craft a story about his own life that he could then strive to make true. That Tarlton did with vigor and imagination. By joining the army, he chose his country over his parents' pacifist God; by marrying a girl from Brooklyn, he chose his heart over practicality and tradition; by putting his faith in Virtue, he chose hope over his brother's skepticism and gloom—and by telling his war not as a quiet matrimonial interlude but as "thrilling anecdotes of military adventure, and hairbreadth escapes," he chose glory over strict accuracy.

Yet the tales that survived him longest, tales told by people who lived surrounded by physical reminders of his long-ago presence, were not *by* him but *about* him. Rooted in the error and disgruntlement of others, those durable stories told of how their ancestor had been fleeced by his country and then slaughtered by Indians. Tarlton Woodson's pursuit of happiness had been trumped by the unhappiness of his heirs.

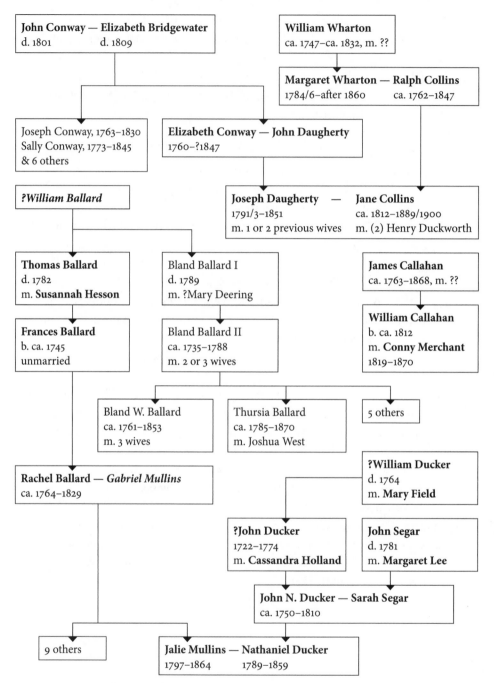

Names in **bold** represent direct ancestors; names in *italics* have been introduced in a previous tree. Other names are included only if relevant. For Payne, Nichols, Roberts, and Hickman, see chapter 5.

CHAPTER 4
The Kentucky Pioneers Speak Out

⁓

The Ballards and Vengeance

IT WAS THE DARK AND BLOODY GROUND, A PLACE OF CONSTANT TERROR and lurking death—and it was like heaven. Or, to be more accurate, heaven was like *it:* the celestial realm was, as the Baptist preacher groping for a comprehensible metaphor told his Virginia congregation, "a Kentucky of a place."[1] Acquiring its first permanent white settlement at almost the same moment the Minutemen were firing the opening shots of the Revolution back in Massachusetts, Kentucky was America's first great West, with all the paradoxes that place—that idea—encompassed. To white Americans it offered a dreamworld vision of happiness: a mythic land that was not meager but bountiful, not bounded but free, not corrupt but natural, not *here* but *out there.* To claim that world for America, to plant a city on a farther hill, and to secure for themselves the profits from so rich and apparently available a country were not just right and proper but also providential. Even those damp-winged Americans whose hopes never quite soared to the celestial heights could look to the West for a balm as modest as it was alluring: a second chance.

But for the earliest of the pioneers who actually pursued the promise of happiness westward, Kentucky often turned into the murky domain of nightmare, where the romantic vision of freedom, plenty, and purity crashed into a reality that seemed to them primitive, uncontrollable, violent, and filled with desperate and unknowable peril. Emigrants found themselves building not cities on the hill but forts against the darkness, and an unwary step outside those magic circles could bring terrible death. And while it would eventually become clear that the westerners most spectacularly cheated were the American Indians displaced by white pursuers of happiness, many of Kentucky's first generations of pioneers, including nearly all of my direct kin, would find themselves following in the footsteps of their great-great-grandparents who had been snookered out of their happy hopes at Jamestown. Their sorrows would often seem relentless, their happiness dim—and, like John and Sarah Woodson's, their encounters with the Indians tragic, for both sides.

Both the heartache and the hope, however, made of Kentucky a place full of amazing adventures, and amazing stories were told to explain them. In fact stories were being told all over America; the new nation was embarked on a great binge of talking about itself. Officially set at liberty to pursue their happiness, and inspired by new political, religious, and philosophical notions about the worth of even a commonplace life, Americans were raring to claim the right (and pleasure) of talking freely *and publicly* about themselves and putting themselves at the center of their own stories. Some of them hungered for a voice not just public but also permanent, a voice captured and preserved in print for the education or delight (they doubtless hoped) of generations and worlds of readers they would never meet. Still nameless but increasingly popular was a new genre rooted in the relatively recent phenomenon of writers willing to explore and share the territory of a unique inner self. Many examples of what would soon be routinely called *autobiography* were written by people who had long ago undergone a typically American uprooting from their childhood homes and whose children and grandchildren were now urging them to preserve the stories of their long and eventful lives.[2]

But more and more often, even the humblest and unluckiest of people could be found taking pen in hand to tell a different kind of story, one just as typically American but rarely before told firsthand. The publishing houses were churning out titles like *Narrative of the Life and Extraordinary Adventures* or *Surprising Adventures* or *Affecting Narrative,* which chronicled the exploits not of fictional heroes but of convicted criminals, beggars, prisoners of war, workingmen, escaped slaves, and women, all of them insisting their tales of endurance and adventure were true to their lives and worthy of attention. At the dawning of the new nation founded so hopefully on the right of every person to pursue happiness, a flourishing new storytelling genre was forthrightly testifying to how complicated and precarious the whole idea of happiness in America really was.[3]

It could be a gutsy move, telling one's stories, in whatever medium, to people one didn't know. It could take a greater measure of self-awareness, even bold-ness, to choose to submit one's self-construction to the scrutiny of strangers than to spin a yarn for a circle of children, friends, or neighbors. The potential benefits were obvious: although explaining how happiness fell short is difficult whoever the audience, explaining it to a public that was unknown and even unseen could grant invaluable liberties, consolations, and sometimes financial rewards to the teller. Some embraced their hardships, some explained them away, some simply bore them. But there were hazards, too, to inviting inspec-tion of one's life, and for other Americans, safety and comfort were best found in reticence.

I came across three sets of stories, in varying versions and often in fragmen-tary form, that involved family members of mine during the first decades of white settlement in Kentucky. All three were written down only much later, and ranged from versions recalled by their own aged protagonists to one shared only recently with me by a distant cousin I have never actually met. Although all three stories were about Indians and fighting, they embody very different relation-ships between the tellers' happiness and their stories, vastly different strategies to come to terms with their smash-ups in paradise. A group of Ballard cousins had a heartbreaking encounter with Indians, but for generations, in fact almost into my own lifetime, descendants and others were reveling in the tale as an epic of vengeance, heroism, and triumph. My Daugherty fourth-great-grandparents and their extended family also suffered tragedies at the hands of Indians, but *their* narrative survived only in nearly unrecognizable shards that throbbed with sorrow and guilt. And although both my fifth-great-grandfather William Wharton and his son-in-law Ralph Collins began their military careers fighting the British in some of the nation's most heroic battles and ended them fighting the Indians in one of its most sordid, Ralph freely told a story that made him look better than he was, while William's reluctant offering left out all the best parts. So as the young nation set about inventing itself, some of my kin were determined to do the very same thing for themselves, while others apparently never mustered either the nerve or the heart to try. One of the great American questions is: What made the difference?

For all of my kin, paradise must have seemed reachable, at first; the very earli-est of the disillusioned and questing great-great-grandchildren of Jamestown to gravitate toward Kentucky had good reason to think it might finally offer a true shot at happiness. It appeared to have all the ingredients of a proper Eden. It was remote, serenely sequestered behind forbidding mountains, and accessible by foot only to those who knew the secret gate—the Cumberland Gap. For a time it was even forbidden, officially (though ineffectually) closed to white settlers by the British in an attempt to pacify the Indian allies of the defeated French. But word trickled out, and that word was irresistible. Beginning in 1750, when the first known organized English exploring party crossed the Gap—working, not surprisingly, on behalf of a newly formed land company—white traders, hunters, scouts, and speculators were telling tales of soil that was deep, black, and fertile, of buffalo and deer that were as plentiful as Tidewater mosquitoes, of bears so fat they were "weary for the rifle shot."[4] If a man was feeling lazy, they said, he could just wait at the foot of the Ohio River falls for dozens of plump geese and ducks, swept over the cataract by the rushing current, to rain down out of the sky, and down at the river bottom swam catfish that could weigh more than a hundred pounds.

Kentucky's earliest promoters—in both the literary and the financial sense, as many of them were speculators in the lands they hymned—consciously perpetuated the Edenic image, often couching their descriptions in biblical cadences, invoking images of paradise, and explicitly promising that out there in the woods would be found real, true happiness. One of the most avid of the promoters was John Filson, a schoolteacher and surveyor from Pennsylvania who moved to "Kentucke" in the early 1780s and began speculating in land. In that wonderful place, he wrote in 1784 in a passage lifted straight from Deuteronomy, "like the land of promise, flowing with milk and honey, a land of brooks of water, of fountains and depths, that spring out of valleys and hills, a land of wheat and barley, and all kinds of fruits, you shall eat bread without scarceness, and not lack any thing in it. . . . [Y]our country, favoured with the smiles of heaven, will probably be inhabited by the first people the world ever knew."[5]

So just as the Woodsons had more than a century and a half earlier, my kin listened to the promoters and struck out to seek their happiness in the wild places. It was, again, a gamble. My fourth-great-grandfather Gabriel Mullins had some Kentucky land due him as a bounty for his military service, all that "marching from one place to another," but my other veterans either hadn't managed to hold on to their warrants or hadn't qualified in the first place. I can imagine husbands and wives probably argued about it, weighing their vague and untested hopes against the rigors of the long journey, the dangers of wilderness life, and the understanding that their farewell to family and friends could well be a sundering as final as death.

Still, the great appeal of the West has always been that anyone can imagine it filled with his or her heart's desire, and that was growing harder and harder for almost anyone to do in the East. The coming of independence and peace had brought Americans little rest and less happiness, at least of the material sort. After eight years of war, the economy of the infant nation was a mess, ravaged by a staggering debt, an unstable currency, plunging commodity prices, and the disruption of trade. Even nature, it seemed, was siding against them: in back-country Albemarle County, where my Ballards and Mullinses and Maupins had wandered in the hope they'd have better luck than in the settled-up Tidewater, the overworked soil was starving the tobacco, weevils were marauding in the wheat, and drought was frizzling the corn one year, downpour drowning it the next. And my fifth-great-grandfather Charles Fleming Payne of Goochland County—scion of all those once prominent Flemings and Woodsons and Bateses, an ever-more-distant cousin of all those Randolphs and Jeffersons—apparently didn't have the opportunity (the sense? the charm?) to jolt the family fortune back to life with the traditional stratagem of marrying money or power. His wife was a local Goochland girl named Adams, a girl so obscure the genealogists can't even agree on whether her first name was Mary or Virginia.

Tobacco was also sucking the soil and frustrating the farmers of Montgomery County in Maryland, where clustered my Duckers, Nicholses, Segars, Robertses, Hickmans, and Trammells, some of whom had not so long before embraced Maryland's own beckoning western frontier as their great escape from the fading fortunes of the Eastern Shore. The Duckers actually did preserve an explanation for their decision to uproot, or at least a legend about it. As one of the immigrant couple's descendants told a local antiquarian in the 1930s, the family had lived in Baltimore and "owned a large tract of land upon which the city was built—had given a long lease—perhaps a 99 year lease on the land. The Baltimore fire destroyed evidence of title of the Ducker heirs." There was nothing left for the bilked landowners to do but start over in the West.[6]

But the Duckers had never lived in Baltimore, the land for which had been bought from members of the powerful Carroll family in the early eighteenth century, when my Duckers were scratching out their livings in rural Maryland as millers, tailors, and the smallest of small farmers. And you'd think that the Duckers of the 1930s, whose fortunes had been subsiding ever since my great-great-great-grandfather Nathaniel Ducker had died in Pendleton County in 1859 with a decent farm, a horde of heirs, and no will, would have been driven to do something about their claim long before the Great Baltimore Fire of 1904 (which in any case had spared the courthouse where land records were kept). The lost title was more likely a Depression-era version of the classic "once we had it all" legend, a fantasy image as shimmery and delightful as Carole Lombard in a bias-cut evening gown, and apparently nearly as popular. On genealogical websites and in bulging cabinets at historical societies, I kept turning up other claimants to that mythic ninety-nine-year Baltimore lease, and to this day the Maryland Historical Society still gets the occasional inquiry from people seeking evidence for their "claims." The librarians there tell me that Lord Baltimore frequently did offer to rent land to early settlers on long-term leases, often ninety-nine years, but title to the land always remained with him, and in any case such leases have not been used since the eighteenth century. The claimants, speculate the librarians, probably bought false titles from a con artist.[7]

So throughout the last quarter of the eighteenth century, my tatterdemalion families joined thousands of other Americans looking for a fresh start for their happiness. A few collateral relatives, including a branch of the Ballard family and of my direct forebears the Conway-Daugherty clan, were genuine trailblazers. They numbered among the earliest and most insanely daring waves of soldiers and settlers, the ones who arrived during the Revolution and had to rely on Harrodsburg and Boonesborough and the other precarious little people-coops to keep out the British enemy as well as the dangers of the wilderness. Two Conways survived the legendary ten-day siege of Boonesborough by Chief Blackfish and some 450 Shawnee warriors in 1778, and through an ancestral in-law by the name of Jesse Oldham I can trace an intimate connection to Kentucky's most rarefied fraternity of all, that tough and tiny band of ur-pioneers who arrived from North Carolina in 1775 with Daniel Boone, were not killed by Indians, and did not give up and flee to their homes back east in terror and despair.

Jesse Oldham's great-great-granddaughter was my great-grandmother's Cousin Jessie Oldham, who died in 1964 at the age of eighty-four. Since my grandmother had stayed with the Oldhams every summer as a child, and my mother and aunt had always visited Cousin Jessie in her sturdy century-old brick house during their trips to Kentucky in the 1930s, you'd think that that personal connection might have yielded us some great stories handed down through the generations directly from old Dan'l's boon companion. You'd think wrong. All my Aunt Gina could remember about Cousin Jessie was that she was "so cheap" she never built an indoor bathroom for the old house, and Doris couldn't recall hearing a single story from her aged relative about the good old ancestors or the good old days. "They were always talking 'adult' talk that ceased when the children were around," Doris remembered later, but she also confessed, "I really don't recall a conversation with her at all. I was a bust as a kid." (I can hardly complain. When I was fourteen, my siblings and I made our own trip to Kentucky with our mother for a family "reunion" in the old hometown we'd never seen before with relatives we had never met. And all any of us can remember is this: there was lots of food, there were lots of cuzzins with funny accents, and the Cincinnati airport is not in Ohio.)

Most of my direct ancestors came later than Boone's band, but nearly all had arrived by the mid-1790s, still in time to confront their share of the darkness and the blood. Charles and Mary (or Virginia) Adams Payne came with the first several of their eleven or twelve children; Gabriel and Rachel Ballard Mullins with the first seven of their ten children; Thomas and Cassandra Roberts Nichols with five little Nicholses; John N. and Sarah Segar Ducker with nine young Duckers; William Wharton with his nameless wife and four daughters; and the bachelors James Callahan and Ralph Collins on their own. They joined a great and sometimes desperate migration that would push Kentucky's population from its first scraggly few dozen pioneers to a reported 180,000 white and 41,000 black residents by 1800. In 1796 a traveler from Virginia named Moses Austin noted in his journal his astonishment that even in the dead of winter he encountered so many destitute families toiling through ice and snow toward Kentucky. He reported that if he asked his fellow travelers "what they expect when they git to Kentuckey the Answer is Land. have you any. No, but I expect I can git it. have you any thing to pay for land, No." No place else along the way was good enough, either. "It will not do its not Kentuckey its not the Promis.d land its not the goodly inheratence the Land of Milk and Honey."[8]

None of my kin, however—and few of their fellow citizens, either—found much sweetness in the new land. If Kentucky was like Jamestown in its evocations of Eden, its tales were also like Jamestown's in promising a happiness they couldn't deliver.

The spoilers of this garden were familiar. Speculators, for one; like Tidewater Virginia's best land, much of Kentucky was soon gobbled up not by the pioneers who risked their lives and their sweat—their only valuables—in the hope of earning a modest stake for themselves and their families, but rather by rich and well-connected men, many of whom didn't even live there and didn't intend to, either. With speculators, settlers, squatters, land jobbers, and military veterans all rushing to claim acreage, whether with bodies or with papers, gaining clear title was complicated enough. The process wasn't helped by the land office's blithe and chronic inattentiveness to precise boundaries when it granted patents and by the ineptitude or venality of many county surveyors. Inevitably, claims fell prey to litigation; in 1786 a traveling French official noted that Kentuckians "would hardly know how to buy a piece of land without involving themselves in a lawsuit, often ruinous, always long and wearing." Clearly the situation offered an advantage to those with long patience and deep pockets—and may also explain the obsession of more than one Kentucky family with that disputed lease to Baltimore. When Kentucky became a state in 1792, only one-third of its adult white male residents owned any land at all. It's a safe bet that close to 100 percent of them had come west in the happy hopes they would.[9]

As at Jamestown, moreover, this paradise wasn't vacant. The Indian name attached to the place didn't actually translate as "Dark and Bloody Ground"— most likely "Kentucky" had something to do with either a meadow or a river— but it should have, as one of the fiercest battlegrounds in the long and ugly clash between the European Americans who wanted the West and the American Indians who had been there first. Deeply involved in that clash was Bland W. Ballard, who was probably a second cousin to my fourth-great-grandmother Rachel Ballard, the child of the unwed Frances Ballard from Albemarle. (The Ballards are a genealogist's nightmare, their relationships impossible to sort out given their relentless mobility, their preposterous fecundity, and their unshakeable habit of naming any son within reach either Thomas, William, James, or the inexplicable Bland.)[10] And Cousin Bland might be my most disturbing kinsman since our mutual forefather Colonel Thomas Ballard, the Virginia governor's double-turncoat councilor. Bland had been elected three times to the state legislature and gotten a county named after himself largely on his renown as an "Indian fighter," as most of his chroniclers labeled him. By the end of his long life he could no longer remember, he said, whether it was thirty or forty he'd killed.

Though the settlers' eventual defeat of the natives may now seem to have been inevitable given their greater numbers, weaponry, economic ambition, and institutional power, to the eighteenth-century Kentuckians on the front lines of the fight, those advantages didn't always seem terribly evident, and their victory didn't seem at all preordained. Until the Battle of Fallen Timbers in 1794, in which General Anthony Wayne's victory over a force of 1,500 warriors near present-day Toledo effectively broke the resistance of the Western Confederacy, the local American Indians had been diligent, determined, and often successful in their efforts to defend their hunting grounds from the interlopers. With the frequent support, both moral and military, of the Americans' British enemy and of white renegades like Simon Girty, Indians attacked settlers in force on the trails, ambushed them from the canebrakes, besieged their forts, assaulted their cabins, snatched their children, stole their horses and guns.

Whites who fell into the hands of the Indians might be slowly and gruesomely tortured to death, or—a prospect that many found scarcely more comforting—adopted by their captors and forced to embrace Indian ways. In the earliest years few pioneers dared live outside the stockades or fortified stations, and a dash beyond the walls to fetch the water or tend the crops required stout hearts, armed guards, or both. Terrible stories were told about the things that happened *out there,* things that challenged the very idea of civilization: entire families butchered within minutes. Happy and well-loved children vanishing while out picking haws and found years later with bear grease in their hair and no memory of their parents, religion, language, or home. Desperate captives grasping at a chance to flee even at the price of leaving their infants behind with the savages. Powerful, mysterious, violent, the American Indians seemed like a different order of human to most of the whites peering out through the chinks and gun loops of their little wooden fortresses and starting at the hooting of an owl. It can certainly be argued the "invaders" shouldn't have made so free with the Indians' land, or that the pioneers used ruthlessly unfair tactics to take what wasn't theirs, or that the ambushed and assaulted settlers were getting what they deserved. But it's also true that in the early years, white Kentuckians had good reason to view the Indians with terror and to see the planting of "civilization" as their only salvation.

The clash between settlers and Indians, however, has led almost inevitably to a clash between memory and time. Later generations of Kentuckians would soon know what the first ones couldn't: they'd won. They would hear the tales, would know how frightening and violent life in frontier Kentucky had been, would, like nearly any group cherishing nearly any collective memory, revere their family stories as illuminations of how they had been made special by challenge, tragedy, and loss. Throughout the nineteenth century, in fact, the wildfire popularity of pamphletized and anthologized and sometimes plagiarized stories of Indian captivity and battle, some of them reveling in almost pornographically explicit violence, testified to the central place taken by those mythic clashes with the savage foe in shaping white Americans' sense of themselves and their manifest destiny. But the readers of those tales would also have understood that the bloody times in Kentucky were over, that the Indians of the Ohio Valley were vanquished, that their ancestors' challenges and tragedies would not come again; they would have known that the story had ended in the definitive triumph of civilization over wilderness. Some Kentuckians nevertheless insisted on leaving that ending unread. Living their comfortable lives in a land long free of any danger from whatever small and cowed population of Indians remained, they sought their happiness and rooted their identity in epics of destruction, telling and retelling the old stories to their children and grandchildren and cementing into family lore an enduring message of bitterness, brutality, and revenge: adventures of unhappiness redressed.

Which is exactly what the descendants of Bland Williams Ballard did.

Bland Ballard, our Indian fighter, our Indian hater, our Indian killer, our teller of many stories and star of many more, gave pride and joy to his many descendants, and to more than a few others who labored fruitlessly to prove their membership in that happy band. Six feet tall Bland was, even in his eighties weighing over two hundred pounds, "strong raw [and] boney," as the frontier historian Lyman C. Draper noted in 1844 after interviewing the old soldier about the settling of Kentucky, "passionate & quick & even over frank." Bland died in 1853, in his mid-nineties and his third marriage, and even at the end of his life as he lay enfeebled in bed, he would grow animated when talking about the old days "of joy and sport."[11]

Ballard's fellow citizens thought he hung the moon. His death was reported as far away as New York, where a brief item in the *Times* of September 21, 1853, noted the "honorable and distinguished part" he had played in Kentucky's earliest days and the "high respect and esteem" he had enjoyed from his compatriots. Major Ballard was "a fine specimen" of "the bold, patriotic men who rescued Kentucky from the forest and the savages," the hometown *Louisville Daily Journal* proclaimed in its own and much lengthier death notice on September 8. "And now that he is gone, we cannot call to mind a single pioneer of Kentucky, who is left. Who shall snatch their memory from oblivion and give us a true history of Kentucky, with its pages all glowing with life-like sketches of the men who redeemed her from the savage, and with stories of adventures, more romantic than even romance itself can furnish[?]"

And who, the *Journal* might have added, would hate that savage so thoroughly? Ballard's claim to Lyman Draper that he had killed thirty or forty Indians all by himself is unverifiable, but whatever the final toll, he went about the business with relish. In the application for a military pension he submitted in 1834, he told the county officials with austere pride that he would "not ennumerate the number of skirmishes & the number of savages that fell by this affiants hands."[12] And the *Journal*'s obituarist recorded for posterity that the major had "never exhibited the slightest compunctions on account of his having killed Indians. His family, and he, in his own person, had received too many injuries from the savages for him ever to feel the slightest sympathy for them. He regarded them as a faithless, treacherous race and the enemy of his own."

He and his family had, undeniably, been injured. In 1779, when he was eighteen or twenty, Bland left his mother and at least four younger siblings behind in Spotsylvania County, Virginia, to join his father, also named Bland, his brother James, and a cousin on a journey to Virginia's Kentucky territory to join the frontier militia fighting the British and their Indian allies. Bland soldiered and scouted for General George Rogers Clark with an enthusiasm that became legendary, once earning from Clark the gift of a linen shirt for having shot three Indians out of their canoe on the Ohio on a misty morning. He reported in his pension application that he had spent fifteen years in military service, most of that time as a hunter and "spy" or scout, but he had also served as a captain under General Wayne at Fallen Timbers. Even at the age of fifty-odd, he couldn't resist enlisting for the War of 1812 to take one more shot at the enemy, but having been badly wounded in the leg, he was captured at the disastrous battle of the River Raisin in the Michigan Territory and suffered "severely" on the march through snow and ice to imprisonment at Fort George.[13]

Shortly after their first arrival in Kentucky, the Ballard men had returned briefly to Virginia to bring out the rest of their family. They eventually settled on Tick Creek near present-day Shelbyville in a log cabin standing just outside the fortified Tyler's station. On March 31, 1788, the Tick Creek household consisted of the elder Bland and his second or third wife; his teenaged sons John and Benjamin; Thursia, who was a toddler; and the infant Elizabeth. An older daughter who was probably married at the time was living elsewhere; the second son, James, was not at home either (his abashed descendants would later explain that he was away at school, not an entirely persuasive alibi for a twenty-four-year-old frontiersman), and the hero Bland, then in his late twenties, was living with his new wife inside the fortified station.[14]

As Bland told the story to the historian Draper fifty years later, early that morning a party of fifteen or twenty Indians launched a sudden attack on the Ballard cabin, shooting young John as he worked at the woodpile and then surrounding the house. Bland, hearing the shot, dashed from the fort with his rifle and from behind a tree fired some shots at the raiders in front of the house, but found himself "treed," unable to move from his shelter, when some of the Indians began shooting back at him. Others went around to the rear of the house, knocked out the chinking between the logs, and through the gaps quickly shot down the father, the other teenaged brother, and the two small girls. As Mrs. Ballard burst through the front door in terror, the Indians broke in through the back and pursued her into the yard, where they clubbed her down, then tomahawked and scalped all the bodies and plundered the house. One attacker, unable to pull little Thursia's shirt over her head because the wristbands had been sewn, tossed her limp body into the waterhole.

Meanwhile Bland got off six shots from behind his tree and "brought an Indian every time. . . . [He] saw each of his six Inds. tumble over." The other men of the station were of little help, occupied with protecting their own families or unable to shoot effectively; but after the attackers were gone, Ballard put together a party to pursue them and found, he later said, six fresh bodies hastily buried within a few miles of the cabin. When Bland pulled Thursia's body from the waterhole, he discovered that despite her terrible injuries the little girl was still breathing. The water may have been cold enough to stop her bleeding, and the clothes over her head had buoyed her well enough that she didn't drown, either. Her brother cleaned and stitched her up himself.[15]

The story circulated for decades. More than half a century later, in the 1840s and 1850s, secondhand versions were still popping up in the recollections of the aging pioneers interviewed by John Dabney Shane, the Presbyterian minister from Cincinnati who traveled the Ohio Valley collecting the stories of anyone old enough to remember life in the first years of the trans-Allegheny settlement.[16] Throughout his life Bland Ballard clearly delighted in telling the tale himself, to anyone who would listen. As his Louisville obituarist would recall, plurally: "We have often seen him on the street dressed in his buckskin hunting shirt, surrounded by crowds of men and boys listening with breathless attention to his stories. We ourselves have listened to them many an hour, and often through the livelong night without fatigue." Lyman Draper had sought out the old soldier for firsthand information about General George Rogers Clark, the subject of one of his intended biographies of frontier leaders and pioneers. Much of what Ballard recounted for Draper concerned his various expeditions with the general, but in the middle of his military recital came pouring out his old, old tale of grievance and heroics. Draper probably could not have stopped it if he'd tried.

No independent eyewitness, though, ever confirmed the episode. As with so many stories of personal heroics—as with the story of Sarah Woodson's defense of *her* family against the Indians—there's no contemporary corroboration of the tale by anyone else who was there at the time. We have only Bland's word for it that he killed six of the attackers (which cleanly exceeded the number of dead Ballards by one), or any attackers at all. And the story was never cast as anything but a celebration of Bland's heroism, the swift and total vengeance of an enraged son and brother against the killers of his relatives. No one ever seems to have mentioned that it had begun as a tale of monumental failure: although Bland had avenged himself on the attackers who had wiped out most of his family in front of his eyes, most of his family was still dead.

Ballard descendants, however, clearly delighted in their ancestor's exploits. A particular champion was Rogers Clark Ballard Thruston, a grandson of the heroic Bland's brother James, who had not been at the fort on the fateful day. Thruston left piles of letters, maps, manuscripts, and photographs to the Filson Historical Society in Louisville and the Kentucky Historical Society in Frankfort describing his efforts to find the sites of the old family cabins, track down gravestones, and interview ancient family members about the event. Christened for his mother's childless great-uncle, General George Rogers Clark himself, Thruston had actually been born a Ballard, but at his mother's request had legally taken her birth surname to prevent its disappearance. (His death in 1946 as a childless bachelor of eighty-eight put an end to that plan.) The preservation and celebration of the paternal name were left to his brothers, who adorned all Louisville with it, holding a series of elected offices, running the well-known Ballard & Ballard flour company—which held the first patent for refrigerated biscuit dough in a popping can and sponsored the beloved Ballard Chefs jug band—and donating an Egyptian mummy that the city science museum still ranks as one of its great treasures.

In a brief unpublished family history he jotted down some seventy years after Bland's death, Thruston noted with no apparent disapproval that his kinsman "rarely failed to kill an Indian when an opportunity afforded. The story is told," he continued, "that when bedridden and only a few days before his death a passing Indian stopped at his cabin door to beg for food. He scented the racial odor of the Indian and asked his wife if that were not an Indian. She answered no, and hastened to get the Indian away. But he crept out of bed, and across the cabin floor, got his rifle and took a parting crack at that Indian as he was crossing the fence." Thruston added that Bland had taken the scalps of the Indians he'd killed after the attack on his family and kept "those trophies" hanging by his fireplace. Thruston had twice tried to get hold of the scalps for himself, but on his first visit to the old man's abandoned cabin he found that the interior log walls had been plastered over, sealing the grisly artifacts inside. Then around 1918 or 1920 he heard that the wrecking crew that tore the old structure down had found the scalps inside the walls. "I went after them," he reported with still-smoldering gusto, "but was never able to locate them."[17]

A visit to another old family homestead was in some ways just as disappointing. On an autumn day in 1921, as he reported in another unpublished set of typed notes, Thruston and a friend hired a car and driver in Frankfort and set out over roads that grew steadily wispier and dirtier until two miles past Head of Cedar, on the border between Scott and Franklin counties. Lugging his camera equipment, Thruston and his friend hiked the final quarter mile up a steep and stony hill to the old cabin where lived an ancient granddaughter of Thursia West, who had borne seven children and died in 1870, aged well into her eighties. She was the former Thursia Ballard, who as a tiny girl had survived being shot, tomahawked, and tossed into the waterhole by the Indians who had killed everyone else in the house.

On that day in 1921, Thruston focused his camera mainly on the scenery: the smokehouse, the water gap, and the family burying ground; the scruffy yard that looked as remote from human habitation as any gothic novel moor; the dogtrot log cabin with the huge stone chimney, where the granddaughter, Mary Rush, lived with her bachelor son J. T. West. The eastern half of the cabin, in which Mary had been born and twice married, had been built a century earlier by her parents, but it was the western half, only thirty years old, that looked like something uncovered by an archaeologist, its inferior logs already starting to rot. Mary, who is seen in one photograph sitting in front of the cabin with her son and her visiting sister, looks like an archaeological relic herself. Swathed in a shawl and long skirt and holding a crutch across her lap, skeletal of face and blank of gaze, every one of her ninety-one years visibly hard-won, she seems barely to belong to the nineteenth century, let alone the twentieth.

The sisters had known their grandmother Thursia long and intimately, but Thruston's conversation with them only reinforced the sad truth that researchers know well: sometimes a relic is only a relic, not a font of historical insight. The old ladies, Thruston noted testily, "do not seem to get along together and each wanted to talk at the same time which materially impaired the benefit I hoped to derive from the interview." Their "meagre" and inconsistent information, he wrote, contributed only a few small nuggets to the family lore. The orphaned Thursia, they said, after living for a while with her rescuer, had been raised mainly by her married half sister Sally, who had been living elsewhere at the time of the killings and who did not accept her new responsibility graciously.

Mary C. Rush (seated center) and her sister Emma Drake (standing), granddaughters of Thursia Ballard, with Mary's son J. T. West and a caretaker, photographed by R. C. B. Thruston during a visit in October 1921. The Filson Historical Society, Louisville, Ky., Rogers Clark Ballard Thruston Collection, TC-817.

Sally treated the girl "with great cruelty" until finally passing her along to "some one else," with whom Thursia stayed until her marriage. According to a much later census, she had never learned to read or write.[18]

Poor Thursia must have looked a fright. She had been "badly disfigured" in the attack, said her granddaughters, her head having been "split open by the Indians, some of her brain oozing out." The sight of a tomahawked or scalped body, or even a survivor of such an attack, was not unusual in those violent days, but it must have been shattering every time. Thursia had been luckier than most, but, said her ancient granddaughters, so sensitive was she about her appearance that although she lived thirty years into the age of photography, she never once allowed herself to sit down in front of a camera.

Thruston's conversation with Thursia's granddaughters, by the way, produced the only acknowledgment I've found in any of the versions of the story that anything ever happened to the little girl other than *being rescued*. Nor did any tellers express concern about what her life might have been like after her family's pursuit of happiness in the West had caused her such devastating injury and loss. It's hard to believe, though, that she ever had much cause to judge her life happy. The simplest questions about her life linger unanswerable: Did her wound continue to pain her? Did it leave her with physical or mental impairments? Did her sister's cruelty turn her hard? Did she find a way to arrange her hair so that sometimes, in the right light, she might look normal? Did her neighbors see her stigmata as a sign of God's displeasure, her presence as something unwholesome or uncanny? Did she hate the Indians until the day she died as much as Bland did? Did she, perhaps, dare to hate God?

It's not even clear that she had authentic recollections of the attack that left her so scarred. In 1870 the census taker gave the ancient lady's age as eighty-six, which could have made her as old as four when the assault took place, but Thursia's brother had told Draper that she was two years old at the time, and her granddaughters would say she'd been three.[19] Since most child psychologists (except for the diehard repressed-memory fringe) hold that children aren't neurologically or cognitively capable of forming lasting and coherent memories, even of traumatic events, until they're between three and four, Thursia's own knowledge of the most shattering event of her life, the one that shadowed her existence every day for more than four score years, may have been no more direct than that of any of the neighbors who flinched at the sight of her face.

Memory, however, is quirky, and many people who feel certain that their vivid mental images of events from very early childhood come from their own direct recollection have in fact assimilated the memories of others as their own, having heard the stories told and retold most of their lives. With Bland around, we can guess that Thursia heard the account of her family's tragedy and her brother's heroics all the time, and its familiarity could well have led her to believe that she herself was recalling the faces of the savages, the snapping of guns, the screaming and the terror and the blood, perhaps even the sound of the tomahawk splitting her head and crunching the bone. But in that case, what she would actually have been "remembering" was Bland's tale, not her own, the tale celebrating the manly hero who ran, who climbed, who fired, who killed, who hated. Poor Thursia spent her life at the heart of a story controlled by someone with a bigger mouth and a better role, someone whose telling as rescuer would always trump hers as rescuee, someone who as a public man in a buckskin shirt had vastly more opportunities than a disfigured orphan girl with her needle and her pots to dazzle a gaggle of awed listeners.

The survival of so vulnerable a child after so brutal an ordeal could easily have been turned into a different and equally classic story: Miracle Girl Found Alive after Family Slaughter! (Something close to that plot worked for the Miracle Woodson Boys, alive in their hidey-holes after the 1644 assault in Virginia.) But even Thursia's granddaughters seem to have given her nothing more than the standard passive female role, that of distressed and damaged damsel pulled out of the water by none other than our hero, still tipsy on the pleasure of those six dead Indians. And in 1936 the newspaper cartoon series "Heroes of American History" added a tingle both lurid and classic to Thursia's distress: the gallant Bland was pictured standing over a heap of dead Indians as he cradled in his arms a drooping female form whose size, shape, and clearly visible breasts lay well beyond the capacity of any three-year-old.[20] Bland's sister was simply the perennial victim, her pain turned into a surefire hit to be told and retold for years, long after she and her brother were both dead. The whole episode is evidence of how even the headliner in a story could be as much a captive to its tellers as any historian two centuries removed—evidence indeed of the awesome power of stories to shape an unhappy life.

Despite, or perhaps because of, the unapologetic violence of the tale, its popularity lasted for generations among Ballard descendants and others who exerted an enormous and creative effort to qualify in that category. In 1941 the eighty-year-old E. N. Ballard wrote down his recollections for posterity since, he said, as Bland's great-grandson, "I think I am the only living person that knows the true story of that fight." (Not quite; at that point he had not yet begun corresponding with R. C. Ballard Thruston, the other old Ballard bachelor obsessed with the family tale, who was still alive in Kentucky, and I am astonished to realize that my life came within about a decade of overlapping both of theirs.) E. N., or Elijah, said he'd gotten the story from his father, also named Bland, who had heard it directly from his grandfather, "Captain Bland," the Indian fighter himself.[21]

Elijah's account was full of colorful details, some of them resounding with you-were-there authenticity while others smacked of romantic embellishment. Captain Bland held off the Indians at the cabin for two solid hours and withstood more than one hundred shots, but the attackers finally managed to crash through the door, and his gun misfired just as he tried to shoot down the raider chasing his stepmother into the yard. "It was all over. He was then at the cabin door, his gun was useless. The Indians were too many for him and he went back to the fort." Only then did he realize that his foot had swollen to twice its normal size, having been badly twisted when he leaped out of bed and caught his toe in a hole in the blanket. Little Thursia had lain in the waterhole for eighteen long hours while the men from the fort were off pursuing the attackers, but upon their return, they "got the baby out and put a piece of silver in its head." Elijah added that his mother, Parthena, had once visited Thursia in her old age. "She said the strip of silver ran from almost between the center of her eyebrow, a little diagonally to the right, up to the edge of her hair. Her scalp never grew back and there was always a spot there some larger than a silver dollar." Though Elijah's father had never managed a peek at poor scarred Thursia, *he* had been shown Captain Bland's collection of Indian scalps, "6 or 7 on a buckskin string."[22]

But some of Elijah's supposedly accurate particulars just don't ring true, and others seem to belong to someone else's story entirely. How could Captain Bland, last seen with a useless gun and a crippled foot in the middle of a yard full of "too many" Indians, have emerged alive to return to the fort? How could Thursia's own granddaughters have spoken with almost lip-smacking relish about the injuries that left the poor woman "badly disfigured" while failing to mention the piquant detail of the silver piece in her head? (John Dabney Shane recorded a similar story about a little girl named Gist, also the terribly injured sole survivor of an attack on her family, who, like Thursia, was supposed to have been patched with silver by some frontier sawbones, and I view that account with the same skepticism I bring to Elijah's.)[23] And how could Elijah have come up with so different a version of Captain Bland's earlier life? According to him, Captain Bland and his father had been "from New York, previously from Virginia," and "at the close of the Revolutionary War" they were in Poughkeepsie working as teamsters for George Washington.[24]

Poughkeepsie? Captain Bland's great-grandson claims to have the only accurate details, handed down directly, father to son, and he has his hero wrangling soldiers' rations in *Poughkeepsie* some four years after military records, eyewitnesses, and other Ballards all agree that the deep-rooted Virginian enlisted with George Rogers Clark to fight the Indians in Kentucky?

Other family details are equally confused. In his memoir and in his voluminous correspondence with the Kentucky Historical Society's librarian and with Thruston, Elijah insisted again and again that the name of his grandfather, who he claimed was the son of old Captain Bland, was William—even though, as he was well aware, all known evidence points to just one son, James, for the Indian fighter Bland. In a huge and labored scrawl Elijah, half-blind from a recent cataract operation, begged his correspondents for help in proving "that James Ballard was not my grand father."[25] The librarian was kind and patient, as was

Thruston, but they remained unconvinced, both of them declining to bestow on Elijah the gift he so desperately wanted—the proof of his membership in the heroic Bland Ballard's family club.

The Indian fighter Bland may indeed have had a second son whose existence entirely escaped the records. In fact, since Elijah mentioned at one point the family "tradition" that his grandfather William "was a very dissipated man," it's possible that a wastrel William had gotten himself disowned by his exasperated family, never to be mentioned by them again.[26]

But another story seems plausible too. Born in Missouri in 1861, Elijah had never known the men he claimed as his grandfather and great-grandfather, and his letters said he'd never set foot in Kentucky. So Elijah's father, Bland, safely remote from the Indian fighter's home turf, embarrassed by his disreputable sire, and secure in the knowledge that anyone who could dispute him was dead, might simply have created a better story for himself by appropriating the distant and distantly related hero as his direct ancestor.

With dozens of Bland Ballards scattered across the country by then, some of them simply christened out of habit with a name that had already been in the family for generations, carrying the Indian fighter's name didn't necessarily make one the Indian fighter's namesake. The odd intrusion of Poughkeepsie into the authentic Ballards' story could even have been a ghostly remnant of Elijah's father's or grandfather's *actual* family history. But whoever he was, as a child in Kentucky Elijah's father could well have known old Captain Bland and heard enough of his stories (apparently it would have been difficult *not* to) to appropriate them for his own and make a choice, even more active and conscious than that of the authentic Ballard descendants, to root his identity in an old story of violence and vengeance and find his happiness in contemplating his kinship with a hero celebrated as a lusty and prolific killer.

Poor Elijah, ancient and solitary and half-blind, the last survivor of his parents' five sons, ending his days in a hotel in Colorado far from the scenes of his birth and his childhood, can perhaps be forgiven for clinging so adamantly to a story possessing such drama and bestowing such importance—a story that was probably his father's last remaining gift. I don't feel nearly as charitable, however, toward the father himself, who seems to have set up his son for so heavy a disappointment. It's one thing to tell a rousing tale of ancestral courage to the bright-eyed young son snuggled on your lap. But it's hardly fair to send that child out all unarmed and unknowing into an unfriendly world where learned librarians lurk.

Some years after the Indian fighter Bland Ballard's parents and siblings were shot, tomahawked, and scalped en masse, his cousin, my fourth-great-grand-mother Rachel Ballard Mullins, arrived in the territory with her husband, Gabriel, and a pack of children. Their eighth child, the first of the family known to have been born in Kentucky, was a daughter whose name in contemporary documents is usually spelled Jalie, Jolie, or Jahily. When it popped up again later on a more literate twig of the family tree, however, I realized that what my kin had had in mind was the biblical name Jael.

As the Book of Judges tells the story, after ten thousand God-kindled Israelites rose up against Jabin the Canaanite and wiped out his entire army, Jabin's general Sisera saved himself by abandoning his chariot and fleeing the rout on foot. Jael was busying herself quietly about her work in her isolated campground far from the rumors of war when the desperate general burst into her tent. Telling him, "Turn aside to me, my lord, and have no fear," Jael offered Sisera a skinful of buttermilk to drink, covered him with a soft rug, and bade him rest. Then Jael took a hammer in her hand and drove a tent peg through his temple as he slept.

When the Israelite general in hot pursuit arrived at her tent, which must have been smoking and reeking with great gobbets of blood, Jael proudly invited him in to show off her handiwork, a mighty blow worthy of any man. "Most blessed of women is Jael," the prophetess Deborah sang, rejoicing. "She crushed his head, she shattered and pierced his temple. He sank, he fell, he lay still at her feet; at her feet he sank, he fell; where he sank, there he fell dead."

It might, I suppose, have been simple devoutness that inspired the Mullinses to name their wilderness-born baby girl after one of the bloodthirstiest hero-ines in the Bible, but none of their nine other children had names as showily scriptural as did the first Kentuckian in their family. Nor would they have been the only Americans to publicly embrace that "most blessed" female. In his great ecclesiastical history *Magnalia Christi Americana,* Cotton Mather himself cele-brated Hannah Duston, who had killed and scalped ten of her "savage" Indian captors, as another Jael rising up against another Sisera.[27] So I can't help but wonder: Was little Jalie a living expression of my family's drive for vengeance, at least symbolic, for the latest example of their eerie propensity for grievous wounds to the head?

The Daughertys and Guilt

Like my Ballard cousins, my Daugherty forebears numbered among the first pioneers to seek their happiness in Kentucky, and like them they encountered catastrophe and grief instead. Unlike the Ballards, however, they noticed full well they were unhappy.

Mystery shrouded my grandmother's paternal relatives when we were growing up. Grace herself, born a Dougherty, knew next to nothing about her father's background because she had barely known her father himself. Arthur Dougherty (who, like his own father, insisted on the maverick "Dougherty" spelling instead of the "Daugherty" preferred by most of the huge clan) had abandoned his family when Grace and her younger sister were tiny, and Grace's mother, Alice, refused ever after to allow her husband's name to be spoken in her house. Grace would later follow suit; she rarely mentioned him to my mother, who gathered only that something dank was hidden behind the silence.

Mystery continued to shroud the Daughertys as I made my first forays into local records and family histories, where the stories I found tended to be fragmentary and vague. But as I gradually pieced the allusions together, it became clear that they were fundamentally different from the tales told by their Ballard contemporaries and by most of my other ancestors as well. The Daughertys didn't yarn about heroic mothers or magnificent pirates or valorous smiters of Indians. There was no triumphalism in *their* tales, no vindication, not even vengeance. Though shot through with bravado and not free from exaggeration and embellishment, they were, at bottom, stories of loss—of land gone, of freedom gone, of treasure gone, of children gone. They seem to have understood: life wasn't supposed to be happy. Things went wrong, and there was no point in pretending anything different.

To be sure, things had not gone right historically for the Daughertys, who had come to Virginia in the early eighteenth century on the floodtide of Scots-Irish immigrants looking for places where they could be left alone. My Daugherty kin left no evidence that fortune had ever defied that desire. A cluster of Daughertys and Dorkertys and Dorathas that probably included my immigrant forebears was caught up in the series of Shawnee raids that terrorized the Shenandoah Valley during the French and Indian War. Charles Daugherty and his whole family were reported killed in one of the attacks on Kerr's Creek; a Daugherty wife (who some family historians say was a Cherokee woman) supposedly leaped on her horse and alerted other settlers of the coming danger in a pell-mell ride through Cowpasture Valley; and a Daugherty child may have been held captive by the Shawnee for a year.[28]

Members of the family began making their way from Virginia into northern Kentucky almost as soon as white settlement began, and populated the region nearly single-handedly, it seems, all of them producing immense broods of twelve or fourteen or even more children. John N. "Slick" Daugherty and his wife, Emily, had sixteen offspring all told, though like so many parents of that era they endured losses that stagger the imagination. One Saturday night at the tail end of summer, the couple tucked seven children into their beds; three Saturdays later they tucked four, having lost ten-year-old Jonathan, six-year-old Mary Ellen, and four-year-old Patrick to the "putrid sore throat." Eighty-seven years after the children's deaths, the clipping from the Frankfort *Yeoman* recording the sad news was still being carefully preserved by the widow of their brother Lewis, who wasn't even born until three years after his parents had watched nearly half their family gasp themselves to death.[29]

But a throng of sturdy Daughertys did survive, many of them bearing those sturdy pioneer names that seem every bit as homemade as anything Grandfather whittled or Sister stitched: Norvin, Orval, Hamp, Parthena, Evaline, Louvisa, Armilda, Salenyalis, and my favorite, A. M. Daugherty, behind whose staid initials lurked the rococo splendor of Arness Mellychamps. I'd guess his mother had been smitten with the fictional character Ernest Mellichampe, the Patriot hero of William Gilmore Simms's romance *Mellichampe,* who tended toward utterances like "Ah, dearest, but for that tory reptile, this rapture would have been mine before." No wonder A. M. preferred to sign his initials.[30]

It was my great-great-great-grandfather Joseph Daugherty, the most vivid character in the Daughertys' surviving stories, who won the blue ribbon as most prolific paterfamilias. For decades he presided over herds of horses, cattle, hogs, sheep, and children on a modest spread taxed as "third-rate" land along the middle fork of Grassy Creek in the almost primeval Pendleton County backcountry. When he took as his second or perhaps third wife Jane Collins, twenty years his junior and a daughter of the tax-defaulting Ralph, he was already the father of as many as ten or eleven minor Daughertys, and Jane was soon contributing lavishly to the Grassy Creek mob. If cholera had not put him down around his sixtieth birthday, heaven knows what cities he would have populated—or rather, heaven knows how many he really *did* populate. Legend has always numbered his spawn at twenty, though I can't make it more than seventeen or eighteen, while of grandchildren he had at least one hundred and nine. Perhaps not surprisingly, Joseph was on record with a nasty temper, too. He was once hauled into court for having assaulted one Oragen Hutchison, who charged that Joseph did "with great violence beat, wound, maim the [plaintiff] by biting the first finger of his left hand by means of which promises the plff was greatly hurt and wounded & became sick sore lame and disordered."[31] The provocation for their battle was not specified, and both sides were ordered to pay costs.

Quarrels and contention were endemic in the Daugherty family, most of whom lived near Joseph on Grassy Creek, which *still* feels like the back of beyond. Like people everywhere who don't have much, they fought and schemed to hang on to the little they had, but the Daughertys seem to have seen their biggest threats in the scrum of their fellow Daughertys. Five siblings sued their brother-in-law for plundering their mother's $105 estate, a pair of cousins got into a round of mutual recriminations over chicken stealing and slander, and an uncle was stripped of the guardianship of his four orphaned nieces and nephews for personal cruelty and financial mismanagement. No one knows anymore why Joseph's nephew Slick got so angry at Preacher Asa Tomlin that he went out and started felling willow trees into the baptizing hole, but Slick's wife was the preacher's cousin, and Slick himself was an in-law several times over. Slick earned his nickname, it was said, from his fondness for the popular fictional character Sam Slick, but there's also a suggestion his fellow citizens considered him as slippery a wheeler-dealer as that shrewd New England clockmaker.[32]

Although the stories about Joseph weren't passed directly down to us, I found some in a source nearly as close to us as my great-grandfather Arthur himself would have been *if* he'd remained on speaking terms. In the 1930s and 1940s the Pendleton County lawyer and amateur historian E. E. Barton spent countless hours gathering up or transcribing official documents (including most of those *Daugherty v. Daugherty* cases, painstakingly copied out, by hand, from the circuit court records) and capturing the memories of old-timers in a vast and disheveled mass of papers that he eventually donated to the local public library. Among these papers I found the recollections of Arthur's first cousin Lawrence Danville Daugherty, neatly typed up in 1938 when he was rising sixty-four, of the family stories he had learned at the knee of his (and Arthur's) grandmother Jane Collins Daugherty. And Jane said she had gotten them straight from her husband, Joseph, himself.

That was no greater a warrant of accuracy than you'd think.

According to Lawrence's recollections, Grandpa Joseph came to Kentucky with Daniel Boone and Simon Kenton—Lawrence still had Boone's own razor—and took up five hundred acres on Grassy Creek, the very same farm where Lawrence was then living, after the Indians "ran them off" their first camp at Ruddles Mills. Soon, however, he was captured with Boone and Kenton at Blue Lick, and watched, helpless, as the Indians carried off his son Jesse. "The Indians got Joe Daugherty's first child, Jesse, and took him to Detroit," Lawrence told Barton. "In a year and one day (afterwards) they went to Detroit and got the child as they were exchanging prisoners then. They got a child at Detroit, but could not be certain that it was their own child. The child they got at Detroit (Jesse) was different from all the other Daughertys; different turned." Later Joseph was elected to a term in Congress, Lawrence continued, but soon after he returned from Washington with his pay, consisting of "from twelve to fifteen thousand dollars in a bag," he was summoned to visit a son who had come down with cholera. Joseph "wanted to put [the money] away in some secure place," so after sending his wife ahead, he went off by himself to the barn, hid his stash, and then hurried on to the sickbed. But Joseph caught the disease himself "in 2 or 3 hours, and died with the cholera. No one ever found the money."[33]

Great stories. Great grandpa. But the signature detail of Joseph's supposed life history is, to put it bluntly, preposterous. My great-great-great-grandfather could not possibly have pioneered with Boone. In 1850 he told the census taker he was fifty-nine years old, which meant he wasn't even born until around 1791, sixteen years *after* Boone and Kenton settled (separately) in Kentucky and thirteen years *after* Boone, surprised by the Shawnee with thirty of his men while making salt at the Lower Blue Licks, surrendered them all in a controversial move he later said was intended to save their lives and avert an attack on the women and children back at the fort. When Boone packed up his worldly possessions, razor probably included, and left Kentucky for good, Joseph was not yet ten years old.[34]

No trace survives of any son of Joseph's called Jesse, but it's less the name than the relationship attached to the lost boy that's the problem: by the time any man born as late as 1791 could have had a child of his own, the Indian threat was long gone from Kentucky, faded into nothing more than an old-timer's yarn. Although Joseph did win public office as a Democrat in 1847, he served not in Congress but in the state assembly, and with legislators drawing the sumptuous stipend of three dollars a day, it goes without saying that any bag filled with fifteen thousand dollars he might have carried home at the end of the session couldn't have been "his pay."[35] But the bit about Joseph's death from cholera was not just accurate, it was also part of an even sadder story. The *Covington Journal* reported on August 23, 1851, that during that sickly season on Grassy Creek, one-third of its residents died of cholera or the flux. Also numbering among the dead were Joseph's oldest son, John M. Daugherty, the one he had been sum-moned to nurse, and John M.'s wife, Elizabeth, who was also his first cousin: three members of the immediate family dead within just days. John M. and Elizabeth moreover left four orphans under the age of eight, the children their uncle Newton, another son of Joseph's, would later be accused of mistreating.

The "came with Dan'l Boone" refrain is only to be expected for such as Joseph. Boone was everyone's hero, and since most people in heavily rural and lightly schooled Pendleton County probably had only a hazy grasp of historical chronol-ogy, anyone as grizzled as Joseph could easily find himself, voluntarily or not, starring in some stretchers about "olden days" far older than his own. That fairy-tale lost bag of money, the equivalent of $400,000 or more in today's currency, could just possibly, I suppose, be genuine after all, a crooked politician's boodle, though that suggestion brought a laugh from a Kentucky native I know. "Our politicians never cost that much," he said. "You could buy a Kentucky legislator for a country ham." But the lost loot was more likely a Depression-era fantasy of Lawrence's on the order of the Duckers' burned deed to all of Baltimore, or even just the wishful thinking of his furious and disappointed heirs. When Joseph's widow, Jane, married her much younger second husband, several of her chil-dren—my great-great-grandfather James, Arthur's father, among them—in fine old Daugherty tradition sued their own mother for withholding their rightful shares of Joseph's estate. Legal documents estimated its value at $1,187.08 and named sixteen heirs eligible for a piece of it. In the end, the only beneficiary seems to have been Jane's no-good second husband, whom she divorced after he frittered away the whole pot within three years of the wedding.[36]

Then there's the lost boy, a tale as irresistibly poignant as it is suspiciously melodramatic. Since Joseph hadn't been a pioneer, hadn't been among the salt makers surprised at the Blue Licks, had probably never been endangered by an American Indian in his life, how could the changeling child be anything but another fairy tale? But my discovery of several other allusions and fragmentary stories involving a Daugherty boy among the Indians, including two separate references to captive ancestors forced to run the gauntlet that came from ancient Daugherty dowagers in the mid-twentieth century, eventually persuaded me that even if the incident didn't happen quite as Barton preserved it, even if it couldn't have happened to Joseph himself or to his own offspring, *something* dramatic or even melodramatic involving captivity among the Indians hap-pened to the Daugherty family.[37] And I became convinced that the *something* was the notorious capture of Ruddell's Station in 1780 by British troops and their Shawnee allies led by Captain Henry Bird. Not only that; the lore provides a suggestive primer on the intricate alchemy that transforms adventure into memory into yarn. Juicy yarn, ripe with meaning and insight into the complex Daughertian relationship with happiness—and perhaps with children.

I found the key to the mysteries when I stumbled on a collection of letters exchanged in the early twentieth century by some remote and hitherto unknown cousins of mine, descendants of my fifth-great-grandparents John and Elizabeth Bridgewater Conway. The letters, copies of which have circulated among Conway family historians for years, were written mainly by or to the couple's great-grandson Henry C. Ogle, and told and retold the adventures of the extended Conway family after they left Virginia for Kentucky during the Revolution. John Conway himself was said to have been a Latin teacher from Dublin, though the little that is known about him makes it more likely that he himself was an *agricola* than that he knew the genitive plural of one. With him and his wife came most of their nine children, including their daughter Elizabeth and her new husband, John Daugherty, and assorted grandchildren and sons-in-law.[38]

In 1780 the clan was living at Ruddle's or Ruddell's Station, a fortified settlement in present-day Harrison County. On a bright June morning the youngest son, Joseph Conway, then sixteen, was sent with some other boys outside the station to drive the cows in for milking. As Ogle told the tale, Joseph had stolen a moment to play with a turtle on the riverbank when without warning a lurking brave shot him in the side, then swiftly tomahawked and scalped the fallen boy before fleeing into the woods. Joseph was carried inside, where his bullet wound was found to be minor and his gory head treated by the congenially named Mrs. Wiseman, who stanched the bleeding with compresses of cobwebs.

Just days afterwards, however, Ruddell's was captured by Captain Bird's British troops and their Indian allies. Marched north to the British garrison at Detroit along with scores of their neighbors were poor Joseph Conway, still heavily bandaged and tormented by fat green flies buzzing around his wound despite the continued ministrations of the angelic Mrs. Wiseman, and the rest of his family, including his newlywed sister Elizabeth Conway Daugherty and her husband. When most of the family was released four years later, Ogle wrote, Elizabeth brought home with her a small son named Jesse who had been born during her captivity. But her little sister Sally, the ninth and youngest Conway child, whose seventh birthday fell just a day or so after the attack, had been adopted by a kindly old Indian couple and was recovered only long afterwards, possibly as much as nine years later. When her father finally came to ransom her, she recognized him instantly and, "true to her race and kindred," eagerly returned home with him despite the entreaties of her Indian parents. Afterwards she married "a man of worthless character" who soon abandoned her and their little boy, but she was adored by the nieces and nephews she helped their sickly mother raise.[39]

Many elements of the Ogle letters are historically verifiable. Captain Bird's capture of Ruddell's Station and nearby Martin's Station was one of the most notorious actions in the western theater of the Revolutionary War, a catastrophe that panicked Kentuckians at the time and haunted their memories for decades afterwards. Bird had launched his expedition from the British garrison at Detroit in the spring of 1780, intending to destroy the American settlements and gain control of the Ohio country. Ascending the rain-swollen Licking River from the Ohio, he came ashore in late June within a few miles of Ruddell's with perhaps 150 British, Canadian, and Loyalist troops, including the renegade "white savage" Simon Girty; a throng of warriors from the Shawnee and other tribes that had reached as many as a thousand by the time they arrived in central Kentucky; and the first six cannons ever turned against the frontier settlements.

Surprised by the sudden appearance of the huge enemy force, unnerved by the cannonballs from the "little gun" that came smashing into the log wall even as the big six-pounder was being pushed into position, Captain Isaac Ruddell quickly agreed to surrender despite the protests of some of the other men who believed they could defend the fort. The terms of the capitulation specifically stated that the British soldiers would protect their captives from the Indians. The minute the gates were opened, however, the Indians, who outnumbered both their British allies and the surrendering Americans, ran wild, killing twenty of Ruddell's men on the spot and seizing other inhabitants willy-nilly as prisoners. Although Captain Bird insisted to his superiors that he had bargained in good faith and had simply been unable to control the Indian warriors, the Americans' fury and bitterness over the "treacherous" British failure to stop the slaughter simmered for decades.[40]

After plundering and burning the fort, Bird's men marched the five miles to Martin's Station and repeated their success there. The original plan had called next for a march on Louisville, but since the warriors had wantonly slaughtered most of the Kentuckians' livestock, which had been intended to feed the expedition, Bird chose to return straightaway to Detroit. Three hundred or more wretched prisoners, most of them still in the Indians' hands, were forced on a six-week journey by foot and boat back to the British garrison, where some of them were separated out and taken farther still to Niagara or to islands in the Great Lakes.

Survivors of the dreadful ordeal told and retold their stories for years, many of those finding their way, decades later and by then usually secondhand, into the notes of the historians Draper and Shane. Small children were brained against trees or tossed into fires when they couldn't keep up. Men and women staggered day after day under the enormous burdens of plunder they were ordered to haul; one woman, forced to carry a large copper kettle on her head, wore a cap for the rest of her life because "the hair never grew again." A young German woman who at first refused to marry the "very ugly" brave chosen for her finally gave in after being forced to swallow a pint of bear oil. Several captives, including a "fleet" young woman named Catherine Honn, were made to run the gauntlet. While the British enjoyed plenty of rations, the American men were allowed just a cup of musty flour a day, the women and children half a cup. One little boy carried papoose-fashion on his mother's back became so hungry he "gnawed through her shoulder."[41]

Once the surviving captives arrived in Detroit, life became somewhat more comfortable, and the British officials generally treated them decently, allowing most of them to live in the community rather than confining them to prison. Even so, anxiety was a constant companion for prisoners who had been separated from their families, and when they were finally freed—most of the group was released in batches between 1782 and 1784—many parents found the joy of liberty eclipsed by the realization of their worst fears: that no one knew where their children had been carried by the Indian families who had adopted them.

Henry Ogle obviously relished his role as the Conways' chief lore keeper. In a letter written in 1912, when he was about seventy-three, he reminisced fondly about the stories "of the old pioneers as often related to me by my mother and uncle around the fireside during the long winter nights." His own specialty was the story of the scalping of his great-uncle Joseph Conway during the roundup of the cows that had preceded the assault on the fort; he told it lengthily, dramatically, and frequently, twice within two months to the same correspondent in 1912. Unlike poor scalped Thursia Ballard, the damaged girl who couldn't bear to sit in front of a camera, as a man in the world of men Joseph Conway was able to wrest a kind of glory from his renown as a survivor of the Indian's blade. A memoirist who as a child in St. Louis had known the aging Captain Conway would later confess that in his "boyish curiosity" he would often "creep around [Joseph's] chair to get a good look at the back of his head, to see where the Indians had taken off the scalps from his head." The boy was convinced that "one of the bravest and noblest men that ever lived in the State of Missouri" had been scalped no fewer than *three* times. So, apparently, was *Ripley's Believe It or Not,* which according to family tradition once included a listing for the triple misfortune of the doughty old pioneer.[42]

Although the Ogle letters are rooted in historical events, like most family reminiscences the collection is rife with inconsistencies, contradictions, and omissions about the Conways' history and personnel. No one could agree on how many Conway daughters there were, for instance, or exactly who their husbands were, with two of the sisters said to have married a variety of Daugherty brothers. Nor did any Daughertys number among Ogle's correspondents, and the letter writers' references to that branch of the family all came from no closer than second or third hand; clearly my direct ancestors weren't part of the little circle of Conway descendants banded together to keep the story alive more than a century after the fact. Nonetheless, the many ways in which the Daughertys' stories about their lost boy rhyme with the Conways' tales of their Indian captivity make a strong case that something like the adventures that Lawrence Daugherty ascribed to his grandfather Joseph Daugherty and to Joseph's "first child," Jesse, are actually a garbled version of what actually happened to Joseph's *parents,* John and Elizabeth Conway Daugherty, and *their* first child, Joseph's big brother Jesse. In fact people named Conway and Daugherty do show up in a British roster of the Ruddell's captives. And although none of the Daughertys' stories made the explicit connection with the surrender of Ruddell's Station, the name had apparently lodged in the familial mind: Lawrence Daugherty named Ruddle's Mills as the campground from which the Indians had driven his grandfather and the other men.[43]

And then there was my fourth-great-uncle Jesse, the former child captive who was "different turned." Like the Ballards', Jesse's story was rooted in a swift and sudden assault on women and children as well as men, and it brought consequences to the family that, while not lethal, were certainly prolonged and grievous, involving years' worth of separation and captivity among enemies who were generally seen as only semi-human. Yet among the Daughertys themselves the tale barely survived, and only in fragmentary, conflicting, and historically dislocated forms.

Unlike the tales told by the Ballards, moreover, who were so inspired by the bloodthirstiness of their Indian-fighting Bland that generations later would-be descendants were still desperate to claim him as their ancestor, the Daugherty stories neither celebrated nor even mentioned any act or thought of revenge against the Indians who first "ran them off" the land they had claimed, then violently and perhaps treacherously took them captive and kept their children for years. No Daugherty on record, in any surviving version of the story, let slip any personal vengefulness toward the Indians. No Daugherty was known to have paraded about the streets proudly retelling his tale to gaggles of awestruck boys, or to have crawled out of his deathbed to take a last potshot at a beggar who smelled wrong, or to have gone poking around decaying log cabins in the undying hope of claiming a bunch of wizened old scalps.

It's impossible to know now the reasons why the Ballards clung to their fury and their martyrdom, choosing to celebrate a heroic act (one confirmed, we recall, by no independent evidence whatsoever) rather than grieving over their losses, while the Daughertys seem to have accepted their unhappy adventure as just another blow from the perennially unkind Fates. Factors could include anything and everything from individual character to family cohesiveness to religious conviction to the Ballards' own misty memory of their former privilege and power, a heritage far grander than the obscure Scots-Irish Daughertys could claim and one that might have nurtured a lingering conviction of their *entitlement* to happiness.

About the life of the wilderness-born Jesse Daugherty himself little is known other than the stories. After their release from Detroit, his parents returned to their old stomping grounds and patented some land not far from the ill-starred Ruddell's Station, where they produced six more children, including my great-great-great-grandfather Joseph, about ten years younger than Jesse. All or most of the seven Daugherty siblings wended their way to Pendleton County, where they established their quarrelsome and litigious little community on the middle fork of Grassy Creek. Jesse Daugherty married a local girl in 1806; he had four or five children, including the crafty "Slick"; he volunteered as a private during the War of 1812. In March 1824 his brother Jonathan was appointed his executor, so when Jesse died he was not yet forty-five, and all of his children were underage. Items sold from his estate included chisels, planes, and other carpenter's tools, but he had also owned nine books, including a two-dollar Bible and a dictionary worth a dollar fifty.[44] Maybe that's what was "different turned" about him.

Or there's another possibility. A suggestive clue is embedded in another version of the story that I was sent, long after I thought I'd heard it all, by a distant Daugherty cousin I'd never met who was still living on part of the patriarch Joseph Daugherty's original Grassy Creek farm. She told me that

Joseph's last child, Norvin, born around 1850, had written a history of the family that was burned some time later by another relative who "didn't like" what it said. Norvin's history had reportedly offered an explanation for why the child Jesse seemed so different from his siblings. "We have heard the story that Jesse Dougherty was born in captivity," this present-day Daugherty descendant wrote me. "He was left when the rest of the family was released and returned to Kentucky. Joseph Daugherty and someone went back and bought his freedom and brought him back home. [A relative said] that Jesse looked different from the other boys, so they figured his father was an Indian."[45]

When I shared that bombshell with my mother, I was surprised to see that she wasn't a bit surprised. "You know," she said, "I thought I remembered Great-Aunt Gertrude hinting something lurid about 'Indian blood' somewhere in the family." So maybe this pale but provocative echo of the story from a second source adds a dollop of credibility to the tale. Maybe something that just about any white American of the day would have seen as deeply shameful had happened to Jesse's mother, voluntarily or not, during her captivity.

And yet it's just as possible—perhaps even more possible—that Jesse's family and neighbors saw him as different simply because they assumed he had to be. Anyone who had sojourned among those mysterious and terrifying Indians must, they would have thought, be forever tainted—darkened—by that association. Jesse, moreover, couldn't even be described as having *returned* to civilization; he'd never been there before, having spent his entire life, literally, among the savages. And his mother, who had come back from captivity with her husband but brought with her living, breathing proof that sexual contact with *somebody* had occurred in the wild places, couldn't have expected to escape the whispers and winks.

If Jesse had in fact been separated from his mother and father, the episode would have been complicated even more by his parents' guilt at not having been able to protect their child from danger. It was a family-wide guilt, too, doubtless shared by Jesse's Conway grandparents over *their* lost child, their youngest daughter, Sally, who, when finally recovered by her father, probably did not come leaping into his arms as eagerly as the family legend insisted. Barely seven years old when she was ripped from her family and somewhere between eleven and sixteen by the time she was reclaimed by people she probably didn't recognize anymore, she would have seen her "rescue" as another uprooting every bit as wrenching as the first had been. As her son later wrote to Ogle, "Concerning her early life, she was not much accustomed to speak."[46]

Her difficult readjustment to white society would have brought a brand of heartbreak familiar to plenty of other American families; Eunice Williams, Mary Jemison, and Olive Oatman were only a few of the most famous of the many longtime captives who strenuously resisted leaving people they had come to care for and returning with strangers to an alien "home." Thirteen-year-old Olive, for instance, was traveling with her family through what is now Arizona when Yavapai Indians killed her parents and four of her siblings, enslaved her, and eventually traded her to the Mojave. But by the time she was ransomed five years later, in 1856, she was wearing the chin tattoos that among the Mojave often signaled marriage, and long after her return she remained a "grieving, unsatisfied woman," one acquaintance noted in her diary, "who somehow shook ones' [sic] belief in civilization. In time we erased the tatoo [sic] marks from her face but we could not erase the wild life from her heart."[47] Both Sally Conway and Jesse Daugherty would have borne a deep imprint from that wild life too.

The different reactions of the Ballards and the Daughertys to their stories suggest something more. The Ballards embraced and enjoyed their tale about their avenging ancestor without questioning it; they were, like latter-day Woodson descendants, happy to accept as a gift from the past a story of the grand sacrifices made by their ancestors on America's epic march to tame the wilderness. The story remained clear and coherent because its meaning was too: murder was avenged with murder. The Daughertys, by contrast, declined to find a message of victory or even endurance in their emotionally murky tale of a child not killed but held captive, a tale that recalled large helpings of bewilderment, helplessness, shame, and guilt as well as grief. The vague, variegated, and splintered state of the Daughertys' story of the lost boy who was "different turned" may reveal the stresses and strains of its heavy use in the hard social work of explaining their selves, their history, and their reality. A story like the Ballards' of murder plain and simple might actually have made the Daughertys happier.

Defeat and Just Deserts

During the American Revolution, the Ballards and the Daughertys pioneered their way to Kentucky looking for paradise and found something more like a hell on earth instead. But when Ralph Collins and William Wharton reached Kentucky in 1791, both were escaping at last from hells of their own that had been growing ever hotter for more than a decade. The stories the two men told about those adventures—the third set of stories I found about the first generations of my Kentucky ancestors—suggest that Ralph and William found very different ways to handle their disappointments and viewed their right to tell their own stories and seize their own happiness in starkly contrasting terms. Both lived lives that were chronically, operatically hapless, but while one forebear apparently forbore from talking about himself even when he had tales of high adventure to share, another revised the story of his very low escapade with such gusto and such success that an edition of it survived for one hundred long years. While one felt his unhappiness deserved no stories, the other told stories to deserve his happiness.

William, the grandfather of Arthur Dougherty's maternal grandmother, was actually, you could argue, a lucky guy, but he used up so much of his good fortune on continually not dying that he had little left to live on. The documentary traces he left are meager, most of them "Musgraves" or not much better, but here's what I was able to find about his life that probably never made it into any fireside stories.

If he was indeed the William Wharton who had been transported to the colonies as a convicted housebreaker, he probably didn't broadcast that information. He would doubtless not have wanted to talk about the straits that drove him to sell or barter the land warrant his arduous military service had earned him, thus giving up, it would turn out, the only chance he would ever have to claim his happiness in the classic American form of land of his own. He could have been equally reticent about the circumstances behind the recurrent suits brought by Pendleton County officials to take away two of his daughters and bind them out to other families, which they finally succeeded in doing in 1805, when one of the girls was about ten. Or why later that same year the county paid Ralph Collins, who had married another of Wharton's daughters, to care for William's orphaned grandchild Agnes, apparently the illegitimate infant of a fourth daughter. (Choosing Ralph was something of a gamble; in 1802 he had again defaulted on his taxes, just as he'd done back in Virginia, and had again resorted to the familiar expedient of flight, this time moving temporarily to next-door Campbell County.) Or where William was lying low in 1809, when county tax collectors marked him down as delinquent and "not found."[48]

When he was over seventy he did open up a little, but that time there was cash in it. In 1818, when Congress decided to grant pension benefits to needy Revolutionary War veterans from the enlisted ranks, William immediately

joined the stream of grizzled and destitute ex-privates who began flocking
to their county courthouses to attest to their "reduced circumstances" and
claim their due. In the pension application he signed with his mark, William
explained that his household consisted of only himself and the orphaned granddaughter, now sixteen (no trace survives of Mrs. William Wharton or her fate);
that he was "very infirm and totally incapable to pursue" his work as a weaver;
and that he possessed no other assets than a forty-five-dollar horse. Someone
owed him fifteen dollars, he added (which is hard to believe), but he himself
was in debt for forty-four (which isn't). Persuaded of his indigence, the government allowed him the standard sum of eight dollars a month. That was
encouragement enough for the tough old bird to make it past eighty-five; he
died after 1835.[49]

To this most lamentable forebear came adventures that may not have been
happy but were certainly memorable. Like many men with no handhold on
the fringes of respectability, he had taken refuge in the military, making his way
in 1776 to the rugged and heavily Scots-Irish backcountry of Pennsylvania to
enlist at the fort in Pittsburgh. His regiment, the Eighth Pennsylvania, which
was praised by General Washington himself as "choice troops," was involved
in some of the most critical and dramatic events of the war. If he was generally with his unit when he was supposed to be—a reasonable if unverifiable
assumption—then the ne'er-do-well who was constantly in debt and constantly
dodging the law turned out to be either phenomenally skillful or phenomenally
lucky as one of those choice soldiers.[50]

In the summer of 1777 a detachment of riflemen from the Eighth was sent to
fight with General Horatio Gates in the campaign along the Hudson that ended
in the stunned and abject surrender of General John Burgyone and nearly six
thousand Redcoats at Saratoga. The Americans' walloping victory would later
be seen as a turning point of the war. Most of the Eighth, however, was assigned
to Washington's army, and endured not just the nasty battles of Brandywine
Creek and Germantown near Philadelphia but also the intervening action at
Paoli, which the Americans, with some reason, called not a battle but a massacre. During the night of September 20–21, 1777, Lord Grey's Redcoats, out-
numbering the Continental troops by more than three to one and under orders
to use only bayonets and swords, attacked General Wayne's encampment as the
soldiers slept, stabbing and slashing the startled troops and setting their crude
huts on fire. Although only fifty-three American bodies were buried on the
battlefield afterwards, the perfidious assault made for excellent propaganda,

and legend insisted that hundreds of Patriots had been slaughtered even as they tried to surrender.[51]

William Wharton also likely numbered among the rare *genuine* members of what would over the years become the most honored and the most overcrowded band in the Revolutionary army. After the Philadelphia campaign, the men of the regathered Eighth Pennsylvania were among the eight or ten thousand soldiers who followed George Washington into winter quarters at Valley Forge during that awful season of 1777–78 and survived the hunger, cold, and disease that killed thousands of their comrades before the dawn of spring. Unlike the countless summer soldiers and sunshine patriots—my allegedly bloody-footed cousin "Tough Daniel" Maupin among them—who either would loft them-selves or would themselves be lofted by eager descendants into the ranks of those claiming a piece of Valley Forge as their own, William could have told a story of that epic campground that was actually true.

Then again, Wharton was probably a bust as a storyteller. The small relic of him that does survive, the sole offprint from the Whartonian mind, is curt almost to opacity. When he petitioned the county justices for a military pen-sion, like all veterans he was required to prove his former service by listing with as much detail as possible the dates and places he'd served, the actions he'd been involved in, and the officers he'd reported to. But in his application, which an old companion in arms signed as a corroborating witness, Wharton gave away almost nothing. "Early in the beginning of the war" he'd enlisted at Fort Pitt under Colonel Aeneas Mackay (who along with dozens of his ragged men had died in the first weeks of 1777 during their ill-equipped march over the wintry Alleghenies to join Washington's army in New Jersey). When his three-year term was up, Wharton had reenlisted, serving about seven years all told through to the end of the war. But, he declared, he had been "mostly engaged in the spy or scouting service on the western waters." The only specific action he mentioned from his seven years of soldiering was "the taking of the Muncey Indian town" in 1779, after the Eighth was sent back over the mountains to Fort Pitt. Offered the wide-open opportunity to talk about his military service, the former Private Wharton neglected to mention his presence at either of the Eighth's epic campaigns, near Philadelphia or at Saratoga, or at the wintertime camp at Valley Forge.

America hadn't quite reached the peak of its romantic reengagement with its past by the time Wharton died; Washington's old campground had not yet been turned into a physical and moral shrine to the "purer devotion, holier sincerity . . . more pious self-sacrifice . . . [and] sublime heroism displayed by the American soldiery at Valley Forge," as the general's biographer put it in 1860.[52] Still, toward the end of his life, my fifth-great-grandfather must have encountered encouragement and inspiration aplenty to tell stories of wartime adventure, sacrifice, and courage. A nation still too fresh and hopeful for a history needed heroes, at least, if it was to succeed in figuring out who and what it was, and heroes of the Revolution were naturals to fill the bill: they had fought in a great cause, they had won a great victory, they had fathered a great nation, and now they were beginning to die off. The reputation of George Washington, dead (and Weems-deified) two decades earlier, had become so lustrous that many who could not legitimately claim its reflected glow simply appropriated it. But Revolutionary herohood was actually open to almost anybody who had picked up a musket. By 1818 newspaper obituarists were taking special and reverent notice of the deaths of veterans, and even some of the most ordinary soldiers were keeping journals or publishing narratives of their own experiences, compositions in which they recognized themselves as authentic, conscious, and worthy actors in an unfolding drama rather than as passive walk-ons in stories under others' control.[53]

But William, who *had* fought with Washington, didn't bother to say so.

It may have been that old age had dimmed his memory and robbed him of a garrulousness his neighbors and grandchildren had become heartily sick of. It may have been the diffidence of a habitual loser unaccustomed to telling officialdom something good about himself. It may have been a posttraumatic reluctance to delve too deeply into old memories of terror and pain, a reticence that would be shared by many veterans of many other wars.

Or Wharton may still have been enmeshed in traditional ideas about the ordinary individual's place in history, his ability (or inability) to control and narrate it, and the strength of his right to pursue, or even expect, happiness. He could have believed that those long-ago years spent being harried and clobbered by enemy invaders were neither noteworthy nor interesting, not especially different from the rest of a down-and-out life spent being harried and clobbered by judges and creditors and courts and tax collectors and daughters pregnant out of wedlock. Unlike the marquee battles that had earned his unit Washington's praise, after all, the Indian skirmish William remembered for forty years had been a resounding victory for *his* side. The destruction of the Munsees' towns on the north branch of the Allegheny River had been a rare romp for the six hundred–odd Pennsylvania troops; they had lost not a single man and had spent most of their time burning down the Indians' villages and hacking up their corn.[54]

In fact it's hard to imagine that Wharton ever forgot *any* victory he'd ever participated in, whether personal or military; they were probably easier to count than his children. Unlike his children, however, for whose creation he could (presumably) take solid credit, history seemed to him to have lain outside his control, open to neither change nor appeal. The great political and military struggle that the ghostwriting John Fleming saw as a fight for republican principles, that Major Tarlton Woodson and his brother George viewed as a referendum on virtue, and that Tarlton ever afterwards used as a source for "thrilling anecdotes of military adventure" rather than fireside tales of matrimonial bliss, was doubtless to Private Wharton just another dirty job that brought him only servile misery, a very tardy eight dollars a month, and no closer to happiness than he'd ever been or expected to be. Some stories are suppressed; some are embroidered or altered. But some—including many of the ones that to a historian with hindsight seem irresistible—simply feel more like *life* than *stories* to those who inhabit them most closely.

Ralph Collins, too, left a tiny fossil imprint of his life story, as a participant in one the most awful adventures in the experience of the new nation. Unlike his father-in-law's story, however, Ralph's tale achieved an odd and inexplicable longevity, which suggests that as unhappy as his life was too, the younger man felt that he had a perfect right to edit it.

In 1791 the young, landless, and illiterate Virginia veteran extricated himself from the importunities of the tax collector with an expedient whose wretchedness is eloquent testimony to the leanness of his options. In a time of relative prosperity, and in the face of the deep-seated American suspicion of standing armies that made it almost impossible to recruit good men into the ranks, Ralph enlisted as a short-term "levy" in the tiny federal military force as it prepared for an expedition against the frontier American Indians who were fiercely resisting white settlement in the Northwest Territory. The pay was lousy—a private like Ralph cleared about two dollars a month after deductions for his supplies—but at least he could count on, or thought he could count on, steady meals, and got himself whisked beyond the reach of the tax man besides.[55]

The frontier army may have been where Ralph met his future father-in-law, if he was the same William Wharton who that year enlisted in Pennsylvania for a short hitch as quartermaster sergeant. At that point William had a growing family to support, including Margaret, born in the mid-1780s, whom Ralph would marry in 1801. And even though William had plenty of experience in the miseries of the martial life, the rank of quartermaster sergeant, with its modest increase in pay and less hazardous duties, might have tempted a middle-aged near-pauper, especially since Major General Richard Butler, who had served for a time as major and colonel in Wharton's old Eighth Pennsylvania Regiment, was the officer in charge of recruiting and organizing the contingent of short-term levies.[56]

So Ralph and perhaps William too took part in the battle that wasn't just, as it is often and accurately called, the American military's worst defeat at the Indians' hands; it is still the American military's worst defeat *ever*, the Indians' best day *ever* against U.S. troops. In a single morning that capped off months' worth of blunders, misfortunes, iniquities, and idiocies, the federal army came close to annihilation on the banks of the Wabash in the awful battle that would be generally known as St. Clair's Defeat.

Major General Arthur St. Clair had fought with credit in the great Revolutionary victories of Princeton and Trenton, but his best-remembered military action came soon thereafter, when he abruptly abandoned Fort Ticonderoga to the much larger and well-positioned army of Redcoat besiegers without firing a shot. A court-martial later cleared him of any blame. In 1791 St. Clair, now the governor of the recently established Northwest Territory, was given command of a motley group of local militiamen, six-month levies, and the two regiments that made up the entire U.S. regular army on an expedition north from Fort Washington near the little settlement of Cincinnati. The stated goal was to set up a military garrison at the Miami towns near present-day Fort Wayne, Indiana, from which the hostile tribes could be intimidated and controlled.

From the start the mission was bungled, exploited, and downright hexed. The contract to provision the army was awarded to a shady financier who was also a good friend and business partner of the secretary of war and whose speculations in state lands were funded in part by U.S. Treasury advances for military supplies. Even though St. Clair's corps fell far short of the three thousand troops sought by the war secretary, there was so little flour on hand that the men were on short rations most of the time. The packhorses kept disappearing or dying, the flimsy tents welcomed in the wind and rain, the men's shoes and clothing disintegrated on their bodies, the gunpowder had been soaked in a riverboat accident, and nobody was getting paid.

"March" sounds too festive a term by far for how this army moved: hacking its way with bad axes through forest and thicket, hauling the big field guns through swamp and mire and heaving them over streams, prodding the skinny cattle and the drooping baggage horses, the column might, on a good day, lumber its way five or six miles forward. Everyone suffered in the constant rain and sleet, but St. Clair himself was so tormented by gout and what he called his "bilious colic" and "rheumatic asthma" that he couldn't endure the saddle. Much of the time the portly commander in chief had to be ignominiously lugged on a litter.[57]

Few of the men seemed any more promising as fighters than their prostrate general. The wretched conditions would have shaken even crackerjack troops, but these soldiers were no one's prize. St. Clair's aide-de-camp, Lieutenant Ebenezer Denny, was shocked at their lack of discipline, noting in his journal that the levies were even "more troublesome [than] and far inferior to" the militia, itself a species of legendary unruliness. Colonel Winthrop Sargent, the haughty adjutant general, was even more contemptuous, dismissing most of the corps as "the offscourings of large towns and cities; enervated by idleness, debaucheries, and every species of vice. . . . An extraordinary aversion to service was also conspicuous amongst them." Many of the soldiers were alarmingly old or young or unskilled or infirm—St. Clair complained about their "rotten legs"—while others had never before been in the woods or fired a gun, and there hadn't been time to teach them anything. Even this pinched and sorry army, however, had *some* standards, as I discovered while browsing through the official service records: on September 4 one Private John Cash of the First Regiment of Levies was "discharged [for] being a fool." As the descendant of another "offscouring" in the same regiment, I took some comfort in this small hint that Ralph Collins couldn't have been *that* bad. He may have been homeless, penniless, unlettered, and unskilled, but if even an army this desperate was able to indulge in the luxury of disposing of its fools, Ralph's continued presence suggests he couldn't have been a complete pumpkinhead.[58]

But he came close.

Ralph hadn't taken long to decide that this army life wasn't for him. His service record notes that he'd enlisted in Major George M. Bedinger's battalion in Winchester, Virginia, in late May, and set out with his unit for the frontier toward the end of July. After a journey of 480 miles by foot and riverboat, his battalion joined the rest of the army on September 5 at Ludlow's Station, the camp established a few miles north of Cincinnati in the hope that "abstracting the men from the debaucheries of the town," as Colonel Sargent noted, "would preserve them in better health and condition for service." Almost immediately they hit the road again—or rather, they *made* the road, chopping their way close to twenty miles in three days to the banks of the Great Miami, where on about September 11 they were set to work building a staging fort that would be named after Alexander Hamilton. There Private Collins lasted a little more than a week. On September 20 Adjutant John Crawford noted in his orderly book that ten men, including Ralph Collins, were court-martialed for desertion.[59]

Getting away shouldn't have been so hard. A week *after* Ralph's court-martial, St. Clair had to tell the commanding officers to stop their troops from "strolling in the invirons of the camp, and sometimes at a great distance from it, in a manner that would be very improper in time of perfect peace"—which one would think could have afforded any soldier with less than half a pumpkinhead ample opportunity to stroll away completely.[60] It wouldn't even have taken much planning or preparation to escape from Fort Hamilton, no more than a long day's journey from the Kentucky border. And scores of men did in fact manage to desert, sometimes ten or twenty of them in a single night, according to Lieutenant Denny's journal. By mid-October the leakage from the corps had become so alarming that St. Clair, to set an example, took two captured deserters, along with a private who'd shot his comrade, and hanged them all in front of the assembled troops. The dramatic gesture didn't have much effect. Just over a week later, no fewer than sixty Kentucky militiamen walked out en masse, declaring they were going to hijack the supply convoy creeping toward the army with desperately needed supplies. St. Clair detached the three hundred men of the First U.S. Regiment of regulars—the most seasoned soldiers in the army—to chase them.

At least Ralph wasn't the only one who didn't make it. Almost every day Adjutant Crawford recorded the court-martial of one man or three or occasionally more who hadn't quite managed to get away. A few were acquitted, for reasons that were never recorded, but most were sentenced to one hundred lashes, the maximum permissible corporal punishment, to be served out in front of their whole company. Among the lashed was Ralph. The circumstances of the expedition were so miserable and the volunteers so badly treated that I can almost admire his enterprise in trying to escape. What bothers me more than his insubordination is how he could possibly have been so—foolish?—as to have failed to stroll free.

On October 4, two weeks after Ralph and his fellow deserters had been recaptured and flogged, the army moved on again. About forty miles past Fort

Hamilton, they halted to build another stockade, which in those bitterly partisan times was shrewdly named Fort Jefferson after Hamilton's archrival in the cabinet. Since, however, the quartermaster had supplied only eighty axes and a single crosscut saw to work with, most of the men spent their days shivering in their leaky tents as the persistent rains turned to hail and their soaked shirts shrank on their bodies. As soon as the walls of the fort had been thrown up, they moved on again, and on November 3, two months and one hundred miles out of Fort Washington, the corps stopped for the night at an old Indian campground perched above the banks of the Wabash River. By then St. Clair's force had dwindled to about 1,400 fighting men and an assortment of servants, laborers, camp followers, and military wives and children.

With the trained regulars of the First U.S. Regiment still out chasing the vanished militiamen and most of the rest of the soldiers slumbering in their tents, a captain who had been leading a scouting party reported back to Richard Butler, the expedition's second-in-command, that he had seen several groups of prowling warriors. Butler, who believed that St. Clair simply didn't understand Indian warfare, apparently took the warning to his own heart at least; family historians would later tell the tale of how that evening he had summoned his subordinate officers including two of his own brothers to his tent, passed the wine, and urged them, "Let us eat, drink, and be merry, for tomorrow we may die."[61]

Early the next morning, not long after reveille and before the sun had quite risen, some sharp ears caught "the damnedest noise imaginable," whose meaning soon became appallingly clear.[62] It was the war whoops of Little Turtle, Blue Jacket, and more than a thousand warriors from the Miami, Shawnee, Delaware, Chippewa, Wyandot, and other nations, who had swiftly disposed of the outer guard of militiamen, sending them into helter-skelter flight, and were surrounding the main camp.

It was not a battle—it was carnage. The fierce and determined Indian warriors knew how to use the woods and ground for cover while constantly moving, never shooting from the same place twice. With ruthless efficiency they concentrated their fire on the officers, most of whom were on horseback and easily distinguishable by their gaudier dress. Left essentially leaderless, the green troops had neither the skill nor the grit to stand up to a massive surprise assault by hundreds of fierce enemies shrieking like banshees and shooting like wizards, and most simply milled about in panic. Survivors described a scene of "the wildest confusion," like a "wild, horrid dream," in which the Indians "fought like hell hounds" against soldiers too dazed and numb to respond.[63]

St. Clair, who was still in bed when the alarm sounded, scrambled quickly into a coarse brown coat and tried desperately with the help of his aides to mount a horse. After two animals in succession were shot dead before he could be heaved aboard, however, the general gave up and on his own two rheumatic feet tottered into battle—where, he later said, the zing of a bullet past his face worked a miraculous cure on his pains. When a retreat was finally ordered, groups of soldiers managed to escape by fixing their bayonets and rushing through a line of attackers too surprised at the sudden outburst of bravado to stop them. Ahead of the exhausted and shell-shocked survivors—many of them bleeding, hobbling, clamping their hands tight over jagged edges of oozing wounds—lay a hundred-mile slog through the rain back to Fort Washington. There they would find no place to sleep, nothing to eat, and not much to do other than go to Cincinnati and get drunk. They did.

Killed in the three-hour battle were 593 soldiers and thirty-seven officers, with another 252 men and thirty-one officers wounded—about two-thirds of the entire corps. Nearly all of the army's equipment and provisions were lost. St. Clair himself survived, suffering damage only to his flowing hair and his coat (as well as his military career). But Butler, badly wounded in the side and too corpulent for easy carrying, ordered his brothers to leave him behind and save themselves. When the Indians found him, they cut out his heart and ate it. Joyous warriors roamed the field of battle, torturing the living, mutilating the dead, and collecting great heaps of abandoned arms and supplies. The freshly scalped heads of the fallen victims steamed in the frigid air. Among the Americans killed or captured were all but three of the women who had accompanied the corps. The Indians' dead were said to number twenty-one.[64]

St. Clair was never officially censured for his part in the defeat. It did not go uncriticized: Washington's private secretary would later tell several friends about how, upon hearing the news, the president strode about the room in anguish, recalling how he himself had warned St. Clair to beware of a surprise attack and finally giving full vent to his "terrible" wrath. "O God, O God," the president raged, "he's worse than a murderer! how can he answer it to his country;—the blood of the slain is upon him—the curse of widows and orphans—the curse of Heaven!" (The secretary's tale was disputed years later by an acolyte who refused to believe that even under such dire provocation the sainted Washington might have displayed a temper.) Yet the president soon regained his composure, swore his secretary to silence about his outburst, and promised that the general should "have full justice."[65]

Although St. Clair was relieved of his commission, he continued to serve as territorial governor and to enjoy the support of many friends and political allies. A congressional investigating committee placed the blame for the debacle largely on the lateness of the season, the failures of the suppliers, and the inexperience of the troops, while St. Clair himself bitterly blamed Richard Butler, who, he said, had failed to give him the scout's warning about the imminent attack. In any case, Butler had the last, if posthumous, laugh, earned by an invincible weapon in the arsenal of public reputation: death on the field of battle. Butler was the one who got to drink that insouciant farewell to life—you can almost see the faint, fleeting smile playing about his lips—as the gouty general snored in his tent. He was the one whose heart the savages chose to eat, in the awful yet epic ritual they intended as a compliment to courage. He was the one who got three whole stanzas to himself in the ballad of "Sainclaire's Defeat," in which, after with his last breath urging his "valiant heroes" to charge, he was conveyed by "blessed angels . . . unto the celestial fields."[66]

St. Clair, by contrast, got a war named not after its location but for its loser, and his reputation was doomed to suffer under the same hopeless disadvantage that Bland W. Ballard's brother James faced after the massacre of his family at Tyler's Station: he didn't die too. A tender legend later arose to explain why St. Clair had survived. The son of the Mohawk chief Joseph Brant, family historians said, having fallen hopelessly in love with St. Clair's daughter, had told his warriors they could shoot at the general's horse but they must not hurt the man himself, the father of his beloved. That's why, the legend went on, St. Clair emerged untouched even though several horses in succession had been shot out from under him and his clothes and flowing hair were riddled with bullets.[67]

Actually, however, his aides hadn't managed to heave their hefty and groaning commander into the saddle until near the end of the battle. Out of uniform and on his feet, he would not have attracted the attention of the warriors, who had been instructed to shoot at the mounted and uniformed officers first. And that is probably what saved the general from a glorious or at least explicable battlefield death: not the timely intervention of a generous lover's hand but his brown civilian coat and a pair of skittish horses.

There are no surviving family legends about my kinsmen Ralph or William. There's virtually no information at all, even in their service records, about their actions that day. As a quartermaster sergeant William should have been busier coping with the ire of his tattered and ravenous comrades than with direct combat duties, but the distinction doubtless dissolved on that chaotic battlefield, where not even the women and children won mercy as noncombatants. Ralph was in Captain Joseph Darke's company of the First Regiment of Levies, which under the command of Captain Darke's father, Lieutenant Colonel William Darke, was in the thick of the action and endured a large proportion of the casualties. The elder Darke emerged as something close to a hero in the action, leading (and surviving) two game but futile bayonet charges, in the second of which he was wounded in the thigh while his son took a musket ball in the face.

Neither of my ancestors, however, was reported to have suffered any wounds, and neither "lost his arms in action," the mishap (or more likely the choice, the faster to run or the lighter to travel) that was charged against the meager pay of so many of their surviving comrades. Their service records say only that Ralph was discharged on the eleventh of November and William on the fifteenth. Which raises the same questions that surrounded St. Clair: Were they lucky, again, or does something else explain how both of my forebears beat the odds and took their places among the fraction of the force that emerged unscathed from the dreadful slaughter?

Even without resorting to tragic lovers, I can imagine some possible scenarios. Maybe they were sharp enough to recognize immediately what the war whoops meant, and slipped away to hide in the woods in the precious few minutes before the warriors fell on the encampment. Maybe they happened to be out in the woods already when the attack came, "strolling" or scrounging or looking for a quiet spot to lower their britches, and, being sensible men, they simply stayed there. Maybe they'd never even made it to the camp on the Wabash: when the army left Fort Jefferson in late October on its final march north toward calamity, a small crew, consisting mainly of the ill and the useless, had been left behind to hold the fort. Or maybe, if they'd had a chance to tell their own stories, they would have emerged as ordinary guys doing their best in a crisis and coming through by the sort of blind luck or amazing coincidence or bizarre accident that in every catastrophe from the Holocaust to the destruction of the World Trade Center seems to extricate more survivors than do planning or skill or just deserts.

We don't know. We don't have their stories. The stories we do have from others on the scene, however, raise uncomfortable suspicions about the conduct of my two kinsmen, one of them a convicted deserter and neither having left a shred of evidence exempting himself from the adjutant general's despised category of the idle, the vicious, and the debauched. For it was Ralph's own commanding officer, the undeniably gallant Lieutenant Colonel Darke, who left the most intimate account of the failures and inadequacies of the common soldiers that day in a long and anguished letter to President Washington relaying the "disagreable news of our defeat." Again and again, he reported, he had tried to rally his stunned troops on the field, but they "would not form in any order in the confution . . . and the whole Army Ran together like a mob at a fair." Some of the officers and even a few of the men had behaved bravely, but many more had thrown away their arms and fled; the levies had taken most of the casualties. "And indeed," Darke told President Washington with a brutality perhaps excused by his grief over his dying son, "many of [the levies] are as well out of the world as in it."[68]

I have no doubt that many of the levies—quite possibly including Ralph and William—were exactly as worthless as the adjutant general said they were and performed exactly as badly as Darke said they did. I'm sure that in the terror of the attack, the wretched and half-starved amateur soldiers did panic, get confused, and huddle or flee. Some of them may have spent the rest of their lives refusing to talk at all about the day, or making up tales of heroics to assuage a secret shame. But I'm also sure that all of them were damn glad to have come out of it alive, delighted to be able to drink themselves stone blind in the scruffy little village of Cincinnati, overjoyed to get home, see little Margaret, and default on their taxes again. And given my deep personal obligations to two particular levies, I'm the last person who should criticize whatever it was they did to keep themselves *in* the world for which Colonel Darke found them so unsuitable.

Neither William nor Ralph went far after that bender in Cincinnati, and they may have gone together. Both ended up in a rolling stretch of knob country on the northern edge of the Bluegrass that was eventually called Grant County, next door to Pendleton, where Ralph soon married William's daughter Margaret, more than twenty years his junior, and both men were soon eluding the tax collector again.

But Ralph was more willing to talk about his wartime experience than William ever was. At least once he seems to have been hoping for some profit out of his tale. More than forty years after the battle on the Wabash, in a pension application he submitted when he was seventy-two, he made a point of telling Grant County officials that in addition to serving in the militia during the Revolution—when he'd participated in the siege of Yorktown and helped guard the British prisoners after their surrender—he'd taken part in "what is generally known as St. Clairs Campaign [and] he was under Captain Dark for nine [i.e., six] months and with him at the defeat of St. Clair."[69]

Although he must have known that postwar enlistments didn't count toward a pension, he may have hoped his story would win him some extra credit. (It didn't, and since his Revolutionary service fell short, he didn't qualify for the government payments.) But he also seems to have simply enjoyed relating his tale, or at least some judiciously selected parts of it. He certainly told it to his children, who were themselves happy to spread the story of their father's survival in so dramatic and lethal a battle. In 1836 Ralph's sixth child, twenty-three-year-old John Collins, left the rest of the family behind and emigrated with his new wife to what would become Scotland County, Missouri. John ended up making a very respectable life for himself as a self-taught judge and seems not to have kept in close touch with his Kentucky kin; his name wasn't even mentioned in his father's 1847 will. But in a local history of Scotland County published in 1887, John's short biography, doubtless written with his own collaboration, carefully mentioned not just his son the congressman and his son the college president but also his father the soldier who "took part in the battle in which Gen. St. Clair was defeated."[70] As inexplicable as Ralph's own unscathed survival is the persistence of a story about a brief century-old battle fought by a man three hundred miles distant and forty years dead, a humiliating butchery of a battle redeemed by no heroics and won by the wrong side, a battle that possessed none of the historic luster of the Yorktown siege in which Ralph had also taken part and that had long since been eclipsed by the monumental conflict in which two of John's own sons had defended the Union, one at the cost of his life.

We don't know exactly *what* Ralph had told his family about his war, though their enduring pride in his participation suggests an emphasis on something a good deal nobler than a court-martial for desertion, something a good deal more complimentary than Colonel Darke's report. So we can presume that whatever the tale, Ralph had felt freer than his father-in-law, William Wharton, to put his own mark on his history.

Knowing nothing about the character of the two men, we can only guess at what made the difference. Ralph was some fifteen years younger than William. He lived long enough to see that the Indians' triumph over St. Clair was the last consequential victory over white America the eastern tribes would ever savor. He had been publicly punished with a stern sentence of one hundred lashes for failing in a desperate malefaction that dozens of his comrades had gotten away with, an event that could well have inspired in him an enduring antagonism toward figures of authority. His children, and perhaps he too, were Baptists, a denomination of increasing importance in Kentucky. His wife outlived him. Maybe most suggestive: his children and grandchildren outdid him. William Wharton's daughters don't seem to have loved any more wisely or chosen any more fortunately than their mother had. Nancy died young and probably "sullied," Jean left no trace past childhood, Margaret married the unprepossessing Ralph, and Elizabeth's husband was both impecunious and illiterate.

But like their brother John, most of Ralph Collins's other children left their father in the dust. In 1850 John's youngest brother, Joseph H. "Hamp," then thirty-four and a farmer, was able to report a respectable net worth of $2,000; ten years later he was worth more than $3,000, and by 1870 a handsome $12,575. He supported his mother until she died in the 1860s at around eighty, and in 1902 he himself was laid to rest in the Oak Ridge Baptist Cemetery in Grant County under a headstone substantial enough to survive to this day. The other Collins brother, William, also reported rising fortunes, and had either education or assurance enough to acquire a license to sell books and maps besides. Their sister Mary married into a substantial farm family, and a third sister, Jane Collins, had one respectable husband anyway, Joseph Daugherty, the father of her children. Though he was famously ornery, he was also generally provident, literate, healthy, her senior in age, presentable enough to win election to public office, and traditional enough to end their union in the old-fashioned way— with his death. All of that would make him look a prize catch compared to the next husband who came along for her.[71]

Since much of the success Ralph's children enjoyed seems to have flowered only after the patriarch's death, it was probably not their rising fortunes that were responsible for emboldening Ralph into some ex post facto raising of his own fortunes as well. But perhaps the relationship between his stories and their happiness was something a bit more subtle and more intricate. William Wharton's children never did any better than their father had any reason to expect; they got, precisely, their just deserts, at least in his eyes. But Ralph, who from somewhere had found the self-assurance to tell his own story his own way, was in effect laying claim to his right to damn the Colonel Darkes of the world and to create not just a story but also a life of his own choosing. Maybe a man with the spunk to recalibrate the justice of his own deserts could provide the jolt of inspiration his children needed to believe they too could succeed in their pursuit of happiness. Maybe creating a family memory had the power to shape the family fortunes as well.

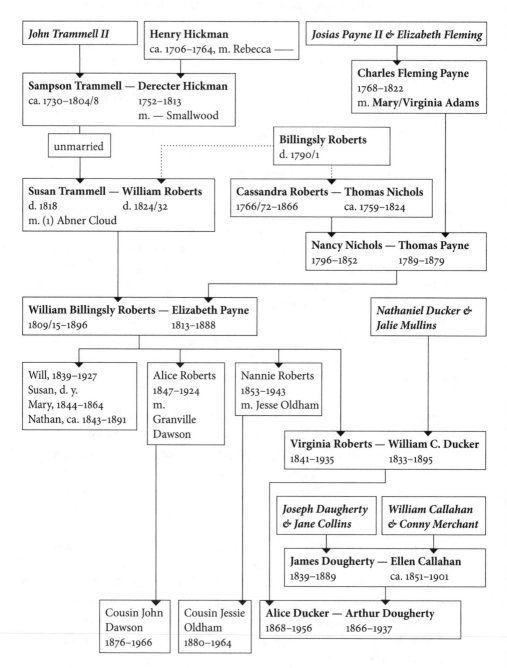

Names in **bold** represent direct ancestors; names in *italics* have been introduced in a previous tree. Other names are included only if relevant. The exact connections to Billingsly Roberts are unclear.

CHAPTER 5
The Civil War, Real and Unreal

⚓

Honor

Two stories about the civil war:

The first is a classic, often retold in the standard histories. About a year and a half after the beginning of the war, southern forces led by General Braxton Bragg and Major General Edmund Kirby Smith mounted a two-pronged invasion of Kentucky intended to win the deeply divided border state for the Confederacy. In mid-September 1862, two southern brigades moved to seize and destroy the long railroad bridge over the Green River at Munfordville, a vital but vulnerable link on the crucial Louisville & Nashville line. The bridge was defended by a Union garrison under the command of Colonel John T. Wilder, a thirty-two-year-old foundry owner from Indiana who brought far more enthusiasm than experience to his military appointment.

To the surprise of both sides, Wilder and his equally raw men briskly fought off the attack, killing or wounding more than seven hundred of the enemy, according to the colonel's (over)estimate at the time, and taking just thirty-seven casualties of their own. Wilder was gracious in his unexpected victory, exchanging half a dozen notes with the defeated brigadier general James Chalmers to arrange the precise terms for the safe retrieval of the wounded on both sides and even lending shovels to the enemy troops so they could bury their dead. "Hoping that when we cross swords again," the southerner wrote his northern foe as he prepared to withdraw his men, "I may be able to render you a similar service, I remain, very respectfully, James R. Chalmers."[1]

J. T. Wilder, Bv't.-Brig. General: the chivalrous warrior. Library of Congress, Prints and Photographs Division, Washington, D.C., LC-USZ62-113167.

Just two days later, however, Wilder's men found themselves again besieged, this time by a much bigger Confederate force led by the irascible Bragg, who sent a note informing the Union men that "in all candor, no chance exists for your escape, successful resistance, or re-enforcement." He offered them an honorable surrender, "which will prevent an unnecessary effusion of blood."[2]

Loath to abandon the vital bridge, hoping to stall long enough for promised reinforcements to get through, Wilder was also uncertain how to tell whether the enemy was bluffing. So the Union colonel asked for advice—from another of his Confederate enemies, Major General Simon Bolivar Buckner, who was commanding some of the very troops waiting out there on the riverbank to kill him. Blindfolded and under a flag of truce, Wilder turned up that night at the southern general's bivouac, explaining that being new to command and anxious to do his duty, and having been assured that Buckner was a gentleman, "I come to you to find out what I ought to do."[3]

Buckner was charmed. Although he declined to offer direct advice, he proposed taking Wilder on a tour of the besiegers' positions so his visitor could judge their strength for himself, and he carefully refused to allow Wilder to tell him anything about the strength of the Union forces. "I wouldn't have deceived that man under those circumstances for anything," Buckner would tell the delegation of Tennessee newspapermen come nearly half a century later to interview "the last surviving lieutenant general" of the Confederacy.[4]

After accompanying Buckner on an inspection of the dozens of guns and tens of thousands of troops prepared to assault the garrison, Wilder came to his unhappy conclusion. "Being satisfied," as he wrote in his official after-action report, "that further resistance was no less than willful murder of the brave men who had so long contested with overwhelming numbers, I determined . . . to surrender the entire force, which I did on Wednesday morning at 2 a.m., marching out of the works at 6 a.m. with all the honors of war, drums beating and colors flying, we being allowed by the terms of surrender our side-arms and all private property and four days' rations."[5] The bridge was destroyed, the captured officers and men were soon exchanged for enemy prisoners and returned to the field, and just days after the capitulation of their garrison, Union forces were back in Munfordville. Wilder's delay in surrendering helped save Louisville for the North, since it distracted Bragg long enough to allow Major General Don Carlos Buell's exhausted and famished Union troops time for a final desperate push that got them to that key city first.

The defender of Munfordville went on to earn more accolades for leading a heroic action at Hoover's Gap during the Tullahoma campaign in Middle Tennessee, and he distinguished himself at the awful battle of Chickamauga as well. He was promoted to brigadier general, though illness forced him to resign his commission six months before the war ended. After the peace Wilder took up residence among his former foes, in Chattanooga, where he served briefly as mayor and ran a successful ironworks. Wilder's own description of the Munfordville siege, which he offered in a talk to a military fraternity around the same time that Buckner had his chat with the Tennessee journalists, included none of the adorable indecision that Buckner had described and much more steely resolve on his own part not to let the enemy hoodwink him, but otherwise the versions were similar. Late in life he took as his second and much younger wife a relative of Robert E. Lee. He died peacefully on a visit to Florida at the age of eighty-seven.[6]

The second story I came across only recently, sitting in the hush of the National Archives' Central Research Room in Washington, D.C., and surrounded by researchers bent reverently over scraps of yellowed paper spread out under bankers' lamps on gleaming wood desks. Out of a flaking envelope I drew the thick sheaf of papers submitted throughout the 1880s by my great-great-grandfather James Dougherty, son of the ornery old pioneer Joseph Daugherty (James chose the aberrant spelling himself), in which he begged the government to compensate him properly for the disabilities he'd been suffering ever since his three years' service as a steadily promoted junior officer in the Eighteenth Kentucky Infantry (U.S.A.).

In a supporting affidavit submitted in 1880, James's former regimental surgeon declared that he'd treated Captain Dougherty for "Camp diarhoea which after continuing on him some time involved his whole digestive apparatus—his liver particularly being obstinate in the performance of its functions." James himself declared in his formal statement that the illness had been brought on by bad food and unhealthy camp conditions during the summer of 1863, when he too was fighting in the Tullahoma campaign in which Colonel Wilder had earned such acclaim. From that time forward, he said, he'd suffered from "sevier Diarrhea" and other digestive troubles accompanied by trembling, "weakness and quaking of the mussels," "coated tongue, sweling around the body, sevier head ache with some nervious feelings," and "hedious dreams when asleep depression when awake." A parade of neighbors, former comrades in arms, and doctors submitted corroborating evidence: yes, before the war he'd been healthy and able-bodied, but now the poor soul was a wreck. He had giddy spells, his appetite was bad, his rectum was "deeply ulcerated and very sensitive on account of internal hemorrhoids," and he was "troubled with a constant flatulence; discharg[ing] gases continuously."[7]

Constant flatulence. There I sat in the National Archives, that great treasury of America's founding documents, and from a paper carefully preserved for 125 years I learned another story about the war for the soul of the nation: it left my great-great-grandfather plagued by chronic hemorrhoids and unable to stop farting.

The Munfordville episode almost made me fall in love with war, or this war anyway. As ugly and brutal as the Civil War was, it could also inspire the occasional episode of gallantry and grace harking back to the ritualized dance of preindustrial cabinet warfare, a high-stakes game governed by stately rules that both winner and loser could be trusted to honor. The deadliest foes could agree on certain eternal truths: even triumph could be temperate, even carnage could be orderly, even defeat deserved its drums, even the most lethal passions were no excuse for bad behavior. As Buckner's biographer later put it, the incident at the bridge proved "not only that both were gentlemen of high order but also that war need not stoop to unnecessary horror."[8] He was writing in 1940, when the appearance of the word "unnecessary" in the same sentence as "horror" and "war" would never again sound anything but quaint. Now, in our era of total war and ephemeral truths, some of our enduring fascination with the Civil War lies in the heartbreaking innocence summed up by the story of General Buckner and Colonel Wilder.

Then again: flatulence for life. James's story is a useful corrective, an indisputable reminder that the same war that brought to some the heady gift of glory and to others the solemn balm of drums also brought ruin to hundreds of thousands of lives. My great-great-grandfather suffered under the double burden of afflictions both risible and debilitating, which obviously cost him dearly in comfort, independence, achievement, and happiness. Every single day they reminded him of the different life the war had lost him—the plain old *ordinary* life that would never be his.

Yet James was one of the lucky ones. He came home, while 750,000 or more others did not—about the same toll, proportional to the population, as if some 7.5 million American soldiers never returned from the wars in Afghanistan and Iraq.[9] Women were widowed before they knew their husbands, children were orphaned without ever meeting their fathers, parents mourned the grandparents they'd never be. That war clawed holes out of the world, and even now, a century and a half later, if you happen upon a newspaper from the era, with its columns and columns of names in tiny type under the heading "KILLED," you can still taste the absence, the *missingness,* that hollowed out the landscape in which so many men were *not there* anymore.

And those absences have never healed; to this day the world is different, shrunken, in ways we can only guess. What tender lovers, what kind neighbors, what inspired teachers never got to leave their gentle footprints on the world? What keen writers, what wise doctors, what courageous politicians, what splendid athletes, what visionary reformers, what quirky inventors were robbed of their destinies by bullets and shells? Mark Twain put his toe into that war and fled it, Oliver Wendell Holmes was wounded three times and survived it—but what more trenchant humorist died in the hospital tent of camp fever before he ever saw action, what more brilliant judge bled out his life trapped in the Sunken Road? How can we ever comprehend how much was lost?

"The real war," wrote Walt Whitman, who on his frequent hospital visits to comfort the wounded witnessed as much loss as anyone, "will never get in the books." Certainly the real unhappiness of the war did not often get in the books, or at least not in the stories told afterwards by one particular breed of people who had the deepest connections to what was probably both the unhappiest and the most storied event in American history.[10]

Like many Kentucky families, mine turned out to have a direct ancestor on each side of the conflict. Both were enthusiastic volunteers, both went into battle and came out alive, both spent brief stints as prisoners of war. Both were longtime residents of Falmouth in Pendleton County. One of them would live just long enough to see a real-life version of that classic curtain-closer of melodrama, when the Reb's granddaughter Alice married Arthur, the Yankee's son. And the stories that survive about their wars were as different in spirit and outlook as their speedily divorcing offspring turned out to be. Only one of the soldiers clearly acknowledged being just as unhappy.

James Dougherty, Grace's paternal grandfather, had been an eager soldier, signing up to defend the Union at almost the first moment he could. During the summer of 1861, when as a deeply divided border state Kentucky was still clinging to the hope that if it didn't officially declare for either side it could stay out of the war, the twenty-one-year-old James joined his county's Home Guard company, formed as protection against the strongly secessionist State Guard militia. And that October, just weeks after the tit-for-tat incursions into the state by both Rebels and Federals that finally killed neutrality and unleashed the recruiters, James traveled down to Paris to enlist as a private in Company D of the Eighteenth Kentucky.[11]

In February 1862, as the war heated up, W. B. Roberts, Grace's maternal great-grandfather, ran away to become a soldier. Like other of his comrades in arms, he seems to have allowed his enthusiasm for that lot to carry him into a lie; if Private William Billingsly Roberts had given his real age, I think the army would have sent our fire-eater straight back home to his family. That's because when Private Roberts enrolled in the service of the Confederate States of America, he was somewhere in the neighborhood of fifty, with a medical practice, a wife, and six children, four of them underage, and to join the Twentieth Arkansas Infantry he had traveled some seven hundred miles from Falmouth to the minuscule town of Centerville in a remote and savage corner of the Ozarks that the word "godforsaken" could have been invented to describe. Though he was far from the oldest private in the army—a North Carolina regiment accepted a seventy-three-year-old as a substitute—his birthdays would always keep him ahead of the increasing draft age, and he would never have been subject to conscription for active duty.[12] W. B. *chose* to enlist.

So I knew right from the beginning of my research: W. B., the loser, would have the better stories. Everyone knows them, the kinds of stories that pay no attention to who won, or rather that redefine the whole idea of "winning" into something so low and distasteful no decent person would want it. Stolidly indestructible, or perhaps perversely irresistible, the dreamy myth of the Lost Cause long ago migrated all the way north to the very homes and hearths of some of the conquerors, and seeped deep into their consciousness, too: no other era of American history has lodged so firmly in the collective memory or so profligately awarded credentials to folks who want to help remember it.

The children and grandchildren of the victors at Gettysburg and Appomattox seem to have been delighted to join the heirs of their defeated foe and to revel together in novels, songs, stage plays, and, eventually, movies, in which The Colonel, splendid in epaulettes and plumes, swings lightly into the saddle on a sun-dappled morning and rides off all doomed and gallant toward his rendezvous with the Peach Orchard or the Hornets' Nest. In which his noble wife, still every inch a lady despite having made a burnt offering of her alabaster skin working like a man to get the cotton in by herself, charms or bamboozles the simian blue-clad marauders away from the hiding places of the family silver and the last surviving pig. In which the faithful darkies, led by a ponderous "Mammy," scornfully reject all that ignorant Yankee nonsense about emancipation and choose instead to stay with the white folks whom in their simple childlike way they love so well. In which the possession that the rosy-cheeked soldier boy most fears to lose is his mother's letter or his sweetheart's curl, not his legs, his nerve, or his griping bowels.

And oh, that cast of leading characters! The saintly Marse Robert, the godly Leonidas Polk, the dapper P. G. T. Beauregard, the dashing Jeb Stuart, the tragic James Longstreet, the nobly dilapidated John Bell Hood, the swashbuckling John Singleton Mosby, the adorable George Pickett, and the magnificently oddball Stonewall Jackson, who sometimes rode into battle holding one hand over his head to keep his blood in balance (and who died after Chancellorsville from the effects of friendly-fire wounds to his left arm). Meanwhile, batting for the Yankees were "Beast" Butler and the monstrous Sherman, "Old Fuss and Feathers" Scott and the dithery McClellan, and Ulysses Simpson Grant, surly, untidy, and drunk, who, the legendeers assured us, prevailed only through luck, greater numbers, and an inhuman indifference to killing his own men as wantonly as he did the enemy's. Yes, it was Grant who had left the little brick house in Appomattox Courthouse with the enemy's capitulation in his hand. But the lasting image of the surrender, with the victorious Union general showing up swordless, rumpled, muddy, and muttering something about his misplaced luggage while Robert E. Lee shone forth all spotless and dignified in red sash and saber, is by itself a perfect icon of the charm of the Lost Cause and the unnarratable grubbiness of victory.

An exemplary son of the Lost Cause was our old friend Henry Morton Woodson, Potato Hole's fifth-great-grandson, who had immortalized the story of John, Sarah, and the American Indians' assault on Jamestown in the big family book he published in 1915, the year of the rebirth of the Ku Klux Klan. While he'd been diligent in mining the archives for bits of information about those earliest ancestors, by the time the elderly Confederate veteran had carried his family tree far enough forward to encompass the generations who had lived through the war, and could gather their tales from their own hands or the hands of their loved ones, Henry's excitement was palpable and his volume full of stories about the Civil War of his kin, and mine.

Those later pages brimmed with model Lost Cause characters. There were the faithful former slaves who after their emancipation proudly clung to the Woodson family name. There was the "sublime devotion" of the fair sex to the Confederate cause, as shown by the Mississippi ladies who tenderly nursed a young Woodson wounded far from his Kentucky home and with "tearful eyes and sorrowing hearts" ensured that the brave "martyr for his country's cause" did not die alone. There was a remarkable number of bold soldier boys who after suffering the mortification of capture redeemed their sullied honor by outwitting the oblivious Yankee with daring stratagems for escape. William David Woodson, for instance, walked out of the Johnson's Island prison with a forged pass and a borrowed blue coat; Henry's own future brother-in-law Joseph Britton Duke strolled out of the Memphis jail after blackening his face and hands with cork and picking up the dinner tray; and the hale and hearty Walter Nelson Woodson didn't seem a whit abashed at how he got out of

Elmira: having traded names with a very ill friend in return for a box of tobacco, he was released in October 1864 in an exchange of the sickest prisoners. The tobacco, probably sold rather than smoked, may actually have done the sick friend some good. He apparently survived long enough to be exchanged a few months later under Walter's name.[13]

Some of the other Woodson stories were completely and confirmably about an *unreal* war, but that seems to have troubled no one. The sister of Hugh Ardinger reported that he'd enlisted at fourteen in the cavalry unit of the dashing raider John Hunt Morgan, was captured and sent to the "prison on 'Bloody Island' in the Mississippi River," and escaped by stealing a skiff and rowing himself to St. Louis. His official military records, however, show that he served only fifteen months, in a unglamorous Tennessee infantry company, before being discharged, apparently because of his youth; there is no record of capture or imprisonment. But by the time Henry Woodson came around asking for family stories, poor Hugh had been gone for decades, having died at thirty-three, childless and unmarried, in a drowning accident while working as a miner in Colorado.[14] Nothing could have been more conventional than for his aged sister to respond to her inquiring kinsman with a tale that added a classically heroic punctuation mark to an abbreviated life of unfulfilled promise.

Then as now, most Civil War stories were about much more than the Civil War itself, which is part of the reason why so many survive to this day and much of the reason why they can still be provocative and defiant. A southern friend of mine recently related a story he'd often been told by a Georgia family so old and tradition-bound that the grandmother had never in her entire life consented to touch her lips to a Coca-Cola, which she ranked right up there with William Tecumseh Sherman as responsible for the extermination of everything that was genteel and gracious about the Old South in general and about Atlanta, the hustling New South city where the stuff is bottled, in particular. The Georgians claim descent from the Confederate officer who was supposed to have shot down the one-armed Union major general Phil Kearny during the wild and storm-drenched battle of Chantilly. According to the Union Army's official report, "General Kearny rode forward alone to reconnoiter in his usual gallant, not to say reckless, manner, and came upon a rebel regiment. In attempting to escape he was killed."[15] In other words: shot in the back off his horse while doing something dumb.

The death of the widely admired Kearny shook even his foes. A. P. Hill mourned that "poor Kearny" had "deserved a better death than this," and

Robert E. Lee himself ordered the body escorted back to Union lines under a flag of truce. The old Georgia family my friend knew, however, has never been guilty of such mawkish sentimentality. They cherish a coda to the tale of their ancestor's deed, a well-known and resolutely imperishable coda, I later discovered, which Kearny's embalmers had tried gamely to refute with a notice in the newspapers just days after his death, which Kearny's grandson was still denying, vociferously, in the biography he published in 1937, and which has even popped up in Internet chat rooms on the Civil War. Although the seat of the dead general's trousers was torn to ribbons, so the deathless story goes, no bloodstains or bullet holes marked his skin. The ball had perfectly and precisely buggered him.[16]

"You want to know what the Civil War was all about?" my southern friend asked me. "I'll tell you. For all the years I knew her, this old grandmother, this perfect southern lady, kept telling that story about exactly how her granddaddy did that Yankee in, and she cackled and gloated about it, too, every time."

Yet while many of these stories are undoubtedly contentious, as artifacts of the great crisis that forever darkened America's cherished image of its own fresh and youthful promise they often carry complex messages about American happiness. That's exactly what the little splinters of stories about my own aging fire-eater Private W. B. Roberts of the Twentieth Arkansas did when I found them in a copy of an old letter that turned up among my grandmother Grace's papers. In 1958 Grace's cousin Lillian had written to an eighty-two-year-old relative from their parents' generation asking for family recollections, and old Cousin John Dawson had responded with a single page of memories of "Grandpa Roberts" and his two soldier sons. Like many of the most interesting stories, his reminiscences about his older relatives ended up revealing a little bit about their ostensible subjects and a great deal more about the storyteller himself, his own relationship to the war, and his family's efforts to recalibrate their happiness when the fighting was over and the boys (and middle-aged men) came home.

Kentucky Graycoats

Cousin John may have been laconic as a storyteller, but he was positively lousy as a biographer; his letter added virtually nothing substantial to the few provable facts we were ever able to unearth about my great-great-great-grandfather William Billingsly Roberts. His life spanned almost the whole of the increasingly well documented nineteenth century, and even sent ripples into mine: I knew people who had known his children. But for a man so nearly modern, his trail remained strangely elusive and his biography full of contradictions, enigmas, and holes.

From what we did know and could deduce, W. B., as he usually called himself, seemed in some ways a perfect embodiment of traditional American values: a self-made man, a defiant individualist, a protector of widows and orphans, a fervent patriot according to his own definition. He also compiled what seems, in retrospect at least, a perfect record of ill luck, bad choices, and missed opportunities: he was orphaned young and widowed too soon, he was summary in his education and unsettled in his profession, he never made any money, he was disappointed in his children, he didn't go west, he sided against the North. He would have had, it seems, every reason to consider his life unhappy. Even though Cousin John doesn't seem to have agreed.

W. B. was born between 1809 and 1815, probably in Montgomery County, Maryland, not far from the swampy new federal city of Washington, D.C., where his mother, Susan Trammell, had lived with her first husband and their five children. His father, William, was a Maryland farmer and trader who had evident but indecipherable ties to a far-flung Roberts clan full of people named Billingsly and Cassandra, but his most common of names makes him almost impossible to trace further with any certainty.[17] The only child of his parents' marriage, W. B. lost his mother when he was a child and his father sometime between 1824 and 1832, whereupon he was sent with his rich uncle Henry Roberts to take up farming in northern Kentucky.

The last of my kin to make the trek inland from the old coastal states, W. B. found Kentucky to be a very different country from the one my Conways and Daughertys and Ballards and Paynes had encountered when they came pioneering over the mountains. Supplanted as "the West" by farther Wests, no longer that last, chaotic place before the untravelable places, Kentucky had become noticeably civilized, its dark ground bloody no longer but instead bursting with tobacco, hemp, and the deep-tinged grass that built the strong muscle and sturdy bone of the Kentucky Thoroughbred. And in the center of the Bluegrass lay the "Athens of the West," as Lexington's hopeful boosters had taken to calling their bumptious town. It was home to dozens of taverns and whorehouses as well as to a philosophical society, a lively book trade, a flourishing industry in hemp processing, the West's first college, and, in 1817, what has often been called the first American performance of a Beethoven symphony, conducted by a wandering Bohemian violinist who was inspired by the fresh romantic grandeur of the West into composing such deathless works as "Yankee Doodliead," the "Barbecue Divertimento," and a soaring, only half-mock-heroic oratorio on the death of Joan Buff, "who died, alas, from taking snuff."[18]

The Athens of the West beckoned the young W. B., too, who as a young man in the early 1830s left his uncle Henry's farm for a job in the big city making rope and bags. But in a familiar reprise of the classic American story, the young man found the promise of city life hollow and the rewards few. With the peak of the hemp boom long since over by then, his first career choice wasn't a terribly perspicacious one, and he soon returned home and succumbed to the family tradition of farming.

In 1838 he married Elizabeth Payne of Woodford County, a second-or-so cousin through the gnarly knot of Robertses, who were also kin to Elizabeth's maternal grandmother, the long-lived Cassandra Roberts Nichols. But on her father's side Elizabeth brought a shred of ancestral glory to the marriage: her Payne forebears "were *somebody*," as my great-grandmother Alice used to tell her granddaughters, dreamily. Exactly *who* that somebody was Alice didn't seem to know, although if she'd thought about it she might have gotten a hint from the persistence of the name "Virginia" through generations of little Payne girls, right down to one of her own granddaughters, my aunt. Everyone seems to have looked on the name more as an accident of birth, however—a family dimple—than as a message from the past.

But within half a century of their arrival, most of the Payne family had given up on Kentucky, too. Around 1840 my fourth-great-grandparents Thomas and Nancy Nichols Payne and as many as eleven of their twelve children followed the path chosen by thousands of other Kentuckians who had grown increasingly unhappy with their promised land, the path embraced by Daniel Boone himself decades earlier, the path that some of my Conway and Collins and Ducker and Nichols and Callahan and Roberts and Hickman cousins were also choosing: they were pursuing their happiness farther west yet, to Missouri this time, where a man could still, perhaps, cherish the hope that there, at last, the milk and honey, or at least a clear title to some fruitful acres, might spring forth for *him*. The Paynes pressed on nearly as far west as they could go without pressing out of the United States entirely, to Lafayette County, by then a well-settled region past its raw youth and abounding with hemp, tobacco, slaves, native Kentuckians, and southern sympathies. There nearly all of the members of the family would eventually die.

All but two. The oldest son, Augustus Payne, who was in his mid-twenties, stayed there only a year or so before changing his mind and going back to Kentucky, where the oldest daughter, Elizabeth Payne Roberts, and her husband, W. B., had stayed all along.[19]

Whatever it was about their new western home Augustus didn't like, his decision was a landmark in the family story. When his chosen West failed him, he didn't try somewhere else fresh, like the newest frontier territories of Wisconsin or Iowa; he didn't root himself more deeply in the South, in the still raw-boned state of Arkansas or even in the foreign country of Texas; he didn't grasp the big chance and join the daring pioneers who were beginning to set out on the great trek to California or Oregon. When the West failed him, he turned around and went back east, back where his sister and her husband had chosen to stay all along. And that decision to return to the very same Kentucky dust the other Paynes had so recently shaken off their feet marked the end of my family's pioneer spirit—their U-turn off America's most classic road to happiness and the end of that great idea that they could fix anything just by *moving on* toward the sunset. The other Paynes never left Missouri, either; not one of my direct ancestors or closest relatives was ever to settle anywhere farther west than the center of the country.

So after 1841 the Paynes and their offspring—the *somebodies'* branch of the family that reached all the way back to some of the very first Europeans ever to stake their lives and futures on North America—would never again have a new family story about moving westward. All they had was the old one about the time Augustus Payne came *back* from a West already well settled and civilized (in an odyssey neither daring nor uncomfortable, most of it possible by steamboat) to the place his sister Elizabeth Roberts had never even left. As other families continued to weave new epics, my family's old stories grew older yet and, in comparison, less compelling. By the 1840s, three of the Payne siblings' grandparents—the generation that had pioneered to Kentucky—were long dead. The last, their interminable grandmother Cassandra Nichols, was so antique as to cast her youthful adventures into America's most useless category: ancient history. When she finally died, her obituary acknowledged briefly that she'd been one of her county's earliest settlers but seemed much more impressed that in her long life she'd never seen a doctor. I wonder whether the Paynes still cherished the belief that *someday* they'd just pick up and go—or whether, as the years went by and the local soil wore out, the sawmills and wool-carding factories went bust, the brimming rivers inundated streets and homes with dismaying regularity, and the burned-out inhabitants dribbled away, the pioneers' offspring looked around northern Kentucky's knob country and said, yes, this is it, we've found our paradise.

W. B. Roberts seems to have been a wanderer of a different sort, on the lookout for frontiers of another kind, but he too eventually found those frontiers to be not gates but fences. In the 1840s, after his Payne in-laws moved to Missouri, my great-great-great-grandfather became the first ancestor to take a stab at an alternative yet also classically American path to happiness, a route that sought to improve the self, not the landscape: after failing at the hemp trade and making a stab at farming, he went back to school. His entry in a local biographical encyclopedia, which was doubtless compiled with his help, states that even as a boy in Maryland and later while busy making rope in Lexington, W. B. had done some reading in medicine "at his leisure . . . with a view to ultimately entering the medical profession."[20] But he was well into his thirties, married, and a father three or four times over by the time he finally took the big step, went back to the city he'd retreated from seven or eight years earlier, and enrolled in the medical department of Lexington's Transylvania University.

Yet this first intellectual ancestor, this first to pursue a life in town rather than in the constant and sequestered drudgery of a farm, doesn't seem to have been one for the honor roll, or even, if I dare judge, to have been very happy in his studies. As a family man he was probably short of both time and money, and he deserves as much credit for perseverance and enterprise as any other grown-up aspirer who has had to carry his adult burdens along in his schoolbag. But the suspicion arises that he had neither much aptitude nor much patience for those books. W. B. told the local biographer he had studied at the university from 1848 to 1850, but Transylvania records suggest that he probably didn't finish even the first of the recommended two years, never wrote the required thesis, and never officially graduated.[21] And even though formal medical degrees weren't mandatory at the time in a profession with a long, strong tradition of practical apprenticeship, W. B.'s few months of classes could scarcely have prepared him to do much more than dose a stomachache and splint a shin.

In 1850 he left the university town and hung out his shingle in Kenton County, where he'd lived as a teenager with his uncle Henry. Eight years later he moved the practice and the family to the Pendleton County seat of Falmouth, a modest and isolated town perched on the finger of land where the South Fork splits from the Licking River. It had only recently welcomed the great wide world in the shape of the Kentucky Central Railroad, which now rumbled its way through town on the way from Covington to Lexington. But in 1861, just three years after the move to Falmouth, W. B. chucked it all again, abandoning his childhood dream of doctoring for his middle-aged dream of soldiering.

Up to that point the Robertses seem to have been reasonably conventional; other than living forever, like the alleged centenarian Cassandra Roberts Nichols, they appear never to have done anything to attract much attention, or to explain what turned W. B. into a gun-toting Rebel when he could have stayed comfortably at home with his boluses and his children. But W. B.'s ancestors on his mother's side had been a different story entirely, and suggest a glimmer of an explanation. That side of the family was a restless and rambunctious lot prone to doing things other people didn't—often things that would have gotten other people arrested. W. B.'s mother, Susan, had grown up in a household highly unorthodox for its time. She was the older daughter of Sampson Trammell and Derecter Smallwood, both of them members of prosperous and respectable landowning families, who for several decades in the late eighteenth and early nineteenth centuries in a thickly settled part of Maryland lived openly and apparently serenely together along with their four children even though they never married each other. W. B., in other words, was a son of a bastard, the offspring of a family that pursued its own particular happiness in proud defiance of the social order.

Derecter Hickman was born on the Eastern Shore around 1752 and as a child moved with her family to Frederick County. By 1776 she had married and already left or lost some unknown Smallwood, but other than her ambiguous marital status, I have never found in any court, church, or newspaper records any hint of the circumstances behind her peculiar relationship with Sampson or any explanation as to how they got away with it.[22] It's yet another of those "Musgraves" that tantalizes the imagination but forever eludes explanation.

One possibility to imagine: Sampson was just too bad-tempered for anyone to dare challenge him. Contrarianism, turbulence, and ill luck do seem to have been family traits. Throughout America, throughout its history, people named "Trammell" in its various spellings—many of them confirmable descendants of one John Trammell, born sometime before Bacon's Rebellion in the rough frontier Virginia county of Stafford and father of seven remarkably fecund sons— have been demonstrating a luxuriant record of defiant or violent behavior. Just the Arkansas and Texas branches of the family alone produced copy enough to populate an entire website of "Trammell Tragedies": Trammells killed by bushwhackers, by Jayhawkers, by drunks, by trains, by policemen, by mad dogs, by stepsons, by jailhouse fires, by Indians, by suicide, by drowning. They were reported to have died in every war, even the most exclusive ones, including the Alamo and the so-called Big Neck War with the Ioway Indians in 1829 at a Missouri settlement named Cabins of White Folks, in which Captain William Trammell accounted for one-quarter of the white death toll. Two of Sampson's nephews emigrated to the Ohio country and were killed by Indians, though their descendants don't agree over whether they were shot down in ambushes, killed in battle, or burned together at the stake. And in the twenty years after the Civil War on a farm in Pope County, Illinois, Harvey Moss's personal harem of Trammell women—his legal wife, née Minerva Trammell; her sister-in-law Susan Trammell Russell; and Susan's two daughters—gave him a total of at least eighteen legitimate and illegitimate children.[23]

Sampson Trammell, W. B.'s unwed grandfather, fit right into the family. He was sued by his siblings over his handling of their inheritance; his bound laborer was taken away by the county because he had treated the boy so badly; he once disciplined a slave for some unknown infraction by cutting off his ear; and when he was deep into his eighties he was apparently expelled for unspecified reasons by the local Methodist conference, which only a year earlier had admitted him to "full connection."[24] But the tempestuous Sampson did his duty by all of his children and by Derecter, too (whose peculiar name had flourished, unexplained, on the Eastern Shore for a century before her birth), and their nonmarital relationship was officially recorded and publicly acknowledged. In a deed of gift signed with his mark in 1793, Sampson, "in consideration of the natural affection I bear for this person hereafter mentioned and two shillings to me in hand," deeded all his real and personal property to Derecter Smallwood, who was to be in charge of managing the estate "for her and my comfortable support" until her youngest child married or reached twenty-one. In 1804 he put his mark to another and even more explicit deed providing for "the said Derecter and for the children of her by the said Trammel begotten." Older than Derecter by about twenty-five years, he died between five and nine years before she did.[25]

W. B. and his ancestors *might* just have been ordinary Americans for their time, average people facing the myriad risks and temptations of life in a youthful nation. But a psychohistorian could suggest another possible explanation for this persistent, generations-long pattern of turbulent and unconventional behavior: a family story. The family therapist John Byng-Hall once explained in an interview that his work exploring the profound influence of family legends and traditions on descendants' behavior—what he called the "family script"—was inspired by his own experience with a story he'd often heard as a child about a notorious fourth-great-uncle who had commanded the under-manned and unaggressive British squadron that was defeated by the French in the battle of Minorca in 1756.

In a court-martial afterwards, Admiral John Byng was convicted of negligence under the Articles of War and sentenced to death by firing squad. Public opinion was widely and vigorously opposed to the execution; it was seen as unfair, a political scapegoating, a draconian overreaction to an error in judgment. Byng's own relatives, however, were made of sterner stuff. According to the story *they* told young Byng-Hall, the admiral had been shot on his foredeck for cowardice. The Byng family's lasting preoccupation with the story, Byng-Hall concluded, had made cowardice and bravery into "a central issue" among his male relatives and had inspired several of them to feats of derring-do as foolhardy as they were conspicuous.[26] Whatever ancient story of provocation and peril the Trammells might have been telling, whatever adventure or misadventure (or misunderstood adventure) of old John and his seven sons anchored their sense of themselves, is now forever lost, but W. B.'s defiant rush toward the fury of battle at his unconventional age seems to have made him, too, a typical Trammell.

Kentucky offered a congenial home for the turbulent spirit; the state that is still about as far north as you can go in the South was a particularly vexed place to endure the war. Though Unionists far outnumbered southern sympathizers and the state never did secede, thousands of its citizens pretended that it had. Confederate supporters set up a capital of their own at Bowling Green and installed two governors in turn, the first of whom was killed in battle and the second forced to flee. As a prize both strategic and symbolic, lusted after by Union and Confederacy alike, the state was invaded by both armies and ravaged by raiders and guerrillas from both sides. Rebels torched courthouses, Federals executed southern recruiters, and freelance renegades took advantage of the confusion to loot anyone and everyone.

In the Robertses' new home county of Pendleton in the northern knob country, where the land was poorer and hillier, the farms smaller, and unfree laborers scarcer than in the socially, economically, and geographically central Bluegrass region, the political passions were particularly heated but also peculiarly balanced. Eighty percent of the county's potential voters turned out for the 1860 presidential election, compared to about 67 percent in the state as a whole. Of them, W. B. Roberts and 806 other Pendletonians, or about 45 percent, chose the breakaway Southern Democrat John C. Breckinridge, who pledged to protect slavery, while nearly as many—758, or about 43 percent—went for the Constitutional Unionist candidate, John Bell, who pledged to protect the Union. (The Northern Democrat, Stephen A. Douglas, had not quite 13 percent of the total, and Abraham Lincoln earned the support of exactly two Pendleton voters. Which wasn't so bad, considering that 36 of Kentucky's 110 counties recorded not a single vote for the native son whose presumed birthplace near Hodgenville would later become, literally, a shrine.)[27]

Pendleton contributed its share of Confederate soldiers as well as sympathizers, activists, and martyrs, among them a handful of DeMossville women who were detained on suspicion of spying for the South and a father of nine randomly executed in retaliation for the murder of a Union supporter. To this day a plaque on the grounds of the state capitol at Frankfort commemorates the official killing of Pendleton's own Thornton Lafferty.[28]

But Pendleton also sent hundreds of its sons, brothers, and fathers to fight for the North, and in the name of the old GAR camp at Falmouth was commemorated another local martyr, this one a Yankee. Abram Wileman had only recently been promoted to major of the Eighteenth Kentucky, leaving his old post as captain of Company D to be filled by James Dougherty. On the evening of October 5, 1863, as the major was recuperating at home from a wound suffered at Chickamauga, a small group of armed men burst into his parlor and hustled him outside. They stripped him nearly naked, beat him with rifle butts, shot him in the head, and then cut a finger off the battered corpse to get at a heavy gold ring. Twenty-year-old Frances Peter, a staunch Unionist who kept a close eye on the war from her home in Lexington, recorded the major's murder in her diary as "only one of many [outrages] that have been committed by the people of Pendleton and the neighboring counties." The "secesh of Pendleton," she wrote, were "perfect savages."[29]

The discord that tortured Kentucky as a whole had its echo in many of Kentucky's families, my extended Nichols-Payne-Roberts clan being a perfect example. The matriarch, Cassandra Roberts Nichols of Harrison County, who was Elizabeth's grandmother as well as a paternal relative of W. B.'s, was certifiably venerable even if she didn't quite make that hundredth birthday she was credited with. As a tiny girl in Montgomery County, Maryland, Cassandra had watched her neighbors in ragged coats take up arms against British invaders in red ones. She spent the very last years of her life watching her great-grandsons in gray coats take up arms against other great-grandsons in blue ones, and died at last less than a year after Appomattox. Her husband, Thomas Nichols, who died more than forty years before she did, may in the end have been the lucky one: he did not, like both his wife and his wife's ancient Trojan namesake, live just long enough to see the cataclysmic destruction of the entire world he knew.

Cassandra's granddaughter Elizabeth Roberts sent her husband, W. B., and both sons to fight in gray and lost a brother in gray at Helena. But shortly before her older boy went off to enlist for the South, her oldest girl, my great-great-grandmother Virgie, married William C. Ducker, of the huge brood produced by Jalie and Nathaniel Ducker, and most of his kin stood on the side of the North; nearly all of William's numerous cousins served in the Union Army and most of his eight sisters married Union men, mothered Union sons, or both. William himself, however, the tenth of his parents' twelve children and the only Ducker brother under thirty when the war began, doesn't seem to have enlisted for either side. He may well have decided, given his awkward position among the fire-eating Rebel kin of his wife, Virgie, that the safest course was to cling more firmly to the strategy that Kentucky itself had tried and failed to follow: to deflect violence from both sides by refusing to embrace either.

W. B. left no evidence as to why he chose the Confederate side, and his life story suggests he could have gone either way. As a Marylander who came to adulthood in Kentucky, he had spent his entire life in border states with generally strong ties to the Union, but his wife's family roots were primordially southern. General Sherman found while recruiting in Kentucky that it was the younger men who tended to be the secessionists, but W. B. joined up six months before his own son, a hale twenty-three-year-old, got around to enlisting. His grandparents had been substantial slaveholders, but he himself owned no humans, no real estate, and not much of anything else, either. Most Confederate volunteers, to be sure, weren't slave owners, and generally saw themselves as fighting to defend home and liberty rather than to preserve the peculiar institution—though in yet one more example of the paradoxical family nature, Elizabeth's uncle Henry Nichols, one of Cassandra's sons, was both a staunch and open Union man and one of the largest slaveholders in Harrison County.[30] The best guess I can make about W. B. is that like many of his fellow volunteers, but also like his grandfather with his defiantly untraditional family, he just didn't care for outsiders telling him what to do.

Also open to guesswork is why W. B. traveled all the way to the remote wilderness of Arkansas in order to enlist even though Kentucky was fielding some Confederate units of its own and other eager volunteers found welcoming recruiters no farther away than Tennessee or Missouri. (Twice in my life, circumstances conspired to place me for a time in Little Rock, and I can attest that even in this day and age it's hard to end up in Arkansas inadvertently.) According to his entry in the local biographical encyclopedia, besides being a man of "great energy and industry," he also displayed "decided and marked traits of character," which could be either a straightforward description of a confident and assertive man or code words hinting at a headstrong, stubborn, and intolerant one. Could my great-great-great-grandfather have been one of those "perfect savages" among Pendleton's secesh (the compelling image here is of his grandfather's savage assault against the slave's ear), a cold-eyed saboteur, perhaps, who crept around in the dark of night tearing up railroad ties or sawing through bridge trusses? Did he take potshots at the local Home Guard? Use his position as the trusted family doctor to eavesdrop on Yankees officers with chilblains and then tell all to the Rebels? Or maybe his trespass was like the one soon to be committed by Dr. Samuel Mudd, sentenced to life in prison because he set someone's leg—someone he insisted he didn't know was the fleeing assassin John Wilkes Booth. Maybe old Doc Roberts, in the humanity of his heart or the passion of his convictions, had treated the wrong person and been forced to roust his family in their nightgowns to escape into the dark just ahead of the law.

The letter from Cousin John Dawson found among my grandmother's things provides no hints about any of these matters, which again condemns—or frees—me to construct my own stories about this exasperating relative. Born in 1876, eleven years after the war ended, Cousin John knew nothing of the great conflict firsthand, but he knew his grandfather W. B. very well. His mother, widowed in Alabama when John was just a baby, brought him and his two older sisters back home to her parents in Falmouth. Then John's grandmother died of consumption when he was about eight, leaving W. B., who had himself been orphaned young, to preside over a household of five in which everyone was mourning either a parent or a spouse.[31]

When Cousin John wrote his letter in December 1958, his grandfather had been dead for more than sixty years, and, as he himself confessed, his memory was fading. The one-page letter is, unfortunately, a typical family reminiscence, a jumble of thoughts and memories jotted down apparently just as they came and showing hardly a sign that the writer was recalling the closest thing to a father he'd ever had. It includes no intimate details, reveals virtually nothing about W. B.'s character or demeanor, and says nothing about his appearance other than that at some point he wore a broadcloth suit, the gift of the "well-off" cousin Sam whose father had raised him. The letter could stand as a model for what honorable family historians should *never* inflict on their descendants.

But Cousin John was himself full of surprises, having in the glum and bereaved world of postwar Kentucky pursued an unusually expansive vision of personal happiness. As a young man he set type at a local newspaper to put himself through Georgetown College, a small Baptist institution just outside Lexington. Despite his long hours at the printer's case he was active on the student newspaper, on the yearbook, and in the Ciceronian literary society, all the while maintaining excellent grades. Graduating at last in 1901, when he was twenty-five, he studied for several months at the University of Caen in France before becoming a professor of modern languages at Howard College in Birmingham, Alabama, the rickety Baptist institution that would later become Samford University. After World War I, the United States Army sent him to the ancient French city of Toulouse to organize a language-training program for American soldiers. From the south of France, Cousin John then made his way to the Upper West Side of Manhattan to finish up his Ph.D. in Romance languages at Columbia. He returned to Birmingham in 1921 to assume the presidency of Howard, where in his ten-year tenure he increased the student body from two hundred to eleven hundred, constructed three new campus buildings, got the college formally accredited, and enjoyed boasting that "an Eastern magazine" had once called his institution "the Amherst of the South." (The southern roots of this Amherst were evident; "Baptists of Alabama," President Dawson said firmly, "are opposed to dancing," and he banned that sinful activity from his campus.) Affectionately called "Long John" by the students, the six-foot-four-inch Dawson possessed a "droll sense of humor" and an "inimitable laugh," recalled a colleague, "that was somewhat boisterous, without being unpleasant."[32]

Adventurous, ambitious, to all appearances *happy:* everything I know about my grandmother Grace and all I can surmise about W. B. persuade me that if Cousin John inherited his character traits from anyone, it must have been someone on the *other* side of his family, his dead father's Alabama kin. Nor do I recognize any family precedent for the sort of self-confidence (or self-indulgence) that made Cousin John, a fatherless Baptist boy raised in a backwater southern town by a pinched country doctor, decide to take up so impractical a study as French in the first place. If he absolutely insisted on pursuing something foreign, he could at least have concentrated his energies on German, the language of serious scholarship as well as a familiar and useful tongue in the nearby immigrant communities of Cincinnati and Covington. But in the 1890s, most rural Kentuckians probably knew little more about France than that it was a place for naughty novels, men in garret studios, and women in unmentionables. Not only that; my cousin, whose older relatives hadn't even liked traveling as far as Missouri, then summoned the nerve (and the funds) to get himself all the way to that naughty foreign place on his own. And Columbia University, where he capped off his studies, was almost as fabulous a destination as the land of the cancan for any Baptist with a drawl.

But while he saw much more of the world than most Kentuckians of his generation ever dreamed of, my droll and learned cousin never permitted his exotic experiences to revise the stories that had shaped his Kentucky childhood. In December 1929, more than four years after the Scopes "monkey trial" in Tennessee made religious fundamentalism a running joke for Americans who enjoyed feeling modern, Cousin John Dawson made a splash on the front page of the *New York Times* for firing a biology professor who had questioned the truth of the biblical stories of Noah's ark and Jonah's whale.[33] And thirty years later, the letter he wrote to his younger cousin showed a faith in his family's stories every bit as pure as his faith in Jonah's.

His letter described a trip taken at the request of his mother's sister Nannie several years before her death in 1943. She wanted to pay a visit to Scott County, north of Lexington, where her mother, Elizabeth Payne Roberts (John's grandmother, my great-great-great-grandmother), had been born. Here's what he wrote to Cousin Lillian about the family's experience in the Civil War:

> We drove to Payne's Depot, to the old pre–Civil War residence of one of the Piatts with whom Aunt Nan had lived during the Civil War. A year or so later that beautiful old house burned to the ground. Grandpa became a surgeon in General Pike's division in Arkansas. I think Uncle Will was a Confederate soldier. Uncle Bud (Nathan) was too young. However, I was told that soldiers, presumably Yankees, strung him up to a tree trying to get information. They didn't kill him, but tried to terrify him into telling what they wanted to know. They burned the house down, and all that was saved was a feather bed. I suppose that was when the family came back to Kentucky, to Independence [in Kenton County], and from there to Falmouth.

Here's every single one of Cousin John's facts I can confirm: Uncle Will was a Confederate soldier.

Other facts of his did come close. I discovered that the Roberts family had indeed spent the war somewhere other than Falmouth, but contrary to Cousin John's recollections, it wasn't down the road in Payne's Depot with the not-yet-related Piatts. Instead, sometime during the first months of the war, W. B. picked up his family and left (or fled) Kentucky for Lafayette County, Missouri, where Elizabeth's parents and siblings as well as various cousins, aunts, and uncles on both sides had moved two decades or so earlier. Unlike those relatives, however, W. B. wasn't looking for a more western frontier. He was looking for a more southern one, and he found it—for a while.

Like its sister border state, Missouri was deeply riven, bitterly fought and schemed over, beset with vicious guerrillas, and loudly claimed for the Confederacy by fervent though outnumbered secessionists. Like Kentucky, Missouri at first attempted to stay out of the war entirely by proclaiming itself officially neutral. But unlike Kentucky, Missouri had been fighting its own civil war for years, between proslavery Border Ruffians and abolitionist Free-Soilers and Jayhawkers along the Missouri-Kansas border. And in the first spring and summer of the war, as Kentucky gamely tried to maintain its neutrality by forbidding the recruiting of troops by either side, Missouri's old tensions kept it boiling.

Lafayette County, where Nichols, Payne, and Roberts kin had been making their home for twenty years, lay in the heart of the most proslavery, Confederate-leaning section of the state. Its soil nourished such legendary Rebel zealots as the bushwhacker William Quantrill, who would unleash the infamous Lawrence Massacre in Kansas, and the Kentucky-born *miles gloriosus* General Jo Shelby, commander of the legendary Iron Brigade of cavalry, who in 1865 would lead hundreds of his unreconstructed comrades into a voluntary two-year exile in Mexico rather than surrender to the Yankees. In September 1861, hundreds of Confederate sympathizers flocked to accompany Major General Sterling Price's State Guard as it struck out northward in a campaign to dislodge the Yankees from the Lafayette County seat of Lexington. The mission was a triumph, as Price and his men besieged the vastly outnumbered Yankees and forced their surrender. Among the Rebel troops celebrating their victory were W. B. Roberts and one or both of his sons. The family had apparently decided to trade the mere chaos of Kentucky for the sheer mayhem of Missouri, which both needed their help more and more openly embraced the southern cause.[34]

In mid-February 1862, the Union Army began its counteroffensive against Price and his Missourians, sending them scurrying south from Springfield so fast that Price left behind heaps of military papers in his headquarters and hundreds of wounded soldiers in their cots. Nipped and harried by the steadily gaining Federals, the shivering graybacks in their tattered uniforms slogged for days down the frontier road to Arkansas, stopping so briefly for meals or sleep that some soldiers learned to snatch both while still on their feet.

By late February, however, the Yankees' supply lines were stretched dangerously thin, and the Confederates were digging in deep in the Boston Mountains in Arkansas's wild and desolate northwestern corner to begin planning their own counterattack against the Yankees. Proclamations in the local papers called for able-bodied Rebels to join the swelling encampment in the mountains. On March 3 two newly organized regiments of volunteers, the Nineteenth and Twentieth (initially called the Twenty-second) Arkansas, turned up raring to have a go at the enemy invaders.[35] One of the new enlistees in the Twentieth was W. B. Roberts, and here at last was the reason he enlisted so far from his Kentucky home: whether under duress or by choice, he had already left home far behind.

That still doesn't quite explain, however, the roots of the passion or the fury or whatever it was that drove him to leave his wife, his three underage daughters, and, apparently, his sons behind in a war zone either to join the wild flight south with Price or to follow soberly on his own in the army's wake. Maybe he was hoping to be taken on as a surgeon, but that didn't happen. And that's another enigma: Why not? Why did W. B. end up in the dirty, disorderly, and dangerous role of a foot soldier instead of the cushier officer's billet you'd think would have been wide open to a middle-aged physician? Twelve years after the end of the war, the local biographical encyclopedia noted that "he spent a great part of his time of service as a physician and surgeon," and Cousin John as well as W. B.'s daughter Nannie and even my grandmother Grace had all been sure that he'd served as a medical man throughout the war.[36] Formal appointment as a field surgeon, however, required the approval of an army medical board and carried the rank of captain, and the service records for Private Roberts, a small-town doctor with a truncated education, show not a hint that he was ever formally accepted, treated, or paid as a doctor.

It's still not impossible that they were telling the truth, or part of it anyway. Surgeons were overworked and hard-pressed throughout the war, and an enlisted man with medical knowledge could have found his way into the ambulance corps or perhaps penetrated even deeper into the medical tents. Certainly any field officer facing scores of screaming soldiers spurting blood would have had good reason to abandon his nice scruples about the bureaucratic qualifications of anyone who was available, uninjured, and able to tell a forceps from a fork.

Or maybe W. B.'s medical story was a later revision, crafted *ex post bello* for an era that had grown tired of bellicosity. Maybe he was glossing over the fact that he just wasn't a good enough doctor to win an appointment, or that true to his contrarian Trammell roots, he had *chosen* to enlist as a private instead of a gentleman. Or maybe back in 1862 he had gone to war in the same spirit of restlessness that had sent him bouncing from county to county and from hemp making to farming to medical school, or to work through the sort of male midlife malaise that later generations would address with either a Porsche or a divorce.

In any case, W. B. and his fellow recruits of the new Twentieth Arkansas, most of them local boys, were doubtless crushed to find that when they presented their eager selves to Major General Earl Van Dorn at the Confederates' encampment, the general wasn't quite so hard up that he was willing to throw such a sorry crew into the breach. Mustered in barely a week earlier, they had had no time for training in anything except how to march from here to there, and most of them were unarmed to boot, with scarcely a usable weapon to be found in the possession of either regiment. The general left the Nineteenth and Twentieth behind and sallied forth to meet the Yankees without them.[37]

So here's my poor old Private Roberts at the end of a long journey of Yankee loathing, a journey that first uprooted him from his old Kentucky home, gave him a taste of military glory during the siege of Lexington, and then precipitated him into a frozen wilderness hundreds of miles from his family. And just as he has finally maneuvered himself to a place where he can scent real battle, just as he is about to unleash his venom against the enemy and measure himself against the supreme test of full-scale combat, he finds that both his arduously earned medical skills and his carefully tended martial enthusiasm have been rejected as unworthy, and he's left sitting in the snow clutching an impotent old gun that, truth be told, the townie doctor probably isn't terribly handy with in any case.

I hope he was grateful.

The battle that W. B. watched from the sidelines, the battle of Pea Ridge, turned out to be the biggest fight of the war west of the Mississippi and a decisive defeat for the South. In the two days of combat, two Confederate generals were killed along with two thousand or more of their thirteen thousand fighting troops, with perhaps five hundred more captured and untold hundreds more wounded. If so pitiful a regiment as W. B.'s had taken the field in so nasty a fight, it's hard to escape the conclusion that his first big battle would probably have been his last. And even if he had managed to survive, Pea Ridge would have been a particularly unpleasant introduction to the sheer barbarism of war. The battle would be forever notorious for the conduct of Brigadier General Albert Pike's Cherokee troops, who early in the fighting simply ran wild, heeding no orders, murdering wounded Yankees as they lay bleeding on the field, and scalping at least eight of their bodies.[38]

My grandmother Grace, the woman who had so few family stories to relate, did tell one about W. B. at Pea Ridge. According to my mother, Grace said she'd often been told by older relatives about how Doc Roberts had worked through the night after the battle, methodically sawing the limbs off screaming soldiers without anesthetic and flinging the discarded arms and legs in a bloody tangle behind him on the floor.

I'd like to believe so dramatic and poignant a story; I'd like to believe that Grace had a genuine family memory and W. B. was a genuine surgeon selflessly, if stoically, ministering to all those poor wounded boys. But so *very* dramatic and poignant—and so familiar—is the tale that I'm suspicious. That gruesome mound of mangled arms and legs showed up unnervingly often in contemporary letters and newspaper accounts as well as memoirs of the fighting written decades later.

One such pile actually helped change the course of Walt Whitman's life and, perhaps, his art as well. At forty-two the poet was beyond draft age and far from the front, but in December 1862, a vague rumor that his brother had been wounded at Fredericksburg sent him rushing from New York to Virginia to search the hospitals for word of the missing George. The first place Walt looked was a large brick mansion on the banks of the Rappahannock, the Lacy house, which had been taken over by Union doctors and filled with Union casualties. Outside, "at the foot of [a] tree, immediately in front," he scribbled in one of the makeshift little notebooks he always carried with him, "a heap of feet, legs, arms, and human fragments, cut, bloody, black and blue, swelled and sickening."[39] Brother George, it turned out, had only the slightest of injuries, but Walt would return again and again in his writings to that haunting image from his first, shattering glimpse of the *real* war. And so shaken was he by the anguish he saw in the camps and clinics, so awed by the brave grace of the broken young men, that he stayed on in Washington to help nurse and comfort the wounded soldiers of both armies.

Non-poets, too, had trouble getting over that sight. Twenty years after the war, the former Confederate private Sam Watkins of Tennessee, whose reminiscences were collected in book form after their publication by a South Carolina newspaper in 1881–82, still remembered visiting a comrade in a field hospital in Atlanta. "Great God!" he wrote.

> I get sick to-day when I think of the agony, and suffering, and sickening stench and odor of dead and dying; of wounds and sloughing sores, caused by the deadly gangrene; of the groaning and wailing. I cannot describe it. I remember, I went in the rear of the building, and there I saw a pile of arms and legs, rotting and decomposing; and, although I saw thousands of horrifying scenes during the war, yet to-day I have no recollection in my whole life, of ever seeing anything that I remember with more horror than that pile of legs and arms that had been cut off our soldiers.[40]

Nor was that horror left entirely to the imagination of the noncombatant: at least one contemporary battlefield photographer preserved for posterity the image of a heap of feet and legs awaiting burial. Reprinted 125 years later in the lavishly illustrated companion volume to Ken Burns's popular PBS documentary series, the image of that grisly jumble of shins and toes, surrounded as it is by dozens of the posed or static battlefield photographs mandated by the cumbersome technology of the day, still feels shockingly, hideously intimate.[41] It was almost a relief when I discovered, while paging through some newspapers of the time, that even a severed leg was good for an occasional laugh. On October 11, 1862, the Unionist *Louisville Journal* reported that "Poindexter, the rebel chief, held as a prisoner in a Missouri village, has had one of his legs amputated. It is to be hoped the young ladies of the village will be considerate enough to invite him to their next hop." You could laugh, in other words, if the stump belonged to the enemy.

But in the new era of the minié ball, the quick-loading cone-shaped bullet that spun wickedly from a rifled bore to shatter and splinter bone, the ubiquity of dismemberment turned the image of the heap of limbs into a sort of iconic shorthand for the horrors of the hospital tent. Especially in the crush of a great battle, medical treatment could be perfunctory, and by today's lights it was appallingly primitive; antiseptics were rare, painkillers crude, transfusions unsafe, and supplies often scanty. Even a modest wound could fester into a death sentence, and the terrified patient who glimpsed a bone saw in the surgeon's hand often tried to fight off the chloroform (or the assistants holding him down), knowing full well that the limb might not be all he'd lose in the agony to come. One study of cases reported by Union surgeons showed that a man's chance of dying from a foot or leg amputation could range anywhere from 5.7 percent to nearly 85 percent, depending on how high up the cut came. Even so, the number of wounded men who managed to survive their ghastly operations was large enough that in 1865, Mississippi devoted one-fifth of its revenues to providing artificial arms and legs for its veterans.[42]

So for my grandmother Grace, and for many children, especially in the South, at the end of the nineteenth century, mutilated elderly men were an everyday sight. That the vision of the pile of limbs may not have been W. B.'s own scarcely mattered; it had become everyone's vision, everyone who could recognize a great-uncle's coming by the distinctive ta-THUMP of his wooden leg, or whose schoolteacher wrote with a left-handed scrawl that never did seem comfortable. The image of the leftover arms and legs was nearly as ubiquitous and as mournful as the men who had left them over, the men who had last been whole on some battlefield half a century ago.

After Pea Ridge, as the spring 1862 campaign season got under way, W. B.'s regiment pulled itself together, moved on with Van Dorn into northern Mississippi, and began to see action. He and his comrades numbered among the troops who slithered out of their entrenchments at the vital rail center of Corinth in the dead of a May night, leaving campfires blazing, dummy guns bristling, and Yankee besiegers confounded. They scuffled at Farmington and Iuka and were scorched in the futile battle to retake Corinth in October. They scurried from Bolivar to Coffeeville to Grand Gulf as part of the Rebels' increasingly frantic efforts to stop the relentless General Grant, who saw the seizure of Vicksburg as critical to controlling the entire Mississippi River. Finally, on the first of May 1863, Private W. B. Roberts was captured at the battle of Port Gibson and sent to the military prison at Alton, Illinois.

It wasn't quite Andersonville, but it was bad enough, beset by leaking roofs, severe overcrowding, a lingering smallpox epidemic, and, worst of all, a small group of Union prisoners even more disreputable than the graycoats. Alton had become "the receptacle," wrote the commander of the prison, for a group of about ninety deserters from the western army who had been sentenced to hard labor with ball and chain. "Many of them are reckless and some of them are desperate men," he reported, who "by their bad conduct give us more trouble than all the Confederate prisoners confined here."[43]

Poor old W. B.! All he had wanted was to help drive the Yankee invaders from southern soil, but at an age when most other men were safe at home in their slippers, there he was jammed into a pestilential penitentiary cheek by jowl with a bunch of Yankee thugs so rotten even their own side didn't want them. He could be forgiven if at that point he finally renounced his old grand notions of the romance and adventure of war. He could also be forgiven if, as appears likely, he never talked about that miserable final adventure in prison to either the local biographer or his family. My mother could not recall that any of the relatives who had known him—not Cousin John or his two sisters, not Aunt Nannie, not her great-grandmother Virgie or her grandmother Alice—ever mentioned it at all. On his release from prison that June he'd apparently had enough mayhem, heading not to Missouri but home to Pendleton. But even there, the deaths didn't stop. In September 1864 his second daughter, twenty-year-old Mary, was laid to rest in the local cemetery, a casualty of typhoid.

Meanwhile "Uncle Will," as Cousin John Dawson called him, William Henry Roberts, the oldest child of W. B. and Elizabeth, was indeed seeing action as a Confederate soldier; that part Long John got right. Will fought with the State Guard alongside his father in the battle of Lexington and enlisted as a private in the First Field Battery of the Missouri Light Artillery almost a year later, in August 1862, by which time W. B. had been skirmishing around Mississippi for six months. And Will's war seems to have been even less glamorous than his father's. Rarely severely tested, his unit took part in a modest string of engagements in Arkansas, Missouri, and Louisiana. Its first captain was Will's cousin Westley Roberts, whose resignation just days after his first battle, the hard-fought stalemate at Prairie Grove, was heartily accepted by the general in command on the grounds that Captain Roberts was "totally ignorant of the duties of an artillery officer." The young lieutenant who was promoted to replace Westley recalled years later that "none of us knew anything about the handling of cannon," resorting to teaching themselves out of an old manual of arms bought from a retired officer for $100 in Confederate bills. The suddenly civilian Westley, meanwhile, started walking home to Lafayette County, surrendered to the first Yankee troops he found on the way, and begged permission to take the oath of allegiance to the Union.[44] But no such softness ever attached to "Uncle Will." Like most of my kin, he died ancient—in 1927, at the age of eighty-eight—and a younger cousin of my grandmother's remembered that every year until almost the end of his life, Will would celebrate Decoration Day by dressing up in his old Confederate uniform.

But Cousin John's tale about Will's brother Nathan, aka "Uncle Bud," the boy too young to be a soldier, raises a host of questions. My cousin said he'd been told "that soldiers, presumably Yankees, strung him up to a tree trying to get information. They didn't kill him, but tried to terrify him into telling what they wanted to know." Exactly what that precious information consisted of we have no clue, but apparently Nathan wasn't the only male in Missouri who knew it. In fact the sportive hanging to extract information from southern sympathizers was a peculiarly Missouri story, told in very similar form in the families of two of the most quintessential Missourians of all.

Here's one:

> Some Northern soldiers . . . went to the house and asked where Frank was. Mother and father didn't know, but the soldiers wouldn't believe them. They took father out and hung him by the neck to a tree. After a while they took him down and gave him another chance to tell. Of course he couldn't. So they hung him up again. They did that three times.[45]

And here's another:

> [Federal troops] tried to make my Uncle Harrison into an informer, but he wouldn't do it. He was only a boy, but he wouldn't turn informer. They tried to hang him, time and again they tried it, "stretching his neck," they called it, but he didn't say anything. I think he'd have died before he'd of said anything.[46]

The first story was told in 1914 by John T. Samuel, the younger half brother of Frank and Jesse James, about the day a patrol of Union militiamen came bushwhacker hunting to the Clay County farm of Zerelda Samuel, mother of the James boys, and her third husband, Reuben. The second was told by the aged ex-president Harry Truman about a Yankee raid on his grandparents' farm that had been witnessed by his mother when she was about eight or nine.

The James family story that Yankees had toyed with hanging the brothers' stepfather seems to be accurate. The incident was reported in the local papers in 1863, long before Frank and Jesse had earned the sort of notoriety that would color so many retrospective accounts—long before anyone had even heard of Jesse James, who at not quite sixteen wasn't even old enough yet to join his big brother among the bushwhackers. In the press report a lieutenant in the Yankee militia was quoted as describing how he and his comrades, convinced that Reuben Samuel knew where to find the bushwhacker band that included his stepson Frank, had placed a noose around their captive's neck and given him "one good swing" from a tree in an effort to scare the truth out of him.[47]

But while it's probably true that the Yankees tortured Reuben Samuel, the story grew as the legend of Jesse James did after the war, and especially after a mercenary young member of his gang shot and killed the bold bandit as he was tidying up his house with a feather duster. Reuben's hanging and the subsequent radicalization of his stepson were described, in person and in print, by other relatives of Jesse's besides his half brother (who had been all of seventeen months old at the time of the Yankees' raid). Jesse's clergyman uncle told it to the *Kansas City Daily Journal* in 1882 just a couple of days after the killing. Jesse's son, Jesse Jr., told it in the book he published in 1899 to "correct the [public's] false impressions" about the outlaw's character. Jesse's daughter-in-law Stella James (who was five weeks old when Jesse was killed) told it in a book posthumously published as recently as 1990. And Jesse's mother told it for the rest of her life to everyone within earshot. Zerelda Samuel, whose loathing of the Yankees and the law was even further inflamed by the Pinkertons' botched 1875 raid on her house, which cost her her right arm and her youngest son, shared her enduring bitterness with a steady stream of reporters and tourists at the family farm until her death in 1911.[48]

But the rousing story told by Jesse's fans was missing the denouement that had topped off the Yankee lieutenant's more contemporary account of Reuben Samuel's capture. Reuben squealed. After just one good jerk of the noose his "memory brightened up," the lieutenant told the local newspaper, and the chastened Rebel led the Yankees to the thicket where his older stepson and the other bushwhackers were holed up playing poker. The Union men killed five of them, scattered the rest, and plundered the Rebels' horses and guns, their spare clothes, and their poker stakes.

Harry Truman's namesake, Uncle Harrison Young, the story went, also faced down the Yankees and their noose; and Uncle Harrison also refused to spill the beans. Harrison's parents, Solomon and Harriet Louisa Young, who had joined the great migration from Kentucky to Missouri years before the war, were clearly in the southern camp. Although Solomon, probably in self-protection, signed a loyalty oath in 1862, his son Will joined the Confederate Army, and his daughter Sallie was married to "Jim Crow" Chiles, a bushwhacker of a savagery spectacularly unhinged. For the rest of her long life, until she died at ninety-one, Truman's grandmother Harriet spun stories of the evil day when Jayhawkers under the command of General Jim Lane, the former border warrior from Kansas whose hot-eyed ferocity earned him as fearsome a reputation among Rebels as Chiles's and Quantrill's among the Unionists, descended on the family farm.

Harriet Young's daughter and grandchildren could fluently recite the indignities of the day: after ordering the woman of the house to bake biscuits "until her wrists were blistered," the Yankee raiders stole the corn and the livestock, torched the barns, purloined the family silver, trampled the best featherbeds in the mud, and butchered four hundred Hampshire hogs, leaving everything but the hams to rot. Family members nursed their fury at the Yankees for decades; as late as 1946, the admiring *New York Times* profile of Truman's ninety-three-year-old mother, Martha Ellen Young Truman, described her as "an unreconstructed Southern Democrat" who indignantly refused her son's invitation to sleep in the Lincoln Bedroom during a visit to the White House. "'What,' she cried, 'sleep in the bed THAT MAN used?'"[49]

But if the anger was consistent, the details of the story were not. In 1890 Harriet Young submitted a formal reparations claim to Congress for "supplies or stores alleged to have been taken by or furnished" to Federal forces "during the late war for the suppression of the rebellion." (Since claimants were generally required to declare that they had been loyal to the Union throughout the war, Harriet must have been crossing her fingers.) No fewer than five different times between May 1861 and September 1864, she stated, Yankees had seized livestock and supplies from the family farm. But though Harriet Young had carefully enumerated the missing property taken by each raiding party—losses that were certainly substantial, including 150 head of cattle, forty-four hogs, 1,200 pounds of bacon, and seven wagons, for a total value of $21,442—her list showed no silver taken and no buildings burned. Jim Lane himself, furthermore, had come only once and seized only a string of horses and mules, while one Colonel Burris, who—as official records confirm—came to the area twice in two consecutive months in 1862, had made off with more than one-third of the claimed property, including the hogs (fewer than four dozen, not "four hundred"), the bacon (which had obviously been liberated from cool repose in the smokehouse, not hacked from steaming carcasses in the barnyard), and the bedding, "1 lot," that featured so vividly in the family account. Clearly the Youngs had suffered and witnessed suffering, but the details that were the most iconic—family silver, burned buildings, rotting pork, Jim Lane—were also the ones most evidently fabricated, exaggerated, or absorbed from the experiences of neighbors or friends, not themselves.[50]

The story of Harrison Young's hanging, an even more iconic story, did not appear in print until more than a century after it was supposed to have happened, when both Harry Truman and his sister Mary Jane told it to the oral historian Merle Miller. Born just two years after Jesse was shot down and just a few miles south of Zerelda's old family farm, Truman couldn't have avoided Jesse worship if he'd tried—and he hadn't. As a child he'd hung around the annual reunions of Quantrill's aging raiders, among whom a grizzled old Frank James could often be glimpsed, and later, while studying at Spalding's Commercial College in Kansas City, he would drop in for an ice cream soda at the candy store owned by Jesse James Jr., who had once trusted him for a nickel when his pockets turned up empty. And one of the worst lickings he ever got from his father, he recalled years later, was sparked by his teacher's report that he had been reading a dime novel hidden in his schoolbook. That mesmerizing paperback had featured Jesse James.[51]

Truman's Uncle Harrison may indeed have been one of the many Missourians to suffer the pain and indignity of torture by noose. Or, given the evident porousness of large parts of the Young family saga, the similarity of Harrison's fate to the widely storied Reuben Samuel's, the ubiquity of the romance of Jesse James, and the special reverence accorded the outlaw by his own neighbors on his own home turf, maybe Uncle Harrison's hanging had been no more real than, and every bit as symbolically resonant as, that great putrefying charnel heap of swine.

Then there's my great-great-great-uncle Nathan Roberts, the "Uncle Bud" who was too young to fight and whose reported fate closely mirrored both Reuben Samuel's and Harrison Young's. And again, maybe the tale as told a century later by Nathan's nephew John Dawson was true. But Cousin John's story, like Reuben Samuel's, has a hole in it. The facts are murky and his exact age is hard to pin down, but Nathan seems to have been plenty old enough to be a soldier, and it's likely that he too, like his brother, his father, and his cousins, had not stayed at home fending off raiders but rather had donned a butternut uniform and gone out to fight for the South.[52] Military records show that in August 1862 a Private Nathan Roberts enlisted on the same day and at the same place in the same battery as Uncle Will Roberts and gave the same hometown Will did. (Both claimed to hail from not Falmouth but Midway, their mother's childhood turf, which reinforces my vague and romantic suspicion that the family might have left Falmouth under some kind of duress.) And in fact Nathan's own sister Nannie Oldham, with whom he lived in the big brick house for some time after the war and who can be presumed to have been a more credible witness than the young Dawson nephew born more than a decade after the last soldiers came home, told the local historian E. E. Barton that her brother Nathan had enlisted with the Confederates. Cousin John apparently got that part of it wrong.[53]

So the question arises: Were any of the other parts accurate? And the answer suggests itself: yes, but not applied to Uncle Bud. Like the Trumans, the Robertses had close ties to the James legend. W. B.'s wife, Elizabeth Payne Roberts, may have known that she was distant kin to Jesse Woodson James himself, whose middle name (and occasional alias) memorialized their common ancestors, the Jamestown immigrants. A much more visible and, probably, satisfying connection came through their local Lafayette County hero, the rabidly "Undefeated" General Shelby, under whom Elizabeth's two brothers had served, one of them making the ultimate sacrifice at Helena. Shelby and his former adjutant Major John N. Edwards, a newspaperman whose biliously luscious prose earned him the title of "the West's own Victor Hugo," were largely responsible for creating the enduring myth of Jesse James as the Confederate Robin Hood.[54]

Of Nathan Roberts's war we know little, of his life after the war too much. He surrendered along with the rest of the battery in June 1865, but just about the only other notation in his typically skimpy Confederate service records shows that in November 1863 he was sent for unspecified reasons to a hospital in Washington—Union territory, though he's not on any extant POW list for that time. Back home in Pendleton after the war, he never seemed quite able to get a grip on his life. Not even in the great throng of widows and bereaved maidens left behind by the slaughter could he, or would he, find one who'd consent to marry *him*. Nor when he was displaced from his own father's house by his widowed sister Alice and her children could he, or did he, strike out on his own, instead moving in with his little sister Nannie and Nannie's husband, Jesse Oldham. Jesse was a prosperous cattle trader and banker, the great-grandson of one of Daniel Boone's pioneering companions, who lived in the imposing brick house his grandfather had built; Nathan was a farmhand and sometimes worked in the mills. And as his young nephew John Dawson with the irresistible laugh, living there in Nathan's childhood home with Nathan's own parents, was pouring his considerable energies into studying and saving for college, Nathan was becoming a drunk.

On Christmas Day 1891, Nathan, staggering and quarrelsome with liquor, picked a fight over a dollar debt with Henry C. Dills, who at twenty-two was less than half his age. As a crowd of equally inebriated rowdies egged the skirmishers on, the spat escalated into a ruckus. Weapons were flourished and insults were flung. Nathan called Dills "a s. of a b," and Dills snapped back that if he said that one more time, "g-d you I will kill you." Nathan did, and Dills did. Shot in the chest, Nathan lingered, spitting blood, for four days, and died on the twenty-ninth of December. He was forty-eight, or thereabouts.[55]

Dills was charged with manslaughter, but during the inquiry several witnesses testified that Nathan had been dangerously out of control. According to Bob Phillips, Nathan had almost seemed to be daring Dills to kill him; he had told the younger man "not to fool with him but to put a hole into him." From his grieving father came a slightly different interpretation. Poor old W. B., by then a widower near the end of his own life, conceded that his younger son had been drunk in the middle of the afternoon but added: "I think a ten year old boy could have whiped [sic] him at that time. He frequently told me that he was about broke down." The authorities, however, seem to have been more persuaded by the picture of Nathan the Dangerous than of Nathan the Doomed, and apparently dropped the manslaughter charges.[56] W. B. lived about another five years, until 1896, but other than the stone in Falmouth's Riverside Cemetery, there is no surviving record of his passing. He was at least eighty-one years old.

The *real* war was lousy to the Roberts clan. Elizabeth and the girls were uprooted, her brother Thomas was killed, her husband W. B. professionally disrespected by his own side and imprisoned by the other, their cousin Westley humiliated, their daughter Mary fevered to death, and poor Nathan, it seems, worn down, wrung out, and eventually destroyed by the accumulated ills and stresses of his long-ago service. Though they'd never been prosperous, by the time they were able to return home to Pendleton, they were very nearly destitute; in 1870 W. B., then in his mid-fifties at least, reported his personal net worth at $100, a shadow of the $400 that had looked paltry enough ten years earlier, and he never did own any real estate. (Meanwhile his rich cousin Sam, with whom he'd been raised and whose gift of a broadcloth suit Cousin John remembered all those years later, was comfortably ensconced on a Kenton County farm he said was worth $117,300.)[57] And on top of all that, when the Robertses went home, they went home losers—a label shared by only half their neighbors and understood by only half their kin.

Cousin John Dawson, who was fifteen years old when his uncle Nathan was shot down in the streets of his hometown, could not have failed to see how unhappy his life and how sordid his death had been, and at that point probably understood perfectly well that the war had worked its ruin on yet another soul. But when, near the end of his own long and remarkably happy and successful life, the scholarly and cosmopolitan cousin was asked about his roots, what he came up with were tales that rewrote the lives of the kinsmen who had been most blighted by a war by then almost a century in the past. Cousin John responded to the younger relative who came seeking his recollections by converting his long-dead grandfather from misfit private to noble surgeon and hauling his wastrel uncle out of the gutter to erect him into a near-martyr in the service of the Lost Cause. That he'd had to borrow all the trappings of nobility and martyrdom from other Losers, some much more famous, scarcely mattered to him, nor, perhaps, did it even register. The stories weren't documentaries; they were benedictions. And no one needed them more than the Robertses.

Kentucky Bluecoats

In the same month that W. B.'s daughter Mary died of typhoid, the Yankee in my family also started his journey home to Falmouth. He'd had a rough war, too, my great-great-grandfather James Dougherty—he of the constant flatulence, he of the obliterated and shameful side of the family, who, almost as soon as he got back to Pendleton, would beget the lamentable Arthur, our black sheep. James had been smack in the middle of two of the most awful battles of the entire war, had been sidelined in two of the most heroic, had been taken prisoner and taken ill, had earned steady promotions even as his comrades were being killed or injured or disgraced. He'd have had plenty to talk about if he'd been so inclined.

But into the black hole that is the Dougherty side of the family have forever disappeared most traces of whatever war stories he might have spun for listeners over Sunday dinner or after the big parade on Decoration Day or on the porch while the katydids cried in the twilight. No noble adventures, no causes lost or honor won, no excuses or validations woven by misty-eyed grandchildren, nothing that came close to those glorious prose poems of southern romance. All we have from him is one tale that many southerners would probably have considered typical of the grubby doggerel of Yankee vulgarity: the one he told county officials years after his military service in the hopes of earning a government check. But grubby or not, it was more *real* than anything Cousin John managed to pass on to Cousin Lillian, to my grandmother Grace, to me.

Even before Kentucky gave up its attempt at neutrality, James had volunteered for the local Home Guard unit, and the minute his state formally entered the war, he rushed to enlist in the army. Within a month he was promoted to first sergeant. Like many young men, James was probably genuinely eager to get into the scrap, but like many of the soldiers on the run into the arms of adventure, he also had plenty to run away *from*—in his case a grotesquely complicated home life.

In April 1858, nearly seven years after James's alarmingly prolific father had died of cholera, his mother, Jane, married again. Her choice of new spouse I take as proof positive that Joseph's big bag of money lost somewhere in the barn was merely mythic; it's hard to imagine what, other than desperation, could have driven the widowed mother of six into wedlock with her neighbor Henry Duckworth, who was, just to start with, a child spouse. Whereas Jane had been twenty years younger than her first husband, now at forty-six she was about twenty years older than her second, and Henry himself was only six or seven years senior to James, the oldest of his new stepchildren.

And Jane was marrying into a family that was every bit as quarrelsome as, and perhaps even less savory than, the Doughertys. Not one of the Duckworths was more than barely literate; on her deathbed Henry's mother disinherited one of her daughters for sleeping with another daughter's husband; Henry's only brother, Perry, had "lost his mind since birth" because of fits and was incapable of caring for himself; and the cruel suspicion arises that Henry himself wasn't much more highly functional than his brother. His chronic inability, revealed in census returns and the various pension forms he filed after the war, to keep straight such basic details of his life as his own age, when his children were born, when he was divorced, the names of his previous wives, or even how many wives he'd had doesn't suggest a man deeply rooted in the affairs of the world.[58]

After Jane's second wedding, in 1858, James Dougherty lived most of the time with older siblings instead of with his mother and her new husband. That's hardly surprising, considering that James was suing her. The official plaintiff was Jasper Daugherty, who, as the legal guardian of his minor half brothers James and Hamp, was demanding their rightful one-sixteenth shares of the $1,187.08 paternal estate. Jane, however, responded that she just didn't have the money. She told the court, pitifully, that James "was sickly for several years after his father's death; that she has fead, cloathed & educated him, . . . and pd. pharysicions for medical attendance for which she has recd. no compensation; that in doing so she has exosted her own means, that she is now old and poor, save the life estate in the house farm—it yields but a scanty support." In the adolescent James's vague and chronic ailments may lie an explanation for Jane's unconventional marriage: she was seeking not a new husband but a sturdier, handier son. And in the belligerent disappointment of those sixteen squabbling heirs bilked of their $74.19 apiece may lie the germ of the legend of the fortune lost to Joseph's untimely death.[59]

But if poor Jane had married the dubious Henry in the hope of replenishing her "exosted" means, she made a bad bargain, and the Daugherty children's concern over their patrimony turned out to be perfectly well justified. After less than two years of marriage Jane sued Henry for divorce, claiming he had "done away with" the remaining property her first husband had left her. The divorce was granted without difficulty, but the quarreling and lawsuits would go on for years.[60]

So my great-great-grandfather James marched off—rushed off—to war. And found himself staying put, right there just a stone's throw from all the relatives and step-relatives and lawsuits and lost legacies he was trying to put behind him. Life in the Eighteenth Kentucky defending the nation must at first have seemed no more adventurous than life on the farm. Most of the regiment spent its first long, grinding winter months of war right at home, standing guard over the Covington & Lexington Railroad where it passed through Pendleton; then in April the troops moved down the road to Lexington to guard it some more—though at least there they were greeted by ladies lavishing strawberries upon them.[61]

Finally, in July, several companies of the Eighteenth Kentucky had their first chance to "see the elephant," as the first taste of combat was widely if obscurely known. Not only that; the elephant they were supposed to see was a guerrilla. They were assigned to join the chase for the daring and beauteous John Hunt Morgan, the darling of Kentucky's beleaguered Rebels, on his first big cavalry raid from Tennessee into Kentucky to destroy supplies, seize horses, wreck bridges and railroads, cut telegraph wires, and, perhaps most important, taunt and tease the Unionists.

Rushing here and there by foot and horseback and railroad and wagon train through the small towns in Lexington's orbit, grouping and regrouping, eating too little and sleeping not at all, desperate for usable intelligence that never came, the Union pursuers kept missing "the marauding chief and his lawless band," sometimes by just hours—a cause of "bitter mortification to us all," wrote Colonel Cicero Maxwell in his official report. Only one small contingent of Union pursuers actually did see their elephant, in an engagement with

Morgan's troops at the covered bridge in Cynthiana, but in a stiff fight of less than two hours the Rebels whipped them. Among the defeated Union soldiers was Cassandra Nichols's grandson Dennis, a local Cynthiana boy who had joined the Seventh Kentucky Cavalry as a private just weeks earlier and whose introduction to warfare was distinctly embarrassing: he was among the hundreds captured in the streets of his own hometown, in front of his own Rebel cousins and in-laws.[62] The prisoners were then immediately paroled, returning to the field as soon as they'd been formally exchanged for Rebel captives of equal rank.

The invasion launched later that summer by Generals Bragg and Kirby Smith brought the Eighteenth Kentucky out to battle again. It would be their first real fight, the first full-sized elephant they would see, and it would be a raging, Jumbo-sized man killer of a beast. Long after the fighting a former Rebel private would remark in his memoir that in the battle "the Confederates gained the most complete little victory of the war."[63] Historians generally agree, though it seems a bit unsporting to gloat over it; no elephant could have failed to complete a victory over a gerbil like the Union Army at the battle of Richmond, Kentucky, on August 30, 1862.

To meet Kirby Smith's army as it advanced north toward Lexington, Union officers gathered at Richmond a motley collection of regiments, most of them except for the Eighteenth Kentucky made up of brand-new recruits who just weeks before had still been lolling safe at home. Among the fresh troops was Henry Duckworth, the youthful wastrel who had married and divorced James Dougherty's mother and squandered James's inheritance and who just weeks earlier had followed James's example, fleeing the complexities of home by joining James's own regiment. Though they weren't in the same company, I cherish a hope that the now seasoned Sergeant Dougherty managed to find an opportunity or two to pull rank over his ex-stepfather, Private Duckworth.

Perhaps not even the soberest and surest commander could have pried a victory out of that sad army, but the inexperienced Brigadier General Mahlon Manson piled up such a tottering heap of tactical blunders that a corporal from the Sixty-ninth Indiana would later conclude that the general was "drunk as a lord and crazy as a loon."[64] The Eighteenth Kentucky, as the senior regiment (even burdened as it was with the recent addition of such desperate characters as Henry Duckworth), actually did quite well for itself; at one point James Dougherty and his companions saved the left flank after both the center and the right fled in panic. Major Frederick G. Bracht of the Eighteenth outdid himself in his bravura official report of the action. "Before we were yet formed," he wrote, "considerable numbers of each company had bit the dust and many more were groaning with ghastly wounds; and yet . . . our men stood boldly up and poured a steady fire into the fence and wood from which the deadly missiles were falling around us." But the battle as a whole was simply "shameful," as the saturnine Brigadier General Charles Cruft put it afterwards. In the end, Federal troops surrendered by the hundreds, and one officer reported to General Kirby Smith that he couldn't even count how many prisoners he had taken. There was, he said, "a ten acre lot full."[65] The victorious Confederates celebrated by occupying Lexington.

Several days passed before the full extent of the disaster became known, but on September 9 the *Louisville Journal* reported that the Eighteenth Kentucky had "fought most gallantly and suffered most severely in the disastrous battle of Richmond. It has won for itself a proud and enduring place in the memory of Kentuckians. . . . The regiment was almost literally cut to pieces." The official records would put the Union's losses on that one day as 206 killed, 844 wounded, and the stunning figure of 4,303 captured or missing. The odds of coming out of the battle of Richmond unscathed had been no better than the odds of coming through the early years of the Jamestown colony alive.[66]

The Eighteenth's colonel, William Warner, was reported mortally wounded in the chest, though he would recover and fight again. James Dougherty was among the captured thousands. So was Henry Duckworth, whom the first accounts had declared dead. So were 235 more officers and men of the Eighteenth Kentucky. So was General Manson. So was Dennis Nichols of the Seventh Kentucky Cavalry, for the second time in six weeks. It was no Babylonian captivity; all were exchanged almost immediately and returned to their regiments, many of which were cowering in Louisville, awaiting the promised coming of General Bragg, the fate from which Colonel Wilder's dilatorily gallant surrender of the Munfordville bridge would help preserve them. The whole episode was scarcely an inviting introduction to the romance and excitement of war.

But my great-great-grandfather stayed on, and returned to the Eighteenth after his formal exchange. That's exactly what he was supposed to do, of course, since he'd enlisted for three years, but those terms didn't stop at least four other Daughertys from deserting: three of James's cousins who had also enlisted in the Eighteenth and his younger brother Orville, who had joined the Thirty-second Kentucky, would skedaddle at various times in 1862 and 1863.[67]

But James seems to have thrived on army life. While all around him his comrades kept dying, ailing, deserting, or disgracing themselves, he kept getting promoted, which in some units was decided by a general vote. Sergeant Dougherty's first advancement came in February 1863, when the second lieutenant, having been given for reasons unrecorded the choice of resigning or facing a board of examiners, gratefully seized the opportunity to quit. Two months later James Dougherty was promoted again upon the resignation of the first lieutenant, who had never recovered from the nasty wound he got at Richmond that had shortened one leg by more than two inches. And in the summer of 1863 the chronically sickly farm boy who had started his military career less than two years earlier as a militia private took over command of Company D when the soon-to-be-martyred Abram Wileman was promoted to major. The war may have marked the first time anyone had ever noticed and applauded a boy who had served his entire childhood in an even more chaotic army: that uncountable swarm of Daugherty siblings.[68]

In June 1863 the Eighteenth Kentucky took the field again, joining Major General William Rosecrans's Tullahoma campaign in Middle Tennessee, a masterly operation long on guile and short on casualties that succeeded in keeping Braxton Bragg from getting reinforcements through to the besieged city of Vicksburg. For most of the men, the eleven-day campaign was notable chiefly for the biblically relentless rain, a constant deluge that turned all the roads to goo and weighted every action with muck. But the campaign offered a resounding redemption for the ubiquitous Colonel Wilder, a chance to graduate from the Honorable Gentleman he had been at the Munfordville bridge to Action Hero. After a heroic pell-mell pursuit of the Rebel pickets through the dangerous four-mile-long Hoover's Gap, he and his mounted troops burst out the other end and held it, new Spencer carbines blazing, until the arrival of reinforcements—including Captain Dougherty, Company D, and the rest of the Eighteenth Kentucky. When Wilder sought out Rosecrans after the battle to confess that he had disobeyed his orders to fall back from the gap, the general pumped his hand with glee and thanked God for the colonel's dereliction. "Promote him, promote him!" Rosecrans exclaimed.[69]

By July 4, when Vicksburg finally fell and Bragg's mission had clearly shown itself a failure, the discombobulated southern commander and his army were retreating to Chattanooga. Cradled by mountainous ridges and enfolded by a generous bend of the Tennessee River, a nexus of railroad lines, the little city was a vital portal to the south, would be a strategic prize for the North, and left no room for maneuver by the Rebels holed up inside. Thus, by the time

Rosecrans and his seventy thousand–man Union Army hove into view, the southern troops had evacuated the city and withdrawn into northern Georgia. Leaving a small garrison to hold the city, the Federals set off again in pursuit.

Yet there the "masterly" and "brilliant" campaign that had been going so well for the Yankees suddenly crashed into disaster, undone by an egregious error in the fog of battle by a moody, exhausted commander and a soreheaded underling: a hole left in the line at precisely the time and place the enemy was poised to attack. After more than a week spent dancing, dodging, and feinting at each other in the ridges and valleys south of Chattanooga, the two armies finally smashed together on September 19 and 20 near Chickamauga Creek. The Cherokee name supposedly translates as "River of Death," as good a name as any: Chickamauga would be the bloodiest battle of the western theater, perhaps even the costliest battle of the entire war proportional to the forces engaged, with even the victorious Rebels emerging heavily damaged. The combat was savage and often at close quarters, more like bushwhacking than battle; neither science nor strategy nor deliberation seemed to have much to do with the matter. As the novelist Thomas Wolfe's ninety-five-year-old great-uncle told the tale, he never knew how many men were killed at Chickamauga: "I only know you could have walked across the dead men without settin' foot upon the ground." It was, he said, "the biggest fight that I was ever in—the bloodiest battle anyone has ever fought."[70]

In the thick of the fighting on both days was the Eighteenth Kentucky. On the first day, Saturday, Captain James Dougherty and the rest of his regiment were under assault for much of the afternoon, "exposed to a heavy and well-directed fire from the enemy, which was warmly returned" until the ammunition ran out. "I saw no cowards," reported the Eighteenth's Colonel Hubbard Milward afterwards, laconically, "nor does the report of any company commander speak of one."[71] The colonel himself, however, had been badly injured in both feet by a runaway horse, while Major Wileman had been hit in the arm. With night came a chilly north wind, an inky black sky barely brightened by a splinter of a moon, and the inevitable, incessant, unbearable wailing of the wounded. The exhausted soldiers had eaten little and drunk even less all day; a late summer drought had dried up most of the creeks and streams, leaving one small cattle pond the only source of water the Federals could readily reach. By the end of the day it had become so foul as to earn a new name: Bloody Pond. When the battle resumed on Sunday morning, neither Colonel Milward nor Major Wileman could take the field, and the regiment fell under the wobbly command of one of James's fellow captains. It was deployed on the left flank with Major General George Thomas, up the line from the Brotherton farm where around eleven in the morning General Longstreet's triumphant southern troops burst through that calamitous gap in the ranks.

But even as whole divisions of panicky bluecoats stampeded toward McFarland's Gap, sweeping along with them teamsters, wagons, caissons, mules, and the occasional general desperately trying to go back in the other direction, General Thomas sturdily covered the chaotic retreat, standing, as legend would have it, like the "Rock of Chickamauga." And the Eighteenth Kentucky had the glum satisfaction of joining the rest of Brigadier General John Turchin's brigade in one small but triumphant parting shot: having finally ordered a general withdrawal in the waning afternoon, Thomas commanded Turchin to "clear out" an enemy brigade that was suddenly threatening their escape. Waving his hat, the "Mad Cossack" Turchin bellowed, "My brigade, charge bayonet, give 'em Hell, God Damn 'em!" They did. More than two hundred prisoners were taken in the wild charge, and the Eighteenth captured two artillery pieces, which had to be left behind because they couldn't be turned.[72]

The Confederates' victory was hideously expensive. Among the thousands of casualties were the star-crossed Major General John Bell Hood, still recovering from the wound that crippled his left arm at Gettysburg, who this time lost his entire right leg, and a brother-in-law of the first lady, Mary Todd Lincoln. But after the long summer's grimness of Gettysburg, Vicksburg, and Bragg's flight through Tennessee, many southerners baptized the victory as the latest incarnation of that splendid mirage, the "turning point." In the aftermath of the terrible battle, some Rebels may have celebrated the renewal of their hopes with an abandon beyond unseemly, or some Yankees may have demonized with a vengeance the authors of their disgrace; more than one Union soldier would report that he'd found mutilated Yankee bodies and severed Yankee heads on the blood-soaked field the next day.[73]

It was a dazed and lacerated Union force that withdrew to what seemed the safety of Chattanooga; even a month later, Lincoln would say, Rosecrans was still "confused and stunned, like a duck hit on the head."[74] But among the men at least the confusion soon gave way to hunger. The Confederates, eager to retrieve the vital city and restore their gangway to the north, settled down and set siege, vowing to starve the Yankees out. Rebel sharpshooters and pickets completely blocked every approach to the city but one, a roundabout, rugged, and ramshackle old wagon road extremely hazardous to negotiate at all, let alone efficiently enough to bring in the great quantities needed to supply more than thirty thousand Yankees with food, clothing, and ammunition. Rations were cut and cut until sometimes a small pane of hardtack was the day's only meal, and guards were set to keep pilferers out of the horses' corn. As autumn advanced, the men tore down houses and fences for fuel and shivered in their tattered summer clothing. Not until late October, when General Grant took command of the reorganized western armies and replaced Rosecrans with General Thomas at the head of the Army of the Cumberland, did the Yankees succeed in opening a much shorter and easier supply route.

The new "cracker line" was made possible by an audacious raid early in the morning of October 27 that gained the necessary foothold by dislodging two Rebel regiments guarding Brown's Ferry west of the city and building a bridge from scratch over the crossing. One of the units involved in the raid was the brigade commanded by the hard-charging General Turchin, with whom the Eighteenth Kentucky had salvaged its last-ditch moment of glory out of the wreckage of Chickamauga. But James Dougherty and his companions didn't get to share in *that* glorious moment. The men of the Eighteenth, still led by the spavined Colonel Milward, had spent the previous weeks up to their knees in mud, mire, and dead mules. The regiment was on detached service for most of October with one of the least glamorous assignments of wartime: road duty. Some of them were standing guard over the invaluable wagon route and the engineering battalions who tended it, but others pitched in and got their hands dirty, cringing at the whistling bullets of Rebel sharpshooters as they helped grade the route and clear it of broken wagons and the emaciated carcasses of the mules that were keeling over by the thousands from starvation and overwork. To have watched their former companions achieve so ardently desired and bloodless a victory while they were out there with the roadkill couldn't have gone far to salve the wounds of Chickamauga for the Eighteenth Kentucky.

In late November, with the troops fattened, heartened, and reinforced by the arrival of Generals Hooker and Sherman, Grant decided it was time for the Yankees to take the initiative and fight their way out of their pen. Over three days they assaulted the Confederates in their perches on the ridges overlooking the city. On Monday they speedily overwhelmed the Rebels on Orchard Knob, on Tuesday they chased them from the foggy slopes of Lookout Mountain, and on the afternoon of Wednesday, November 25, a mass of bluecoats, four divisions and more than twenty thousand strong, stood staring up at the crest of the forbidding five-hundred-foot-high Missionary Ridge, which was crowned with Rebel batteries and infantry units. At the signal the Yankees spilled forward toward the rifle pits at the base of the ridge and overran them, sending the Confederate shooters scurrying upward in retreat.

What happened next is legend. After taking the rifle pits, the Yankees, to the surprise of the high command, simply kept surging up the ridge, straight into and through the frantic firing of the enemy clustered at the top, driven, it seemed, by their own martial ardor and a passion to avenge the disaster of Chickamauga. "The enemy were fleeing up the slopes and we were bound to follow them," a soldier from Ohio said afterwards. "We didn't stop to think whether we could carry the crest or not—we didn't think at all!" In places the slope was so steep that soldiers had to scuttle and clamber using arms and legs both, hauling themselves up by the late-autumn scrub. Order disintegrated in the mad rush, and as "the atmosphere seemed filled with the messengers of death, and shells burst in every direction," as Brigadier General Absalom Baird put it in his after-action report, "the strongest men and the bravest men" sprang to the lead. Staff officers stationed across the way on Orchard Knob watched in awe as sixty regimental flags jostled their way to the crest, not one, they said, ever touching the ground, since the moment one color bearer faltered or stumbled, someone else was there to seize the flag and forge on. Amazed, exultant bluecoats began to reach the crest of the ridge, overwhelming Rebel batteries and killing, capturing, or driving off the defenders. They had done the impossible: they had climbed up straight into the face of enemy fire and stopped it.[75]

It was, the legend insists, a spontaneous uprising of mass valor ordered by no one. When an astonished Grant asked his officers who had given the command to advance, the story goes, no one claimed credit, but one responded, "When these men get going, all hell can't stop them!" And it spawned legendary heroes, like First Lieutenant Arthur MacArthur, the eighteen-year-old adjutant of the Twenty-fourth Wisconsin, who, as his son would later tell the story, seized the regimental standard after the first color bearer had been shot down, the second bayoneted, and the third beheaded by a flying shell, shouting "On Wisconsin!" as all bloody and tattered he planted the flagpole at the crest of the ridge. The young hero's cry gave heart to the faltering blue line, the story went, and "eyes blazing, lips snarling, bayonets plunging," they reached the top and won the ridge.[76] Participants, observers, and historians have described the charge ever since with words like "sublime," "spectacular," and "exhilarating"; it was the "miracle of Missionary Ridge"; what the Yankees had done was both impossible and decisive, the deathblow to the Confederacy's hopes of protecting the Deep South.

All that is inarguable, but the whole thing also fell somewhere on the scale

between an understandable error and a career-ending offense. While the legendeers insist that no one gave the order to charge, afterwards no one seems to
have agreed on exactly what the actual orders had been, and the attack on the
rifle pits in the first place appears to have been driven by Grant's misunderstanding about how Sherman's army was faring in a separate action at the north end
of the ridge. The simple reality of the assault was that once the men had overrun
the pits, they were left fully exposed to the bullets and shells raining down from
above and facing a lethal quandary: retreat, under fire; stand still, under fire; or
keep going up, under fire, but also, perhaps, protected somewhat by the steep
angle of the mountainside. They could either die advancing honorably or die
retreating shamefully. Many men saw no real choice.[77]

On the extreme left of the line Colonel Edward Phelps's brigade, to which
the Eighteenth Kentucky had been reassigned, did its duty manfully. After
taking the rifle pits under a furious fire, "the officers and men became wild
with enthusiasm and desire to advance," reported the commanding officer of
the Tenth Kentucky afterwards, "although it seemed from there that it would
be to a harvest of death." When the bugle sounded, "one wild yell went up,
and forward they swept, over an open plain, through the camp of the enemy,
and gained the foot of the ridge under a terrible enfilading fire of artillery from
Tunnel Hill, knocking down the huts of the enemy's camp and tearing up the
ground in every direction, but the men never wavered or faltered." At the crest
of the ridge the "gallant" Phelps himself was killed.[78]

But yet again, the Eighteenth Kentucky sat on the sidelines while others got
the glory—or, as in Phelps's case, *went* to glory. For whatever reason—their
colonel's injury, their small numbers, their ongoing guard duty, their bad luck,
their good luck—the men of the Eighteenth weren't included in the order of
battle, and from the sidelines watched their companions in one of the single
most heroic actions of the war.

So what would a man like James Dougherty do who had missed glory by
a whisker, who had sacrificed a laurel wreath to his colonel's swollen ankles?
When Jimmy finally came marching home again, what would he tell the teenaged sweetheart waiting for him? Could any man have resisted the temptations
offered by an audience that included as many as ten older siblings who had
stayed at home, a younger brother who was a deserter, a mother who was a scandal, and a wastrel ex-stepfather who had developed a diseased "back side" that
was keeping him miles from the battlefield? Nothing would have been more
human or less surprising than if James Dougherty, like his grandfather Ralph

Collins after St. Clair's defeat and like tens of thousands of other soldiers and sailors in dozens of wars unhappy with what they'd done or not done in that supreme test of manhood, had performed some repairs on his own personal after-action report.

In fact, even some of those with perfectly good reason to feel happy about their conduct have been known to do some later tinkering and polishing. The legendary color bearer Arthur MacArthur did, or at least others did on his behalf, as the promising young soldier went on to become a decorated officer, a military governor, and the father of an even more glorious (and grandiose) son, General Douglas MacArthur. The story grew in the telling. According to the official after-action report, the gallant young soldier had actually scored his triumph in the wake not of a pile of progressively mangled bodies but of a single color sergeant merely "exhausted," not killed. But by the time Lieutenant General Arthur MacArthur dropped dead in 1912 while addressing a reunion of his old regiment, the Twenty-fourth Wisconsin's sole and weary color sergeant was showing up in some of the general's obituaries as two dead ones, both "shot down."[79] That in his son's canonical version of the story there were *three* dead, that archetypal number redolent of wishes, brothers, and little pigs, does sound like something of a giveaway.

Yet whatever vanished tales my great-great-grandfather James might have told of glory or adventure on the battlefield, it turns out that one story *did* survive him, one story that was in its own way just as iconic of Yankee victory. It was the story I discovered in the same grand pedimented and columned building where I had turned up the tiny narratives of war told by James's own grandfather and great-grandfather, by Ralph Collins about St. Clair's defeat and by William Wharton about his Revolution. This story of James's was supported and confirmed by a chorus of friends, neighbors, family, doctors, and former comrades in arms and performed for a select and particular audience using language almost as formulaic as Homer's. Similar stories would be told by other Union veterans backed by other neighbors and relatives throughout the length and breadth of the victorious northern states. In the pension bureau files tenderly preserved in the National Archives in Washington—three cheers for government bureaucracy!—tens of thousands of Union soldiers tell their stories not of winning but of what *they* had lost in the war.

After Chattanooga, James's shooting war was just about at an end. He was granted a medical leave to tend to a case of the ubiquitous and debilitating "camp diarrhea," one of the more polite names applied to the range of bowel disorders—caused or compounded by dirty water, poor hygiene, bad food, close quarters, and perhaps some overenthusiastic dosing with opium or strychnine—that ran riot through the ranks, killing more soldiers than any other single malady and leaving countless others haggard, enfeebled, and disheartened. In late September, with his three years nearly up, Atlanta taken and torched, and the Eighteenth Kentucky about to end its stint of garrison duty and rejoin Sherman's army, James submitted his letter of resignation. In a tidy and practiced hand he explained that he had been "in every battle and skirmish and in almost every march in which my command has participated. My services are needed at my home in Ky. where lawless bands of guerrillas are pillaging the country."[80] His resignation was accepted, just in time to save him from earning his own personal part of the venom that Sherman's scorching march to Savannah would draw from southerners for generations to come. Dozens of other Pendleton boys from the Eighteenth did accompany the general as he blasted his merciless path to the sea.

So home James went, to embrace the old life he'd been so eager to escape in the thrilling summer of 1861. On December 29, 1864, just three months after his discharge, he married Ellen Callahan, who was fifteen or sixteen; among the wedding guests may have been her grandfather James Callahan, who had pioneered from the Carolinas to the savage Kentucky frontier seventy-five years earlier and who at the age of 101 still had four more years to live. Ellen herself would set no records for longevity: according to family legend she was a nasty-tempered "shrew" who in her early fifties burst a blood vessel in her throat during a tirade at a tradesman and keeled over on the spot. She had yelled herself to death.

After his return from the war my great-great-grandfather James farmed for a while, then in 1875 set up a law practice. Like his father, the old pioneer Joseph, he was heroically fecund, siring ten children. Like his father, he dabbled in local politics, losing at least one election for county attorney before serving a term as mayor of Falmouth in 1884–85. And again like his father, he seems to have had a propensity for entangling himself in personal difficulties. As the *True Kentuckian* reported on December 31, 1879, James's own brother-in-law C. C. Cram once pulled out a pistol in the courtroom and fired a shot at him, which missed its target and grazed a bystander in the forehead.

But even as he appeared to be settling down to a normal life in the years after the war, his health grew no better, and in 1879 he began to gather the stack of service records, medical certificates, and corroborating statements from friends and relatives that were required in an application for the veteran's pension offered by the federal government to Union soldiers who could prove they'd been disabled in the service of their country. Also required, as it had been of his grandfather and great-grandfather before him, was a personal statement, the soldier's own story.

The ritual of narrating one's war to officialdom had changed markedly in the decades since William Wharton omitted Valley Forge from his diffident little summary and Ralph Collins seemed to be bragging about being at St. Clair's devastating defeat. For William, Ralph, and James the purpose was the same: to persuade the government to reward their sacrifices with money. Each performed his statement for an audience, which in James's case included the county clerk who took his statement down in writing and who must have been recommended for his post by other talents than his spelling. But unlike his reticent forefathers, James gave every indication in the statement he dictated on January 24, 1881, that he was enjoying his time in the spotlight, relishing the role of narrator, and understanding what was expected of a war story. Five full pages long, the statement was articulate and self-confident, its language and tone often echoing the hearty style of the classic after-action report. And while the wording of the written version may have been massaged a little by the clerk, that inky official also showed signs here and there of how deeply he himself had been caught up in James's dramatic telling.

It had all started at Hoover's Gap in Tennessee, where the dauntless Colonel Wilder pulled off his grand charge. Captain Dougherty, however, was moving nowhere; his command was ordered to support a battery even as "the rain poured down in torrents all knight and fell in showers all next day he was officer of the night and took charge of the pickets when in close range of the enemy. Dawn found affiant and his command water soaked for 10 hours and in close range of the enemy in heavy force."[81]

As James's description of the situation grew more dire, the clerk fought valiantly against the temptation to transform himself from amanuensis to comrade in arms. "The battle of artilery opened with fury the 18th Ky lying in front of our cannon," the affidavit continued, wobbling back and forth between the first and third person,

> and laid in the mud and water all day except when they would rise to drive back the enemies infantry at night they were relieved and slept without shelter and no covering except their wet and muddy clothes next

day we were ordered forward through rain mud and swollen streams; and continued on the campaign in the field for 16 days it raining each day; our clothing being dried by warmth of our bodies and the sun to again be drenched by rain. At the end of this time my clothes were moulded and, I felt my heath failing Indigestion Camp Diarhea and inaction of the liver were troubling me for the first at the end of this campaign.

A brief recovery during the lull at the end of the Tullahoma campaign was followed by a relapse, and he fought the dreadful battle of Chickamauga while "completely exhausted" and with his "nervous system . . . greatly impared." Soon thereafter he was granted his medical leave and later that year his discharge.

His return home didn't restore him. As his older half sister Martha Bullock told the pension officials, James had become so ill in the summer of 1866 that "his life [was] dispaired of for a long time." Afterwards, Martha said, James's hair turned "one half gray" even though their father, Joseph, had been "but little gray" when he died at sixty of cholera, James's mother was still hearty at seventy, and "his family is noted for longevity." Near the end of his own statement James supplied the details of what ailed him: a range of digestive troubles, weakness, headaches, muscles that trembled so much he could barely lift a cup of water to his mouth, and "hedious dreams when asleep depression when awake." Hoping for an improvement in his health, he had not at first, he claimed, "demand[ed] of the government what is justly due me." But, he continued, as the clerk, caught up in the drama of the grand peroration, embraced the first person for good, "the prospect of want and beggary on myself and family has compelled me to ask the gov. to perform its contract placing me on the rolls to partially compensate me for the loss of my manhood in helping to preserve my benefactor."[82]

James's story paid off. His eloquence, or at least his documents and medical reports, persuaded his benefactor to appraise his lost manhood at $8.50 a month, the payments beginning in 1881 but retroactive to his discharge seventeen years earlier. Within six years, however, he had begun submitting a steady stream of additional medical documents and affidavits to request an increase on the grounds of ever-worsening "chronic diarrhoea and disease of liver; resulting dyspepsia and . . . nervous prostrations; irregular circulation of blood on left side; epilepsy and hemorrage of bowels and weakness of mind."[83]

But this time James's story ran smack into a counternarrative, a dissenting tale told by the part of his audience that mattered most. The three doctors from

Maysville who conducted the official medical examination evaluating James's request for the increase, and who immortalized his chronic flatulence, told a very different story about the seriousness of his complaints. Yes, they conceded, he had a range of symptoms: various pains and swellings, an irregular heartbeat, poor appetite, constipation alternating with diarrhea ("sometimes 15 or 20 actions daily"), a congested and ulcerated rectum, that chronic gas, and "fits of an epileptic character." But he was also "erect, dark-haired, fresh complexioned, and for an incurable or chronic dyspeptic, fairly well nourished . . . physical strength fairly good. . . . no gastric tenderness . . . no hepatic or splenic enlargement." The whole description is hard to square with the broken-down soul of the earlier witnesses' pictures; even something as basic as the color of his hair was in contention. Although the doctors rated James at seventeen-eighteenths disability, which eventually qualified him for a pension of $17 a month, they refused to recognize his nervous troubles among his war injuries and showed no sympathy for his pains. "The claimant," they wrote, "is a *dyspeptic* and a *hypochondriac;* he is suffering from irritable heart—but the fundamental trouble is evidently the diseased rectum—the *ulceration* and the *internal piles.* As for 'weakness of mind' we should scarcely look for it in a clever attorney."[84]

Cynical the doctors had some reason to be, especially regarding an attorney who might be clever. Ever since 1879, when Congress revised the pension laws to allow new applicants to claim lump-sum arrears payments covering all the years since their discharge, the scramble for pension funds had become unseemly. Some Americans were seeing the system as a massive boondoggle. By 1889 *The Nation* was complaining that annual spending on veterans' pensions was exceeding the prewar cost of the entire government, while the colossal new palazzo-style brick Pension Building in downtown Washington, where eight of the largest Corinthian columns in the world march in two rows across a fifteen-story-high interior courtyard, only reinforced a widespread impression of bloat. Nearly two-thirds of the Union's surviving soldiers were on the pension rolls in 1895.[85]

James was no malingerer; his physical suffering seems undeniable. Some doctors at the time were using the diagnosis of "irritable heart" to describe the consequences of overexertion and the exhaustion brought on by weeks-long stretches of hard marching and intense fighting.[86] The hemorrhoids and digestive complaints, moreover, which must certainly have been painful, constant, and debilitating, were clearly war injuries, a direct (and common) consequence of camp diarrhea and its associated disorders.

But his weren't the only doctors who looked on the much fuzzier gamut of "nervous" complaints, the headaches and giddy spells and bad dreams, with suspicion and disfavor. Nor were his doctors the only Americans who saw fortitude as a prime virtue and considered it unmanly to complain or despond. With psychiatric medicine in its infancy and the Victorian emphasis on self-reliance and moral strength in full flower, medical boards tended to be dismissive of mental or emotional troubles that didn't seem to have originated in some kind of overt and evident physical trauma. Psychiatrists as well as historians have concluded that many Civil War soldiers and veterans showed symptoms consistent with the kind of severe psychological distress that has come to be known as posttraumatic stress disorder, or PTSD. In 2006 a psychiatric journal published a study of the old pension records that noted a clear statistical correlation between service in regiments with high mortality rates and later reports of heart, digestive, and nervous disease. Under the conventions and assumptions of the time, however, sufferers were generally treated as if they were shirking, whining, or crazy. Even the most severely impaired men were frequently denied pensions because doctors saw no obvious physical link between their nervous condition and their wartime service. Their ailments were, in other words, their own fault.[87]

So James and the government's medical advisers had good reason to tell their different stories. It's also very possible that James could have been embellishing or exaggerating his physical symptoms in an attempt to win some allowances for his less acceptable ones. Perhaps it's unfair to point out that a man supposed to be so disabled he "cannot do anything" nonetheless managed to father ten children, a new baby appearing like clockwork every other year throughout his marriage until his wife was nearing forty—but one does wonder.

Still, James's war had been as rich as anyone's in the stuff that "hedious dreams" are made on. Each of his promotions, while doubtless gratifying, also brought increasing responsibilities and anxieties; not for him the almost liberating impotence of the foot soldier who only had to follow orders, never worrying about issuing the right ones. The fates of the three officers whose places he successively took were also vivid reminders of how various the catastrophes of war could be: the first had done something unacceptably stupid or dangerous, the second never walked normally again, and the last was seized in his own home in front of his wife by guerrillas who then shot him down in the mud and mutilated his body. In James's three years of active service, moreover, the Eighteenth Kentucky had been on or near the ground for several skirmishes and four major actions. Both Richmond, where he ended his first battle experience as a prisoner of war, and Chickamauga, where he'd stayed on the legendarily gruesome field until almost the very end, ranked high among the Union's most crushing disasters. After enduring the miseries of the long siege at Chattanooga, he had then watched from the sidelines as the rest of his brigade joined in one of the Union's most glorious triumphs. And the victory at Hoover's Gap that had brought renewed renown to Colonel Wilder bestowed on James only a moldy uniform and the beginning of what would be a quarter century of illness, embarrassment, inconvenience, and unhappiness. It would also be a quarter century of increasingly urgent attempts to demonstrate that even though he might not be displaying the unambiguous pathos of a stump or scar, his war had *hurt.*

He finally did prove his point. On the fifth of May 1889, less than two and a half years after the doctors called him a hypochondriac, Captain James Dougherty offered the most persuasive possible rebuttal to the medical board's skepticism: he died. The physician's certificate submitted by his widow to the pension board (and, yes, she was asking for survivor's benefits) described the cause as "Apoplexy, the result of a long existing or chronic gastritis, chronic Diarrhoea and disease of the liver."[88] This scion of the family "noted for longevity" was not quite fifty years of age.

At least the poor man had had company throughout his long misery. The pension files are full of war stories by formerly healthy men, including several other Yankee connections of mine, claiming to have been unmanned by disabilities both evident and obscure. Henry Duckworth, James's ex-stepfather, "had to walk with two canes in going down a hill," according to a neighbor's affidavit in 1901. "At the present time he is not able to work any at all, when he exerts himself any in the least he will turn blind and fall down." After several tries Henry was awarded a small sum for his rheumatism, but pension officials refused to compensate him for his heart disease, his chronic diarrhea, his fits, and the deafness that he sometimes reported in his right ear and sometimes in his left. Despite all his ailments, he outlived his stepson by a quarter century, dying at ninety-two of chronic kidney disease at the old soldiers' home in Ohio.[89] Dennis Nichols's application reported that he was "nervous" and had chronic diarrhea, congestion of the stomach and bowels, and an inflamed rectum with "3 internal piles 1/4 inch in diameter—2 external piles 1/4 inch in diameter." But after he was awarded $17 a month in 1890, officials rejected his constant pleas for an increase, arguing that the piles and the congestion had been covered under the award and the nervousness wasn't the government's problem.[90] The ubiquity of complaints about bowel and digestive problems suggests to any attentive reader of the pension files an entirely new vision of post–Civil War America as a land full of middle-aged men preoccupied with their rectums and frequently to be found groaning in the outhouse or fleeing from the horsehair settee.

But the reader also finds a vast, insistent, and collaborative story of woe rising from the statements made to the pension bureau by all those returned veterans and their friends, neighbors, and kin. Yes, I know him, he used to be fine and strong and healthy, but *now* look at him. Yes, I was a soldier when I was young and hearty, but *now* look at me. The Union pension system accomplished all sorts of feats, some intended and some not: it bound the vast army of ex-soldiers into a community of common interest, it encouraged a sense of gratitude toward the government, it planted deep roots for the controversial idea of federal responsibility for individual and family welfare, it served as a mighty tool for political patronage and an incitement to profiteers and cheats. But there was something else, too. To all those veterans who had come home from the war injured or sick, but particularly to the ones who, once home, found themselves troubled, out of sorts, dreaming bad dreams, disdained by their manlier neighbors, generally unhappy in ways for which both medicine and words seemed lacking, the Union's pension process offered more than the admittedly magnetic possibility of money; it was also a golden chance to tell their stories. In fact it absolutely required the tellers to insist on the depth of their suffering and to focus their attention on everything they had lost. Even as the United States put its war behind it and officially embraced a public story of reconciliation, enterprise, and progress, the government's establishment of the federal pension bureau—the winner's generosity toward the soldiers who had made its victory possible—ended up encouraging and often rewarding a genre of storytelling that wove a more subdued alternative epic not of triumph but of unhappiness and loss: Listen while I tell you what the war cost me. *Just listen to me!*

Few of the war's *official* losers were invited to join this particular storytelling circle. Pensions for ex-Confederates tended to be rare, small, and long in coming. The federal government, understandably, did not extend its general postwar spirit of reconciliation so far as to pay people for the hurts they had suffered in rebelling against it. That left the granting of pensions up to the individual states, but the southern and border governments were either too burdened or too ambivalent to offer their ex-Rebels much support. W. B. Roberts, his wife, and their hapless son Nathan were all long dead by 1912, when Kentucky finally got around to offering modest pensions to resident Confederate veterans or their widows, but like most of its sister states, it relieved only the poorest and sickest. W. B.'s older son, Will, did apply immediately, but the process was perfunctory in the extreme. After filling out a two-page application form, the old soldier, by then seventy-three, underwent a brief interview at the county courthouse in which he testified to both his poverty and his precarious health and presented a couple of witnesses who said they were pretty sure Will had been in the Confederate Army. He spun no tales about his days in the army half a century gone and supplied no details of his service other than the dates of his enlistment and his surrender. The application was approved without discussion, no story required.[91]

Federal pensions would never have stopped southerners from indulging in their Lost Cause, and in fact some southerners found yet another confirmation of their moral superiority in what they dismissed as Yankee handouts to graspers and grumblers.[92] Nor did Confederate veterans and their families suffer any less keenly than the Yankees did from the lingering physical pains of war. But in the surviving stories about my fighting kinsmen lies one elucidation of the conundrum of the impossibly romanticized but ardently embraced Lost Cause. It was Nathan Roberts, ne'er-do-well, drunkard, and defeated Rebel, who lived on in his family's stories as a martyr on par with some of the South's most cherished heroes. It was James Dougherty—mayor, family man, officer, and victorious Yankee—who left me with more information about his ruined bowels than I really care to know.

Only the winners could afford to acknowledge what had been lost in the *real* war.

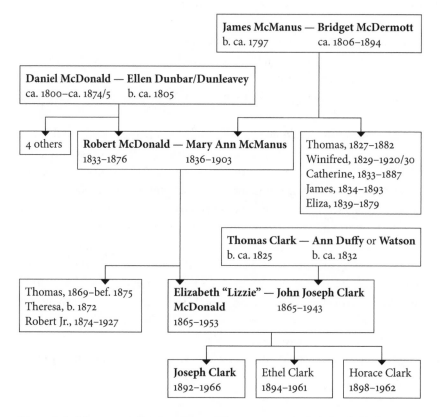

Names in **bold** represent direct ancestors. Other names are included only if relevant.

CHAPTER 6
Damned Yankees

⚮

NANA C. WAS THE LAST PERSON IN THE WORLD YOU'D SUSPECT OF HAR-boring any kind of secret, let alone a shockingly unhappy one. I didn't quite know her myself—born just weeks after Abraham Lincoln died, my mother's paternal grandmother, Lizzie McDonald Clark, died just weeks before my first brother was born—but as a child I certainly knew about her. She seemed a classic representative of the *other* side of the family, the kin my grandmother Grace acquired through her radically un-Kentuckian marriage to Joseph Clark, the cautious, prim, and frugal New Yorker she'd met in 1918 while doing war work in Washington during what was probably her first-ever venture more than fifty miles from home. Compared to the tales of generations of roving, brawl-ing, feckless, luckless, scalped, and stolen southern pioneers who preceded my mother's mother into the world, everything Lizzie and the rest of my mother's father's forebears had said about their lives seemed almost aggressively decorous.

They were Yankees, first of all—not even ambiguous border-staters but gen-uine Yankees like me—which meant, I presumed, that I wouldn't have to grap-ple with them or excuse them or figure them out: I could just *understand* them. They had lived in good Yankee towns like Albany and Troy, in upstate New York, and they did the sorts of things happy Yankees do. From my grandfather's family came tales of a math professor, a piano teacher, a prominent physician, a breeder of racehorses, a munitions mogul, and a member of the "landed aris-tocracy" who was a friend of Governor Franklin Roosevelt. Most glorious of all was Lizzie's uncle Thomas McManus, a "brilliant" lad who as a mere boy had ripsnorted his way all the way through Euclid's *Elements* and whose storybook life included coups both entrepreneurial and matrimonial. Starting out at four-teen as a lowly clerk, in no time at all he had become the handpicked heir to the great Hudson River shipping firm of the childless Colonel James Hooker, and he married the future great-aunt of Wallis Warfield Simpson, the woman King Edward VIII would love. Through no fault of his own, Uncle Thomas eventually suffered some cataclysmic business failure, and my mother had a vague impression that he made amends with an honorable suicide. But that only added a touch of authenticity to his tale: after all, *we* weren't rich.

Lizzie herself, the first native-born American in the clan, used to tell my mother tales of a conventional and comfortable childhood, carefully bounded by firm rules of decorum and propriety—all her life she was such a demon for white gloves that in 1972 my mother dutifully packed me off to my historically all-male college with a pair—but leavened by visits to Uncle Thomas's fine house on the park and carefree sledding parties on the wintry hills of Troy. She grew up to be an ample, sweet-faced, double-chinned, fluffy-haired old lady, a solid if not ardent convert to the Episcopal Church, a dutiful wife to the diminutive husband she overtopped by half a head, a careful but affectionate mother to Joseph, Ethel, and Horace, and a confidante, ally, and storyteller to Joe's younger daughter, Doris.

But when we finally discovered that sweet-faced Nana C. in her prim white gloves was the most audaciously revisionist of all my kin in her stories about her American pursuit of happiness, the most unreliable narrator of the bunch, we also had to acknowledge that she had every reason to be. It had taken my grand-mother Grace's family three hundred years, starting with their arrival near the very dawn of the English American experience, to accomplish a fully rounded cycle of aspiration, prosperity, misfortune, violence, and decline. My grandfa-ther's family arrived in America two and a half centuries later, and within the span of a single generation had done the same thing.

It was good Yankee tragedy, too—*modern* tragedy, smartly accomplished at a brisk modern pace—that did them in. Its setting was as modern as could be. The two hustling melting pot cities facing each other across the Hudson River were connected by canal and rail to just about everywhere else and devoted to the tireless production and transportation of *things:* of beer and shirt collars, horseshoes and iron stoves, stagecoaches, stockings, and great cast-iron bells weighing as much as six tons. Not for Lizzie's family the raw and casual brutality of the frontier; not for them the eerie menace of the faintly rustling forest, the daily horror of the disfigured daughter, the never-ending grief for the stolen son.

And not for them the beguiling melancholy of the Lost Cause, that exquisite solvent of tedious Yankee virtues like grit, ambition, and push. My northern kin had grit aplenty and earned a resounding success in their ambitiously charted path toward happiness, but in the end they lost everything modern life had given them, and more: fortune, their pride, their past, all hope, and, spectacularly, one rather repugnant life. Unlike my Rebel ancestors, however, they had no grand master narrative to explain, soothe, and spread the burden of their bereavement, no covenant with a finer unhappiness. The narrative Lizzie's family came up with was a complicated knot of familiar stories shot through with silences and trepanned by secrets. Especially that one about the murder.

Although secrets seem the polar opposite of stories, they serve many of the same purposes that stories do: secret keeping is in effect *selective* storytelling in which the tellers organize reality in a meaningful way and create the self they desire by claiming the right *not* to share some crucial elements of their experience. But secrets are black holes for historians (and for descendants, too), who rarely have enough information to expect or even suspect the presence of one. That they exist at all is usually itself the deepest secret; like a body buried in the backyard, they tend to be uncovered only by accident, if the rain falls hard enough or the neighbor's nosy dog gets through the fence. It had long ago occurred to me that all those generations' worth of southern forebears had plenty of secrets of their own, too, ranging from the trivial to the terrible, but I had never really expected I could find a window into the heart and soul of our turbulent Colonel Thomas Ballard, for instance, the wealthy slave owner and political opportunist dead now for three and a half centuries. There is dispensation in distance, I decided, and I was content to let sleeping ancestors lie.

But Lizzie and her family were telling their stories to, and keeping their secrets from, *me*. The tales that she and her only daughter, Ethel, bestowed on my mother, and through her on me, were largely unmediated by either the long slippage of time or the nostalgic yearnings of descendants; they came directly to us from familiar people who had lived them. Doris knew her grandmother Lizzie well, lived near her on New York's Staten Island all her life, honored her, loved her. Of course she never thought her kin would look her in the eye and lie to her. Why on earth should she have expected that an ordinary old nana with her double chins and her sensible shoes had anything untoward buried in the tidy little backyard where her husband pottered among the hydrangeas and harvested Concord grapes for his homemade wine?

Even I had known my great-aunt Ethel, who died when I was six. And

Lizzie Clark, "Nana C.," keeping secrets in her backyard in Staten Island, N.Y., ca. 1950.

although I was too young to understand or remember much of what she'd said, I still have the little sheaf of penciled notes and reminiscences that in her self-appointed role as family storyteller—something my southern kin had entirely lacked—she had late in her life begun to write down. The notes were to be the basis for a book that, she was confident, would restore the fortunes that

Saturday, January 9, 1954

9th day—356 days follow

<u>Mc Manus</u> mothers family
Came here (maternal pide
from Ireland — sailing
vessel 1839. Parents
and several small children
Landed in Lachine Can..
A fishing part. Conticles
and fish were sold in
the town. Trip across — 8 wks

The head of family
who had been a
professor of math, in
Dublin university opened a
private school in
town of Lachine Later moved
down to Montreal where
they lived for a time.
Barges were then

Ethel Clark's notes toward a family history, 1954.

219

Ethel Clark, publicity photograph, early 1920s.

had been lost to some unexplained and personally malignant fate, and restore the rightful luster of our family name.

"Poor Aunt Ethel," my mother always called her.

Lizzie's pride and joy, Ethel had at a very young age been discovered to be "musical," and was promptly signed up for singing and dancing lessons. When she made her recital debut at the age of nine, a local reviewer called her a "child wonder," praising her voice as "very firm and sweet" and her enunciation as "most perfect." Unlike her two brothers, she was not entrusted to the local public high school, receiving private instruction instead, and at nineteen was admitted to the Institute of Musical Art, the pioneering conservatory founded by Frank Damrosch that would later merge with the newer Juilliard School. There Damrosch himself judged Ethel's "high flexible soprano" voice as "bright, intelligent, [and] musical." But she was also "unrhythmical and careless" at the piano, she struggled in ear training, she failed her Italian class, and she left the conservatory after a year without graduating. (That didn't stop her from forever afterwards making frequent and casual mention of her degree from Juilliard.) Her talents seem to have been both noteworthy and limited.[1]

As an adult she performed with several light opera companies and made a specialty of Gilbert and Sullivan's lesser ingénue roles. We still have a couple of the scrapbooks she kept, crammed with photographs, programs, fan letters, reviews, and clippings, including one from the *Evening Post* of December 19, 1931, displaying Ethel Clark's picture from *The Mikado* right next to one of Gloria Swanson in *Tonight or Never* at the Rialto. The notice Ethel drew in the reviews was generally as modest as her parts, running heavily to adjectives like "dainty," "charming," "sweet," and "winsome," though one reviewer found her "fluttery coyness" a bit overdone. Ethel had definitely found her niche, but as her co-diva Gloria Swanson herself would show the world years later in *Sunset Boulevard,* it had the potential to be a cruel one. When on May 5, 1931, the powerful *New York Times* drama critic Brooks Atkinson blessed Ethel's portrayal of Pitti-Sing as "splendidly girlish," my great-aunt was nearly thirty-seven years old. A year earlier she had told the census takers she was twenty-eight.[2]

In fact Ethel would be spared the fate of the petrified ingénue Norma Desmond, but by a providence that was no less unkind: in what would reveal itself as a family pattern, she lost everything to a string of sudden misfortunes and reversals when she was barely entering middle age. In 1922, when she was twenty-eight for real, she had placed her happiness into the keeping of "Dr." Walter Cleveland from exotic Palm Beach (the ironic quotes are mine but, I would wager, entirely appropriate), a chiropractor and "naturopath" who according to his business card offered "manipulative and ultra violet ray treatments" and whose tales of high social connections were catnip for poor Aunt Ethel. He became her manager and established an apartment for them in Atlantic City that was entirely decorated in white, including the chow dog.

My mother could summon no recollection of Walter at all, but she never forgot that apartment.

I don't know whether Ethel ever knew, as I easily discovered through a brief foray into the federal census returns under the guidance of Ancestry. com's secret-busting search engine, that her fancy husband was actually the son of a small farmer and a former hired girl from the mountains of northern Pennsylvania.[3] What did become quickly clear, though, was that Walter was either an inept manager or a venal one, and much too fond of the ponies besides. He had managed to run through just about all of Ethel's money by the time he was "dispatched," as my mother put it, by his brother-in-law, my grandfather Joe, who had mistrusted his motives and morals from the start.

Then, just as Ethel was starting over as a divorcée in reduced circumstances, her singing voice was ravaged by a bad throat infection. By the time she reached her forties she had retired from the stage and entered into the genteel drudgery of giving lessons and singing for churches and charities, and even though this second career was "rather routine and dull for one at the peak of attainment in an artistic world," as she put it in her reminiscences, she "dug in." Throughout her life Ethel carried like an offering of frankincense or myrrh her conviction that she had been tragically wronged, that blind and uncontrollable forces had somehow robbed her of her rightful happiness and dragged our entire family down from the heights we had once occupied. "How could this all have fallen to the Grand niece of one Thomas McManus," she jotted, not quite coherently, in her notes, "whose career in shipping, with a N.Y. office at #20 Coenties Slip—the New York office of Hudson River Day Line, which Thomas McManus inherited from the original owner, Col. Hooker." She reached no conclusion, at least in those notes, which she compiled when she was sixty (for real). But she had pinned a pile of hopes on that proposed book—not only that it would right the injustices visited upon our family, but also that it would, with any luck, win her her heart's desire: membership in the Daughters of the American Revolution.

That quest was hopeless, and given all the genealogical work she'd done, she must have known it, too. My mother and I discovered almost as soon as we began poking into my grandfather's family that the roots of all four of Joe's and Ethel's grandparents ran deep in Irish soil and that all four had arrived in the United States around the middle of the nineteenth century. That's also when we realized that one whole side of the family, the relatives of Lizzie's father—my great-great-grandfather Robert McDonald—had essentially been torn out of the family scrapbook. As with Grace's father, the deplorable Arthur, just about the only information we were able to find about Robert and his family came not from kin but from strangers, in this case the hardworking drudges of the various census bureaus who had periodically gone knocking on my relatives' doors to ask them about their jobs, their children, their heritage, in some years even about their income or education or general health.

It was from Scottish drudges I learned that shortly after their marriage, Robert's parents, Daniel and Ellen McDonald, both Irish natives, moved to Paisley, Scotland, on the outskirts of the smoky and often squalid industrial city of Glasgow. There five surviving children were born to them between about 1832 and 1849, and there Daniel plied the lowly trade of bootmaker. The first visible signs of the McDonalds' presence in the United States were the listings in the 1856 *Albany Directory* showing that they'd essentially brought the Old World with them; most of them were still working as shoemakers or dressmakers. But Robert, the second son, was a maverick who broke ranks with his family and took an entirely different professional path. No awls for him, no days spent hunched over lasts and shoe leather; my great-great-grandfather quickly found his way into the liquor trade, a booming business if ever there was one and a chance for a man with gumption to smash right through that Old Country tradition that you'd never make more of yourself than your father had. Robert was married by 1860 and living in a houseful of women—wife, mother-in-law, and two-year-old daughter—but all three of them had vanished without explanation by 1864, when my great-great-grandmother Mary Ann McManus became his second wife.[4]

For the other side of Lizzie's family, her maternal relatives, the McManuses, the problem wasn't that there was *no* story; it was deciding which of the many stories were worth trusting. On guard against the dangerous combination of grandiosity and calculated silence that was Ethel's legacy, I was initially inclined to doubt everything she said. And some of her assertions were indeed demonstrably inaccurate. While she had always insisted, for instance, that her great-grandfather James McManus had been a math professor at "Dublin University," there's not a single mathematical McManus in the impressive records kept by Trinity College, Dublin.[5] But my task became both more interesting and more difficult when *some* of her stories turned out to have roots, however shallow, in reality.

Her notes didn't say where the family had come from, but, pondering hard, both my aunt Gina and my mother, when queried separately, offered up the same hazy memory. Roscommon, they said; they seemed to remember hearing something about Lizzie's roots in County Roscommon. That part fit: McManus was (and still is) a common name in the region, Roscommon does turn up as the birthplace on the death certificate of the woman who was almost certainly my great-great-great-grandmother, and the register of Boyle parish in Roscommon does include entries for a McManus family with six children that generally conforms to the scattered and sometimes conflicting information I've been able to tease out, from both family tradition and documentary evidence, about my ancestors' later life in New York. In the McManuses' day Boyle was a bustling market and garrison town serving a fertile hinterland dotted with tiny farms raising mainly potatoes and oats. But as an agent from the Royal Dublin Society noted on a surveying visit in 1830, the town was also known for public houses "to an extent injurious to the health, morals, and best interests of the lower classes," and he was appalled by both the disproportionately large size of Boyle's beggar population and the "disgusting depravity" of its habits.[6]

Like many mid-century immigrants with misspellable names, the McManuses left no clear traces anywhere, anytime, of how and when they made it to America. Ethel said the family arrived in Canada in 1839 and soon made its way south, which is not the story you'd expect in an Irish American family of the McManuses' vintage. You'd expect—or I expected—them to have left home between around 1846 and 1851, for the same reasons a million or more other Irish people did: in headlong flight from the misery brought by the relentless blight rotting the potatoes that were a mainstay of the peasant diet, and from the parsimony and contempt that government officials were offering in response.[7] To my surprise, however, the New York State census of 1855 captured my McManus relatives in a two-family house in West Troy, where, they said, they'd been living for twelve years—that is, since 1843. And the 1849 *Prescott & Wilson's Troy City Directory* listed Lizzie's uncle Thomas as a clerk in a waterfront firm, a position that seems inconceivable for someone who'd only recently arrived as a desperate famine emigrant.[8]

In fact I found all sorts of evidence suggesting that for a while at least, Ethel hadn't been exaggerating (much) about the fortunes of the McManuses in America. One confirmation came from a welcome but problematic source for any family historian: photographs. Ethel, we found, had tucked away a collection of about two dozen *carte de visite* portraits dating from the early or mid-1860s, all showing thriving, well-turned-out people and most bearing inked annotations, sometimes cryptic, on the back: "Thomas McManus, Mother's uncle" or "Robert McDonald, My Grandfather" or "One of the

Warrens of New York" (who on earth?). Finding Ethel's little collection was a vivid reminder that while old photographs can be the most intimate of historical sources, they can also be the most inscrutable. Because my great-aunt happened to have labeled them, I could not only use them as evidence that these ancestors were confident and conventional-seeming middle-class people alive at a particular moment in time; I could also indulge in the mystic pleasure of holding "Robert" in my hand and looking into the eyes of one of the thousands of long-gone people absolutely essential to my appearance on this earth. But if Ethel had never gotten around to picking up her fountain pen, someone would long ago have tossed those photographs away as just a bunch of "Musgraves."

When I looked critically at Ethel's claims of ancestral glory, I realized that cranking them down by just a couple of notches usually did the trick. Although no James McManus ever taught math at Trinity College, a man with that name did keep a modest-sized and prosperous pay school in Boyle in 1824, and according to one account he later worked as a teller in a local bank.[9] Uncle Thomas's precocious mastery of mathematics remains unconfirmed, except perhaps in the amazing ability of his great-nephew Horace, Ethel's younger brother, to add endless columns of figures in a flash. But even though his mother couldn't sign her name, Thomas did have enough education to land a job as a clerk in the thriving shipping firm of Colonel James Hooker, remembered in an obituary as a "wonderful business man" who conducted the affairs of his "immense concern . . . with such admirable method, excellent tact, and complete success." In 1850 Hooker was presiding over eleven barges, 120 canal boats, a dozen steamboats and propeller-driven ships, eleven sailing vessels, one thousand draft horses, and offices in five cities.[10]

When the colonel died a year later, however, that "wonderful business man" left no will, which meant that, contrary to Ethel's insistence, he didn't bequeath his firm to Thomas, or to any of his other 1,395 employees, either. But after several years of clerking elsewhere, in 1860 Thomas and a partner had the resources as well as the confidence to form a firm of their own, the Hudson River Transport Company of Troy and New York (not, as Ethel had it, the long-lived and well-beloved Hudson River Day Line, which had been established by Commodore Alfred Van Santvoord in 1856). As another sign of his increasing civic importance, he got himself elected that same year to the first of six consecutive one-year terms as alderman from the city's eighth ward, and in the early 1870s came back after a redistricting to serve three more terms from the twelfth.[11]

The rest of the family was thriving too. Thomas's sister Eliza, the reputed piano teacher, married a young American-born medical man named Alexander McDonald, who was no relation to the Scottish immigrant who would become Mary Ann's husband, and who was appointed city physician for the northern district of Troy (Ethel said he was director of the Board of Health.) Their sister Catherine's husband, Lawrence Grattan, was progressing from baker to grocer to farmer to running a livery stable (Ethel said he was a "gentleman farmer" and racehorse breeder). Winifred's husband was another recent Irish immigrant, Thomas Behan, who "prospered exceedingly" in the liquor trade. Ethel wasn't entirely wrong when she linked the Behans to their "close friend" Governor Franklin Roosevelt, who in 1931 would appoint a son of Thomas and Winifred to the post of state insurance inspector. The new bureaucrat enjoyed the honor for just two months before dropping dead. But the Behans weren't exactly the "landed aristocracy" she said they were, unless you count as "land" the plot in St. Agnes's cemetery in the Albany suburb of Menands that the family bought when it first opened and where Thomas Behan spent his last years as superintendent. The family matriarch, meanwhile, seems to have celebrated her arrival in the United States by changing her name to something more suitable to her new estate: Thomas and Mary Ann's mother, known as Bridget back in Ireland, was now calling herself Betsey.[12]

But even though Ethel wasn't always completely wrong, there was a lot she wasn't telling. It wasn't just the entire paternal side of the family, Robert's side, that went unmentioned by her and by Lizzie too. As far as my mother could recall, neither Ethel nor Lizzie had ever said a word about Lizzie's own mother, Mary Ann, and the gallery of family photographs that Ethel cherished includes not a single image identified as that of her grandmother.

It was completely by accident that my mother and I figured out why, tipped off by a fleeting reference buried deep in a breadbox-sized bicentennial history of Albany that we had heaved off a library shelf on a whim.[13] Soon we were sitting under the glare of the microfilm reader marveling as the *Albany Evening Journal* unspooled its lurid tale. Doris was torn between fascination on the one hand and pity, chagrin, and dismay on the other; to come along and rip open the secret her beloved grandmother had guarded so faithfully in life seemed an affront no less brutal than reaching into the casket and stripping the white gloves from her clasped dead hands.

For me, though, whom chronology had made Lizzie's historian rather than her mourner, the pity and dismay came in third. First was a sense of profound gratitude to the gods of chance that we'd found the volume in the first place. And following as a close second was a resurgence of the dark questions that can keep the researcher awake at night: If I could find out something so momentous entirely by luck, what other lucky strikes have I missed? What kind of utterly wrongheaded story would I be telling about my own family's lives and happiness if we had simply galumphed right past the tiny clue pointing to how as an eleven-year-old girl my great-grandmother watched her mother shoot her father in the head?

Once we knew where the story ended, it was easy to work backwards and retrace the steps that brought the McDonalds and McManuses to their moment of crisis. The public sources from the 1860s were continuing to tell a story of happiness and success. The Civil War that engulfed Kentucky in grief, terror, and anguish brought little but high times to the Yankee side of the family, no member of which seems to have gotten around to serving. According to Ethel, Mary Ann's brother James McManus "made a fortune in munitions at the [Watervliet] arsenal during the war," though I've found no confirmation of that; more likely, given Ethel's pattern, James, who left fewer contemporary traces than any of his siblings, was just one of the two thousand minions working at the busy arsenal at the height of the war. Ethel did go on to note that "they were not a money wise family—it did not seem to remain with them," and that part certainly has the ring of truth to me.

Uncle Thomas, however, was thriving. In the early 1860s he began buying land in the Albany suburbs, took up residence in a house in an upscale Troy neighborhood, and launched the pride of his Albany–to–New York fleet, a one-cylinder wooden-hull steamboat the brand-new mogul exuberantly named after himself. The *Thomas McManus,* which carried both passengers and freight and measured 170 feet long, was distinctive for its unusually large size as well as its tasteful furnishings.[14] Around the same time, Thomas married Isabella Montague, the older daughter of Troy's leading merchant tailor. (Ethel's fantasy was flightier than usual here: although Wallis Warfield's mother was a Montague too, the future duchess of Windsor's roots ran deep in Virginia and Baltimore, while Isabella's father was yet another immigrant from Ireland.)

Later it was said that Thomas had been "at one time" worth $100,000—well over two million dollars in today's currency—and this was probably that time. The photograph from Ethel's collection shows a confident and substantial man, his watch chain straining across a well-filled waistcoat, his face composed. It's

Great-great-great-uncle Thomas McManus, the family mogul, early 1860s.

a quirky face, with one eyebrow arching tidily while the other shoots up at an angle and a goatee that looks as if it has been pasted on crooked, but it seems to survey the world with quiet happiness.

My great-great-grandfather Robert McDonald, too, found an opportunity in the war years to join the ranks of the entrepreneurs: with a couple of partners he opened a liquor dealership. Their invaluable commodity probably helped soothe his grief over the death of his first wife after less than five years of marriage, as well as, perhaps, their baby daughter. But he also managed to find a more tangible comfort: Mary Ann McManus, whom he had probably first met in 1858, when she was about twenty-two and he a lowly bookkeeper working for her brother-in-law Thomas Behan's liquor firm. Mary Ann's intended spouse didn't quite measure up to her siblings', to Thomas's merchant princess or to Winifred Behan's Thomas, who was clearly flourishing in the business his erstwhile clerk was still struggling to master. Maybe it was Robert's widowerhood that appealed to Mary Ann, the chance to heal and comfort a broken heart. Or maybe with the war dragging into its fourth year there just weren't many other men for a woman closing in on thirty to choose from. In any case, Robert and Mary Ann were married on July 7, 1864, as General Sherman was marching on Atlanta and the war was lurching toward its chaotic close. Ten months later, just weeks after Abraham Lincoln died, Mary Ann bore their first child, a daughter they named Elizabeth. She was always called Lizzie.

Even if he couldn't yet compete with the prosperity of his in-laws, Robert must have seemed a tycoon to the rest of his own family of shoemakers and dressmakers. Ethel's photograph shows an ordinary, respectable man of affairs, well brushed and maintained, and not even a historian with the unfair advantage of hindsight can discern in his stiff posture and direct stare any foreshadowing of doom. (A single photograph may be worth a thousand words, but all it can tell you is the middle of a story, never the beginning or the end.) In the first years of his marriage he did well enough to supply his wife with the standard middle-class accessory of a live-in Irish servant and his daughter Lizzie with the standard middle-class garniture of piano lessons, which much later she would pass on to her little granddaughters, Doris and Gina. But the first signs of trouble didn't take long to show. By 1867 Robert and his two partners had already fallen so deeply into debt that his brother-in-law Thomas had to bail them out, becoming assignee of their floundering firm. Two years later, when Mary Ann and Robert had their second child, they named the boy for their benefactor. It was doubtless a bittersweet tribute for Thomas, since he and

Great-great-grandfather Robert McDonald, the family disgrace, early 1860s.

Isabella would not produce any surviving children of their own to share in their growing prosperity.[15]

By 1870 Mary Ann could have had little doubt that Robert was a chronic loser. After running through at least four partners, he crashed yet another firm, this one indebted for well over $10,000, including $3,652.48 owed to Thomas. He also owed more than $1,200 in damages and court costs to a seventy-five-year-old woman named Margaret Foy who had been "cut, hurt, wounded, bruised and greatly paralized [*sic*], & her life despaired of" when Robert's horse ran away with the delivery wagon and knocked her down.[16] After losing his firm, Robert traded for a while on his own in a seedy waterfront neighborhood, but soon even that effort crumbled. At the age of around forty, and with four young children at home, he became a hireling again, taking a job as "superintendent" for a downtown restaurant called the Marble Pillar. The suspicion is inescapable that he had become much too fond of his own merchandise.

Adding to the troubles of Robert and Mary Ann at this point was the string of calamities that visited all of the Thomases of the McDonald-McManus clan. The little boy, their firstborn son, died before the age of six of causes unknown. Winifred's husband, Thomas Behan, lost that "exceedingly" prosperous liquor firm of his to the financial turmoil of the early 1870s.[17] And in the years leading up to 1876, Thomas McManus, the family's mainstay, endured all the trials of Job, but there was no deus ex machina in the end to tell him he hadn't really meant it.

Thomas must have been staggered in 1871 by the death of his young wife only six or seven years after their wedding, but the will she left hints strongly at deep stresses in their marriage and a profound mistrust of her husband's financial competence. She bequeathed him "my brick dwelling house and lot" on Seventh Street in Troy (not *our* house, though they'd both been living there), but went on to "expressly" charge him with repaying $3,000 to her estate within six months of her death. That sum represented "the amount he owes me for monies of mine lately taken by him to invest for my account," and if he couldn't raise the cash, as she scolded from the grave in her will, he would have to sell the house. She didn't even trust him to administer her estate; her executors were her mother and sister, to whom she left the rest of her property.[18]

Isabella's doubts seem to have been justified. After apparently making a deal with his mother-in-law to retire his debt with a payment of only $2,000, Thomas immediately mortgaged the house to the Merchants and Mechanics Bank of Troy for $12,000, then within two years lost it in a sheriff's sale. Also deep in debt to the Delaware, Lackawanna, and Western Railroad, Thomas schemed to protect his property from his creditors by transferring title to his large lot in Cohoes to his mother. With its legendary cutthroat persistence, however, the railroad eventually managed to wrest a chunk of the lot from Betsey and auction that off too. Murky traces of a tangle of other suits and judgments against Thomas float throughout the deed books and court records, and by 1875 his firm, which had never been formally incorporated or registered, had disappeared from sight.[19] At nearly fifty years of age, the widowed Thomas moved back into lodgings in Troy and started all over again as a lawyer. (Ethel said he was district attorney. "The young McManus had many bad breaks," she noted, "but he always used them as stepping stones.")

Ethel put it all down to the bad luck that stalked the McManus family. The federal government had commandeered and ruined three of his barges during the Civil War, she recalled in her notes, then refused to make restitution even after his claim for $250,000 "went as far as a bill which was introduced on the House floor." On top of that, two more of his vessels just happened to have been tied up in Chicago when Mrs. O'Leary's cow kicked over the lantern, and had burned up in the spectacular fire of 1871.

Again, Ethel's recollections aren't entirely outside the penumbra of truth. Not the part about the Great Chicago Fire, I think—it's difficult to imagine that vessels constructed for river traffic would have braved (or found profit in) the long trip all the way to Chicago through the high seas and choppy waves of most of the Great Lakes—but in May 1862 Troy had a relatively great fire of its own. After sparks from a locomotive ignited the wooden railroad bridge over the Hudson, the flames, driven by a high wind, quickly engulfed much of the waterfront business district and whirled inland to devour houses, banks, orphanages, and churches, 507 buildings in all. Neither Thomas's home nor his office stood in the path of the conflagration, but some of his barges may have: the burning debris from the collapsed bridge floated down the river, endangering the boats lying moored at the wharves.[20]

And during the Civil War the army quartermaster did lease (not commandeer) four (not three) of Thomas's barges and a steamboat besides, which did indeed see hard usage during service that included transporting troops and supplies to Bermuda Hundred in Virginia in the spring of 1864. In a suit filed with the United States Court of Claims in 1868, T. McManus & Co. detailed a litany of sins committed against the *S. Warren*, the *Iowa*, the *Oregon*, the *Patterson*, and the propeller-driven *General Wool* while in the government's care: careless captains neglected their boilers, worms ate through their bottoms, schooners collided with them, ammunition boats exploded next to them, tugboats towed them into dangerous open waters, waves and larger vessels battered them against the shore as they unloaded their cargo. Not only that, but also the government arbitrarily cut the leasing fees it had contracted to pay.

Government lawyers, however, had rebuttals for every cent of the $51,345.66 (not a quarter of a million dollars) that Thomas's firm claimed in restitution. Most of the arguments about responsibility for the damage turned on fine points of maritime and military law, but Thomas's claim that he'd been underpaid was trumped by the government's evidence that his firm had consented to the reduced fees at the time and had itself paid for all the necessary repairs without demur, even returning the vessels to government service afterwards. The court ruled for the government, and when in 1878 Thomas appealed to the Supreme Court (not the House of Representatives), the justices affirmed the verdict.[21]

The perennial bad luck that Ethel saw stalking her great-uncle was probably simply his fatally shaky business judgment. To be sure, the postwar period was economically tumultuous for many others besides our two Thomases, notably the financier Jay Cooke, who had so overextended himself building railroads that in 1873 his bank collapsed. In the ensuing Panic, hundreds of other banks, brokers, and businesses went down with him, and the economy did not fully recover for more than twenty years. But while the general hard times must have made it even more difficult for Thomas McManus to recoup his losses, his own troubles had taken hold sometime before the great crash, so he hadn't needed Cooke's help to go down in the first place.

The war boom may have disguised the fact for a while, but Thomas had entered the inland shipping business at exactly the wrong moment, as the railroads were muscling out the riverboats and canal barges as the fastest, cheapest, and most direct way to ship goods. Passengers, too, were abandoning ship for the fast new railroad route from New York to East Greenbush and over the river to Albany, and by 1869 Commodore Vanderbilt was presiding over one of the largest trunk lines (and one of the most powerful companies) in the country, essentially controlling railroad transportation from New York City to Chicago. So Thomas's lawsuit against the government, launched more than four years after the fact and just when his finances were starting to raise doubts in the mind of his wealthy wife, was probably just a forlorn Hail Mary pass that surprised no one in its failure to raise a little cash.

But I have to feel a bit sorry for my hapless great-great-great-uncle. Plenty of other shippers who struck deals with the army made out like bandits: quartermasters were notorious for paying outrageous prices in their desperate or ignorant or corrupt efforts to wangle enough serviceable transport to handle the endless task of moving soldiers and supplies from here to there. Even the oldest and most decrepit boat, complained one government official, could inspire its owner with visions of "a fortune in its rotten ribs," and not infrequently those dreams came true.[22] Except for Uncle Thomas. As Ethel had said, for once with pinpoint accuracy, we were "not a money wise family."

All of this turmoil meant that Thomas was no longer able to offer his sister financial help just when Mary Ann's family was sinking fastest. Still, it would turn out a piece of luck for Mary Ann that he had been forced to change his profession. A lawyer in the family would soon be exactly what she needed.

Here is where my family's paper trail thickens into a superhighway. The *Evening Journal,* the *Daily Times,* and the *Daily Argus* were among the Albany papers carrying full and detailed accounts of what happened next between Robert and Mary Ann. Over the last two weeks of the centennial year, supposedly a year of celebration and triumph for the entire nation, the intimate details of the lives of my great-great-grandmother and my great-great-grandfather were splayed open for everyone they knew to see.[23]

By 1876 Robert had lost even his marginal job at the Marble Pillar restaurant and was subsisting mainly on handouts from John Gernon, an old friend who ran a tavern and charitably allowed Robert to call himself the bookkeeper. Even the thriftiest family with young children couldn't feed, clothe, and house itself in the Albany area for less than $300 a year, and that allowed nothing for such necessities and comforts as carfare, medical care, or liquor. It was difficult enough to *earn* that much consistently in the aftermath of the Panic, with wages slashed, workers laid off, and dollar-a-day factory hands relying on the even more meager day's pay earned by their children to make ends meet.[24] If in those tough times Gernon's charity was expansive enough to guarantee the minimal six dollars a week plus hooch to a man who was basically a bum, he was a prodigal indeed.

Besides that, there was the Other Woman, or so Mary Ann claimed. Kate Mandeville was her name, and she was a dressmaker half Robert's age (and some seventeen years younger than the forty-year-old Mary Ann). She lived in nearby Greenbush, where her family was connected with a soda water company, an ironic attraction indeed for someone as fond of drink as Robert was. Mary Ann was positive he was spending whatever little money he did scrounge on Kate and the two illegitimate children they had had together.

Maybe. But it seems more likely that poor Mary Ann conjured the affair, or at least the bastards, out of her own fevered imagination; no one else ever acknowledged having seen or heard of any offspring, and I've found no documentary evidence of their existence. And Mary Ann's imagination clearly *was* fevered. In October 1876 Robert went home to his mother in Bath-on-Hudson, told her his twelve-year marriage was over, and stayed there for nearly two months. Mary Ann, left to fend for herself in their flat on Morton Street, sent their middle child, four-year-old Theresa, to live with relatives in West Troy and showed up frequently at her mother-in-law's door in Bath to demand money and food for the two other children, Lizzie and the baby, Robert Jr., who was two. Several times she threw stones at the house; once she followed Robert to the ferry and threw stones at him, too. "I'll fix him," she told her husband's mother and his sister Maria. "You are low people and my people are high, and if he comes back I'll shoot him like a dog." The women called the police and had their highborn in-law arrested for breaking their windows.

Three weeks before Christmas, Mary Ann and the children were evicted from Morton Street for nonpayment of rent, and when they moved into an even smaller and shabbier flat on Clinton Street, Robert came with them. But the reconciliation, if that's what it was, didn't last. Husband and wife continued to quarrel violently, Mary Ann pressing him to give the other woman up and Robert insisting there was no other woman.

The McDonalds' new neighbor Mary Streebel, the wife of a junk dealer, later said that Mary Ann McDonald had at first "acted nice," but then suddenly began to behave in a "very strange" manner. On December 13 she seemed to be "unusually wild" and "out of her head," and at one point came into the Streebels' apartment to talk about how good-looking she had been, what a "nice lady," before she married Robert. Then Mary Ann stood before the window parting her hair on one side, said Mrs. Streebel, until "her head looked wild; never saw a person look so."

Robert was gone all that afternoon, leaving scarcely a mouthful of food in the house, and twice Mary Ann went around the corner to Gernon's in a vain search for him. Finally, around seven or eight o'clock, he came home "with his collar button missing and his manner disturbed." Again they began to quarrel, again she insisted he leave the woman, again he denied seeing anyone and struck or threatened to strike her. Then suddenly the old familiar quarrel veered violently off course. "Do you see this?" Mary Ann demanded, pulling a tiny silver-handled Smith & Wesson revolver from her pocket. Robert dismissed it, profanely, as a mere trifle. Mary Ann pointed the gun at her husband's head and fired.

The baby bullet embedded itself in Robert's temple. He sat down hard, then managed to put on his hat, stagger downstairs, and make his way around the corner to Gernon's, where he told his friend "She has shot me at last" and demanded a drink. Upstairs Mrs. Streebel, hearing a noise like a lamp exploding, put her head into the corridor to ask what was the matter. "Nothing," my great-great-grandmother said calmly; "I have shot my husband."

Leaving the two children behind in the apartment, Mary Ann descended to the street, found a police officer, handed him the gun, and told him the same thing. The officer found Robert at Gernon's and took them both to the station house, where Mary Ann was locked up overnight and Robert sent on to City Hospital. The children were turned over to relatives.

For the first day or two after the shooting the doctors were cautiously optimistic about Robert's chances for recovery, but soon he took a turn for the worse. The wound itself was shallow and they had gotten the bullet out, but "both tables of the skull were found to be fractured," Dr. William A. Hall told the police investigators, and to make matters even more dire, the patient had been suffering from delirium tremens when he was admitted. "Should the injury result fatally," the *Evening Journal* rumbled on December 14, "it will be due mainly to his previous habits and a constitution impaired by the excessive indulgence in liquor."

Four days later the investigation into the shooting did indeed become an investigation into a homicide. Robert was dead. Less than a week before Christmas, my great-great-grandfather, aged forty-three, was laid to rest in St. Mary's churchyard—not, for obvious reasons, in the still empty family plot in St. Agnes's cemetery that his mother-in-law, Betsey, had providently bought four years earlier. The handsome silver-handled rosewood casket that contained his mortal remains was probably contributed by the United Irishmen's Association, which, according to the *Daily Argus* of December 21, turned out in force at the funeral of the Scots-born victim of the "Irish curse" of drunkenness.

At the preliminary examination by police officials and at the coroner's inquest to determine the cause of Robert's death, key testimony came from the sole eyewitness to the shooting, the one other person besides the couple who had been there as the quarrel escalated into a crisis. That was Lizzie, my mother's Nana C., aged eleven years, who had seen the whole thing. First to the police and then to the coroner Lizzie described the moment when her mother shot her father in the head. She was in the front room, she said. She heard the quarrel, she heard the accusations, the threats, and the curses, and then she saw "a little red blaze" flicker. "I said 'Oh, Mama,'" Lizzie told the court officials. "She said nothing to me. . . . As long as I can remember, he has abused her awful; he has not furnished food or support; he said he would reduce her to a shadow."

Other witnesses at the inquest painted no prettier a picture of the McDonalds' home life. Gernon told the coroner's jury that whatever he paid Robert "was mere charity," and Gernon's son James, who worked with his father at the tavern, declared that Robert was "a drinking man, and a little drink would intoxicate him." Mary Ann, he said, he had never seen drunk, though once she took a glass of ale. Mrs. Streebel described poor Mary Ann's wildness during the days just before the final quarrel. A pawnbroker named James McDonough said a lady had come into his shop the day before the shooting, picked out a silver-plated single-barreled pistol, and paid a dollar and a half for it. He could not say for sure that the lady had been Mary Ann.

Public opinion seemed firmly on Mary Ann's side. "Among those who know the family great sympathy is felt for the unfortunate wife," reported the *Evening Journal* on December 14, because of Robert's habit of "carousing with his boon companions." The *Daily Times* generally agreed, noting on the same day, "For years, it is said, she and her children have been abused by her husband until she was goaded almost to madness by his brutal treatment." The next day the *Times* did note judiciously that "while many sympathize with Mrs. McDonald, there are others who think the blame should not be all on one side. A doctor states that not long ago McDonald came to him with his head badly cut, the effects of an assault committed by Mrs. McDonald with a stove-lid lifter." That, however, was the last newspaper hint of any shadow on Mary Ann.

One possible reason for the public's united sympathy became evident during the inquest. Robert's doctor testified that the postmortem showed a severely diseased brain, "soft and of unhealthy color," and he revealed that he had treated Robert for syphilis. He had also, he added, treated Mary Ann for the same then-incurable disease. It's not hard to guess who had given it to whom.

Mary Ann's illness may explain her strange wildness, her fevered imagination, and also what came next. After four evenings' worth of testimony interrupted by a four-day break for Christmas, the coroner's jury was sent out to deliberate on the cause of Robert's death. The six-man panel was a cross-section of Albany society: a teamster, a carpenter, a fruit seller, an assistant city surveyor, a hotel

proprietor, and, as foreman, a restaurant owner. They returned the same evening with the finding: "That Robert McDonald came to his death from a pistol
shot, the said pistol being fired by the hands of his wife, Mary A. McDonald."

The coroner discharged the six with thanks, but half an hour later five of
them, all except the foreman, regathered in the courthouse and delivered a
second finding. This time they determined that the said Robert McDonald
"came to his death by means of a pistol shot, caused by a pistol in the hands of
his wife Mary A. McDonald . . . and that said pistol was fired by said Mary A.
McDonald in self-defense, and not feloniously or with malice aforethought."

That was, as the *Daily Argus* put it on January 3, 1877, a "queer action." The
second finding was clearly unofficial and legally invalid; the *Evening Journal*
described it as a "so-called verdict" rendered "of course without any color of
right, as [the jurors] had already signed a verdict, and been discharged." The
Daily Times supplied a provocative detail: that when the five dissident members regathered, they were "accompanied by Hugh Rielly, counsel for Mrs.
McDonald," and they "announced to coroner Fitzhenry that they had rendered
the verdict under a misunderstanding and wished to revise their action. The
coroner held that the case was closed, and declined to re-open it." Whether or
not Mary Ann's counsel was applying pressure, the public would clearly have
gotten the message that five of the six jurors were going to extraordinary lengths
to publicize their disagreement with the foreman and to express a consensus
that Robert had gotten exactly what he deserved.

In the end, the unofficial finding seems to have carried the day. In January
1877 Mary Ann was indicted on the relatively toothless charge of manslaughter
in the third degree, and after pleading not guilty was released on bail. Her lawyer
won a postponement until the next Court of Sessions, arguing that he needed
more time to prepare for "the long and protracted examination of questions of
medical jurisprudence, both as to the condition of the deceased and the cause of
his death, concerning which there was much conflict of opinion." In June, Mary
Ann's ingenious lawyer won another delay, until October, on the grounds that
her case involved "intricate and novel questions of law" and thus should properly
be heard in the higher-level Court of Oyer and Terminer. In October, nothing. In 1878, nothing. In 1879, nothing. Nothing survives in the court records
through the end of the decade to show that Mary Ann's case ever went to trial;
nothing shows that it was ever formally dismissed, either. The 1886 history of
Albany that had opened our eyes to the episode in the first place noted only that
Mary A. McDonald had been "tried and acquitted" on the manslaughter charge,

an imprecise memory perhaps influenced by what had been the prevailing public sentiment at the time.[25] My best guess is that prosecutors, warned by the newspapers' sympathy and the jurors' revolt that they were unlikely to win a conviction against a wild-haired woman of uncertain mental health whose drunken husband had abused her, starved her, and infected her with an unspeakable disease, quietly decided to forget the whole thing.

And Thomas McManus—Mary Ann's brother Thomas, newly turned lawyer—probably helped them to their decision. He did not represent his sister officially and was never mentioned in the newspaper accounts, but as an ex-alderman with political connections, he was surely working behind the scenes on her behalf. He notarized her lawyers' June application to move the trial to a higher court, and earlier, in February, Thomas had also formally witnessed Mary Ann's petition to the Surrogate Court to be appointed administratrix of the $100 estate left by her late husband. The deceased, the petition affirmed, had "died a natural death."[26]

In view of that bald-faced lie, I can't help but regard with suspicion some other quirks I've turned up in the public record. Even though Albany had begun back in 1870 to require that official reports be filed for all deaths in the city, the nice young woman I spoke to in the Bureau of Vital Statistics at City Hall tried three times without success to find a death certificate for Robert, which presumably would have revealed a cause of death that was highly unnatural. Nor could the staff at the Albany County Hall of Records explain the only significant gap in their holdings of police blotter records for the McDonalds' precinct in the 1870s. Missing were the records from July 1876 through March 1877, exactly when Mary Ann and Robert's home life was spiraling into violence. Thomas may have had very well placed friends indeed.

But even politically connected friends could go only so far. Even if they were able to clean up the record of Mary Ann's desperate remedy for her unhappiness, there wasn't much they, or anyone else, could have done to stop the unhappiness in the first place.

Obviously she couldn't have divorced Robert; she was a Catholic. She couldn't have gotten much practical help from her church; a married woman, even one as wracked and tormented as Mary Ann, would probably have been advised just to go home and do her duty by her husband. She couldn't just leave him; like many wives she was a hostage to her children, and like most women in those economically depressed times, she had no decent way to support herself and them. She couldn't sic the law on him; wife abuse wasn't a crime and nonsupport wasn't actionable. And for material help she couldn't count on her family, either; the McManus family's day in the sun had turned out to be a fleeting winter solstice. Brother Thomas, the family mogul, was spectacularly broke. So was the family's other Thomas, Winifred Behan's husband, who after the loss of his liquor business was supporting their nine children as the superintendent of a graveyard. Another of Mary Ann's brothers-in-law, Catherine's husband, Lawrence Grattan, had put up part of her bail, but that seems to have been the extent of his ability or inclination. And while the third sister, Eliza, was married to a doctor, medicine was not then the lucrative profession it would become, especially for public health practitioners like her husband. In any case, the doctor would die just three months after the shooting, aged thirty-three, and Eliza would follow him less than three years later.

All Mary Ann could do with her drunken husband, in the end, was plead with him, shout at him, beg him, shame him, threaten him, follow him, lob stones at him, and when all that failed, kill him. In the end, murder was no more or less unthinkable than divorce.

Here the paper trail begins to peter out.

Thomas continued working as an attorney, but he was ominously peripatetic, moving from boardinghouse to hotel to another boardinghouse, and his office in the stately Harmony Building soon gave way to a room in the much less imposing Wotkyns' Block. In October 1882, nearly six years after the murder, he was admitted to a Manhattan charity hospital. Three days after checking into St. Vincent's, he was dead. His obituary back home in Troy set his onetime worth at $100,000, and kindly said he had gone to the city seeking treatment for consumption. According to his death certificate, however, the primary cause of his death was alcoholism, with asthenia, or general weakness and debility, as a secondary cause. At only fifty-five he had drunk himself to death. Perhaps that old rumor my mother vaguely recalled about his suicide was technically true after all.[27]

Misfortune continued to cut a swath through the McManus ranks. When Thomas and Mary Ann's widowed sister Eliza died in 1879, she left a seven-year-old orphan daughter who had been suffering all her life from tuberculosis of the spine and who would survive her mother by only six years. Then, just five days after the sickly little orphan finally faded away, another young cousin, twenty-eight-year-old Katie Grattan, succumbed to some kind of heart trouble. Less than two years after that, Katie's mother, Catherine, was dead too, of a kidney complaint. Everyone in the family, it seems, was chronically ill.[28]

Or chronically drunk. Just as Lizzie's uncle Thomas had, her uncle James

McManus took his troubles to New York and died of them there. At the city hospital on Blackwell's Island, a charity institution devoted mainly to sufferers from alcoholism and venereal disease, James, not yet sixty, died in 1893 of pulmonary edema and delirium tremens. Finally, in 1894 and at the reported age of eighty-eight, Lizzie's grandmother McManus, having seen both of her sons die drunkards, two of her four daughters die young, and a third daughter publicly exposed as a syphilitic murderess, succumbed to "senile gangrene" at the Little Sisters of the Poor. Her gravestone in the family plot in St. Agnes's that she had bought during their better days renounced the American hopefulness of being Betsey: there lay Bridget McManus.[29]

Mary Ann herself, the murderess, lived for another quarter century but left few traces of her passage on earth. We don't know what happened to her in the aftermath of the murder; we don't know where or how she lived; we don't know how in those pre-penicillin days she survived her disease for so long. But the first few years following the shooting were grim. In 1880 Mary Ann's six-year-old son was living at the city asylum for destitute children and her younger daughter, Theresa, then not quite eight, was in a Catholic orphanage.[30] Mary Ann was so financially, physically, or emotionally incapable of caring for her two younger children that she had to hand them over to charitable strangers.

Mary Ann resurfaced in the records in 1900, living in Manhattan with her surviving son, twenty-five-year-old Robert, who bore the name of the man she had killed. He was working as an express driver and renting modest quarters in a seedy uptown neighborhood populated largely by asylums and almshouses. Just three years later, in 1903, Mary Ann died and was buried in her mother's plot back in Albany. Her doctor listed the cause of her death as broncho-pneumonia, with senility as a contributing cause, but perhaps he couldn't spell "tertiary syphilis."[31] My great-great-grandmother's passing left her sister Winifred Behan in Albany to live at least another twenty years as the sole survivor of the eight McManuses who had left Ireland together so long ago.

Also living with Robert and Mary Ann in 1900 was one "Beatrice McDonald, foundling," aged one year. Where exactly this child had been "found," and what became of her later, are a mystery, but since neither Mary Ann nor Robert would have been in a position to take on the burden of a child just for the goodwill of it, a dark suspicion falls on Robert. We don't know much about what happened to him, either, but he seems to have inherited more than his name from his father. Much later, as my grandmother Grace would recall, Robert, who had not been seen for years, showed up uninvited and drunk at the house of his sister Lizzie. She summoned her son Joe to throw him out. In 1927 Robert, fifty-three and unmarried, died of tuberculosis. Like his two uncles, he met his end in a Manhattan charity hospital, having lingered in that grim institution for six months, and the body was sent upstate to join the throng in St. Agnes's.[32]

The other McDonald sibling, Theresa, managed a definitive rejection of her own family, its sordid past, and men in general. Theresa became a nun. Given her childhood stay in the Catholic orphanage and her dismal experience with the male sex, it isn't, perhaps, surprising that she should have taken her vows, but my mother sometimes wondered whether her great-aunt didn't come to regret her choice. Doris once said she *thought* she could summon a dim recollection of a hectic day when Aunt Theresa tried to run away from her Staten Island convent. She was pursued, apprehended, and returned immediately.

Maybe—it occurs to me only now—the "foundling" Beatrice was Theresa's.

That leaves Lizzie. My mother's grandmother, the ample and sweet-faced old lady Doris loved dearly and saw often. The lady who assured her daughter and then her granddaughters that standing up straight, wearing white gloves and plenty of underwear, remembering to say "glow" instead of "sweat," and maintaining a healthy distrust for the blandishments of men would equip them for any possible situation they might meet in life. The lady who years earlier in a shabby flat in the heart of a cheerless Christmas season had watched her mother shoot her father in the head.

Lizzie's life in the few years after the murder is as obscure as her mother's. According to Ethel, Lizzie soon "struck out on her own" and came to New York City by herself. I'm sure it would have been tempting for any young woman to look for her happiness in some place far away from where the only adult relative who wasn't either sick or dead was a crazy mother under a cloud for killing her dissolute husband. But the family Bible records her wedding in 1891 at her mother's "residence" in Troy. Her son Joe believed that Lizzie moved to Manhattan only after she married the stiff and diminutive John J. Clark, one of the seven children of an illiterate Scottish mother and Irish father who had settled near the Brooklyn Navy Yard in the mid-1850s and moved after 1860 to a Queens neighborhood close to the increasingly foul and sludgy Newtown Creek.[33]

Which leaves us wondering: How and where on earth could a woman from a fallen middle-class family in Troy have managed to meet a man from an uneducated immigrant family in an outer borough of New York City? Nothing about

John and Lizzie seems to have been particularly well matched. My mother remembered her grandfather Clark as cold, prone to flashes of fury, and strict with the women in the family. She told us that Grace had never forgiven her father-in-law for refusing to allow her to train as a teacher—her place was at home with her husband, he said, though "home" at that point was a room at her in-laws' house—and he forbade his little granddaughters to whistle, which he considered an unseemly habit for girls. Given the public knowledge we all had about my Clark great-grandparents, if asked to guess which of the two was hiding a lurid secret about the ultimate in family dysfunction, I would *not* have chosen sweet-faced and affectionate Lizzie.

Yet for all we know, John was harboring lurid secrets of his own. "Both of our grandparents were so buttoned-down," my aunt Gina told me, "that we never knew a thing about either of them—except that our grandfather once ran away to join the circus." He was sent back immediately. John grew up to work, like his father, on trains, but whereas Thomas Clark had only tended the switches on the Long Island Railroad, my grandfather always said that John had once cut a more glamorous figure as an engineer or conductor on the Third Avenue El. Sometimes I try to imagine a meaningful look, maybe even a thrilling touch, passing between him and Lizzie one morning as she stepped aboard his train on a visit to New York. But it's nearly impossible for me to picture the delirious dereliction of good breeding that would have had to overtake both of my buttoned-down forebears for him, a stranger, to have had the audacity to speak to her.

However it happened, the newlyweds Lizzie and John took up residence in an apartment building on Edgecombe Avenue in Harlem that, family legend has it, had been George M. Cohan's birthplace. (Which was actually in Rhode Island, but then again, the songmeister himself wasn't actually "born on the Fourth of July," either, as his family always claimed.) But her husband, too, like her father, her brother, and her uncles, failed Lizzie in the end. John drove the El for only a few years, until some obscure crisis—some "breakdown," perhaps, as his daughter-in-law Grace later mused darkly—forced him off the line and into the less strenuous career of custodian at an elementary school in the least dashing borough in New York. Lizzie never quite forgave him for carrying her into the wilderness that was Staten Island and the shame of being a janitor's wife.

She poured her heart into her three children. Horace, the youngest, had some sort of spinal problem as a child, and she carried him in her arms to Manhattan every week for treatment, no small feat at a time when boarding the ferry required an agile scamper across a temporary gangplank that bobbed up and down with the motion of the boat. But while she obviously loved her boys, they were congenitally members of that suspect half of humanity, and it was Ethel, her only girl, who carried all her hopes. Ethel would win renown and respect in her singing career; Ethel's talents would earn her the love of a worthy man; Ethel would redeem the family's lost honor. In the end, however, Ethel ended up almost as unhappy in life and in love as her mother and grandmother.

I last saw my great-aunt Ethel at a family Christmas gathering, where she had arrived embarrassed and upset: the bagful of carefully wrapped gifts she was bringing had somehow been switched with someone else's bag at the bus stop, and she had nothing to put under the tree for us. The right bag was soon recovered and the presents distributed, but by the time I unwrapped the baby-doll pajamas she had picked out for me, she was dead. She had been stricken with a heart attack, alone at home on the Friday before the long New Year's weekend, and no one had found her until Monday. She was sixty-seven. I was six; it was the first family bereavement I can remember. And even at six I could tell: poor Aunt Ethel had had a poor death.

After our moment of discovery over the microfilm reader, my mother struggled to fit her new knowledge into the old stories her beloved grandmother and her grandiloquent aunt had told her about their family. But as she told me later, eventually she could only marvel at the "grace" with which her Nana C. had lived after so searing a tragedy. She "drew upon her inner strength," Doris told me, "to live a 'normal' life," and became more of an anchor to her family through war and the Great Depression than her husband managed to do.

When I asked her whether she thought Lizzie had ever told her children the truth about the whole awful roster of McManus miseries, Doris wasn't sure. "I doubt my father would have been interested in family history in any case," she said. "He always believed that you make yourself who you are, and what came before doesn't matter." What he made himself was steady, responsible, prudent; whether subconsciously or by design, he built a life that reversed everything his male forebears had done. Resisting the high-flying risks of entrepreneurship, he methodically planned his route to the security of a practical profession. His acceptance at the Cooper Union, the distinguished Manhattan institution offering a free education in engineering, art, or architecture, made him the family's first college man. Deciding after two years that he'd learned enough about engineering to earn his living, he went on to spend his entire career in the same modest but safe niche, editing a technical journal for a professional association of mechanical engineers, and weathered even the depression without serious hardship. The one wild moment when, as my mother recalled, he considered taking a job in Mexico passed by quickly.

Joe drank rarely, never to excess, and took pride in being "money wise"; he was pushing fifty by the time he indulged in either a checking account or a mortgage. A doting father, he was also a painfully cautious one. When his daughters were small, he surprised them with the gift of a Silver King Monarch bicycle, a generous present indeed in those penny-pinching days. But he bought only one bike, which the girls were expected to share. Years later Gina and Doris realized that it was less a financial decision than a containment strategy: providing only one bike would mean he couldn't lose more than one daughter at a time.

About Ethel my mother was more certain. "I bet she knew all about the tragedy," Doris said. "Ethel and her mother talked about everything, and I can't imagine Nana didn't tell her that, too. That was probably why all her life she tried so hard to make us look so grand: she was compensating."

So our family storyteller was also our family liar.

And lies, we all know, are bad. Ethically and philosophically they raise a host of questions about exclusion, manipulation, and control. For Ethel's family— for her two nieces, a nephew, and their children—these lies for years denied us information about people whose lives are deeply implicated in our own, and by the time we finally found out the truth for ourselves, it was too late to ask them any questions about it. For historians they are yet one more example of how challenging it can be to find our way into a past that now lodges mainly in the words of others—yet one more nagging reminder that no matter how diligent our research, sometimes only luck will tell us how wildly wrong we almost were.

But for Ethel it was a chance to get things right at last. Like most storytellers—like most of those other family liars—she was simply claiming her right to narrate her own life and make her own sense of an American dream that ended up including much more horror and pain than happiness. Her choice to substitute the consolation of lost glories for the implacable wretchedness of murder and ruin was, I don't doubt, another gift besides the baby-doll pajamas that my great-aunt Ethel chose to give to me.

GRANDMOTHER GRACE

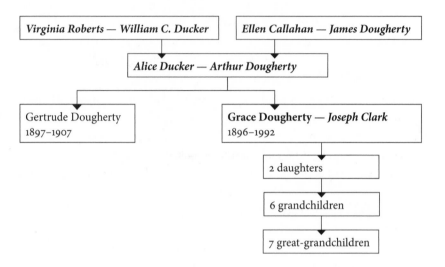

Virginia Roberts — William C. Ducker

Ellen Callahan — James Dougherty

Alice Ducker — Arthur Dougherty

Gertrude Dougherty
1897–1907

Grace Dougherty — Joseph Clark
1896–1992

2 daughters

6 grandchildren

7 great-grandchildren

CHAPTER 7

Grandmother Grace

⚜

FOR TWELVE GENERATIONS, MEMBERS OF AN AMERICAN FAMILY HAVE BEEN telling stories to *me*. From the moment nearly four centuries ago when my fore-bears first set foot in the brave New World, they did all the things that typical American pursuers of happiness have always done: they left families and old lives behind, they moved west and west again, they sought wealth in land, they reinvented themselves, they took risks, they sacrificed, they schemed. And they told stories about what happened, stories they hoped would make sense of it all for themselves, for their families, for their descendants—and, therefore, for me. Along with a handful of old papers and photographs, a ruby ring of Aunt Ethel's that is missing a stone, and my grandmother's hand-sewn wedding dress, this my legacy from the thousands of faceless people essential to getting me born: a clutch of stories about the most important moments in their lives.

It's no sweeping generational saga, no magisterial *Buddenbrooks* capped off with a resolution and a moral. These pages sound much closer to *To the Lighthouse:* episodic, personal, and often mysterious, as when Mrs. Ramsay, the center of attention in the first part of Virginia Woolf's novel, is abruptly and offhandedly dead in the second. But that's also much closer to the way most people engage with the world from within the absorbing ambit of their own lives. And it's hardly surprising that in any family, the stories most likely to have been preserved are the ones that reflect their tellers' attempts to under-stand, explain, and perhaps justify the saddest or most joyous or most tragic or most surprising things that happened to them. It takes the rare and obsessive energy of a Henry Morton Woodson to bother seeking out and preserving the random scenarios of everyday life—that a great-grandson of Potato Hole was nicknamed "Poplar Foot," for instance, because of his "unusually large feet," and a great-great-grandson of Tub was called "Turkey" because of the way he walked, that an infant Woodson received a "fatherly kiss" from the British general Cornwallis when he made his headquarters at her parents' house, that a Civil War veteran had a "sunny nature" and could play his banjo behind his back.[1] For most of the people who preceded us in the world, what their friends teased them about or what they could do at parties is forever lost. It's the poignant or conflict-ridden stories that seize the emotions, lodge in the memory, and tell the most about how to live.

What my own family's stories can tell us now about their lives is that even in this nation devoted to the pursuit of happiness, disappointment and heartbreak and injustice could be lurking around any corner. Sarah Woodson watched her husband meet a terrible death. Mary Randolph died heartbroken and "doubtless deranged." Captain Jack Fleming perished at Princeton at only twenty-one, in a brutal engagement forced by error and surprise. Tarlton Woodson was imprisoned by the British and then shortchanged by the Americans. Bland Ballard's enemies scalped and killed or scarred nearly everyone in his family. The Daugherty clan spent years searching for their lost children. William Wharton battled all his life with creditors, penury, and his neighbors' disapproval. Ralph Collins was regularly defeated by his own debts. W. B. Roberts ended up as worn out and disgraced as his "country" did. James Dougherty finally managed to persuade the government that he really did deserve an increase in his invalid's pension only by going ahead and dying. Nathan Roberts didn't survive a death threat from a drunken street brawler. The McManus family's American dream was destroyed by murder and bankruptcy.

Some of the family storytellers acknowledged unhappy endings, but theirs were the stories whose main plot point most directly involved money, or rather the lack of it. Tarlton Woodson himself, according to a grandson quoted in Henry Morton Woodson's big book, loved telling his "thrilling anecdotes of military adventure, and hairbreadth escapes"; it was four generations' worth of impoverished and embittered descendants brooding together in his increasingly dilapidated old house who memorialized him as the government's chump.[2] William Wharton, who would have left virtually no trace in his descendants' hearts (or on the world itself, for that matter) if the government hadn't offered the old veteran a cash reward for talking about himself, also had one of the least fortunate American lives of all my kin. James Dougherty was essentially written out of my own branch of the family after he foisted his lamentable son Arthur on it, but no one else in the huge swarm of Daughertys and Doughertys seems to have had anything much to say about him either, leaving the pension office alone to tell his tale.

Most of my family's stories, however, had a very different message. They gave us to understand that even though Sarah Woodson watched her husband meet a terrible death, with daring and guile she saved the lives of her sons. That even though Mary Randolph died heartbroken and "doubtless deranged," she had lived out a romantic drama worthy of a best-selling novel. That even though Captain Jack Fleming perished at Princeton at only twenty-one, in a brutal engagement forced by error and surprise, he perished a hero. That even though Bland Ballard's enemies scalped and killed or scarred nearly everyone in his family, he hunted down those violent enemies and saved his community from further heartbreak. That even though the Daugherty clan spent years searching for their lost children, those children were absolutely thrilled when they finally came back home. That even though William Wharton and Ralph Collins were regularly defeated by their own debts, they came out alive from the worst military defeat in American history. That even though W. B. Roberts ended up as worn out and disgraced as his "country" did, he had gone above and beyond the call of duty in volunteering his skills to the service of that country. That even though Nathan Roberts hadn't survived a death threat from a drunken street brawler, he had defied the one from the blue-coated tormentors. That even though the McManus family's American dream was destroyed by murder and bankruptcy, nobody had to know, and nobody could stop them from starting fresh somewhere else. That even though disappointment and heartbreak and injustice could be lurking around any corner, so could a ray of hope.

Not surprisingly, my family's stories also tell us that the route to hope often entailed making a wide detour around the kind of empirically verifiable facts that would satisfy a disinterested historian. By the time generations of Woodson descendants had finished reshaping the history of John and Sarah to make sense for their own particular moments in history, it had entirely lost touch with the real world of Virginia in the 1640s. Bland Ballard grew more heroic with each new storyteller. Cousin John Dawson repaired the reputations of his uncle and his grandfather by (innocently or not) pilfering somebody else's better stories. Aunt Ethel left out the sad parts. Mrs. Pittman just made stuff up. Revisionist historians like to describe their exploration of the lives of ordinary and often voiceless people as "doing history from the bottom up," but what storytellers like mine did is more like history from the inside out: their own accounts in their own voices of how they saw their own place in the stream of events, accounts based less on *facts* than on what felt like the *truth* about sorrow, recompense, love, pain, and the pursuit of happiness in America. With their stories they created the world they wished for, and in their stories they revealed something about their relationships with the world they had.

And like most family stories, mine did something that the more ephemeral tales of everyday life don't: they worked in two directions. People tell stories to create the selves they'd like their descendants to know—to touch the future. It was probably Ralph Collins himself who told his children as well as the pension office about his service in the melee on the Wabash; it was doubtless Bland Ballard himself who launched the deathless tale of how he avenged the massacre of his family. But when the descendants do come along, they inevitably put their inheritance to uses of their own. Most of my family stories show clear evidence of progressive emendation: the heroic Sarah Woodson who drove away the alien invaders, the Flemings and Savages who left behind their Old World castles but not their innate nobility, the tycoon whose business failure was an undeserved bolt from the blue. Creating the ancestors of one's dreams can be a less contestable way of claiming the present and the future one prefers.

And then my family stories crashed into the brick wall that was my grandmother Grace. Exactly three centuries after John and Sarah Woodson arrived in Jamestown and became our first Americans, Grace became the family's last southerner, and left that past and its stories entirely behind. It wasn't even that she was keeping secrets, as her sister-in-law Ethel had done; she wasn't changing crucial details or creating attractive distractions. Grace simply wasn't talking about herself or her past at all.

At first I found Grace's indifference to her history astonishing, not to mention a betrayal of all those generations' worth of ancestors who hoped they'd be talking to *us*. It seemed particularly odd, given that everything about her age and heritage seemed to mandate that she be a crack storyteller. Born in 1896, she was surrounded throughout her childhood by a beehive of grannies, great-aunts, and antique female cousins (their men were shiftless, missing, or dead) whose own memories would have spanned most of the nineteenth century and whose grandparents could plausibly have recalled Valley Forge or Yorktown. She grew up during a gamy era in which the present had become so confusing to so many that connecting to the past, by whatever means necessary, had become something of a national obsession. And she inhabited a place suffused with the beguiling melancholy of the Lost Cause, that philosopher's stone that made of failure a grace and of the future a mean and alien land—a place with more stories than people. Storytelling is what southerners did, after all; the South's master storyteller, William Faulkner, told his stories about southerners telling stories.

But since family stories work in two directions, it seemed only natural that I should tell my own tales about Grace. And when I began exploring her life and past—a recent, well-witnessed, well-documented past much easier to enter than, say, the Camelot of the tobacco fields—it became clear that if indeed the most insistent stories are those inspired by life's sorrows and disappointments, her nearest relatives and neighbors were certainly providing raw material aplenty that she could have used. In the years after the Civil War, as the McManuses and McDonalds of upstate New York were casting their lot with the other industrialists and merchants who were willing to be bold, lucky, and "modern," their future in-laws, the Robertses, the Doughertys, and the Duckers, were miring themselves more and more deeply into a sort of misfortune and unhappiness closer in spirit to the primordial perils of Jamestown than to a noisy steam-powered nation moving so fast that it was literally, as the physician George Beard insisted in his 1881 treatise on neurasthenia, making people sick.

To be sure, Kentucky was not a terribly happy place for anyone after the war, as the state that had *almost* seceded went on to be *almost* Reconstructed, and the dismantling of the edifice of slavery through a process delicately known as "readjustment" ended up radicalizing and sometimes impoverishing many of the state's loyal Unionists. Former secessionists, meanwhile, nursed their resentment and hardened their resistance, sometimes under the masks and robes of the Ku Klux Klan. And one of America's biggest and boldest storytelling projects ever, the myth of the Lost Cause, was offering a chance to indulge in the "adoration of a fictitious past," as a tart but affectionate southern-born critic of the South put it, and providing "a magnificent alibi" for all the region's many faults. At least one member of my family took his own direct aim at the new order. Grace's great-uncle Will Roberts, who throughout her entire childhood would pull out his old Confederate uniform to wear on special occasions (and whose great-grandfather Trammell, it may not be unfair to recall, had many years earlier slashed off his slave's ear), was charged in 1877 in the Kenton County Criminal Court with "shooting at an insolent negro, on Seventh street, in Covington, some time ago." The act apparently earned him more accolades than admonitions from his neighbors and friends. The *Falmouth Independent*

Great-great-great-uncle Will Roberts (with hat), the diehard Confederate, and members of his family, early 1920s.

of November 29 reported that he was "very properly let off with one cent and cost."[3]

But Grace's people carried other burdens besides the loss of their Cause. None of them, for instance, had any money. That's hardly surprising for a clan that ran so heavily to small farmers with big families, but even the "professional" men of the bunch, Dr. W. B. Roberts and James Dougherty, Esq., found pickings slim in the little back-country community of Falmouth, which felt every year more remote from the rush of the wider world. None of them seems to have expected anything for themselves, either, a trait that apparently persists among some of Falmouth's inhabitants to this day. In 1997, when the latest in a long series of devastating Ohio Valley floods reserved its usual special wallop for the little town on the forks of the Licking River, this time killing five people and causing more than $40 million in damage, the locals were apparently neither surprised nor aggrieved, and most dismissed the perennial suggestion that the whole town move to higher ground. "People here have lost their homes before and now they've lost them again," Falmouth's mayor said. "But we've got strong people here. We're country people and we can handle it."[4]

None of Grace's people in that postwar era seems to have been very healthy, either, given all those veterans from both sides who spent their days trembling, wasting away, reeling into fits, running for the outhouse, turning blind and falling down, daring death in drunken brawls. But in her family you didn't have to be an ex-soldier to suffer, either physically or emotionally. That's what happened with her own parents, Alice Ducker and Arthur Dougherty, in the inexplicable and awful marriage that in June 1895 finally linked the aggrieved former Tidewater *somebodies* with the perennial Scots-Irish nobodies and then combusted so quickly that Grace, born precisely nine months and nine days after the wedding, had no real memory of her father. She *did* know that Alice suffered, constantly and vocally, under the mortification of being an abandoned wife, the discomforts of bunking in her mother's little rented house in Covington with as many as four grown siblings, and the drudgery of supporting her two daughters as a sales clerk at Pogue's department store across the river in Cincinnati. Grace's little sister, Gertrude, suffered too, dying at nine after a three-week bout of "acute gastritis."[5] Grace would outlive her only sibling by eighty-five years almost to the day.

Little Gertrude's was only the latest in the gruesome parade of postwar deaths and accidents that mowed down my kin with a fearsome regularity. Some were by any measure heartbreaking, like the loss of the vigorous young newlywed,

Grandmother Grace Dougherty (right), who lived to be nearly ninety-six, and her only sibling, Gertrude, who died at nine, ca. 1906.

"the beau ideal of manliness" as the newspapers called him, who went up in flames in front of dozens of children at a church Christmas party when the raw cotton trim on his Santa Claus costume grazed a lighted candle. But many of the family's afflictions, while undoubtedly searing for those involved, seem to the dispassionate eye more Punch and Judy than Götterdämmerung. A cousin found dead outdoors in his nightshirt had probably stumbled and killed himself accidentally with his own gun—or at least that's how the coroner chose to rule it—while he was chasing thieves from his orchard. Another cousin with a jumpy trigger finger, this one a teenager, mangled his own arm. Cunning old "Slick" Daugherty slipped off a fence while he was out on a surveying job and died of a broken neck. George Ducker was shot in the stomach and killed by his good friend John Murphy during a drunken quarrel in the blacksmith's back room.[6]

And then there was Grace's poor snakebit grandfather William C. Ducker, who had sat out the Civil War after marrying Virgie Roberts, daughter and sister of fire-eating volunteers in gray. William had never amounted to much, scratching a minimal living for Virgie and their ten children as a farmer and odd-job man—and a tottery one at that, it seems, since in 1880 the census taker marked down the forty-seven-year-old with an unspecified "general debility."[7] Five months before Grace was born, William took a job blasting out a well. On October 29, 1895, he and a black man named Uncle Mose laid the explosives and then "retired to a safe distance to await the discharge," reported a local paper. But "as the fuse was slow in its progress to reach the cartridge they became impatient and went to the excavation, and just as they looked in to see if the fuse had gone out, an explosion occurred sending a rock through the brain of Mr. Ducker, killing him almost instantly. His entire forehead was crushed in and his brains scattered promiscuously over the ground."[8] Uncle Mose made a narrow escape with his life.

Another star-crossed forebear felled in the midst of an ordinary day by a grievous wound to the head. But this time, none of my great-great-grandfather William's kin bothered to make up and pass along the sort of tale that had transfigured poor tomahawked John Woodson into a martyred medico, or poor scalped Joseph Conway into a local tourist attraction, or poor scalped Thursia Ballard into the bearer of a silver skull plate, or even poor war-shattered Nathan Roberts into the fellow sufferer of a beloved outlaw's defining trauma. Before we came upon the unlabeled clipping from an unnamed paper squirreled away in Grace's house, my mother had never heard a word about her great-grandfather's fate from her mother or any of the other Kentucky kin—including William's widow and his daughter Alice—whom she herself had known well. William's brainless end was too inglorious even to embellish into a story.

It was the women of the family who seem to have borne most of life's burdens. My mother's strongest memories of her maternal grandmother, Alice, besides her stewardship of the vague but insistent family tradition that we were *somebody*, involved her "long and gloomy" face and her "black and moody" disposition, but everything I knew and learned about my female kin suggests that even a thundercloud like Alice wouldn't have been an anomaly among them. All of those former somebodies *knew* that expecting happiness was either vulgar or dangerous; they *knew* that Fate wasn't impish or capricious. Awful things were bound to happen, and they would be your own fault. Whatever misfortune you suffered was not some random affliction but rather cosmic justice, your own just deserts; it was brought down on you by something you had done, and your own personal happiness or hopes had nothing to do with it.

And there was no use complaining about your fate, either, no matter how unhappy it happened to be. Alice's cousin Jessie Oldham, a great-great-granddaughter

Great-great-grandmother Virgie Roberts Ducker, widow of the hapless well-blaster William C. Ducker, early 1930s.

Grandmother Grace and her mother, Alice Ducker Dougherty, who was somebody, ca. 1920.

The old Oldham place, built ca. 1825 on the Licking River across from Falmouth. Cousin Jessie bequeathed it to a local church, but the planned youth camp was never built there, the property went to seed, and soon after this photograph was taken (by the author) in 1996, the house was torn down as a hazard.

through her father's side of Boone's pioneering companion, and herself the last of the Oldhams, was a childless spinster whose two siblings had died in infancy. By the end of her very long life she had outlived all her friends, contemporaries, and closest kin, lost her father to a spectacular suicide leap off Falmouth's brand-new bridge and an uncle to a lonely noose in the barn, and endured the Great Flood of 1937 that had inundated the whole first floor of the sturdy brick house built by her great-grandfather, leaving the piano wedged halfway up the stairs and an egg, perfectly whole, resting gently atop the lintel of the front door.

But after Cousin Jessie's death another female relative wrote to my grandmother with something resembling pride that whenever the old lady fell to lamenting her sad lot she would chide her, reminding her that she wasn't the only person in the world to have troubles and that others' were even worse. "I'm sure she thought all the terrible things that happened to her shouldn't have," the relative marveled to Grace. "I don't know why she felt she should be the exception."

Grace talked about none of this. Yet even though she wasn't making this parade of misfortune and sorrow into stories, she did construct an ending of sorts—and all things considered, it was an astonishing one. Sometime after the United States entered World War I, when she was about twenty-one, she took herself downtown, sat for the civil service exam, earned one of the highest scores in the commonwealth, and accepted a job in the wartime Department of Agriculture in faraway Washington, D.C., where in a flu shot line she met Joe Clark from the New York City borough of Staten Island. Like Sarah Woodson, who sailed off with her husband to the terra incognita of Virginia; like Mary Randolph, who ran off and married the overseer; like the Ballards and Conways and Daughertys, who trekked over the mountains to the forbidding wilderness of Kentucky; like John Dawson, who jaunted off to the fleshpots of France; indeed like Ishmael of the *Pequod,* Huck Finn, Jay Gatsby, and other heroes of America's best fiction, Grace claimed the right to adventure off to someplace new. She didn't *tell* a story about her life; she *lived* one.

She herself even became a story that inspired other young women to write new stories of their own. My grandmother's younger cousin Dot confided to me late in her life that Grace's grand flight to wartime Washington had directly inspired her to seek her own adventure when the next big conflagration came around, and during World War II she made it all the way to Japan as an officer in the Women's Army Corps. Once while on leave in Kentucky, Dot told me, she dropped in on the nearby defense plant where her brother was working, and the smart uniform she wore and the brisk salutes she received so impressed the young women toiling on the assembly line that twenty of them quit on the spot to join the WACs too.

By putting all of her past behind her—the profound, relentless unhappiness of her hapless family, hobbled by generations-old poverty, humiliated by Arthur's abandonment, hammered again and again by stupid accidents and tragic misfortunes, deeply rooted in the tradition-bound inertia of tiny rural Falmouth but increasingly dependent on modern, bustling Cincinnati—Grace also repudiated the classic prefabricated story system that her heritage entitled her to and resisted the cultural tradition that valued even the saddest history because it *was* history. She never betrayed the slightest interest in the Lost Cause, which Uncle Will and the rest of her primordially Rebel relatives must have been trotting out daily, making sense of their defeat by telling themselves they were happier being unhappy. I would guess that Grace didn't find Staten Island a hospitable place to moon over that mythic South, "perpetually suspended in the great haze of memory," in W. J. Cash's wonderful phrase, "poised, somewhere between earth and sky, colossal, shining, and incomparably lovely."[9] If people use stories to organize reality, then the gap between the reality of New York City, a reliable husband with a steady professional job, and a crew of Irish American in-laws with grandiose ideas on the one hand, and that lovely, hazy myth on the other, could have loomed too large to have any traction in her daily life or to help her make sense of anything in the world around her. People tell stories as long as they're useful, and then they don't tell them anymore. Grace's old stories made no sense for the new life she was making.

My grandmother's break with tradition, expectation, and mythology reminds us of yet another characteristic of how family stories work. They explain the important things; they offer hope and recalibrate happiness; they form a bridge to the past and send up a signal flare to the future. And then, in the end, most of them die. Most of the family stories those three centuries' worth of ancestors wanted to share with their progeny, after all, are only relics now; I came across them embalmed in print, not shared on the porch at twilight. Some, like the enduring tale of Sarah Woodson's heroism, had been rediscovered, reembraced, and repurposed more as curiosities than as life lessons. Others, like the blood-thirsty and long-lived tale of Bland Ballard's revenge, make a good case that some stories really *ought* to die, that it's a step forward for humankind when they do. And none of the stories would have been embalmed in the first place if they hadn't been important once upon a time. But if stories from the past can tell us something about what their tellers hoped and feared, about what they valued and where they found their happiness, then the way the stories ended can tell us something about how those tellers—and their hearers—changed.

All stories yearn toward conclusions, whether "the rest is silence" or "they all lived happily ever after." Ending this book with our family's last southerner and her renunciation of her past makes for a tidy narrative with a clear arc and a satisfying resolution. But that's only one way to look at Grace's story. She was also, of course, one of our family's first New Yorkers—and her six grandchildren and seven great-grandchildren will have stories of their own to tell.

ABBREVIATIONS

❦

ACHOR	Albany County Hall of Records, Albany, N.Y.
Barton	E. E. Barton Collection of Northern Kentucky Families, Pendleton County Public Library, Falmouth, Ky. (microfilm also available at KHS)
BFC	Ballard Family Correspondence, SC 839, KHS
CSR-Confed	Compiled Service Records of Soldiers Who Served in Confederate Organizations, 1861–1865, War Department Collection of Confederate Records, Record Group 109, NARA
CSR-PostRev	Compiled Service Records of Volunteer Soldiers Who Served from 1784 to 1811 (Post-Revolutionary Period), Records of the Adjutant General's Office, Record Group 94, M905, NARA; citations are given to both the NARA microfilm holdings and the online images available through the subscription database Ancestry.com
CSR-Rev	Compiled Service Records of Soldiers Who Served in the American Army during the Revolutionary War, War Department Collection of Revolutionary War Records, Record Group 93, M881, NARA
CSR-Union	Compiled Service Records of Soldiers Who Served in Volunteer Organizations during the American Civil War, Records of the Adjutant General's Office, Record Group 94, NARA
CWP	Civil War Pension Files, Records of the Department of Veterans Affairs, Record Group 15, NARA
DFAN	*Daugherty Family Association Newsletter*
DM	Lyman Copeland Draper Manuscript Collection, WHS

FCHQ	*Filson Club History Quarterly*
KDLA	Archives Research Room, Kentucky Department for Libraries and Archives, Frankfort
KHS	Kentucky Historical Society, Frankfort
LDS	Church of Latter-Day Saints microfilm genealogy collections
LVA	Library of Virginia, Richmond (formerly Virginia State Library)
MSA	Maryland State Archives, Annapolis
NARA	National Archives and Records Administration, Washington, D.C.
NYCMA	New York City Municipal Archives
NYSDH	New York State Department of Health, Albany
NYSL	New York State Library, Albany
NYT	*New York Times*
OR	*The War of the Rebellion: A Compilation of the Official Records of the Union and Confederate Armies,* 70 vols. (Washington, D.C.: Government Printing Office, 1880–1901); all references are to series 1 unless otherwise noted
PCCC	Pendleton County Circuit Court, Ky.
PCHGS	Pendleton County Historical and Genealogical Society, Falmouth, Ky.
RCC	Rensselaer County Clerk's Office, Troy, N.Y.
RCSC	Rensselaer County Surrogates Court, Troy, N.Y.
RWP	Revolutionary War Pension and Bounty-Land Warrant Application Files, Records of the Department of Veterans Affairs, Record Group 15, M804, NARA; citations are given to both the NARA microfilm holdings and the online images available through Ancestry.com
USFC	United States Federal Census; citations are given to both the NARA microfilm holdings and the online images available through Ancestry.com
VHS	Virginia Historical Society, Richmond
VMHB	*Virginia Magazine of History and Biography*
WHS	Wisconsin Historical Society, Madison
WMQ	*William and Mary Quarterly*
Woodson Papers	Woodson Family Papers, 1740–1945, accession 29437 (LVA)
WPHM	*Western Pennsylvania Historical Magazine*

NOTES

❧

Introduction

1. Harry G. Frankfurt, *On Bullshit* (Princeton: Princeton University Press, 2005), 53–56.

2. Charles Tilly, *Why?* (Princeton: Princeton University Press, 2006), 65. I also draw here on Jerome Bruner, "Life as Narrative," *Social Research* 54 (1987): 11–32; Bruner, "The Narrative Construction of Reality," *Critical Inquiry* 18 (Autumn 1991): 1–21; Alasdair MacIntyre, *After Virtue: A Study in Moral Theory,* 2nd ed. (Notre Dame: University of Notre Dame Press, 1984); and William Cronon, "A Place for Stories: Nature, History, and Narrative," *Journal of American History* 78 (1992): 1347–76.

3. Mechal Sobel, "The Revolution in Selves: Black and White Inner Aliens," in *Through a Glass Darkly: Reflections on Personal Identity in Early America,* ed. Ronald Hoffman, Mechal Sobel, and Fredrika J. Teute (Chapel Hill: University of North Carolina Press, 1997), 167; see also Sobel, *Teach Me Dreams: The Search for Self in the Revolutionary Era* (Princeton: Princeton University Press, 2000), 3–7; Rhys Isaac, "Stories and Constructions of Identity: Folk Tellings and Diary Inscriptions in Revolutionary Virginia," in Hoffman, Sobel, and Teute, *Through a Glass Darkly,* 206–37; Isaac, *Landon Carter's Uneasy Kingdom: Revolution and Rebellion on a Virginia Plantation* (New York: Oxford University Press, 2004).

4. Pauline Maier, *American Scripture: Making the Declaration of Independence* (New York: Vintage, 1998), 175–89.

5. Jefferson to Henry Lee, May 8, 1825, in *The Basic Writings of Thomas Jefferson,* ed. Philip S. Foner (New York: Wiley, 1944), 802; Maier, *American Scripture,* 133–35; Darrin M. McMahon, *Happiness: A History* (New York: Grove, 2006), 314–31.

6. "The Pursuit of Happiness," *NBC Nightly News,* March 5, 2007. On August 9, 2013, the then current version of the iPhone app was showing a rating of fewer than two stars out of five on its iTunes preview page, http://bit.ly/14X7ANs.

7. Andrew Delbanco, *The Real American Dream: A Meditation on Hope* (Cambridge: Harvard University Press, 1999), 2.

8. John Smith, *The Proceedings of the English Colonie in Virginia Since Their First Beginning from England in the Yeare of our Lord 1606 . . .* , in *The Complete Works of Captain John Smith (1580–1631)*, ed. Philip L. Barbour, 3 vols. (Chapel Hill: University of North Carolina Press, 1986), 1:203.

9. "Wm. Ducker, of this Place, Meets His Death While Blasting in a Well," undated clipping from an unidentified newspaper formerly in my grandmother's possession.

1. Seeking Paradise in the New World

1. Henry Morton Woodson, *Historical Genealogy of the Woodsons and Their Connections* (Columbia, Mo.: By the author, 1915), 21–22.

2. The census or "muster" is reprinted in John Frederick Dorman, comp. and ed., *Adventurers of Purse and Person, Virginia, 1607–1624/5*, 4th ed., 3 vols. (Baltimore: Genealogical Publishing Co., 2004–2007), with the Woodsons at 1:23.

3. Woodson, *Historical Genealogy*, 134–35, 246–47, 147–48, 125 (these claims are widely confirmed); "The Woodson Descent of Frank & Jesse Woodson James," *Woodson Watcher Plus Allied Lines* 1, no. 3 (July 1983): 108–11.

4. Woodson, *Historical Genealogy*, 43–44. The manuscript list is held in the Woodson Papers and is reprinted, with slight variations that suggest the existence of other copies of the list, in R. A. Brock, "Descendants of John Woodson, of Dorsetshire, England, Who Settled in Virginia in 1624," *Richmond Standard*, January 17, 1880, and Lyon G. Tyler, "Woodson Family, Continued: Additions and Corrections," *WMQ*, 1st ser., 11 (July 1902): 54–57.

5. Undated clipping by "T. J. G." captioned "Special correspondence of The State, Prospect, VA., October 13," Woodson Papers; the publication year has been derived from internal evidence, while T. J. G. was doubtless Thomas J. Garden, the husband of Charles Van der Veer Woodson's niece Nannie Venable: Woodson, *Historical Genealogy*, 227, 365.

6. Mrs. H. D. Pittman, ed., *Americans of Gentle Birth and Their Ancestors: A Genealogical Encyclopedia*, 2 vols. (St. Louis: Buxton & Skinner, 1903–1907), 1:i–ii.

7. Ibid., 1:ii.

8. Ibid., 1:342; John A. McClung, *Sketches of Western Adventure* (Maysville, Ky.: L. Collins, 1832), 210–11; Niel Johnson and Verna Gail Johnson, "Rooted in History: The Genealogy of Harry S. Truman," Harry S. Truman Library and Museum, Independence, Mo., http://bit.ly/1cFBcFo; *The Hereditary Register of the United States of America, 1972* (Washington, D.C.: U.S. Hereditary Register, 1972), 213.

9. Woodson, *Historical Genealogy*, 10 (citing John Camden Hotten, *The Original Lists of Persons of Quality; Emigrants; Religious Exiles; Political Rebels, . . . 1600–1700 . . .* , originally published in 1874), 132.

10. See, for example, the *Woodson Watcher*, especially the first several issues (undated, 1982–83); the Woodson Family Forum at http://genforum.genealogy.com/woodson; and the Woodson family e-mail list on Rootsweb.com, archived at http://bit.ly/1clahfx. See also Linton Weeks, "At the Beginning," *Washington Post*, December 26, 1996, on discovering he was a Tub Woodson by surfing the Web.

11. Two widely used and generally careful sources, Dorman, *Adventurers*, 3:712, and Virginia

Lee Hutcheson Davis, *Tidewater Virginia Families: A Social History* (Baltimore: Genealogical Publishing Co., 1989), 399, also cite Henry Woodson, sometimes gingerly.

12. Among the historians who cite Woodson are Jacqueline Goggin, *Carter G. Woodson: A Life in Black History* (Baton Rouge: Louisiana State University Press, 1993), 1, accepting the Woodsons' slave ownership in 1619, and *Revolutionary Virginia: The Road to Independence,* 7 vols. (Charlottesville: University Press of Virginia, 1973–83), 2:358–59, on the descent of John Woodson, burgess from Goochland, 1769–1776, from "Potato Hole"; Fred E. Woodson, M.D., "Sara, Beloved Wife of a Physician," *Southern Medical Journal* 57 (June 1964): 687; Josephine Rich, *Women behind Men of Medicine* (New York: Messner, 1967), 23–35, citing Fred Woodson.

13. Alessandro Portelli, *The Death of Luigi Trastulli and Other Stories: Form and Meaning in Oral History* (Albany: State University of New York Press, 1991), 15–16.

14. Woodson's cited source, Hotten's *Original Lists,* omits the property inventories from the second muster and reproduces the haphazard organization of the names in the first, but the second makes clear that the Africans belonged to Peirsey's household. On Pott, see Dorman, *Adventurers,* 1:30, and the Virginia Company's letter to the governor and council dated July 25, 1621, in *The Records of the Virginia Company of London,* ed. Susan Myra Kingsbury, 4 vols. (Washington, D.C.: GPO, 1906–1935), 3:485–86. On Peirsey and on Yeardley's tenants, see Dorman, *Adventurers,* 1:23–24; Edmund S. Morgan, *American Slavery, American Freedom: The Ordeal of Colonial Virginia* (New York: Norton, 1995), 120, 122; and James Deetz, *Flowerdew Hundred: The Archeology of a Virginia Plantation, 1619–1864* (Charlottesville: University Press of Virginia, 1993), 47.

15. Henrico County Miscellaneous Court Records [Deeds, Wills], 1650–1717, 13–14, quoted in Catherine E. Whitten and Joida Whitten, "Is This Sarah Woodson, Widow of Dr. John Woodson?" *Virginia Genealogist* 20 (January–March 1976): 4–5.

16. Brian J. Given, *A Most Pernicious Thing: Gun Trading and Native Warfare in the Early Contact Period* (Ottawa: Carleton University Press, 1994), 15–23, 38–41, 100–110; Major-General B. P. Hughes, *Firepower: Weapons Effectiveness on the Battlefield, 1630–1850* (Staplehurst: Spellmount, 1997), 26–29; [William D. Ligon], *The Ligon Family and Connections* [New York?, 1947], 306–13.

17. For example, a traditional story of a woman who hid under a tub during the Mohawks' attack on Deerfield, Massachusetts, is cited in John Demos, *The Unredeemed Captive: A Family Story from Early America* (New York: Knopf, 1994), 21; on an alarm over Redcoats in Yarmouth, Massachusetts, see Sears Family Association, "Eleazar Sears (Capt.)," http://bit.ly/14lRQk9; on hiding from the Yankees, see "Yadkin County and Caswell County" under James Richard Jeter, http://bit.ly/1cXyQ38; on the concealment of Harriet Tubman, see Sarah H. Bradford, *Harriet: The Moses of Her People* (New York: Lockwood, 1886), 42; on three children protected from a windstorm in 1890, see "Grayson Co. Edwards Family Tied to Two State Governors," *Grayson County (Ky.) News Gazette,* October 29, 1992; and on a boy who survived the great Miramichi fire in New Brunswick, Canada, in 1825, see Jesse E. Lincoln, "Through Flame and Tempest," *Youth's Companion* (New England ed.), October 11 1894, 451.

18. James C. Kelly, Assistant Director for Museums, VHS, e-mail message to author, June

28, 2001; Woodson, *Historical Genealogy,* 22. The VHS's website (viewed June 6, 2013) describes the musket without mentioning the family story, but as of that date the label in the exhibition itself did include the judicious reference.

19. Alexander Brown, *The First Republic in America* (Boston: Houghton Mifflin, 1898), 308; Lady Wyatt to her sister Sandys, April 4, 1623, in Kingsbury, *Virginia Company,* 4:232. On the Jamestown settlement, see generally Karen Ordahl Kupperman, *The Jamestown Project* (Cambridge: Belknap Press of Harvard University Press, 2007); James Horn, *A Land as God Made It: Jamestown and the Birth of America* (New York: Basic Books, 2005); Helen C. Rountree, *Pocahontas, Powhatan, Opechancanough: Three Indian Lives Changed by Jamestown* (Charlottesville: University of Virginia Press, 2005); Morgan, *American Slavery.*

20. Rachel B. Herrmann, "The 'Tragicall Historie': Cannibalism and Abundance in Colonial Jamestown," *WMQ* 68 (2011): 47–74; Kupperman, *Jamestown Project,* 166–72.

21. Nicolás Monardes, *Ioyfull Nevves out of the Newe Founde Worlde, Wherein is Declared the Rare and Singuler Vertues of Diuerse and Sundrie Hearbes, Trees, Oyles, Plantes, and Stones . . .* (London, 1577), fol. 5r–5v, 35r–38v, 49v.

22. Karen Ordahl Kupperman, "Apathy and Death in Early Jamestown," *Journal of American History* 66 (1979): 24–40.

23. [Robert Beverley], *The History and Present State of Virginia, in Four Parts . . . By a Native and Inhabitant of the Place* (London, 1705), 38.

24. James, King of England, *A Counterblaste to Tobacco* (London, 1604), D2r.

25. Morgan, *American Slavery,* 120–23.

26. Edward Waterhouse, *A Declaration of the State of the Colony and Affaires in Virginia, With a Relation of the Barbarous Massacre,* in Kingsbury, *Virginia Company,* 3:551; William Capps to Dr. Thomas Wynston, March or April (?) 1623, ibid., 4:38. See also Bernard Bailyn, *The Barbarous Years: The People of British North America: The Conflict of Civilizations, 1600–1675* (New York: Knopf, 2012), 100–111.

27. [Alderman Johnson or Sir Nathaniel Rich], "Parts of Drafts of a Statement Touching the Miserable Condition of Virginia," May or June 1623, Manchester Papers no. 347, in Kingsbury, *Virginia Company,* 4:179; Wesley Frank Craven, *The Dissolution of the Virginia Company: The Failure of a Colonial Experiment* (Gloucester, Mass.: Peter Smith, 1964), 273–74.

28. Dorman, *Adventurers,* 1:23.

29. Estimates of the total number of settlers sent by the Company vary from about six thousand to about eight thousand. The 1624 list may have been undercounted by as much as 20 percent; see Morgan, *American Slavery,* 395–97; and Irene W. D. Hecht, "The Virginia Muster of 1624/5 as a Source for Demographic History," *WMQ* 30 (1973): 65–92.

30. [Ligon], *Ligon Family,* 365, 373; Woodson, *Historical Genealogy,* 70; *Journals of the House of Burgesses of Virginia, 1766–1769,* ed. John Pendleton Kennedy (Richmond: Virginia State Library, 1906), 124–25 (April 11, 1767); Rind's *Virginia Gazette,* May 12 and June 16, 1768.

31. Bessie Thompson, "Survey Report, Brooklyn, 1936 Nov. 24," and "Survey Report, The Shultz Place, 1937 Mar. 5," Works Progress Administration of Virginia Historical Inventory, available through the LVA online catalogue, http://lva1.hosted.exlibrisgroup. com/F. Thompson's informant, Charles A. Garden, was both a stepson and a half nephew

of Charles Woodson's great-great-granddaughter Nannie Venable Garden, whose aged spinster sister Mollie Venable was the last of the Woodson line to inhabit the house.

32. Charles Taylor, *Sources of the Self: The Making of the Modern Identity* (Cambridge: Harvard University Press, 1989), 286–88; Peter Brooks, *Reading for the Plot: Design and Intention in Narrative* (New York: Knopf, 1984), 5–7; Rhys Isaac, "Stories and Constructions of Identity: Folk Tellings and Diary Inscriptions in Revolutionary Virginia," in *Through a Glass Darkly: Reflections on Personal Identity in Early America*, ed. Ronald Hoffman, Mechal Sobel, and Fredrika J. Teute (Chapel Hill: University of North Carolina Press, 1997), 206–9, 216–17; Mechal Sobel, "The Revolution in Selves: Black and White Inner Aliens," in Hoffman, Sobel, and Teute, *Through a Glass Darkly,* 165–70.

33. Greg Sieminski, "The Puritan Captivity Narrative and the Politics of the American Revolution," *American Quarterly* 42 (1990): 39–42.

34. Laurel Thatcher Ulrich, *Good Wives: Image and Reality in the Lives of Women in Northern New England, 1650–1750* (New York: Vintage, 1991), 167–77; June Namias, *White Captives: Gender and Ethnicity on the American Frontier* (Chapel Hill: University of North Carolina Press, 1995), 29–36.

35. Woodsons including Charles's grandfather John appear throughout Society of Friends, Henrico County Monthly Meeting, "Friends' Records, 1699–1834" (available from LDS, reel 0031762). William Wade Hinshaw, *Encyclopedia of American Quaker Genealogy,* vol. 6 (1950; Baltimore: Genealogical Publishing Co., 1993), 220, cites records showing three Woodson brothers disowned in 1775 for enlisting, as was a sister in 1771 for marrying out of unity. On Major Woodson's captivity, see Major Tarlton Woodson, Continental Troops: Hazen's Regiment, M881, roll 91 CSR-Rev; and Tarlton Woodson to Sally Clark, November 9, 1777, Woodson Papers. For the brothers' letters about the possibility of virtue, see chapter 3.

36. Michael Kammen, *Mystic Chords of Memory: The Transformation of Tradition in American Culture* (New York: Vintage, 1993), 215–24; Eric Hobsbawm, "Mass-Producing Traditions: Europe, 1870–1914," in *The Invention of Tradition,* ed. Eric Hobsbawm and Terence Ranger (Cambridge: Cambridge University Press, 1983), 292–93; Robert M. Taylor Jr. and Ralph J. Crandall, "Historians and Genealogists: An Emerging Community of Interest," in *Generations and Change: Genealogical Perspectives in Social History,* ed. Robert M. Taylor Jr. and Ralph J. Crandall (Macon, Ga.: Mercer University Press, 1986), 6–8.

37. Woodson, *Historical Genealogy,* 471–73; H. M. Woodson, Thirty-fourth Mississippi Infantry, M269, roll 360, CSR-Confed.

38. Woodson, *Historical Genealogy,* 114, 11, 10. Both Carter Woodson's family and several white Woodson families had roots in Fluvanna County, Virginia.

39. On the anachronism, see Virginia Lee Hutcheson Davis, *Tidewater Families: Generations Beyond* (Baltimore: Genealogical Publishing Co., 1998), 123; [Marilyn Goza Longobardi], "Critical Note on Woodson Family Traditions," *Woodson Watcher* 1, no. 2 (March 1983): 61.

40. David Carr, *Time, Narrative, and History* (Bloomington: Indiana University Press, 1991), 163.

41. H. Porter Abbott, *The Cambridge Introduction to Narrative,* 2nd ed. (Cambridge: Cambridge University Press, 2008), 86–90.

2. Camelot in the Tobacco Fields

1. Mrs. H. D. Pittman, ed., *Americans of Gentle Birth and Their Ancestors: A Genealogical Encyclopedia*, 2 vols. (St. Louis: Buxton & Skinner, 1903–1907), 1:354; "The Mullins Family in Europe," http://mullinsclan.webs.com/.

2. Franklin Miller Jr., *The Mellett and Hickman Families of Henry County, Indiana*, 2 vols. (Gambier, Ohio: By the author, 1974), 1:120, on the Earl of Bute, citing a story that "may have been quoted from *Our Forefathers* (1946) by Vinetta Burke, a book which is in the NSDAR [National Society Daughters of the American Revolution] library" (though Vinetta Wells *Ranke*'s self-published book by that title does not include such a story); on Ferris: Pittman, *Americans,* 1:358–59, and the Ferris Family Genealogy Forum, http://genforum.genealogy.com/ferris, which also cites Adelle Bartlett Harper, *Family Lines: A Loving Tribute to Our Southern Heritage* (1973).

3. Claims for (and refutations of) the Ballards' connection to Richard II's household surface frequently in online discussion boards and forums, especially the Ballard family e-mail list archived on Rootsweb.com, http://bit.ly/1dUfIn8; on Thomas Savage's descent from Charlemagne: Evelyn Kinder Donaldson, *Squires and Dames of Old Virginia* (Los Angeles: Miller Printing, 1950), 247–48; on the Savages' connection to the noble Irish family, see the Savage family e-mail list archived on Rootsweb.com, http://bit.ly/17pjLD8; on the Earl of Wigton, see, e.g., Henry Morton Woodson, *Historical Genealogy of the Woodsons and Their Connections* (Columbia, Mo.: By the author, 1915), 30; Pittman, *Americans,* 1:350, 360; and frequent references (pro and sometimes con) on the Fleming Family Genealogy Forum, http://genforum.genealogy.com/fleming/.

4. Edward E. Lanphere, *Bates: Descendants of Bates Ancestors Who Lived in Virginia* (Chapel Hill: By the author, 1973), vi.

5. In their intensive survey of the ways Americans use history in their everyday lives, Roy Rosenzweig and David Thelen found that people put more trust in personal accounts of the past by their own older relatives than in almost any other historical source. "People I don't know—a professor, a movie—could be telling me any old thing," one respondent explained, "but grandparents get my complete trust." Roy Rosenzweig and David Thelen, *The Presence of the Past: Popular Uses of History in American Life* (New York: Columbia University Press, 1998), 91, 95.

6. Kunhardt Productions, *African American Lives, with Henry Louis Gates, Jr.,* episode 2, "The Promise of Freedom," produced and directed by Leslie Asako Gladsjo, DVD (Alexandria, Va.: PBS Home Video, 2006).

7. J. H. Plumb, *The Death of the Past* (Boston: Houghton Mifflin, 1970), 29–33.

8. James C. Cobb, *Away Down South: A History of Southern Identity* (Oxford: Oxford University Press, 2005), 22–23.

9. For a brisk summary of views of the Puritan/Cavalier dichotomy, see ibid., 9–33, 43–47.

10. Charles Taylor, *Sources of the Self: The Making of Modern Identity* (Cambridge: Harvard University Press, 1989), 159–84; John R. Gillis, *A World of Their Own Making: Myth, Ritual, and the Quest for Family Values* (New York: Basic Books, 1996), 12–15.

11. David Hackett Fisher, *Albion's Seed: Four British Folkways in America* (New York: Oxford University Press, 1991), 216.

12. Alex Shoumatoff, *The Mountain of Names: A History of the Human Family* (New York: Vintage, 1990), 231; Steve Olson, "The Royal We," *Atlantic Monthly,* May 2002, 62–64, citing a paper by Joseph Chang giving the 1400 date; and Mark Humphrys, "Common Ancestors of All Humans," HumphrysFamilyTree.com, http://bit.ly/15AAnu, suggesting the 1000 date.

13. A. Roger Ekirch, *Birthright: The True Story That Inspired "Kidnapped"* (New York: Norton, 2010).

14. Some Fleming descendants have launched a DNA project on dna.ancestry.com, but their efforts have been frustrated by the apparent failure centuries ago of the male Fleming line.

15. Thomas Haskell, *Objectivity Is Not Neutrality: Explanatory Schemes in History* (Baltimore: Johns Hopkins University Press, 1998), 282–83.

16. On the Huitts: JoAnn Riley McKey, *Accomack County, Virginia, Court Order Abstracts,* vol. 1, 1663–1666 (Bowie, Md.: Heritage, 1996), 19–20, 33; on Tarlton: York County Deeds, Orders, Wills, vol. 3 (1657–1662), 175, 181 (LVA); on Smith: Susie M. Ames, ed., *County Court Records of Accomack-Northampton, Virginia, 1640–1645* (Charlottesville: University Press of Virginia, 1973), 298–300; on Ballard: quoted in Jon Kukla, *Speakers and Clerks of the Virginia House of Burgesses, 1643–1776* (Richmond: Virginia State Library, 1981), 76.

17. Ralph T. Whitelaw, *Virginia's Eastern Shore: A History of Northampton and Accomack Counties,* 2 vols. (Richmond: VHS, 1951), 108–14, 968–71.

18. Ibid., 110–11, 116–17; "A Marriage Agreement: Original Draft of an Agreement on File at Eastville, Northampton Co., Virginia," *VMHB* 4 (1897): 64–66; "Editor's Drawer," *Harper's New Monthly Magazine* 32 (January 1866): 270.

19. Russell R. Menard, "From Servant to Freeholder: Status Mobility and Property Accumulation in Seventeenth-Century Maryland," *WMQ* 30 (1973): 39–40; Lois Green Carr, "Introduction," in *Colonial Chesapeake Society,* ed. Lois Green Carr, Philip D. Morgan, and Jean B. Russo (Chapel Hill: University of North Carolina Press, 1988), 36; James Horn, *Adapting to a New World: English Society in the Seventeenth-Century Chesapeake* (Chapel Hill: University of North Carolina Press, 1994), 154; Thomas J. Wertenbaker, *The Planters of Colonial Virginia* (New York: Russell & Russell, 1959), 73.

20. Most of these names (with allowances for the era's casual spelling) appear in volumes 1 and 2 of Nell Marion Nugent, *Cavaliers and Pioneers: Abstracts of Virginia Land Patents and Grants* (Richmond: Dietz; Virginia State Library, 1934–1977), among the lists of servants and others for whose transportation the grantees claimed headrights. The names also belong to men I've otherwise identified as my ancestors and fit with whatever else I know about their lifespans, locations, and connections. See Savage claimed in 1671 by Captain Edmund Bowman and Southy Littleton (2:94), and again in 1673 by Roger Michaell (2:139); Via in 1677 by John Webb and John Rea (2:178–79); Ferris in 1636 by Robert Hollom (1:41); Payne in 1642 by Daniel Gookins (1:138); Roberts in 1652 by Arthur Upshott (1:286); Fleming in 1653 by Joseph Croshaw (1:249); Hickman in 1655 by John Dorman (1:326); Merriman and his wife in 1664 by George Vezey and others (1:514); and Mullins in 1666 by Cornelius Dabney (1:558). Smith testified in court in 1635 about his indentureship (Susie M. Ames, ed., *County Court Records of Accomack-Northampton, Virginia, 1632–1640* [Washington, D.C.: American Historical Association, 1954], 37); Watson was under indenture in 1651 (Northampton County Deeds, Wills, etc., vol. 4

[1651–54], fol. 47 [LVA]); Pemmet was transported to Maryland in 1663 (Gust Skordas, ed., *The Early Settlers of Maryland* [Baltimore: Genealogical Publishing Co., 1968], lib. 6 f. 290). A Thomas Trammell was indentured in Stafford County around 1671 (*Minutes of the Council and General Court of Colonial Virginia, 1622–1632, 1670–1676*, ed. H. R. McIlwaine [Richmond: Virginia State Library, 1924], 405), but his connection to my ancestor John Trammell, a slightly younger resident of the same county, is unclear. The origins of Tarlton (first appearing in York County around 1659) and Huitt (on the Eastern Shore beginning in the mid-1650s) are unknown; on Ballard, see my discussion later in this chapter.

21. Kenneth Morgan, *Slavery and Servitude in North America, 1607–1800* (Edinburgh: Edinburgh University Press, 2000), 8–25; David W. Galenson, *White Servitude in Colonial America: An Economic Analysis* (Cambridge: Cambridge University Press, 1981), 23–78; Horn, *Adapting,* 19–77.

22. Don Jordan and Michael Walsh, *White Cargo: The Forgotten History of Britain's White Slaves in America* (New York: New York University Press, 2008), 127–36.

23. George Alsop, *A Character of the Province of Mary-Land* (London, 1666), 33; John Hammond, *Leah and Rachel: Or, The Two Fruitfull Sisters Virginia and Mary-Land* (London, 1656), 7, 12, 9, 17.

24. Alsop, *Province of Mary-Land,* 38.

25. On the "chattelisation" of the servant: Jordan and Walsh, *White Cargo,* 108–12; for citations to varying estimates of the mortality rates, see John Ruston Pagan, *Anne Orthwood's Bastard: Sex and Law in Early Virginia* (Oxford: Oxford University Press, 2003), 15, 156n17.

26. Horn, *Adapting,* 257.

27. Orphan: Ames, *Court Records, 1640–1645,* 271–72; Hinman: J. Douglas Deal, *Race and Class in Colonial Virginia: Indians, Englishmen, and Africans on the Eastern Shore during the Seventeenth Century* (New York: Garland, 1993), 41–42; Mikell (also spelled Michaell, Makeel, etc.): JoAnn Riley McKey, comp., *Accomack County, Virginia Court Order Abstracts,* vol. 6, 1678–1682 (Bowie, Md.: Heritage, 1997), xxi–xxiii; Jones: Ames, *Court Records, 1640–1645,* 290–91; Thomas's suicide: James Handley Marshall, *Abstracts of the Wills and Administrations of Northampton County, Virginia, 1632–1802* (Rockport, Me.: Picton, 1994), entry dated October 25, 1656, citing Northampton County Deeds, Wills, etc., vol. 7, no. 7 (1655–1657), 26 (LVA).

28. Kukla, *Speakers and Clerks,* 74. No evidence, however, ties Colonel Ballard to King Richard II's lavishly rewarded underling, and his offspring are almost as difficult to sort out as his ancestry is. He may be my ninth-great-grandfather, not my eighth; see my discussion in chapter 4.

29. See generally James D. Rice, *Tales from a Revolution: Bacon's Rebellion and the Transformation of Early America* (Oxford: Oxford University Press, 2012); and Morgan, *American Slavery,* 235–92.

30. Paul G. E. Clemens, "Reimagining the Political Economy of Early Virginia," *WMQ* 68 (2011): 393–97, rounds up recent scholarship on the displacement of indentureship by slavery.

31. Morgan, *American Slavery,* 238.

32. Quoted in Kukla, *Speakers and Clerks,* 76.

33. Will of Josias Payne, Pittsylvania County, Virginia, dated January 12, 1785, proved December 19, 1785; quoted in "The Payne Family of Goochland, &c. (continued)," [i.e., pt. 3], *VMHB* 7:80–81.

34. Dorman, *Adventurers,* 1:206–8; York County Deeds, Orders, Wills, vol. 15 (1716–20), 605–7 (LVA).

35. "The Ancestors and Descendants of John Rolfe, with Notices of Some Connected Families: The Fleming Family," *VMHB* 23 (1915): 214, 325–26; Virginia Lee Hutcheson Davis, *Tidewater Families: A Social History* (Baltimore: Genealogical Publishing Co., 1989), 420–21; "Rock Castle (Queen Anne Cottage)," *Goochland County Historical Society Magazine* 1 (Autumn 1969): 12–14.

36. "Petition of Stephen Tarleton of New Kent County to the Commissioners for Virginia," March–May 1677, *Calendar of State Papers, Colonial: North America and the West Indies, 1574–1739,* item 162, vol. 10 (1677–80), 53, CO I/40, no. 31 (available on CD-ROM [London: Routledge, 2000]).

37. Pittman, *Americans,* 1:ii, vi.

38. Pittman quoted in Joseph Y. DeSpain, "Kentucky Biographical Notebook: Hannah Daviess Pittman, Neglected Kentucky Author," *FCHQ* 70, no. 2 (April 1996): 194; Thomas Paine, *Common Sense* (Philadelphia, 1776), 43.

3. Declaring Independence

1. Cassandra Nichols, USFC, 1860, Kentucky, Harrison County, roll M653_372, 80, http://bit.ly/1800lZR. My count of all obvious spellings of the name (e.g., Cassandria, Casandra) is based on Bettie Stirling Carothers, comp., *1776 Census of Maryland* (Westminster, Md.: Family Line Publications, 1986).

2. Mechal Sobel, *Teach Me Dreams: The Search for Self in the Revolutionary Era* (Princeton: Princeton University Press, 2000), 3–7; Carol Z. Stearns, "'Lord Help Me Walk Humbly': Anger and Sadness in England and America, 1570–1750," in *Emotion and Social Change: Toward a New Psychohistory,* ed. Carol Z. Stearns and Peter N. Stearns (New York: Holmes & Meier, 1988), 44–45; Thomas Haskell, *Objectivity Is Not Neutrality: Explanatory Schemes in History* (Baltimore: Johns Hopkins University Press, 1998), 340–41.

3. The rich literature addressing this topic includes, e.g., Jan Lewis, *The Pursuit of Happiness: Family and Values in Jefferson's Virginia* (Cambridge: Cambridge University Press, 1983), 9–20; Jack P. Greene, *Pursuits of Happiness: The Social Development of Early Modern British Colonies and the Formation of American Culture* (Chapel Hill: University of North Carolina Press, 1988), 195–98; T. H. Breen, *Tobacco Culture: The Mentality of the Great Tidewater Planters on the Eve of the Revolution* (Princeton: Princeton University Press, 1985), 85–91; and Rhys Isaac, *The Transformation of Virginia, 1740–1790* (Chapel Hill: University of North Carolina Press, 1982), 115–38.

4. Breen, *Tobacco Culture,* 125–28; Landon Carter, *The Diary of Colonel Landon Carter of Sabine Hall, 1752–1778,* ed. Jack P. Greene, 2 vols. (Charlottesville: University Press of Virginia, 1965), 1:548 (March 12, 1771).

5. Thomas Jefferson, *The Autobiography of Thomas Jefferson, 1743–1790, Together with a*

Summary of the Chief Events of Jefferson's Life, ed. Paul Leicester Ford, new intro. by Michael Zuckerman (Philadelphia: University of Pennsylvania Press, 2005), 4.

6. Will of Tarlton Fleming [Senior], Goochland County Deed Book, vol. 6 (1748–1755), 113–14 (LVA); *Journals of the House of Burgesses of Virginia, 1758–1761,* ed. H. R. McIlwaine (Richmond: Virginia State Library, 1908), 141–42.

7. "British Mercantile Claims, 1775–1803, Continued," *Virginia Genealogist* 24 (1980): 125–26, citing records in London's Public Records Office; Goochland County Deed Book, vol. 12 (1777–1779), 102–8, vol. 15 (1788–1791), 421–32 (LVA); Martha Randolph quoted in Jonathan Daniels, *The Randolphs of Virginia* (Garden City, N.Y.: Doubleday, 1972), 225–26.

8. Inventory and Appraisement of the Estate of Col. Tarlton Fleming deceased, Goochland County Deed Book, vol. 12 (1777–1779), 102–8 (LVA).

9. Kenneth A. Lockridge, *The Diary, and Life, of William Byrd II of Virginia, 1674–1744* (Chapel Hill: University of North Carolina Press, 1987), 127–43.

10. William Byrd, "A Progress to the Mines in the Year 1732," in *The Prose Works of William Byrd of Westover: Narratives of a Colonial Virginian,* ed. Louis B. Wright (Cambridge: Belknap Press of Harvard University Press, 1966), 342–45.

11. Ibid., 342.

12. Jean Edward Smith, *John Marshall: Definer of a Nation* (New York: Henry Holt, 1996), 24–25, citing letters from contemporary clergymen to the bishop of London.

13. W. M. Paxton, *The Marshall Family, or a Genealogical Chart of the Descendants of John Marshall and Elizabeth Markham, His Wife* (Cincinnati: Robert Clarke, 1885), 3, 25.

14. Ibid., 25–26, 45.

15. Ibid., 25–26.

16. Ibid., 45, 16–17.

17. Ibid., 16–17.

18. Ibid., 15–16 quoting Green.

19. H. F. Rankin, *The Golden Age of Piracy* (Williamsburg, Va.: Colonial Williamsburg, 1969), 54–55.

20. Details of the pirate's death vary from account to account; this comes from the *Boston News-Letter,* February 23/March 2, 1719.

21. Paxton, *Marshall Family,* 226–27.

22. Albert J. Beveridge, *Life of John Marshall,* 4 vols. (New York: Houghton Mifflin, 1916–1919), 1:17–18n7; Smith, *Marshall,* 24–25.

23. Christie's novel is *Taken at the Flood,* published in the United States as *There Is a Tide* (1948); the Cary Grant movie, *My Favorite Wife* (1940), is a gender-reversed version in which Grant's character, called Nick Arden, discovers on his second wedding day that his "late" first wife (Irene Dunne) has been rescued from a desert island.

24. "The Maupin Family," *VMHB* 8 (1901): 216–18; Dorothy Maupin Shaffett, comp., *The Story of Gabriel and Marie Maupin, Huguenot Refugees to Virginia in 1700* (Baltimore: Gateway, 1994), 44–51, 58, 60–62; H. Bullock, "The Magazine (LL) Historical Report, Block 12 Building 9," Colonial Williamsburg Foundation Library Research Report series, no. 1248 (Williamsburg, 1990), 91, http://bit.ly/1eKVvha.

25. Shaffett, *Gabriel and Marie Maupin*, 58.

26. "John C. Collins," in *History of Lewis, Clark, Knox, and Scotland Counties, Missouri, from the Earliest Time to the Present* . . . (St. Louis: Goodspeed, 1887), 1158–59; Robert Y. Clay, "Some Delinquent Taxpayers, 1787–1790," *Virginia Genealogist* 20 (July–September 1976): 202.

27. James Webb, *Born Fighting: How the Scots-Irish Shaped America* (New York: Broadway Books, 2004); James G. Leyburn, *The Scotch-Irish: A Social History* (Chapel Hill: University of North Carolina Press, 1962), 157–223; David Hackett Fischer, *Albion's Seed: Four British Folkways in America* (New York: Oxford University Press, 1991), 605–39.

28. Peter Wilson Coldham, *The Complete Book of Emigrants in Bondage, 1614–1775* (Baltimore: Genealogical Publishing Co., 1988), 859.

29. A. Roger Ekirch, *Bound for America: The Transportation of British Convicts to the Colonies, 1718–1775* (Oxford: Clarendon Press, 1987), 134–37, 28–29, 33–35; Don Jordan and Michael Walsh, *White Cargo: The Forgotten History of Britain's White Slaves in America* (New York: New York University Press, 2008), 247–50; Old Bailey Proceedings Online, June 30, 1770, trial of John Underwood and William Wharton (t17700630-23), http://bit.ly/140tnFM.

30. Shaffett, *Gabriel and Marie Maupin*, 247.

31. ["Tough"] Daniel Maupin, W556, and Daniel Maupin, S5733, both roll 1655, RWP, http://bit.ly/1riATGg (["Tough"] Daniel) and http://bit.ly/1gfr33J (Daniel).

32. Lorett Treese, *Valley Forge: Making and Remaking a National Symbol* (University Park: Pennsylvania State University Press, 1995), 11, 73–47, 130; Barry Schwartz, "Social Change and Collective Memory: The Democratization of George Washington," *American Sociological Review* 56 (April 1991): 224, citing Gustave de Beaumont in 1832 on Washington's divinity; George B. Forgie, *Patricide in the House Divided: A Psychological Interpretation of Lincoln and His Age* (New York: Norton, 1979), 22–35; David Lowenthal, *The Past Is a Foreign Country* (Cambridge: Cambridge University Press, 1985), 117–21.

33. Hinshaw, *Quaker Genealogy*, 6:220.

34. George Woodson to Frederick Woodson, August 6, 1778; [September 1779?]; November 7, 1779 (including quote), Virginia Revolutionary War Correspondence, 1778–1779, accession number 8352-b, Albert and Shirley Small Special Collections Library, University of Virginia.

35. George Woodson to Tarlton Woodson, May 19, 1776, Woodson Papers.

36. Gordon S. Wood, *The Creation of the American Republic, 1776–1787* (New York: Norton, 1969), 68–69; Adams quoted at 570.

37. George Woodson to Tarlton Woodson, May 19, 1776, Woodson Papers.

38. "Ancestors and Descendants of Rolfe, with Notices of Some Connected Families: The Fleming Family," *VMHB* 24 (1916): 94–97, 206–10, 440–43.

39. Mrs. H. D. Pittman, ed., *Americans of Gentle Birth and Their Ancestors: A Genealogical Encyclopedia*, 2 vols. (St. Louis: Buxton & Skinner, 1903–1907), 1:350.

40. Thomas S. Kidd, *Patrick Henry: First among Patriots* (New York: Basic Books, 2011), 52, calls the defiant response "almost certainly apocryphal," although "the words seemed like something the Patrick Henry who is known to history would indeed have said."

41. William Wirt, *Sketches of the Life and Character of Patrick Henry* (1836), 9th ed. (Freeport, N.Y.: Books for Libraries Press, 1970), 75–76, quoting Henry.

42. Robert Douthat Mead, *Patrick Henry: Patriot in the Making* (Philadelphia: Lippincott, 1957), 168–70, 383–86n36, 39–41, quoting at 169 the former House member Paul Carrington; Edmund Randolph, *History of Virginia*, ed. Arthur H. Shaffer (Charlottesville: University Press of Virginia, 1970), 169.

43. Attributed by Curtis Carroll Davis, *The King's Chevalier: A Biography of Lewis Littlepage* (Indianapolis: Bobbs Merrill, 1961), 21–22; originally published in Purdie's *Virginia Gazette,* March 14, 1777.

44. George Bancroft, *History of the United States, from the Discovery of the American Continent,* 3rd ed., vol. 9 (Boston: Little Brown, 1873), 248.

45. David Hackett Fischer, *Washington's Crossing* (Oxford: Oxford University Press, 2004), 332.

46. Quoted in *A Brief Narrative of the Ravages of the British and Hessians at Princeton in 1776–1777: A Contemporary Account of the Battles of Trenton and Princeton,* ed. Varnum Lansing Collins (Princeton: University Library, 1906), 43–44n.

47. Shaffett, *Gabriel and Marie Maupin,* 394; Henry Morton Woodson, *Historical Genealogy of the Woodsons and Their Connections* (Columbia, Mo.: By the author, 1915), 72, 110–11.

48. Gabriel Mullins, S30608, roll 1787, and William Wharton (with land warrant 10661 assigned to Daniel Vertner, May 9, 1797), S37534, roll 2541, RWP, http://bit.ly/1fRZc4F (Mullins) and http://bit.ly/NGM2AG (Wharton).

49. Charles Patrick Neimeyer, *America Goes to War: A Social History of the Continental Army* (New York: New York University Press, 1996), 24.

50. Mullins, RWP.

51. An early appearance in print of the Rock Castle story is in Robert A. Lancaster Jr., *Historic Virginia Homes and Churches* (Philadelphia: Lippincott, 1915), 183, and it still appears often online. Robert D. Bass, *The Green Dragoon: The Lives of Banastre Tarleton and Mary Robinson* (New York: Henry Holt, 1957), 442–48.

52. Major Tarlton Woodson, Continental Troops: Hazen's Regiment, M881, roll 91, CSR-Rev; Allan S. Everest, *Moses Hazen and the Canadian Refugees in the American Revolution* (Syracuse: Syracuse University Press, 1976), 47–48, 52.

53. Andrew Lee, "Sullivan's Expedition to Staten Island in 1777: Extract from the Diary of Captain Andrew Lee," *Pennsylvania Magazine of History and Biography* 3 (1879): 172–73.

54. Tarlton Woodson to Sally Clark, November 9, 1777, Woodson Papers.

55. George Woodson to Tarlton Woodson, Henrico County, September 29, 1777, and May 31, 1778, Woodson Papers.

56. George Woodson to Tarlton Woodson, May 31, 1778.

57. *Names of Persons for Whom Marriage Licenses Were Issued by the Secretary of the Province of New York, Previous to 1784* (Albany: Weed, Parsons, 1860), 470.

58. E. B. O'Callaghan, comp., *Documentary History of the State of New York,* 4 vols. (Albany: Weed, Parsons, 1850–51), 3:514. Jeromus Van der Veer was named as Anne's father in the handwritten Woodson family history in the Woodson Papers.

59. Tarlton Woodson, CSR-Rev; on his presence at Cornwallis's surrender, see U.S. Congress, Senate Committee on Claims, *Heirs of Maj. Tarleton Woodson,* 56th Cong., 2d sess., Report 2024, January 24, 1901, 1; Woodson, *Historical Genealogy,* 81.

60. Woodson, *Historical Genealogy,* 81.

61. Nancy Woodson, USFC, 1850, Virginia, Prince Edward County, roll M432_970, 11, http://bit.ly/1asm2U2.

62. Bessie Thompson, "Survey Report: The Shultz Place, 1937 Mar. 5," Works Progress Administration of Virginia Historical Inventory, 3; available through the LVA online catalogue, http://lva1.hosted.exlibrisgroup.com/F.

63. U.S. Congress, Senate, *Heirs of Maj. Woodson,* citing some of the earlier congressional actions; U.S. Congress, Senate, *A Bill for the Relief of the Heirs at Law of Major Tarleton Woodson,* S3365, 58th Cong., 2nd sess., January 12, 1904; see also, e.g., *House Journal,* 1st Cong., 3rd sess., February 16, 1791, 380 (here and in some nineteenth-century entries his forename is spelled "Tarlton"); on officers' pensions, see John Resch, *Suffering Soldiers: Revolutionary War Veterans, Moral Sentiment, and Political Culture in the Early Republic* (Amherst: University of Massachusetts Press, 1999), 208–9.

64. Thompson, "Survey Report: The Shultz Place," 3.

4. The Kentucky Pioneers Speak Out

1. Quoted in Arthur K. Moore, *The Frontier Mind: A Cultural Analysis of the Kentucky Frontiersman* (Frankfort: University of Kentucky Press, 1957), 24.

2. Joyce Appleby, ed., *Recollections of the Early Republic: Selected Autobiographies* (Boston: Northeastern University Press, 1997), xix–xx.

3. Mechal Sobel, "The Revolution in Selves: Black and White Inner Aliens," in *Through a Glass Darkly: Reflections on Personal Identity in Early America,* ed. Ronald Hoffman, Mechal Sobel, and Fredrika J. Teute (Chapel Hill: University of North Carolina Press, 1997), 166–70; Ann Fabian, *The Unvarnished Truth: Personal Narratives in Nineteenth-Century America* (Berkeley: University of California Press, 2000), 2–7; Michael O'Brien, *Intellectual Life and the American South, 1810–1860* (Chapel Hill: University of North Carolina Press, 2010), 162–66.

4. Quoted in Stephen Aron, *How the West Was Lost: The Transformation of Kentucky from Daniel Boone to Henry Clay* (Baltimore: Johns Hopkins University Press, 1996), 6.

5. John Filson, *The Discovery, Settlement and Present State Of Kentucke . . .* (Wilmington, 1784), 109.

6. "John Nathaniel Ducker Sr.," filled-in form with information from James L. Kirby, December 30, 1936; James L. Kirby, "John Nathaniel Ducker," June 12, 1936, Ducker folder, box 195, Barton.

7. Jennifer Copeland, assistant librarian, H. Furlong Baldwin Library, Maryland Historical Society, e-mail message to author, January 5, 2005.

8. Moses Austin, in *Running Mad for Kentucky: Frontier Travel Accounts,* ed. Ellen Eslinger (Lexington: University Press of Kentucky, 2004), 179.

9. Aron, *How the West Was Lost,* 70–83; quotation at 82.

10. Rachel Ballard Mullins was the granddaughter of Thomas and Susannah Hesson Ballard of Albemarle, and while family historians continue to debate who exactly Thomas's father was and whether Thomas was a grandson or great-grandson of the emigrant Colonel Thomas Ballard, the evidence is strong that Bland Ballard I—the grandfather of the Indian fighter

Bland W. Ballard—was this Thomas's brother. The Bland name may have entered the Ballard family through marriage to a female offspring of the prosperous and prolific Bland family of Virginia, but no such union has been recorded.

11. Bland W. Ballard interview, DM 8 J 170–72, from which version I quote here; the interview and Draper's comments are reprinted (with some spelling and grammar corrected) in Margaret Morris Bridwell, "Notes on One of the Early Ballard Families of Kentucky, Including the Ballard Massacre," *FCHQ* 13 (1939): 56, 59–60.

12. Bland W. Ballard, W20655, roll 129, RWP, http://bit.ly/1lZv2lg.

13. Lewis Collins, *History of Kentucky: Embracing Prehistoric, Annals for 331 Years . . . ,* rev. Richard H. Collins, 2 vols. (Covington, Ky.: Collins, 1878–82), 2:40–42.

14. Bridwell, "Ballard," 55.

15. Ballard interview, DM.

16. Shane interview with Samuel Graham, DM 11 CC 297; with Jeptha Kemper, 12 CC 132, transcribed in *FCHQ* 12 [1938]: 151–61. On Shane, see Elizabeth A. Perkins, *Border Life: Experience and Memory in the Revolutionary Ohio Valley* (Chapel Hill: University of North Carolina Press, 1998), 15–22.

17. [Rogers Clark Ballard Thruston], "Our Ballard Family," undated, signed in pencil "R. C. T. B.," Ballard Family Files, 4–5, Filson Historical Society, Louisville, Ky.; quoted by permission of the Society.

18. Rogers Clark Ballard Thruston, "Ballard Massacre 1788 and Theresa Ballard West," attached to his letter to KHS dated September 19, 1921, BFC; Whitfield West (Thursia's son), USFC, 1870, Kentucky, Franklin County, roll M593_462, 191, http://bit.ly/13tLMKy.

19. Whitfield West, USFC.

20. Clipping, Sunday, November 22, 1936, headed "America's greatest comic weekly," BFC.

21. KHS holds voluminous correspondence from E. N. Ballard, including several manuscript versions of the story, all very similar, in addition to the typescript quoted here, "Incidents in the Life of Captain Bland Williams Ballard," which was "written April 15, 1941 and recopied in September 29, 1945. This copy was made July 22nd, 1946." BFC.

22. Ibid.

23. Shane interview with John Hanks, DM 12 CC 138–44, transcribed in *Register of the Kentucky Historical Society* 92 (1994): 131–48.

24. E. N. Ballard, "Incidents in the Life of Captain Ballard."

25. E. N. Ballard to KHS, La Junta, Colorado, July 23, 1941, BFC.

26. E. N. Ballard to R. C. B. Thruston, October 9, 1941, BFC.

27. Cotton Mather, *Magnalia Christi Americana, Or, The Ecclesiastical History of New-England* (London, 1702), bk. 7, 91.

28. William C. Stewart, "The Doughertys of Kentucky," in *Genealogies of Kentucky Families from the Register of the Kentucky Historical Society,* vol. 1 (Baltimore: Genealogical Publishing Co., 1981), 233–46; Joseph Addison Waddell, *Annals of Augusta County, Virginia,* 2nd ed. (Staunton, Va.: Caldwell, 1902), 172; Oren F. Morton, *Annals of Bath County, Virginia* (Staunton, Va.: McClure, 1917), 84; Bill Stupak, "William Daugherty and Elizabeth Bunch," http://bit.ly/1ad1YEf, noting there is no source for the traditional identification of Elizabeth Bunch Daugherty as Cherokee; William S. Ewing, "Indian Captives Released

by Colonel Bouquet," *WPHM* 39 (1956): 193, referring to "Dorothy's son," an oddly familiar reference if it's to a woman but less so if it's to an Irish surname no one spelled the
same way twice. I link my ancestors to the Shenandoah Valley Daughertys through their
relationship with the Conway family.

29. Typed copy taken March 18, 1945, from a clipping in the possession of Ida J. Dougherty
and said to be from the *Yeoman,* noting the children's deaths between September 12 and
October 2, 1858, John N. "Slick" Daugherty folder, box 193, Barton.

30. W. Gilmore Simms, *Mellichampe: A Legend of the Santee* (1836), new rev. ed. (New York:
Redfield, 1854), 123.

31. Ms. copy, *Hutcheson v. Daugherty,* PCCC Criminal cases, pkg. 67, filed June 29, 1832, July
term, Joseph Daugherty Sr. folder, box 193, Barton (original at KDLA).

32. Ms. copy, *John Grant v. Thomas Belew,* PCCC Civil cases, pkg. 39, filed April 9, 1824;
William Daugherty v. J. Daugherty, pkg. 13, filed July 18, 1816; Newton Daugherty, pkg.
26, 1852–56 (originals at KDLA); on "Slick": filled-in form with information from Enoch
Daugherty, September 23, 1941, Joseph Daugherty Sr. folder; undated ms., "Slick"
Daugherty folder, Barton.

33. L. D. Daugherty, February 8, 1938, typed statement, Joseph Daugherty Sr. folder, Barton.

34. Joseph Daugherty, USFC, 1850, Kentucky, Pendleton County, roll M432_216, 345, http://
bit.ly/17gXed3.

35. Jane Minder, reference librarian, KDLA, e-mail message to author, August 15, 2003, citing
the *Annual Report of the Auditor of Public Accounts for the Year Ending October 10, 1847.*

36. Ms. copies, petition, Jasper Daugherty, February 14, 1859, PCCC, pkg. 209; *Jane C.
Daugherty plff. v. Henry Duckworth and John Daugherty,* January 2, 1861, PCCC, pkg. 160;
Joseph Daugherty Sr. folder, Barton (originals at KDLA).

37. Mrs. Alice Daugherty, July 8, 1943, Jonathan Daugherty folder, box 193, Barton; Arline Stith
Dougherty, "Running the Gauntlet," *DFAN,* December 1984, 124, 132. Alice Daugherty, who
married a grandson of Joseph Daugherty's brother Jesse, names the gauntlet runner as her
husband's grandmother rather than his chronologically more plausible great-grandmother.
Arline Dougherty, who said she had "no idea as to when or where" her unnamed relative
faced his gauntlet, noted that her family was descended from Joseph's brother Jonathan.

38. Copies of many Ogle letters were donated to WHS by George Pohlmann in 1917, but
the current owner and the whereabouts of the originals are unknown; Harold L. Miller,
reference archivist, WHS, to author, July 9, 2003. Copies of a few other letters not in
the WHS Conway Family Collection, which were also signed by or addressed to Ogle
around the same time and are consistent in style and content with the library's letters,
have been privately circulated among family members and have been posted with the
WHS letters online; see, e.g., PCHGS, "The Letters of Henry C. Ogle, Sr., transcribed
and submitted by Sherida Dougherty," http://bit.ly/19zooOY. One descendant tells me
the originals are owned by a woman in Quincy, Illinois, but I have been unable to trace
her. See also Virginia Walton Brooks, "The Triumphant Trials, Toils, and Tribulations of
Revolutionary Pioneer Mother, Elizabeth Bridgewater Conway: A Biography to Show
the Human Portrait of This Heroine of the Western Frontier," *Ansearchin News* 10 (July
1963): 99–110; Ruby Bogner, "It's Really a Daugherty Story," *DFAN,* June 1985, 34. The

letters get some of the genealogical details wrong; on the basis of other sources I am here correcting the number of Conway children (nine, not ten) and the first name of Elizabeth Daugherty's husband (also given as Joseph or William).

39. T. J. Underwood to Henry C. Ogle, Dawson, Sangamon County, Illinois, September 19, 1888; Ogle to Pohlman, Chicago, July 2, 1912, typed copies in WHS Conway Collection.

40. Daniel Trabue, *Westward into Kentucky: The Narrative of Daniel Trabue*, ed. Chester Raymond Young (Lexington: University Press of Kentucky, 1981), 80–81; Milo Quaife, "When Detroit Invaded Kentucky," *FCHQ* 1 (January 1927): 53–67.

41. On the woman's cap: William Albert Galloway, *Old Chillicothe Shawnee and Pioneer History: Conflicts and Romances in the Northwest Territory* (Xenia, Ohio: Buckeye Press, 1934), 52, quoting a 1928 letter from Mrs. W. T. Lafferty; on the bear oil: Draper interview with John Tofflemire, DM 20 S 218–20; on running the gauntlet: Draper interview with Mrs. Ledwell, DM 17 S 200; on the flour: Shane interview with Mrs. Wilson, DM 11 CC 276–79, transcribed in *FCHQ* 16 (1942): 227–35; on the papoose: Bob Francis, "Ruddell's & Martin's Forts," List of Captives at Martin's Station, s.v. John Loveless, http://bit.ly/1d-v8t7B, citing "family stories."

42. Ogle to Pohlman, July 2, 1912; the story is told again in Ogle to Pohlman, Paris, Ky., September 5, 1912, both typed copies in WHS Conway Collection; John F. Darby, *Personal Recollections of Many Prominent People Whom I Have Known* (St. Louis: G. I. Jones, 1880), 84; on the entry in *Ripley's:* Brooks, "Triumphant Trials," 102.

43. Haldimand Papers, Add. Mss. 21, 843, roll A-765, 289, transcribed online at Chris McHenry, comp., "Rebel Prisoners at Quebec, 1778–1783," http://bit.ly/15MFVMZ; see also *Pennsylvania Gazette,* August 13, 1783, for a list including Betsey Doherty and a number of other Ruddell's names. Two Conway brothers mention their captivity in their pension applications: John Conway, W8622, and Jesse Conway, W10674, both roll 632, RWP, http://bit.ly/1gJs5QA (John) and http://bit.ly/1hSre2E (Jesse).

44. "Appraisement," March 25, 1824, Jesse Daugherty folder, Barton.

45. Mildred Belew to author, DeMossville, Ky., August 15, 2003; see also "Daugherty, Jim," undated form, Joseph Daugherty Sr. folder, Barton.

46. Underwood to Ogle, September 19, 1888.

47. Diary of Susan Parrish, cited in Lillian Schlissel, *Women's Diaries of the Westward Journey,* expanded ed. (New York: Schocken, 1992), 69; Brian McGinty, *The Oatman Massacre: A Tale of Desert Captivity* (Norman: University of Oklahoma Press, 2005), 98–102; on Eunice Williams, who was Sally's age when taken, see John Demos, *The Unredeemed Captive: A Family Story from Early America* (New York: Knopf, 1994).

48. Janet K. Pease, *Pendleton County, Kentucky, Order Book A, 1799–1805* (Moline: By the author, 1972), 13, 14, 27, 45; Pease, *Pendleton County, Kentucky, Order Book B, 1805–14* (Moline: By the author, 1972), 1 (*bis*), 9.

49. William Wharton, S37534, roll 2541, RWP, http://bit.ly/NGM2AG. Through either impatience or some mix-up, he applied twice, submitting a statement to the county court on June 15, 1818, and another, essentially the same, on September 3. On August 21, 1820, he filed the required inventory of his personal property.

50. Paul W. Myers, *Westmoreland County in the American Revolution* (Apollo, Pa.: Closson

Press, 1988), 165–79; Washington on "choice troops" quoted in Frank F. Carver, *Fort McIntosh: The Story of Its History and Restoration of the Site,* 2nd ed. (Beaver, Pa.: Beaver Area Heritage Foundation, 1993), http://bit.ly/16irxiV, "The Troops."

51. Movements of the Eighth taken from John B. B. Trussell Jr., *The Pennsylvania Line: Regimental Organizations and Operations, 1776–1783* (Harrisburg: Pennsylvania Historical and Museum Commissions, 1977), 102–10.

52. Benson J. Lossing, *Washington: A Biography* (New York, 1860), quoted in Lorett Treese, *Valley Forge: Making and Remaking a National Symbol* (University Park: Pennsylvania State University Press, 1995), 9.

53. Michael Kammen, *Mystic Chords of Memory: The Transformation of Tradition in American Culture* (New York: Vintage, 1993), 65–66; Janice Hume, *Obituaries in American Culture* (Jackson: University Press of Mississippi, 2000), 33; Sobel, "Revolution," 165–69.

54. Rufus Stone, "Brodhead's Raid on the Senecas," *WPHM* 7 (1924): 88–101.

55. Ralph Collins, U.S. Organizations: U.S. Levies, First Regiment (Darke), roll 3, CSR-PostRev, http://bit.ly/1h6mogF.

56. William Wharton, Second Regiment, roll 6, CSR-PostRev, http://bit.ly/1rc3fSH; Wiley Sword, *President Washington's Indian War: The Struggle for the Old Northwest, 1790–1795* (Norman: University of Oklahoma Press, 1985), 148.

57. St. Clair to Henry Knox, November 1, 1791, in Arthur St. Clair, *The St. Clair Papers: The Life and Public Services of Arthur St. Clair . . . with His Correspondence and Other Papers,* ed. William Henry Smith, 2 vols. (Cincinnati: Clarke, 1882), 2:249.

58. Ebenezer Denny, *Military Journal of Major Ebenezer Denny, an Officer in the Revolutionary and Indian Wars* (Philadelphia: Lippincott, 1859), 161; Winthrop Sargent, "Winthrop Sargent's Diary While with General Arthur St. Clair's Expedition Against the Indians," *Ohio Archaeological and Historical Quarterly* 33 (July 1924): 242; Arthur St. Clair, *A Narrative of the Manner in Which the Campaign Against the Indians, in the Year One Thousand Seven Hundred and Ninety-One, Was Conducted . . .* (Philadelphia: Aitken, 1812), 196; John Cash, First Regiment, roll 3, CSR-PostRev, http://bit.ly/1h6l5hG.

59. Sargent, "Diary," 240; "Adjutant Crawford's Orderly Book," September 20 1791, William D. Wilkins Papers, Burton Historical Collection, Detroit Public Library, 23 (in the library's typescript reference copy); quoted by permission of the Detroit Public Library.

60. St. Clair cited in "Adjutant Crawford's Orderly Book," September 28, 1791, 30 (in type-script copy); quoted by permission of the Detroit Public Library.

61. William David Butler, John Cromwell Butler, and Joseph Marion Butler, *The Butler Family in America* (St. Louis: Shallcross, 1909), 157.

62. Sword, *Washington's War,* 178.

63. Ibid., 180–83.

64. Denny, *Military Journal,* 171; Sargent, "Diary," 260, has a slightly different count and notes the three surviving women at 268–69.

65. Quoted in George H. Moore, *Libels on Washington, with a Critical Examination Thereof* (New York: For the author, 1889), 10–12, but Moore disputes the truth of the account.

66. Quoted in William L. Stone, *Life of Joseph Brant—Thayendanegea, Including the Indian Wars of the American Revolution,* vol. 2 (Albany: Munsell, 1865), 550–51.

67. John F. Meginness, *The Family of General Arthur St. Clair: Reprinted from Dr. Egle's Notes and Queries* (Harrisburg, Pa.: Harrisburg Publishing, 1897), 26.

68. William Darke to George Washington, November 9, 1791, Gilder Lehrman Collection Documents, http://to.pbs.org/14QOeoQ.

69. Ralph C. Collins, R2182, roll 614, RWP, http://bit.ly/1ioYrVg.

70. *History of Lewis, Clark, Knox, and Scotland Counties, Missouri, from the Earliest Time to the Present* (St. Louis: Goodspeed, 1887), 1158–59.

71. Joseph H. Collins, USFC, 1850, Kentucky, Grant County, roll M432_201, 350, http://bit.ly/15MGsP9; 1860, roll M653_368, 461, http://bit.ly/15I6sSA; 1870, roll M593_463, 583, http://bit.ly/1aVMhSc; William C. Collins, 1850, roll M432_201, 354, http://bit.ly/17gYvk9; 1860, the same as Joseph; Janet K. Pease, comp., *Grant County Order Book H, 1855–63,* in *Kentucky County Court Records: Grant, Harrison, Pendleton,* vol. 3 (Williamstown, Ky.: Grant County Historical Society, 1986), 101.

5. The Civil War, Real and Unreal

1. *OR* 16(1):959–63, 977.

2. Ibid., 969.

3. Marmaduke B. Morton, "Last Surviving Lieutenant General: Visit to the Home of Gen. S. B. Buckner," *Confederate Veteran* 17 (February 1909): 85, excerpted from the original article in the *Nashville Banner.*

4. Ibid.

5. *OR* 16(1):962.

6. Samuel C. Williams, *General John T. Wilder: Commander of the Lightning Brigade* (Bloomington: Indiana University Press, 1936), 49; Wilder's talk is in Appendix B, 56–64.

7. Affidavit from Joseph Fithian, surgeon of the Eighteenth Kentucky, May 15, 1880; "Invalid Pension of J. L. Dougherty: Statement of Claimant," June 24, 1881; "Surgeon's Certificate," December 28, 1887, signed by board of surgeons, Maysville; James L. Dougherty pension file, cert. 204387 (filed under Charles M. Dougherty, minor child, cert. 509667), CWP.

8. Arndt M. Stickles, *Simon Bolivar Buckner: Borderland Knight* (Chapel Hill: University of North Carolina Press, 1940), 200.

9. J. David Hacker, "A Census-Based Count of the Civil War Dead," *Civil War History* 57 (2011): 307–48, draws on newly digitized census data to revise the traditional figure of about 620,000 deaths upward to a "realistic probable range" of between 650,000 to 850,000 deaths "with a preferred estimate of 750,000" (348).

10. Walt Whitman, *Prose Works, 1892,* vol. 1, *Specimen Days,* ed. Floyd Stovall (New York: New York University Press, 1963), 115.

11. James L. Dougherty, Eighteenth Kentucky Infantry (U.S.A.), M397, roll 311, CSR-Union.

12. W. B. Roberts, Twentieth Arkansas Infantry, M317, roll 172, CSR-Confed; Bell Irvin Wiley, *The Life of Johnny Reb: The Common Soldier of the Confederacy* (Indianapolis: Bobbs-Merrill, 1943), 332.

13. Henry Morton Woodson, *Historical Genealogy of the Woodsons and Their Connections* (Columbia, Mo.: By the author, 1915), 10, 259, 299, 470, 423–24. Official records for Duke

and William David Woodson confirm that each man did escape, but the bureaucratic documents, typically, include no details about how their escapes were managed; Woodson: Twenty-eighth Virginia Infantry, M324, roll 751, and J. B. Duke: Twelfth (Green's) Tennessee Cavalry, M268, roll 50, CSR-Confed. The papers for Walter Nelson Woodson, Twenty-first Virginia Cavalry (Peters's Regiment), M324, roll 169, CSR-Confed, show his exchange in February 1865, while the man whose name he said he took, Michael James Taylor of the Forty-ninth Georgia Infantry, M266, roll 503, CSR-Confed, was exchanged in October 1864.

14. Woodson, *Historical Genealogy,* 410; Hugh L. Ardinger, Thirty-fourth Tennessee Infantry (Fourth Confederate Regiment Infantry), M268, roll 257, CSR-Confed; USFC Mortality Schedules Index, 1880, MRT197_7613, http://bit.ly/14zOoKW (under Hught [*sic*] Ardinger).

15. *OR* 12(2):414.

16. Allen Christian Redwood, *Memoir of Allen Christian Redwood,* in *Battles and Leaders of the Civil War,* vol. 2 of the Century War Series (New York: Century Co., 1887), 537n. Thomas Kearny, in *General Philip Kearny: Battle Soldier of Five Wars* (New York: Putnam, 1937), 389–90, refutes the "vulgar gossip" about the wound by quoting a report by the two doctors who had embalmed his grandfather's body: the minié ball had entered "through the gluteous muscles a little back of the hip joint" and lodged near the breastbone. The vulgar gossip persists; it was discussed in depth in an undated chat about "KIA generals" (no longer available) at www.us-civilwar.com.

17. Much of the biographical information here comes from "Roberts, William Billingsly," in *Biographical Encyclopedia of Kentucky of the Dead and Living Men of the Nineteenth Century* (Cincinnati: J. M. Armstrong, 1878), 242–43; census records, his gravestone, and other contemporary sources show conflicting birthdates and birthplaces for W. B.

18. On the Bohemian composer Anthony Philip Heinrich, see Gilbert Chase, *America's Music: From the Pilgrims to the Present,* 3rd ed. (Urbana: University of Illinois Press, 1992), 266–84.

19. William Henry Perrin, ed., *History of Fayette County, Kentucky, with an Outline Sketch of the Blue Grass Region* (Chicago: Baskin, 1882), 851–52.

20. "Roberts," 242.

21. According to B. J. Gooch, special collections librarian, university archivist, Transylvania University Library, Lexington, e-mail message to author, January 28, 2005, records show that in 1844 and again in 1849, a William B. Roberts enrolled for the "first course" in the medical school (whether it was the same man enrolling twice is impossible to say), but neither registrant completed the course.

22. Will of Henry Hickman, Frederick County Wills, February 6, 1764, Liber A, no. 1, fol. 195 (MSA); Bettie Stirling Carothers, comp., *1776 Census of Maryland* (Westminster, Md.: Family Line Publications, 1986), 77, where Derecter is listed as living near brothers and other relatives but in her own household. Smallwood left no sign of his existence in any other document I've seen. See also the Hickman Family File, Montgomery County Historical Society, Rockville, Md.

23. "Trammell Tragedies," ed. Larry Anderson, formerly at http://laanderson.com/; on the (disputed) connection of Alamo defender Burke Trammell to the Virginia family, see the

Trammell Family Genealogy Forum, http://genforum.genealogy.com/trammell/; on the Big Neck War, *History of Caldwell and Livingston Counties, Missouri* (St. Louis: National Historical Co., 1886), 687–88; on the deaths in Indian country, Franklin Miller Jr., *The Mellett and Hickman Families of Henry County, Indiana*, 2 vols. (Gambier, Ohio: By the author, 1974), 1:111; on the harem, Thomas W. Jones, "'A Solid Gang of Them': An Illinois Morse-Trammell Family's Reactions to a Scandal," *National Genealogical Society Quarterly* 92 (June 2004): 105–18.

24. Loudoun County Court Order Book F (1773–1776), April 30, 1773, 4 (LVA); Malick W. Ghachem, "The Slave's Two Bodies: The Life of an American Legal Fiction," *WMQ* 60 (2003): 832–24; see also Loudoun County Order Book E (1770–1773), September 29, 1772, 418, referring to testimony about Trammell's maiming of his slave (LVA); and *Minutes of the Annual Conferences of the Methodist Episcopal Church, for the Years 1773–1828*, vol. 1 (New York: Mason and Lane, 1840), 143, 155, though it's possible this Sampson was the unwed couple's son Sampson, who usually appears in the records with his mother's surname but seems occasionally to have used his father's.

25. Montgomery County Land Records, August 10 1793, Liber E:382; April 5, 1804, Liber L:306 (MSA). Early federal census records listed only the name of the head of the household, but in the 1790 USFC for Montgomery County, Maryland (M637, roll 3, 54, http://bit.ly/16Lh3Wb), Sampson's household included three free white women of unspecified ages, one man over sixteen (presumably Sampson himself), two free white boys, and eleven slaves. Sampson's death date is unrecorded but must have come after April 1804 or, if he was the ex-Methodist, 1808; Derecter's will was probated in January 1813 (Montgomery County Will Book H:33).

26. John Byng-Hall interviewed by Paul Thompson, "The Power of Family Myths," in *The Myths We Live By*, ed. Raphael Samuel and Paul Thompson (London: Routledge, 1990), 216–24.

27. Jasper B. Shannon and Ruth McQuown, *Presidential Politics in Kentucky, 1824–1948: A Compilation of Election Statistics and an Analysis of Political Behavior* (Lexington: Bureau of Government Research, University of Kentucky, 1950), 35–36; W. B.'s vote noted in "Roberts," 243.

28. On the DeMossville women, see Lewis Collins, *History of Kentucky: Embracing Prehistoric, Annals for 331 Years . . .* , rev. Richard H. Collins, 2 vols. (Covington, Ky.: Collins, 1878–82), 1:123, for June 3, 1863; on Lafferty, see ibid., 1:145–46, for November 2, 1864, and Kentucky Historical Marker no. 504.

29. Major Abram Wileman, Eighteenth Kentucky Infantry (U.S.A.), M397, roll 318, CSR-Union; *Louisville Journal*, October 17, 20, 21, 1863; *OR* 30(4):469; Eric C. Nagle, "The Life and Death of Major A. G. Wileman," *PCHGS Newsletter* 1, n.d., http://bit.ly/1d2JIi3; Frances Peter, *A Union Woman in Civil War Kentucky: The Diary of Frances Peter*, ed. John David Smith and William Cooper Jr. (Lexington: University Press of Kentucky, 2000), 166.

30. Sherman quoted in Lowell H. Harrison, *The Civil War in Kentucky* (Lexington: University Press of Kentucky, 1975), 15; on Henry Nichols's Unionist sentiments, see Lucius Desha to Eliza Desha, October 28, 1862, quoted in William A. Penn, *Rattling Spurs and Broad-Brimmed Hats: The Civil War in Cynthiana and Harrison County, Kentucky* (Midway, Ky.:

Battle Grove Press, 1995), 60; Henry Nichols, USFC Slave Schedules, 1860, Kentucky, Harrison County, 127a–b, http://bit.ly/15gM2cg.

31. James F. Sulzby Jr., *Toward a History of Samford University* (Birmingham, Ala.: Samford University Press, 1986), 449–51. Alice Roberts Dawson and her three children are in William Roberts's household in USFC, 1880, Kentucky, Pendleton County, Falmouth, roll T9_438, 365, http://bit.ly/181ZhAu; Elizabeth Roberts's unsourced obituary "copied from Mary Elizabeth Wood's Scrapbook" at Carrie Baugh, "Mrs. Roberts," online posting, October 23, 1998, Pendleton County Message Board, Rootsweb.com, http://bit.ly/1728SJk.

32. Glen Taul, director, Office of International Programs/Archives, Georgetown College, e-mail messages to me, October 19 and December 20, 2006; "Dr. John Dawson, Ex-Falmouthite, Dies at Alex., Va.," *Falmouth Outlook,* April 15, 1966; "John Dawson, College President," *New York Herald Tribune,* April 10, 1966; Sulzby, *Samford University,* 454; Hul-Cee Marcus Acton, *Chalk, Termites, and God's Country* (Birmingham: Banner Press, 1967), 108, 136, 101–2.

33. "Baptist College Drops Professor Who Doubted Stories of Noah's Ark and Jonah and the Whale," *NYT,* December 14, 1929; see also "Professor Ousted for Bible Slur," *Los Angeles Times;* "Teacher Questions Bible; Resigns Job," *Washington Post;* and "Drop Professor Who Discredits Bible Stories," *Chicago Daily Tribune,* all December 14, 1929.

34. Missouri State Parks and Historic Sites, "Battle of Lexington State Historic Site—Southern Forces," http://on.mo.gov/15tSVxY, listing William, William H., Nathan, and A. Clay Roberts, all from Lafayette; "Roberts," 243, notes that W. B. fought at Lexington.

35. William L. Shea and Earl J. Hess, *Pea Ridge: Civil War Campaign in the West* (Chapel Hill: University of North Carolina Press, 1992), 58–59.

36. "Roberts," 243; Nannie Payne [Roberts] Oldham, "Wm. Billingsly Roberts," filled-in form, June 5, 1936, Roberts folder, box 238, Barton.

37. Shea, *Pea Ridge,* 58–59.

38. Ibid., 102, 270–71.

39. Walt Whitman, *Notebooks and Unpublished Prose Manuscripts,* vol. 2, *Washington,* ed. Edward F. Grier (New York: New York University Press, 1984), 504; see also Whitman, *Specimen Days,* 32, which includes citations to other published versions.

40. Sam Watkins, *"Company Aytch" or, A Side Show of the Big Show and Other Sketches,* ed. M. Thomas Inge (New York: Plume, 1999), 171–72.

41. Geoffrey C. Ward, *The Civil War: An Illustrated History* (New York: Knopf, 1990), 296.

42. U.S. Surgeon General's Office, *The Medical and Surgical History of the War of the Rebellion (1861–65),* 12 vols. (1870–1883; repr., Wilmington, N.C.: Broadfoot, 1990–91), 12:877; Eric Foner, *Reconstruction: America's Unfinished Revolution, 1863–1877* (New York: Harper & Row, 1988), 125.

43. Roberts, CSR-Confed; *OR,* ser. 2, 5:652–53.

44. William H. Roberts, Westley Roberts, both First Field Battery, Missouri Light Artillery, M322, roll 83, CSR-Confed; Capt. S. T. Ruffner, "Sketch of First Missouri Battery, C.S.A.," *Confederate Veteran* 20 (September 1912): 417.

45. Julian Street, "The Borderland: Chapter X," *Collier's Magazine,* September 26, 1914, 19.

46. Merle Miller, *Plain Speaking: An Oral Biography of Harry S. Truman* (New York: Berkley, 1973), 75.

47. *Saint Joseph Morning Herald,* May 29, 1863, quoted in Ted P. Yeatman, *Frank and Jesse James: The Story behind the Legend* (Nashville: Cumberland House, 2000), 40.

48. "Missed His Mark," *Kansas City Daily Journal,* April 6, 1882, quoted in Jesse James Bank Museum, *Good Bye, Jesse James: A Reprinting of Six of the Best News Stories Concerning the Career and Death of America's Most Famous Outlaw . . .* (Liberty, Mo., 1967), 106–7; Jesse James Jr., *Jesse James, My Father: The First and Only True Story of His Adventures Ever Written* (Independence, Mo.: Sentinel, 1899), 4, 29–31; Stella F. James, *In the Shadow of Jesse James,* ed. Milton F. Perry (Thousand Oaks, Calif.: Revolver Press, 1990), 39–40. On Zerelda Samuel and on the hanging story in general, see Yeatman, *Frank and Jesse James,* 38–40, 275–76, 383nn31–32. See also Frank Triplett, *The Life, Times, and Treacherous Death of Jesse James* (1882), intro. and notes by Joseph Snell (New York: Swallow Press, 1970), 4–5, for a version allegedly told by Jesse's mother and his widow; the women later denied cooperating with Triplett.

49. Miller, *Plain Speaking,* 74; Harry S. Truman, *The Autobiography,* ed. Robert H. Ferrell (Boulder: Colorado Associated University Press, 1980), 28; Meyer Berger, "Mother Truman—Portrait of a Rebel," *NYT,* June 23, 1946.

50. U.S. Congress, House, *Harriet L. Young, Administratrix,* 59th Cong., 1st sess. [1906], Doc. 901; *OR* 13:253–55, 267–68, 345–46; see also David McCullough, *Truman* (New York, 1992), 31.

51. Randy Sowell, archivist, Harry S. Truman Library, Independence, Mo., e-mail message to author, January 18, 2005, cites the appearance of the hanging story in Miller's 1973 book and in the notes of his 1961–62 interviews, adding, "I'm not aware that this incident is further documented in our manuscript collections or oral history interviews." McCullough, *Truman,* 53; Miller, *Plain Speaking,* 77–78; Truman, *Autobiography,* 21; "Harry S. Truman and the Jameses," *James Farm Journal* 2 (August 1984): 1.

52. William B. Roberts family, USFC, 1850, Kentucky, Kenton County, roll M432_208, 126, http://bit.ly/181ZCD9; USFC, 1860, Kentucky, Pendleton County, roll M653_392, 537, http://bit.ly/1dnjIig; USFC, 1870, Kentucky, Pendleton County, roll M593_494, p. 405, http://bit.ly/14B2R5T; for 1880 census, see note 31. Nathan's presumptive birth year ranged in the censuses from 1843 to 1852.

53. Nathan Roberts, First Field Battery, Missouri Light Artillery, M322, roll 83, CSR-Confed; William H. Roberts, Capt. Westley Roberts, and A. Clay Roberts are in the same unit on the same roll. Nannie Oldham, "Roberts," Roberts folder, Barton.

54. Daniel O'Flaherty, *General Jo Shelby: Undefeated Rebel* (Chapel Hill: University of North Carolina Press, 1954), 366–67; Thomas Payne, Dennis Payne, both Fifth Missouri Cavalry, M380, roll 11, CSR-Confed.

55. *Commonwealth of Kentucky v. R. C.* [*sic*] *Dills,* December 30, 1891, PCCC Criminal Cases, pkg. 67, box 18 (KDLA).

56. Ibid.

57. W. B. Roberts, USFC, 1870; Samuel F. Roberts, USFC, 1870, Kentucky, Kenton County, roll M593_478, 296, http://bit.ly/18iz1kf.

58. Ms. copies, *John N. Daugherty, admrs. of the will of Amelia Duckworth, decd., v. Children and*

Heirs of Amelia Duckworth, January 19, 1868; *Commonwealth v. Robert Perry Duckworth,* Writ of Lunacy, August 4, 1868, PCCC, pkg. 274; Duckworth folder, box 195, Barton (originals at KDLA). Henry S. Duckworth pension file, cert. 679090, CWP, includes a mass of contradictory information about names and dates both internally and measured against other public documents; Henry seems to have married at least three times.

59. Ms. copy, Jasper Daugherty, Petition, PCCC, pkg. 209, February 4, 1859; in Joseph Daugherty Sr. folder, box 193, Barton (original at KDLA).

60. Ms. copy, "Daugherty-Duckworth" [heading], *Jane C. Duckworth, plff. v. Henry S. Duckworth and John N. Daugherty,* PCCC, pkg. 160, January 2, 1861; in Joseph Daugherty Sr. folder (original at KDLA).

61. Peter, *Union Woman,* 18.

62. *OR* 16(1):763; Dennis Nichols, Seventh Kentucky Cavalry (U.S.A.), M397, roll 82, CSR-Union.

63. William Edgar Hughes, *The Journal of a Grandfather* (St. Louis: Nixon-Jones, 1912), 85.

64. Quoted in D. Warren Lambert, "The Decisive Battle of Richmond, August 29–30, 1862," in *The Civil War in Kentucky: Battle for the Bluegrass State,* ed. Kent Masterson Brown (Mason City, Iowa: Savas, 2000), 121, noting that "oral history in Madison County" also held that Manson was probably drunk.

65. *OR* 16(1):927, 920; Lambert, "Richmond," 128.

66. *OR* 16(1):909.

67. Sanford M. Daugherty, George Daugherty, Henry A. Dougherty, all Eighteenth Kentucky (U.S.A.), M397, roll 311, CSR-Union; Oval [*sic*] L. Dougherty, Thirty-second Kentucky (U.S.A.), M397, roll 401, CSR-Union. Sanford and George were eventually pardoned and taken back, but Henry disappeared from sight and Orville apparently managed to dodge the army until the end.

68. James H. Johns, Samuel S. Patterson, Eighteenth Kentucky (U.S.A.), M397, rolls 313 (Johns), 315 (Patterson), CSR-Union.

69. Michael R. Bradley, *Tullahoma: The 1863 Campaign for the Control of Middle Tennessee* (Shippensburg, Pa.: Burd Street Press, 2000), 59–67; Peter Cozzens, *This Terrible Sound: The Battle of Chickamauga* (Urbana: University of Illinois Press, 1992), 18.

70. James Lee McDonough, *Chattanooga: A Death Grip on the Confederacy* (Knoxville: University of Tennessee Press, 1984), 13; Thomas Wolfe, "Chickamauga," in *The Hills Beyond* (Baton Rouge: Louisiana State University Press, 2000), 106, 107; Wolfe to Hamilton Basso, July 13, 1937, in *The Letters of Thomas Wolfe,* ed. Elizabeth Nowell (New York: Scribner, 1956), 625, saying he wrote the sketch "in the old man's language."

71. *OR* 30(1):477–78.

72. Cozzens, *Terrible Sound,* 492–94; *OR* 30(1):474–76, 479.

73. McDonough, *Chattanooga,* 17.

74. Ibid., 45.

75. Ibid., 164–98; Ohio soldier quoted in Wiley Sword, *Mountains Touched with Fire: Chattanooga Besieged, 1863* (New York: St. Martin's, 1995), 277–78; *OR* 31(2):508–9.

76. McDonough, *Chattanooga,* 168; Douglas MacArthur, *Reminiscences* (New York: McGraw Hill, 1964), 8–9.

77. Sword, *Mountains Touched with Fire*, 263–70.

78. *OR* 31(2):547–48.

79. *OR* 31(2):208; "Arthur MacArthur," *The Outlook*, September 21, 1912, 95–96.

80. James L. Dougherty to Gen. Wm. D. Whipple, September 13, 1864, in Dougherty pension file, CWP.

81. Except where otherwise noted, quotations are from "Statement by Claimant," in Dougherty pension file, CWP.

82. J. C. and Martha Bullock, affidavit, February 7, 1882.

83. Quoted in Surgeon's Certificate, December 28, 1887, Maysville, in Dougherty pension file, CWP.

84. Ibid.

85. Claudia Linares, "The Civil War Pension Law," CPE Working Paper no. 2001-6 (Chicago: Center for Population Economics, December 2001), 3–5, 13, formerly at www.cpe.uchicago.edu; "The New Pension Policy," *The Nation*, May 30, 1889, 438; Theda Skocpol, *Protecting Soldiers and Mothers: The Political Origins of Social Policy in the United States* (Cambridge: Belknap Press of Harvard University Press, 1992), 143–45, 109.

86. Eric T. Dean Jr., *Shook Over Hell: Post-Traumatic Stress, Vietnam, and the Civil War* (Cambridge: Harvard University Press, 1997), 130–31.

87. Ibid., 143–44, 202–3; Lisa A. Long, *Rehabilitating Bodies: Health, History, and the American Civil War* (Philadelphia: University of Pennsylvania Press, 2004), 4; Judith Pizarro, Roxane Cohen Silver, and JoAnn Prause, "Physical and Mental Health Costs of Traumatic War Experiences among Civil War Veterans," *Archives of General Psychiatry* 63 (2006): 193–200.

88. Melvin Wheeler, "Physician's Affidavit," June 1, 1889, Dougherty pension file, CWP. The General Affidavit, May 20, 1889, submitted by the widow herself gave the causes of death as "chronic diarroea and disease of liver and resulting dyspepsia," with no mention of apoplexy.

89. Robert Fogle, "General Affidavit," July 31, 1901, Duckworth pension file, CWP; Henry S. Duckworth: Certificate of Death, State of Ohio, Montgomery County, November 10, 1914, no. 64049.

90. James W. Cromwell, "General Affidavit," June 19, 1890; Nichols's invalid pension application, July 23, 1903; surgeon's certificate, October 7, 1891; Dennis Nichols pension file, cert. 667465 (filed under widow Mary S. Nichols), CWP.

91. William H. Roberts, Confederate Pension Application no. 2012, issue date August 19, 1912, http://hdl.handle.net/10602/8352 (KDLA).

92. Jeffrey E. Vogel, "Redefining Reconciliation: Confederate Veterans and the Southern Responses to Federal Civil War Pensions," *Civil War History* 51 (2005): 69.

6. Damned Yankees

1. "Enjoyable Recital Given by the Pupils of J. N. Forest," unlabeled and undated clipping formerly in Ethel Clark's possession; Ethel Agnes Clarke, transcript, Institute of Musical Art, October 13, 1913–May 30, 1914 (copy obtained from the Office of the Registrar, the Juilliard School). Ethel added the terminal *e* to her surname because, my mother said, she thought it was more refined.

2. Ethel Cleveland, USFC, 1930, New Jersey, Atlantic County, Atlantic City, roll T626_1309, 3A, http://bit.ly/14GT5vV.

3. Flora Mc Curroy (his mother, a domestic in the household of attorney D. L. Deane), USFC, 1880, Pennsylvania, Tioga County, Wellsboro, roll T9_1198, 459, http://bit.ly/17MoTU3; N. R. Cleveland, USFC, 1900, Pennsylvania, Tioga County, Shippen, roll T623_1490, 2B, http://bit.ly/1aZdAes; Flora's parents named in her household, USFC, 1910 Pennsylvania, Tioga County, Shippen, roll T624_1422, 5B, http://bit.ly/18KhJht.

4. Daniel McDonald, 1851 Scotland Census, Paisley Low Church, ED 3, roll CSSCT1851_124, 10, http://bit.ly/1axOlk7; Daniel McDonald, USFC, 1860, New York, Rensselaer County, Greenbush, roll M653_848, 113, http://bit.ly/17lSanO; Daniel Mc Donald, USFC, 1870, New York, Rensselaer County, North Greenbush, roll M593_1083, 135, http://bit.ly/1aZaTtb; Robert McDonald, USFC, 1860, New York, Albany County, Albany, roll M653_719, 8, http://bit.ly/1aZ8cbd. The family Bible formerly in Lizzie Clark's possession includes among the handwritten list of Robert's children an entry for "Mary Ellen, April 11, 1859, by first wife."

5. George Dames Burtchaell and Thomas Ulick Sadlier, eds., *Alumni Dublinenses: A Register of the Students, Graduates, Professors and Provosts of Trinity College in the University of Dublin (1593–1860)*, new ed. (Dublin: Thom, 1935).

6. James McManus and his wife, the former Bridget McDermott, entered four names that correspond to most of the known family: Thomas, baptized in 1827; Catherine, in 1833; Mary Ann, in 1836; and Elizabeth, in 1839. Two other McManus-McDermott couples whose first names may have been mistranscribed entered a Winifred in 1829 and a James in 1834; they match the other two known siblings. Catholic Church, Parish of Boyle (Roscommon), Parochial Registers of Boyle, 1792–1881; available on microfilm from LDS, reel 0989743. The names are rendered in Latin and the film is extremely difficult to read; more legible but not always consistent are the transcribed entries for the same names on Ancestry.com; on the LDS's genealogical website, www.familysearch.org; and in Rose McManus, Peter McManus, and Michael McManus, comps., *Where Rest Our Genesis: An Historical Note on the Noble and Ancient Clan McManus of North Roscommon, Ireland . . .* (Durham City: McManus Family History Society, 1997). Isaac Weld, *Statistical Survey of the County of Roscommon* (Dublin: Graisberry, 1832), 201–7, 196–99.

7. The estimates of mortality and emigration during the famine vary; see Cormac Ó Gráda, *Black '47 and Beyond: The Great Irish Famine in History, Economy, and Memory* (Princeton: Princeton University Press, 1999), 85, 105–6.

8. Elizabeth McManus, New York State Census, 1855, Albany County, Watervliet, district 3, 219 (available as a searchable CD-ROM at NYSL).

9. Commissioners of Irish Education Inquiry, *Second Report* (London, 1826), 18, 1290–99 (with McManus at 1292); Cuyler Reynolds, ed., *Hudson-Mohawk Genealogical and Family Memoirs*, vol. 4 (New York: Lewis, 1911), 1684 (though this entry about Winifred McManus's husband states both that she was born in 1831 in Plattsburgh, New York, and that her father, James McManus, the teacher and bank teller, came from Ireland to New York in 1850).

10. "Death of Col. James H. Hooker," *Troy Daily Times,* December 29, 1851; A. J. Weise,

History of the City of Troy, from the Expulsion of the Mohegan Indians to the Present Centennial Year . . . (Troy, N.Y.: Young, 1876), 205.

11. Thomas's obituary noted his youthful employment with Hooker: *Troy Daily Times,* October 24, 1882; Weise, *City of Troy,* 291–94; Surrogate Record Book 42, 409, RCSC, granting letters of administration for Hooker's estate.

12. On Behan's prosperity: Reynolds, *Hudson-Mohawk;* "Thomas F. Behan, Insurance Head of State for 2 Months, Dies Suddenly at His Home," undated clipping [1931] formerly in Ethel Clark's possession. In a few documents, including the Boyle register, the name of Mary Ann's mother was given as Bridget, but in most New York records her name appears as Betsey or Elizabeth. A deed that referred to "the said Bridget McManus (under the name of Betsey McManus as appears in Albany County clerk office records)" strongly suggests she was the same woman. Rensselaer County Deed Book 356, 24–25, recorded February 4, 1884, RCC.

13. George Rogers Howell and Jonathan Tenney, *Bi-Centennial History of Albany: History of the County of Albany, N.Y., from 1609 to 1886* (New York: Munsell, 1886), 308.

14. Arthur G. Adams, August 18, 1996, to author, with an undated clipping, "Hudson River Steamboats . . . Written from the Collection of George W. Murdock . . . No. 88: Thomas McManus," and a copy of a photograph of the *Thomas McManus* from the Charles Parslow Collection; both from the collection of the Steamship Historical Society of America at the Hudson River Maritime Museum, Kingston, N.Y.

15. Robt. Mc Donald, USFC, 1870, New York, Albany County, Albany Ward 2, roll M593_898, 173, http://bit.ly/1fSltAb; Albany County Deed Book 206, 365–66, February 26, 1867, recorded March 22 1867, ACHOR; Thomas's birth was recorded in the family Bible.

16. Albany County Deed Book 242, 64–65, May 10, 1870, recorded May 22, 1871 [*sic*], ACHOR; *Margaret Foy agt. Robert McDonald,* March 1, 1874, Albany County Supreme Court Records, 1874, box 531, 90-00034, ACHOR; "Runaway Accident," *Albany Evening Journal,* November 29, 1870.

17. Reynolds, *Hudson-Mohawk.*

18. Will of Isabella McManus, Surrogate Records Book 72, 465–66, probated June 14, 1871, RCSC.

19. On the Troy house and lot: Rensselaer County Deed Book 154, 51, recorded September 16, 1871; Mortgage Book 130, 308–9, recorded September 25, 1871; Deed Book 159, 284–85, March 3 1873, RCC. On the Cohoes lot: Albany County Deed Book 274, 411–12, December 28, 1874, recorded January 2, 1875; Sheriff Certificates Book 1, 420–21, January 23, 1875, recorded May 11, 1876; Deed Book 288, 453–55, May 12, 1876, recorded June 6, 1876; Deed Book 336, 4–5, July 28, 1881, ACHOR.

20. Weise, *City of Troy,* 235–38.

21. *T. McManus & Co. v. The United States,* United States Court of Claims, Gen. Jur. Case File 3728, boxes 265 (folders 1–2) and 266 (folder 3), Record Group 123, NARA.

22. Erna Risch, *Quartermaster Support of the Army: A History of the Corps, 1775–1939* (Washington, D.C.: U.S. Army Center of Military History, 1989), 406–7.

23. The coverage in these three papers, especially when relying on official court documents, was generally similar. I draw here on all three between December 14, 1876, and January 15, 1877, citing specific issues only when one paper contained information lacking in the others.

24. Daniel J. Walkowitz, *Worker City, Company Town: Iron and Cotton-Worker Protest in Troy and Cohoes, New York, 1855–84* (Urbana: University of Illinois Press, 1981), 103–7, 145–49.

25. *Evening Journal,* January 8 and 15, 1877; *The People v. Mary A. McDonald,* Application for Trial, Court of Oyer and Terminer, filed June 23, 1877; Supreme Court Records and Minute Books, ACHOR; Howell and Tenney, *Bi-Centennial History,* 308.

26. Petition for Letters of Administration, In the Matter of . . . Robert McDonald, Deceased, filed February 2, 1877, Albany Surrogate's Court, ACHOR.

27. Thomas McManus, obituary; Certificate of Death, City of New York, October 23, 1882, no. 439330, NYCMA.

28. Mary A. McDonald: Certificate of Death, County of Rensselaer, State of New York, August 21, 1885, no. 19477; Katie M. Grattan: Certificate of Death, West Troy, August 28, 1885, no. 19918; Catherine Grattan: Certificate of Death, Albany, June 16, 1887, no. 17302, NYSDH.

29. James McManus: Certificate of Death, New York, April 3, 1893, no. 12621, NYCMA; Brigite McManus: Certificate of Death, Rensselaer, February 6, 1894, no. 6129, NYSDH; lot card, St. Agnes's Cemetery, Albany [i.e., Menands], New York, Lot 37, south half, sect. 28, owner McManus, Bridget (Mrs.), formerly in Lizzie Clark's possession.

30. Robert Mc Donald [Jr.], USFC, 1880, New York, Rensselaer County, Troy, roll T9_920, 322, http://bit.ly/17MphBS; Theresa Mc Donald, USFC, 1880, New York, Rensselaer County, Troy, roll T9_920, 367, http://bit.ly/14GR5Ui.

31. Mary Mac Donald, USFC, 1900, New York, New York, roll T623_1105, 16A, http://bit.ly/186vCu7; Mary MacDonald: Certificate of Death, New York, November 28, 1903, no. 33732, NYCMA.

32. Robert McDonald [Jr.], Certificate of Death, New York, March 29, 1927, no. 8221, NYCMA.

33. Thomas Clark, USFC, 1860, New York, Kings County, Brooklyn, roll M653_767, 300, http://bit.ly/17lSOBw; Thomas Clark, USFC, 1870, New York, Queens County, Newtown, roll M593_1080, 6, http://bit.ly/1fSl5kW; Thomas Clarke, USFC, 1880, New York, Queens County, Long Island City, roll T9_918, 24D, http://bit.ly/186vf2v.

7. Grandmother Grace

1. Henry Morton Woodson, *Historical Genealogy of the Woodsons and Their Connections* (Columbia, Mo.: By the author, 1915), 65, 78, 150, 147.

2. Ibid., 51.

3. Jonathan Daniels, *A Southerner Discovers the South* (New York: Macmillan, 1938), 337. Will Roberts was clerk of the Pendleton County courts at the time he was charged; a search through seven boxes of Kenton County court documents for 1877 (KDLA) failed to turn up any official record of the case. The Covington *Daily Commonwealth* noted on July 7, 1877, that he was "arraigned on charge of shooting with intent to kill."

4. Andrea Tortora, "Home and Hearts Torn Apart," *Cincinnati Enquirer,* March 6, 1997.

5. Alice Dougherty, USFC, 1900, Kentucky, Kenton County, roll 534, 10A, http://bit.ly/18yD7Vz; USFC, 1910, roll T624_488, 4A, http://bit.ly/1a1Yulh; Gertrude Lillian

Dougherty, Certificate of Death, City of Covington, Kenton County, February 15, 1907, no. 21815, KDLA.

6. On the Christmastime tragedy of Fred Jaynes, married to an Ingels cousin: Paris *True Kentuckian*, December 31, 1879; on Joseph B. Ingels's death in the orchard: Paris *True Kentuckian*, August 17, 1870; on the accident to teenaged Thomas Oldham: *Falmouth Independent*, June 20, 1878; on "Slick," who died in 1872: Enoch Daugherty, Joseph Daugherty Sr. folder, Barton; on George Ducker's shooting, *Cincinnati Enquirer*, May 7, 1913, and "George Ducker: Shot by John Murphy at Butler and Died Later—No Excuse Given for the Rash Act," article dated May 9, 1913, transcribed from an unidentified Falmouth newspaper and posted in the Family Tree area on Ancestry.com, http://ancstry .me/1ilY9LR.

7. W. C. Ducker, USFC, 1880, Kentucky, Pendleton County, roll 438, 395B, http://bit .ly/199EFuM.

8. "Wm. Ducker, of this Place, Meets His Death While Blasting in a Well," undated clipping from an unidentified newspaper formerly in my grandmother's possession; other sources give the date of Ducker's death as October 29, 1895.

9. W. J. Cash, *The Mind of the South* (1941), new intro. by Bertram Wyatt-Brown (New York: Vintage, 1991), 124.

INDEX

of

Andie Tucher is an associate professor at the Columbia University Graduate School of Journalism. In previous lives she was a journalist (Public Affairs Television and ABC News), a campaign speechwriter (Clinton-Gore '92), and a rare-book librarian. Her first book, *Froth and Scum: Truth, Beauty, Goodness, and the Ax Murder in America's First Mass Medium* (1994), won the Allan Nevins Prize from the Society of American Historians. Born in Plainfield, New Jersey, she studied classics at Princeton and earned a Ph.D. in American Civilization from New York University. She lives in Manhattan.

✄